高 橋 和 希

VOLUME 30...! (NOTE: YU-GI-OH!: DUELIST VOL. 23
WAS PUBLISHED IN JAPAN AS YU-GI-OH! VOL. 30. --THE
EDITOR) ABOUT SIX YEARS SINCE YU-GI-OH! STARTED. I
CAN'T BELIEVE IT'S LASTED SO LONG.

I DIDN'T INITIALLY ENVISION YU-GI-OH! AS A CARD BAT-
TLE MANGA. THE CARD GAME WAS ONLY SUPPOSED TO BE
TWO CHAPTERS (IN VOLUME 2 OF THE ORIGINAL YU-GI-OH!
MANGA SERIES), AND I CAME UP WITH THE RULES FOR THE
GAME IN ONE NIGHT. HOW AMAZING THAT IT TURNED OUT
TO BE THE HEART OF THE STORY!

IT'S ALL THANKS TO THE PEOPLE WHO'VE SUPPORTED
YU-GI-OH! THAT IT'S BEEN THIS SUCCESSFUL. THANK YOU
SO MUCH!
 -KAZUKI TAKAHASHI, 2002

Artist/author Kazuki Takahashi first tried to break into
the manga business in 1982, but success eluded him
until **Yu-Gi-Oh!** debuted in the Japanese **Weekly
Shonen Jump** magazine in 1996. **Yu-Gi-Oh!**'s themes
of friendship and fighting, together with Takahashi's
weird and wonderful art, soon became enormously
successful, spawning a real-world card game, video
games, and two anime series. A lifelong gamer,
Takahashi enjoys Shogi (Japanese chess), Mahjong,
card games, and tabletop RPGs, among other games.

YU-GI-OH!: DUELIST VOL. 23
The SHONEN JUMP Manga Edition

STORY AND ART BY
KAZUKI TAKAHASHI

Translation & English Adaptation/Joe Yamazaki
Touch-up Art & Lettering/Eric Erbes
Design/Andrea Rice
Editor/Jason Thompson

Editor in Chief, Books/Alvin Lu
Editor in Chief, Magazines/Marc Weidenbaum
VP of Publishing Licensing/Rika Inouye
VP of Sales/Gonzalo Ferreyra
Sr. VP of Marketing/Liza Coppola
Publisher/Hyoe Narita

In the original Japanese edition, YU-GI-OH!, YU-GI-OH!: DUELIST and
YU-GI-OH!: MILLENNIUM WORLD are known collectively as YU-GI-OH!.
The English YU-GI-OH!: DUELIST was originally volumes 8-31
of the Japanese YU-GI-OH!.

Printed in the U.S.A.

Published by VIZ Media, LLC
P.O. Box 77010
San Francisco, CA 94107

SHONEN JUMP Manga Edition
10 9 8 7 6 5 4 3 2 1
First printing, October 2007

PARENTAL ADVISORY
YU-GI-OH!: DUELIST is rated T for Teen
and is recommended for ages 13 and
up. Contains fantasy violence.
ratings.viz.com

THE WORLD'S
MOST POPULAR MANGA

www.viz.com

www.shonenjump.com

SHONEN JUMP MANGA

Vol. 23
RA THE IMMORTAL
STORY AND ART BY
KAZUKI TAKAHASHI

THE STORY SO FAR...

YUGI MUTOU/
YU-GI-OH

When 10th grader Yugi solved the Millennium Puzzle, another spirit took up residence in his body...Yu-Gi-Oh, the King of Games, a dark avenger who challenges evildoers to "Shadow Games" of life and death!

YUGI FACES DEADLY ENEMIES!

Using his gaming skills, Yugi fights ruthless adversaries like Maximillion Pegasus, multimillionaire creator of the collectible card game "Duel Monsters," and Ryo Bakura, whose friendly personality turns evil when he is possessed by the spirit of the Millennium Ring. But Yugi's greatest rival is Seto Kaiba, the world's second-greatest gamer—and the ruthless teenage president of Kaiba Corporation. At first, Kaiba and Yugi are bitter enemies, but after fighting against a common adversary—Pegasus—they come to respect one another. But for all his powers, there is one thing Yu-Gi-Oh cannot do: remember who he is and where he came from.

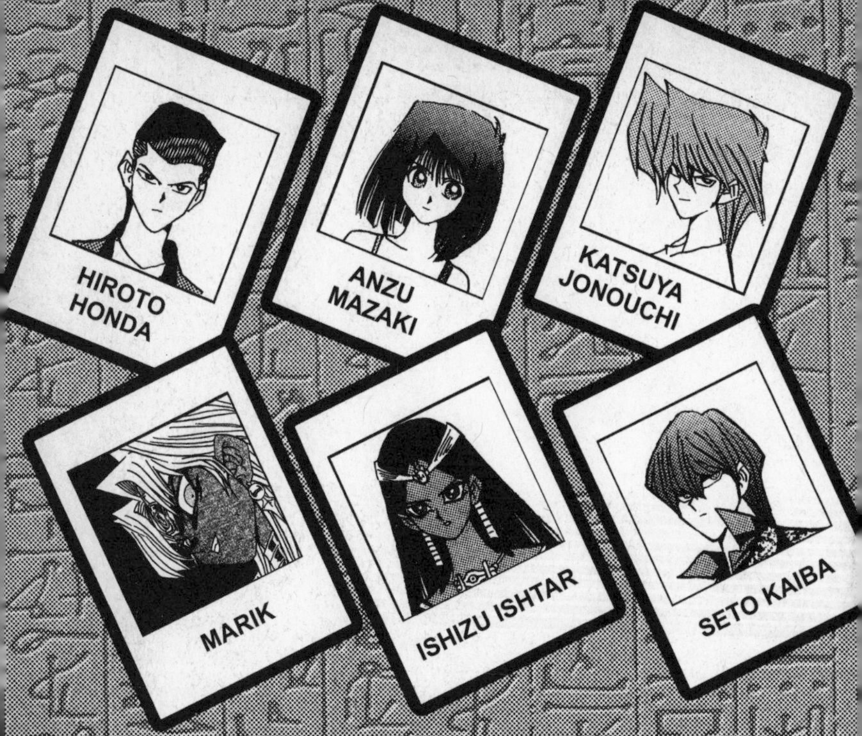
HIROTO HONDA
ANZU MAZAKI
KATSUYA JONOUCHI
MARIK
ISHIZU ISHTAR
SETO KAIBA

THE TABLET OF THE PHARAOH'S MEMORIES

Then one day, when an Egyptian museum exhibit comes to Japan, Yugi sees an ancient carving of himself as an Egyptian pharaoh! The curator of the exhibit, Ishizu Ishtar, explains that there are seven Millennium Items, which were made to fit into a stone tablet in a hidden shrine in Egypt. According to the legend, when the seven Items are brought together, the pharaoh will regain his memories of his past life.

THE EGYPTIAN GOD CARDS

But there is another piece of the puzzle—the three Egyptian God Cards, the rarest cards on Earth. To collect the God Cards, Kaiba announces "Battle City," an enormous "Duel Monsters" tournament. Attracted by the scent of blood, the most powerful God Card wielder comes to Tokyo: Ishizu's insane brother Marik, who wants to murder the pharaoh to satisfy a grudge. Using his sadistic torture deck, Marik climbs to the tournament semi-finals, where he defeats Yugi's friend Jonouchi, leaving him in a deathlike state. Now, only one semi-finals match remains: the last duel between Yugi and Kaiba, as foretold 3,000 years ago on an ancient Egyptian carving!

Vol. 23

CONTENTS

Duel 201 Red Spirit 7

Duel 202 Beyond Hatred 27

Duel 203 As a Friend 47

Duel 204 The Monster of Victory or Defeat 67

Duel 205 The Entrusted Card 87

Duel 206 Showdown in the Heavens! 107

Duel 207 The Quick Attack Trap 127

Duel 208 Slifer vs. Ra! 147

Duel 209 Ra the Immortal 167

Master of the Cards 186

Previews 190

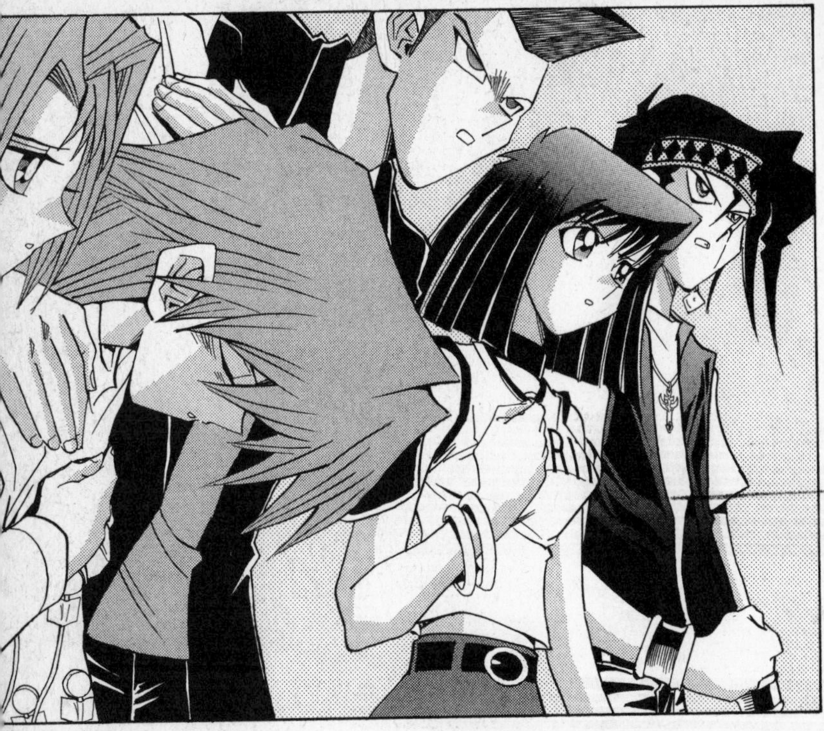

Duel 201: Red Spirit

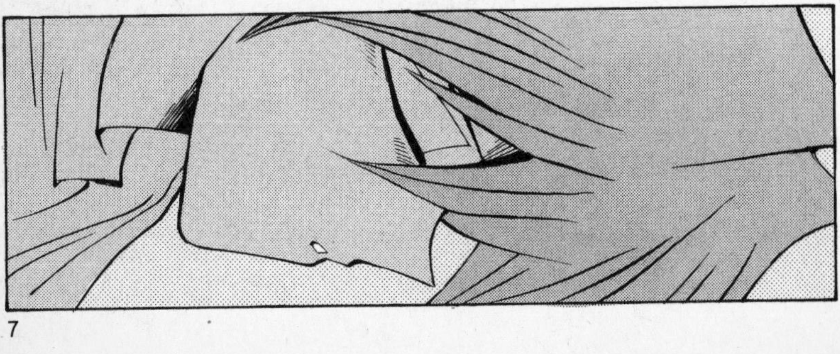

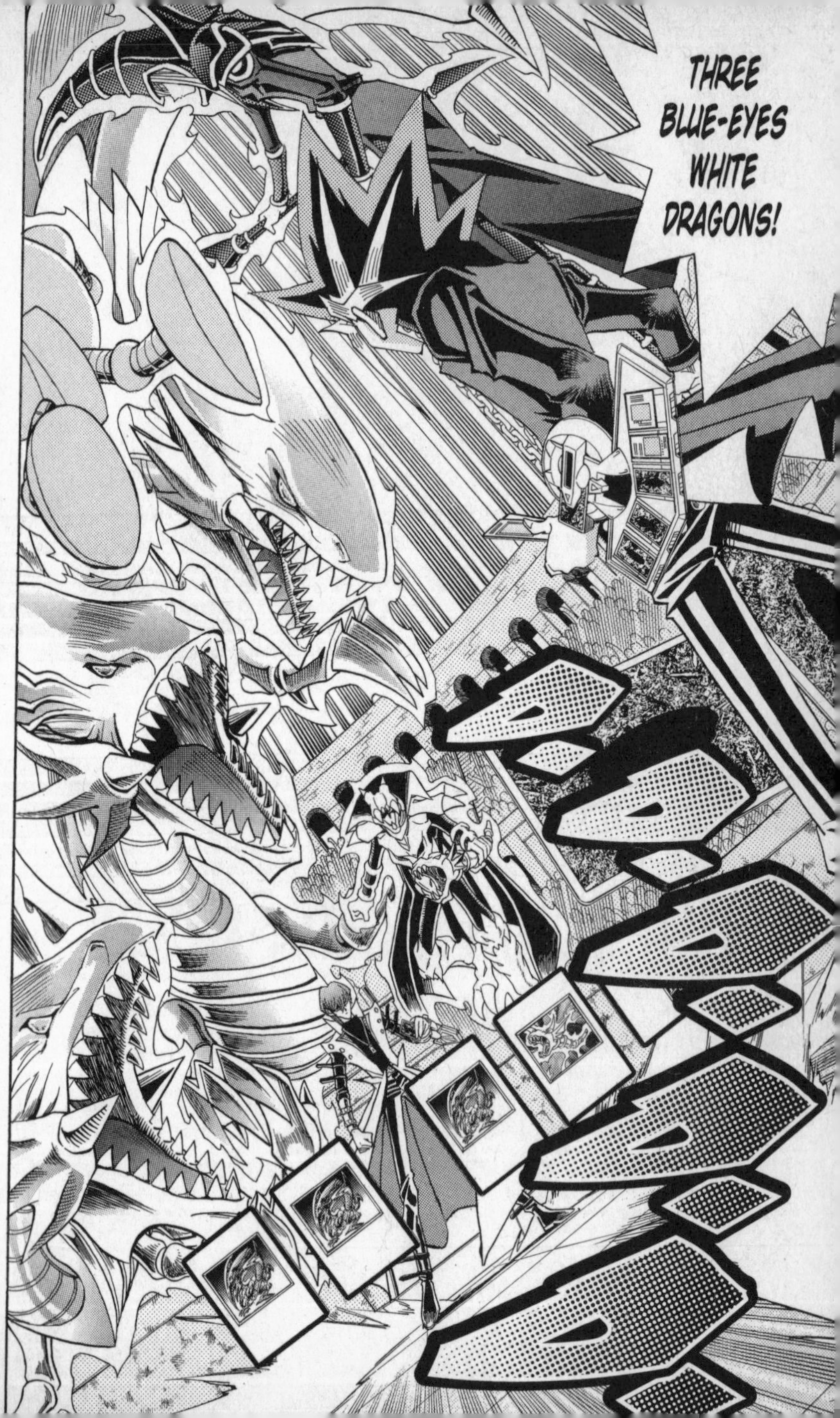
THREE BLUE-EYES WHITE DRAGONS!

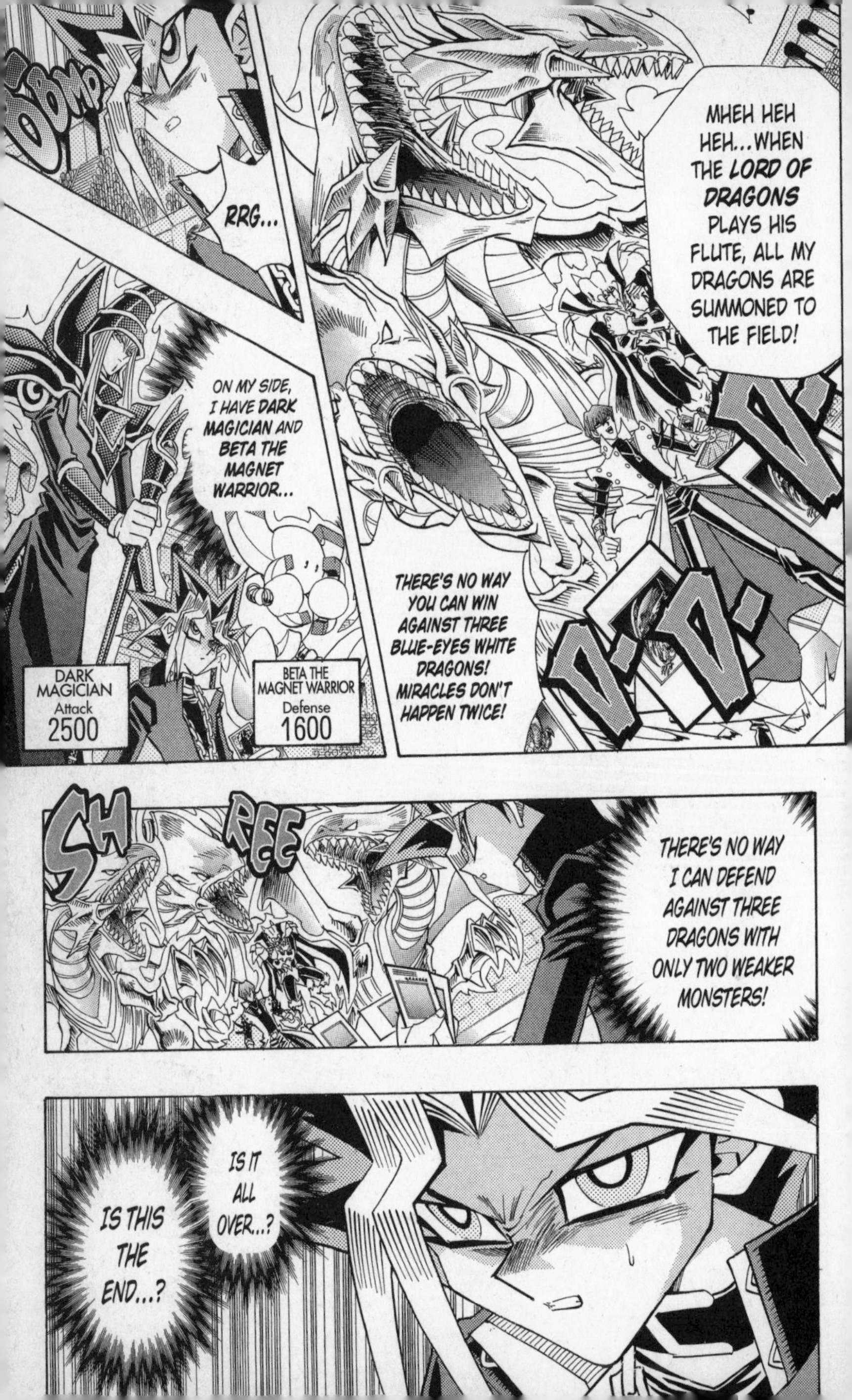
MHEH HEH HEH...WHEN THE LORD OF DRAGONS PLAYS HIS FLUTE, ALL MY DRAGONS ARE SUMMONED TO THE FIELD!
THERE'S NO WAY YOU CAN WIN AGAINST THREE BLUE-EYES WHITE DRAGONS! MIRACLES DON'T HAPPEN TWICE!
RRG...
ON MY SIDE, I HAVE DARK MAGICIAN AND BETA THE MAGNET WARRIOR...
BETA THE MAGNET WARRIOR Defense 1600
DARK MAGICIAN Attack 2500
SH REE
THERE'S NO WAY I CAN DEFEND AGAINST THREE DRAGONS WITH ONLY TWO WEAKER MONSTERS!
IS IT ALL OVER...?
IS THIS THE END...?

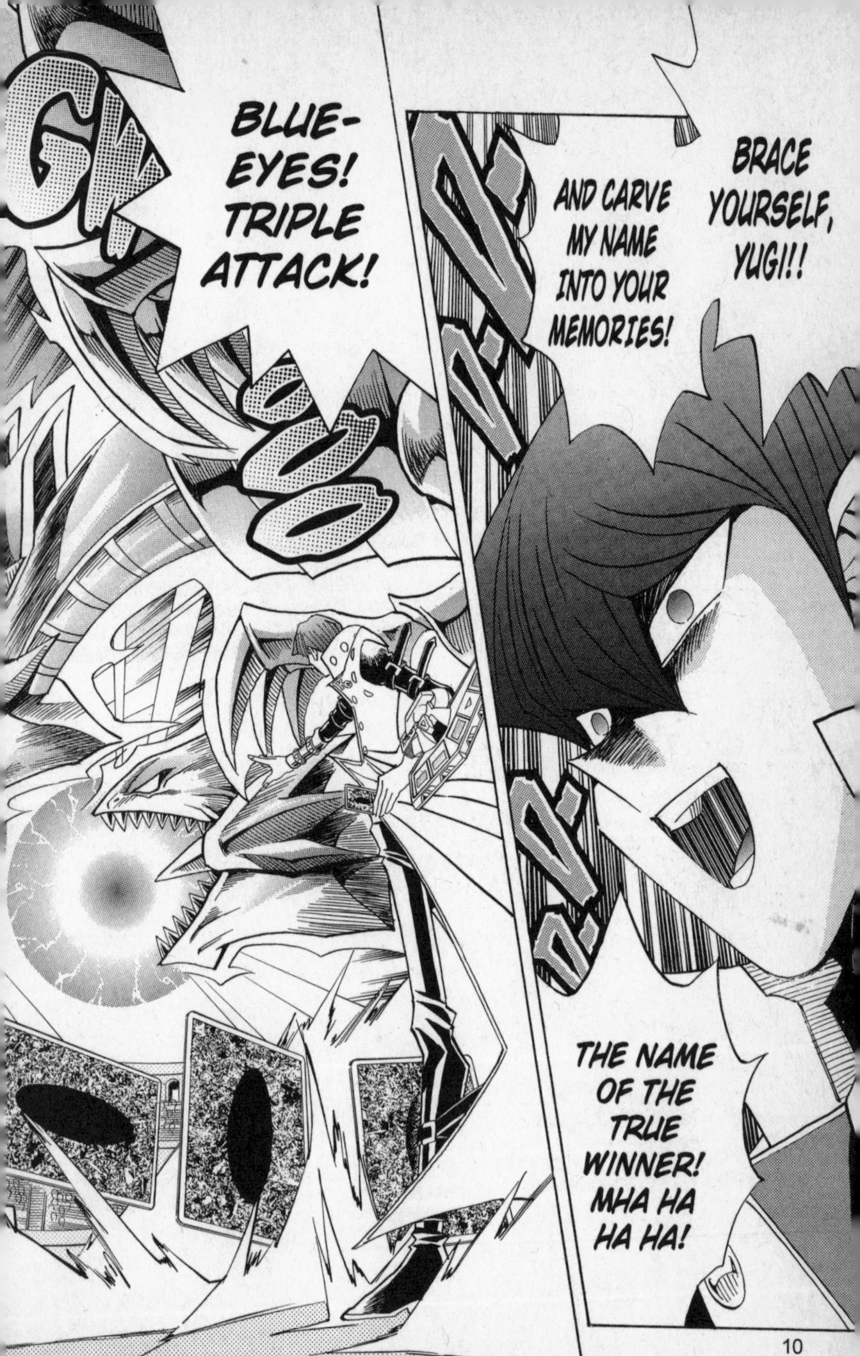
BRACE YOURSELF, YUGI!!
AND CARVE MY NAME INTO YOUR MEMORIES!
THE NAME OF THE TRUE WINNER! MHA HA HA HA!
BLUE-EYES! TRIPLE ATTACK!

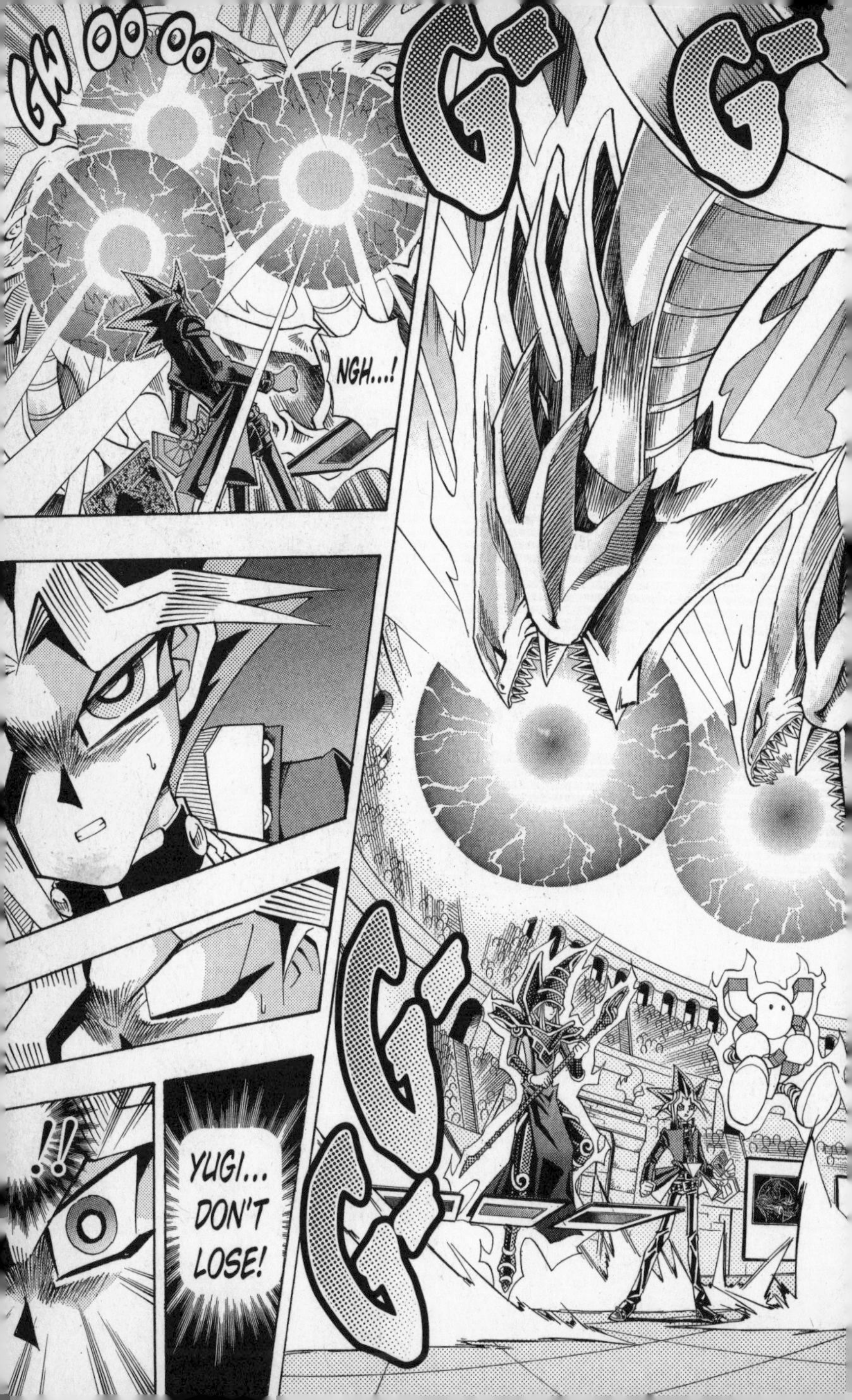
G G
G G G
GWOOOO
NGH...!
!!
YUGI... DON'T LOSE!

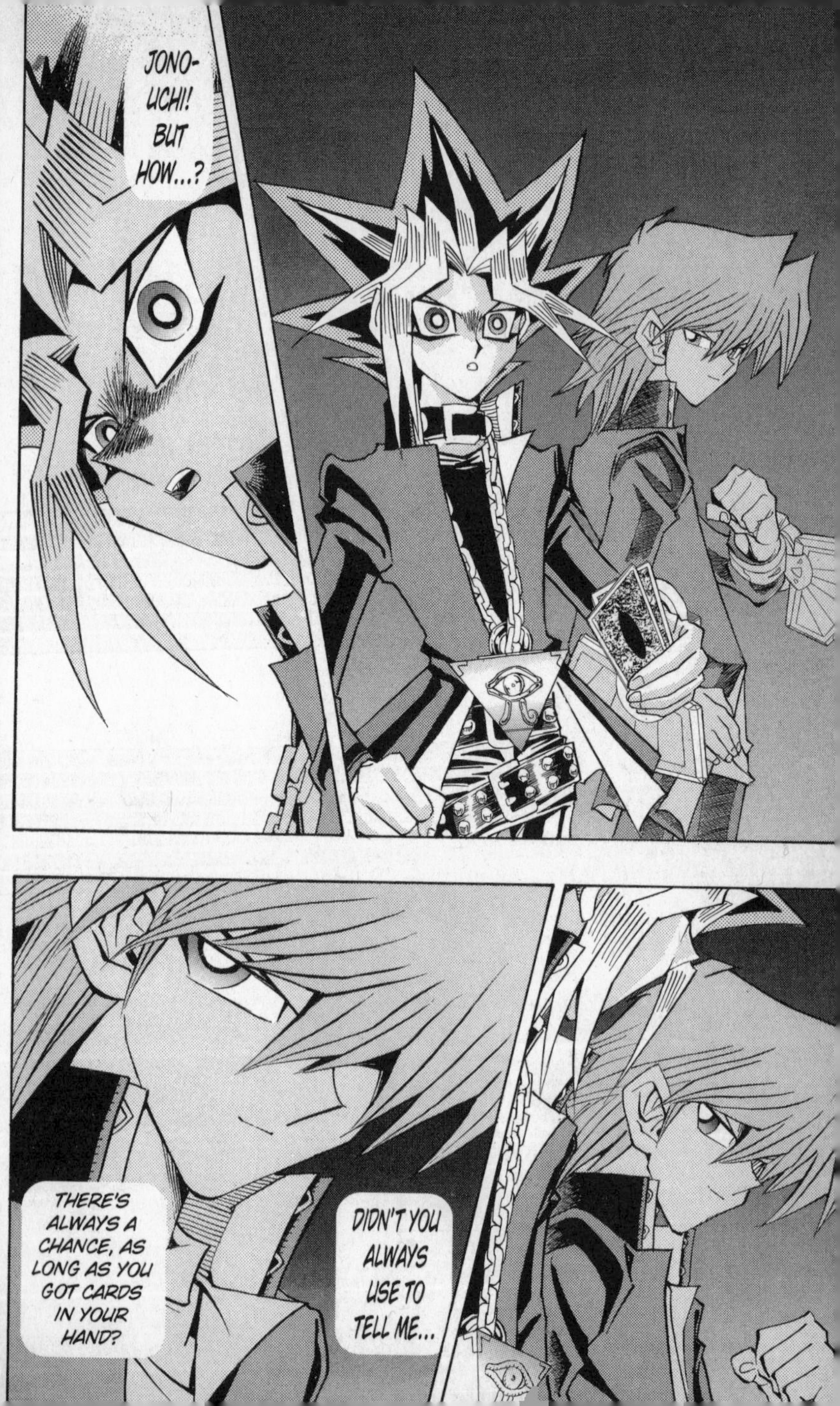
JONO-UCHI! BUT HOW...?
DIDN'T YOU ALWAYS USE TO TELL ME...
THERE'S ALWAYS A CHANCE, AS LONG AS YOU GOT CARDS IN YOUR HAND?

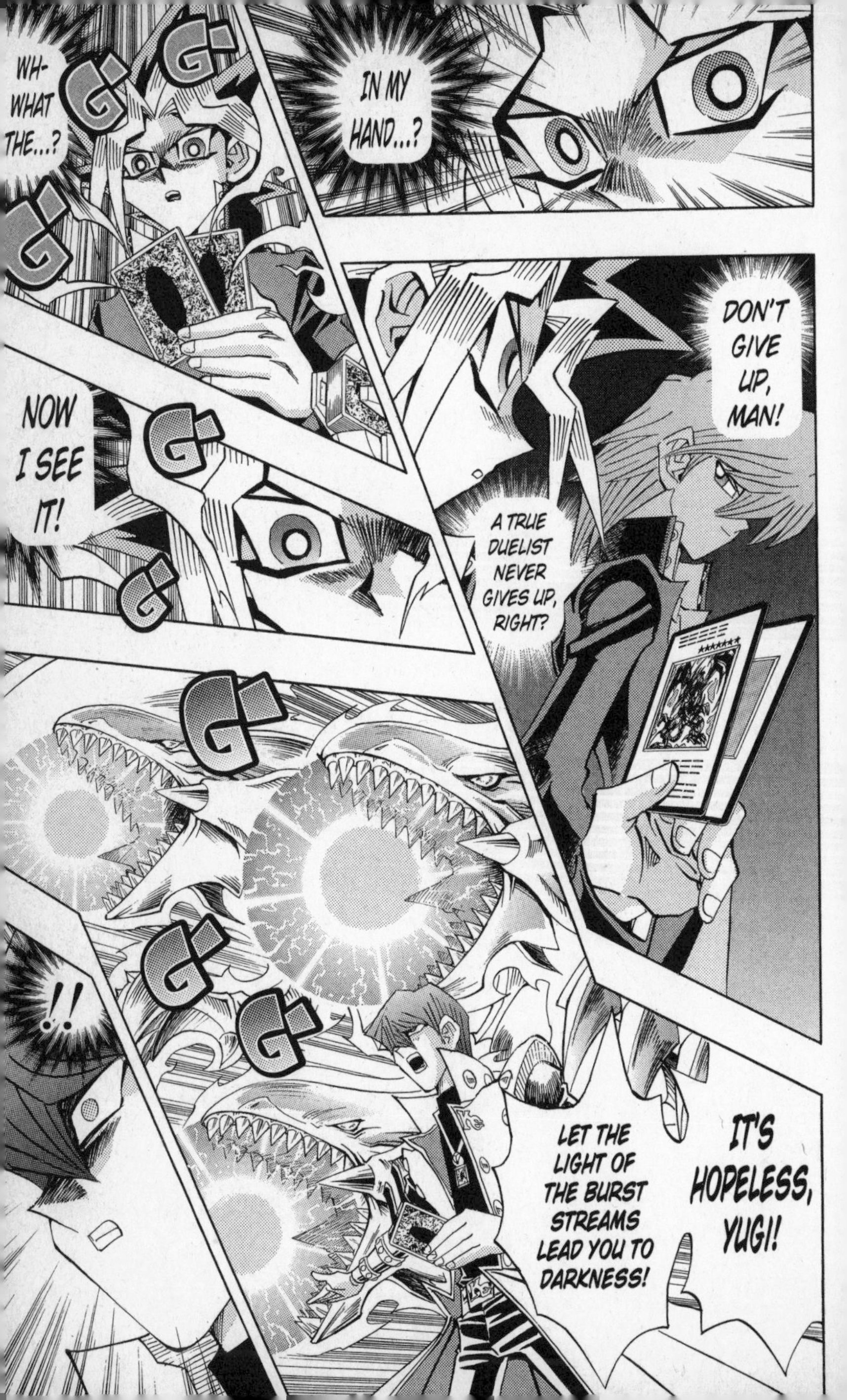
IN MY HAND...?
WH- WHAT THE...?
G G G G
DON'T GIVE UP, MAN!
A TRUE DUELIST NEVER GIVES UP, RIGHT?
NOW I SEE IT!
G G
IT'S HOPELESS, YUGI!
LET THE LIGHT OF THE BURST STREAMS LEAD YOU TO DARKNESS!
G G G
!!

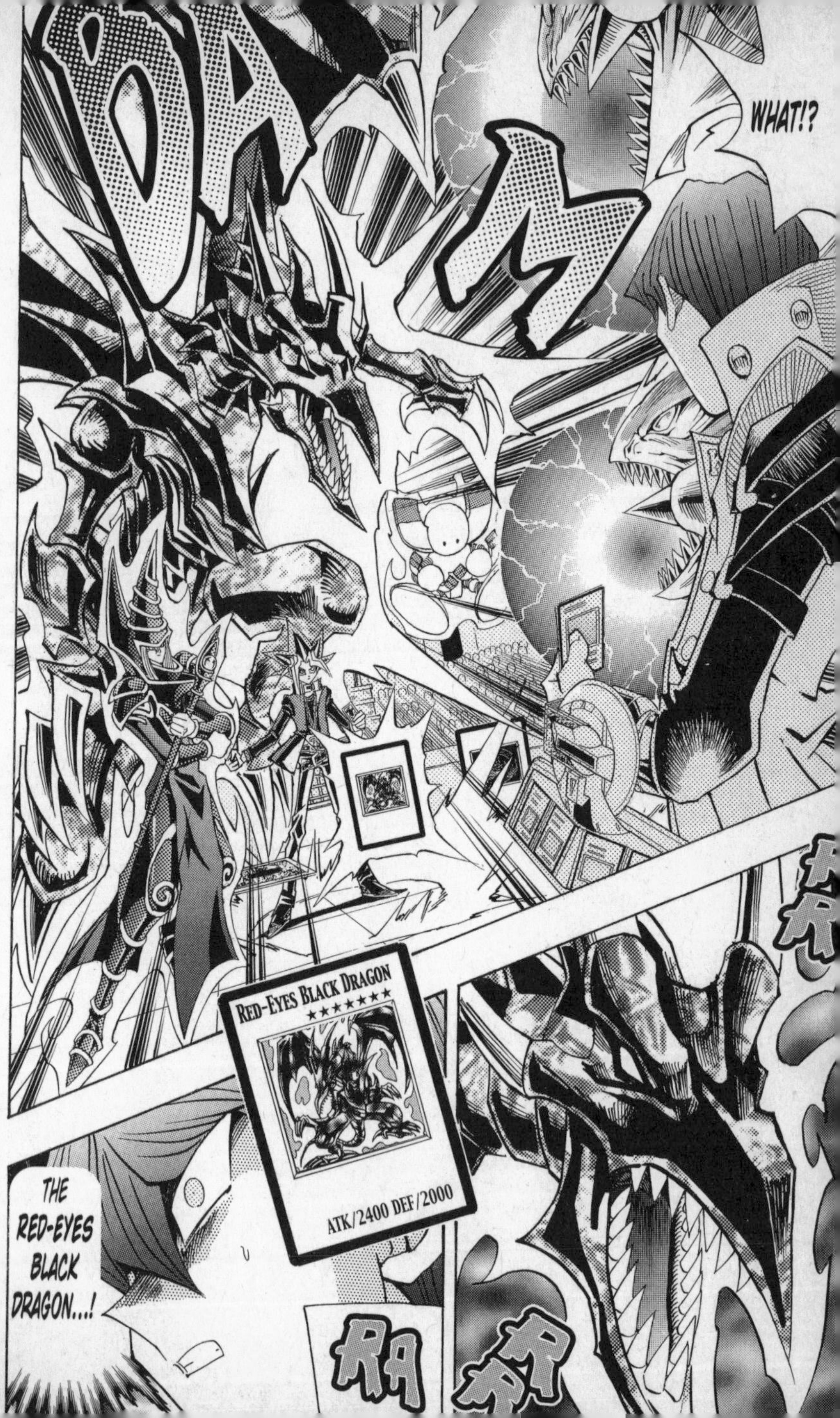

WHAT!?
RED-EYES BLACK DRAGON
ATK/2400 DEF/2000
THE RED-EYES BLACK DRAGON...!

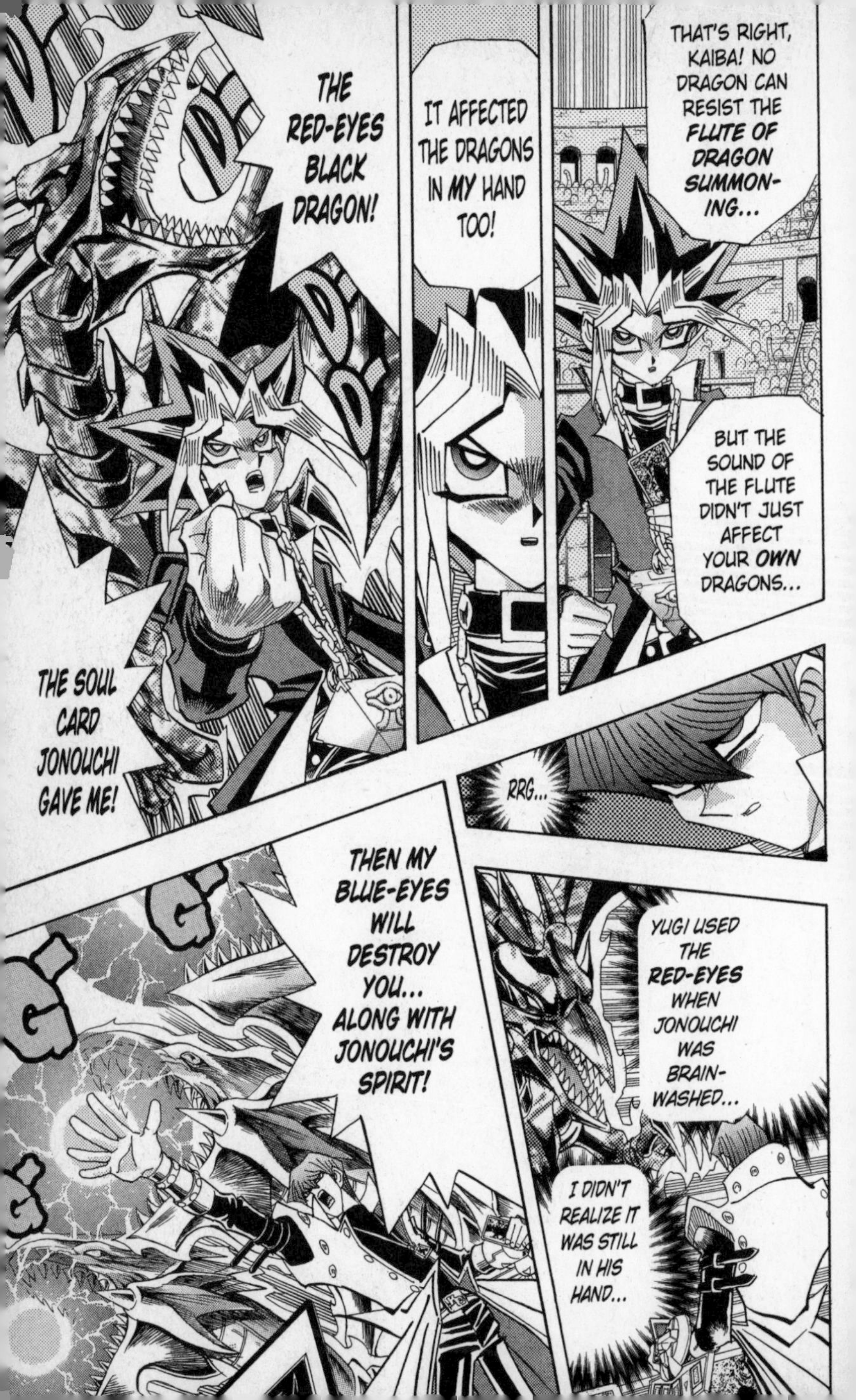

THAT'S RIGHT, KAIBA! NO DRAGON CAN RESIST THE FLUTE OF DRAGON SUMMONING...
BUT THE SOUND OF THE FLUTE DIDN'T JUST AFFECT YOUR OWN DRAGONS...
IT AFFECTED THE DRAGONS IN MY HAND TOO!
THE RED-EYES BLACK DRAGON!
THE SOUL CARD JONOUCHI GAVE ME!
RRG...
YUGI USED THE RED-EYES WHEN JONOUCHI WAS BRAIN-WASHED...
I DIDN'T REALIZE IT WAS STILL IN HIS HAND...
THEN MY BLUE-EYES WILL DESTROY YOU... ALONG WITH JONOUCHI'S SPIRIT!
G
G
G
G

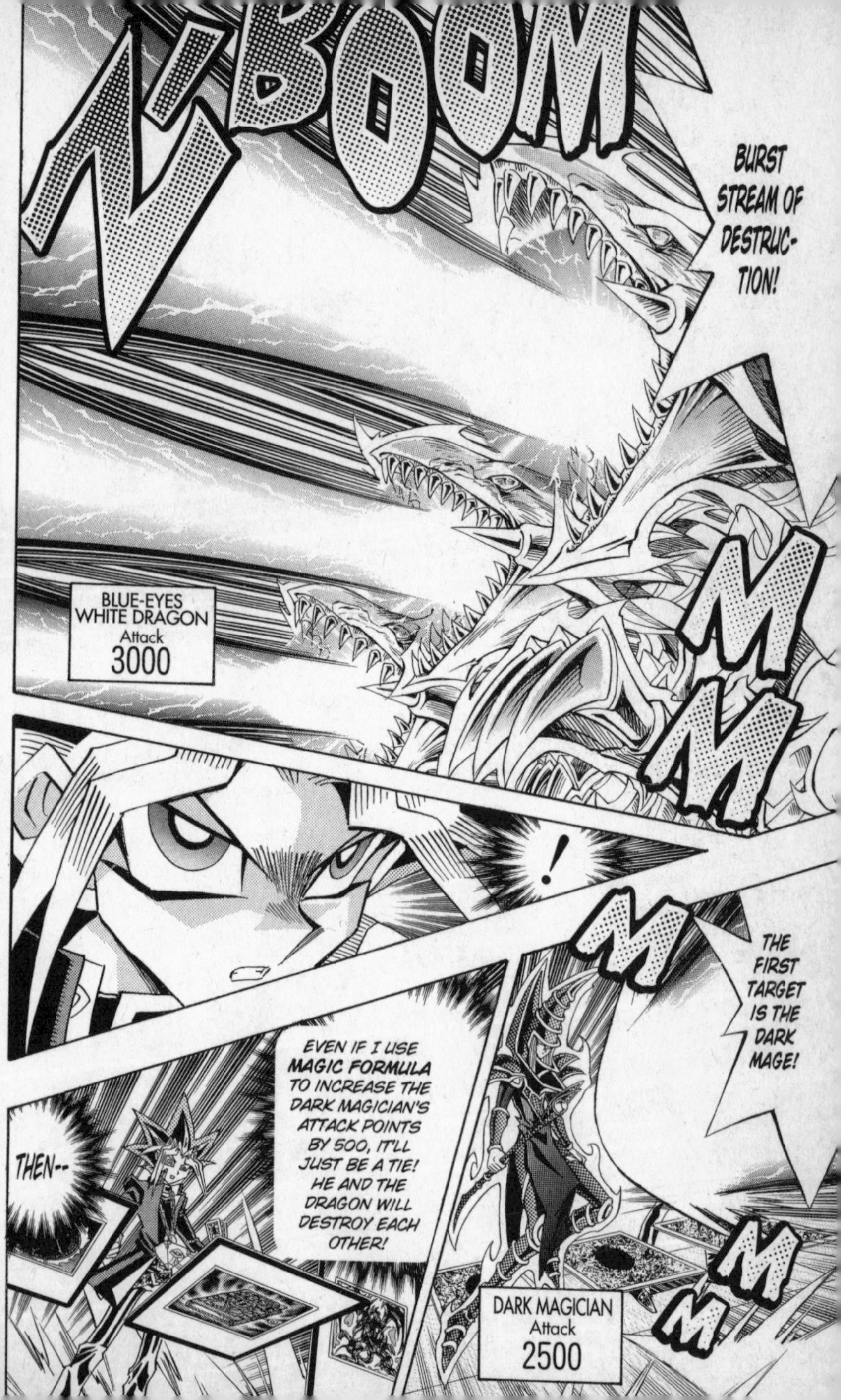

Z'BOOM
BURST STREAM OF DESTRUC-TION!
BLUE-EYES WHITE DRAGON Attack 3000
MMM
!
MM
THE FIRST TARGET IS THE DARK MAGE!
EVEN IF I USE MAGIC FORMULA TO INCREASE THE DARK MAGICIAN'S ATTACK POINTS BY 500, IT'LL JUST BE A TIE! HE AND THE DRAGON WILL DESTROY EACH OTHER!
THEN--
MM
DARK MAGICIAN Attack 2500

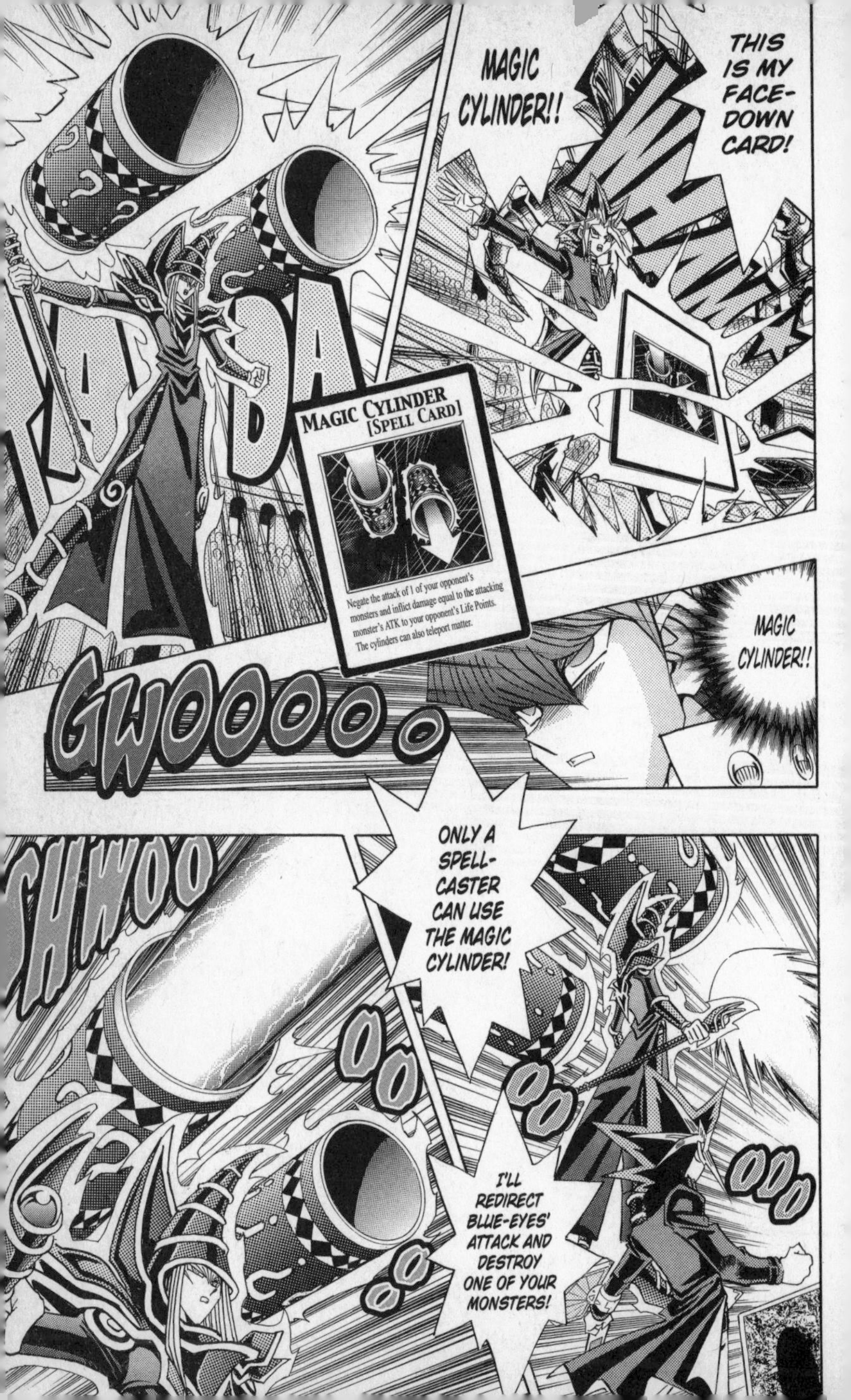
THIS IS MY FACE-DOWN CARD!
MAGIC CYLINDER!!
MAGIC CYLINDER
[SPELL CARD]
Negate the attack of 1 of your opponent's monsters and inflict damage equal to the attacking monster's ATK to your opponent's Life Points. The cylinders can also teleport matter.
GWOOOOO
MAGIC CYLINDER!!
ONLY A SPELL-CASTER CAN USE THE MAGIC CYLINDER!
I'LL REDIRECT BLUE-EYES' ATTACK AND DESTROY ONE OF YOUR MONSTERS!
SHWOOOOOOOO

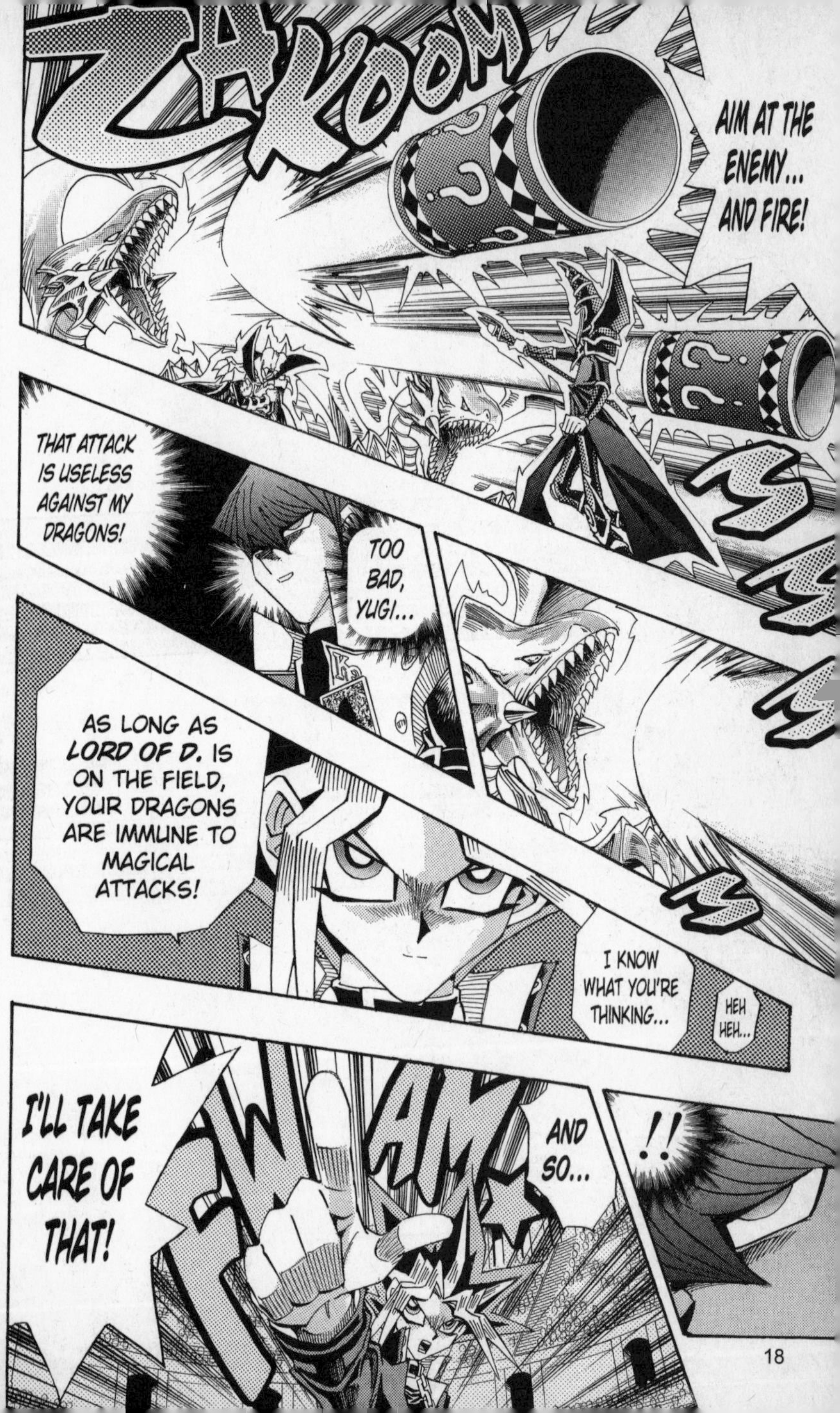

AIM AT THE ENEMY... AND FIRE!
ZAKOOM
MMMMM
THAT ATTACK IS USELESS AGAINST MY DRAGONS!
TOO BAD, YUGI...
AS LONG AS *LORD OF D.* IS ON THE FIELD, YOUR DRAGONS ARE IMMUNE TO MAGICAL ATTACKS!
HEH HEH...
I KNOW WHAT YOU'RE THINKING...
!!
AND SO...
I'LL TAKE CARE OF THAT!
WHAM

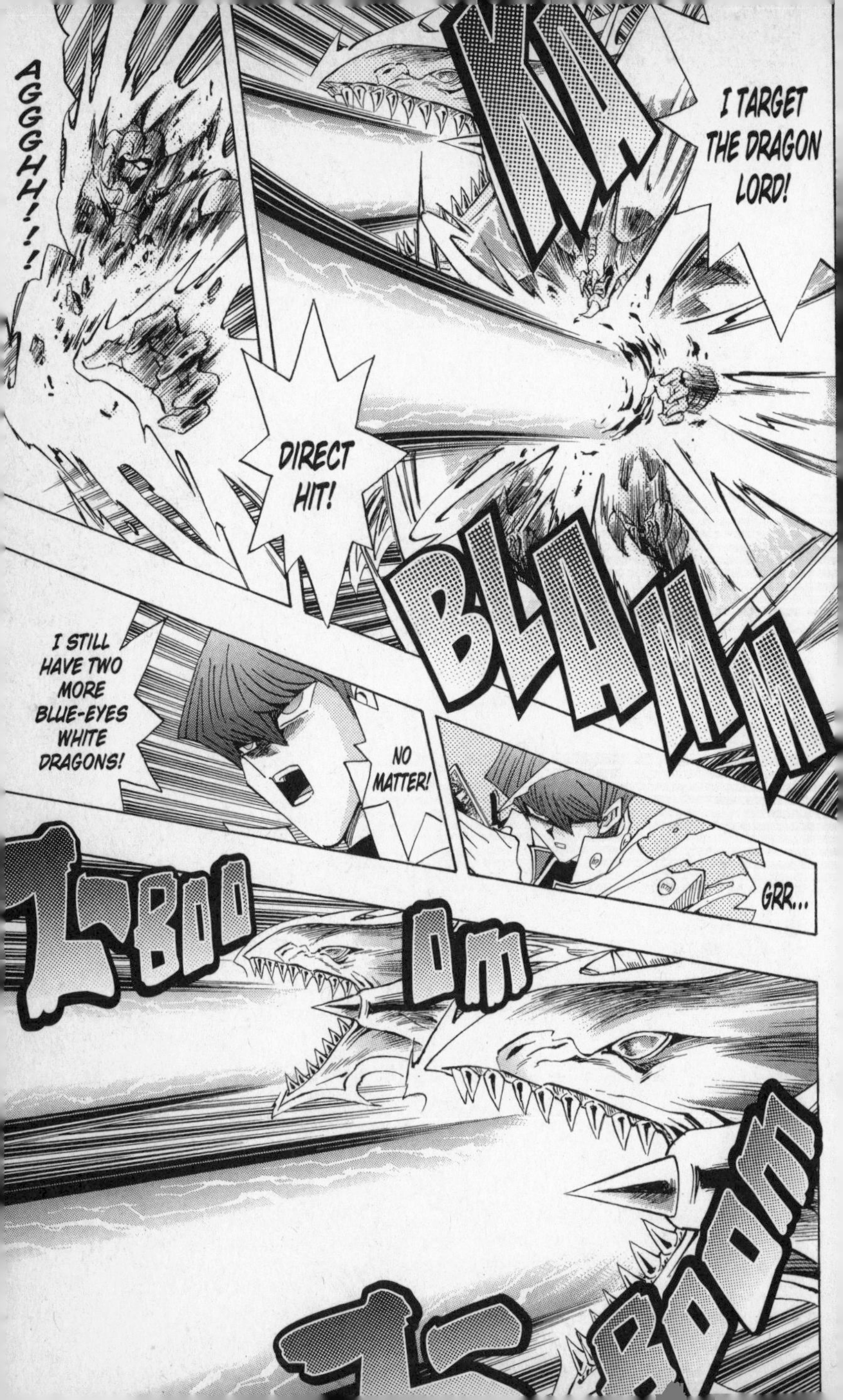
I TARGET THE DRAGON LORD!
AGGGHH!!!
DIRECT HIT!
BLAMMM
GRR...
NO MATTER!
I STILL HAVE TWO MORE BLUE-EYES WHITE DRAGONS!
BOOM

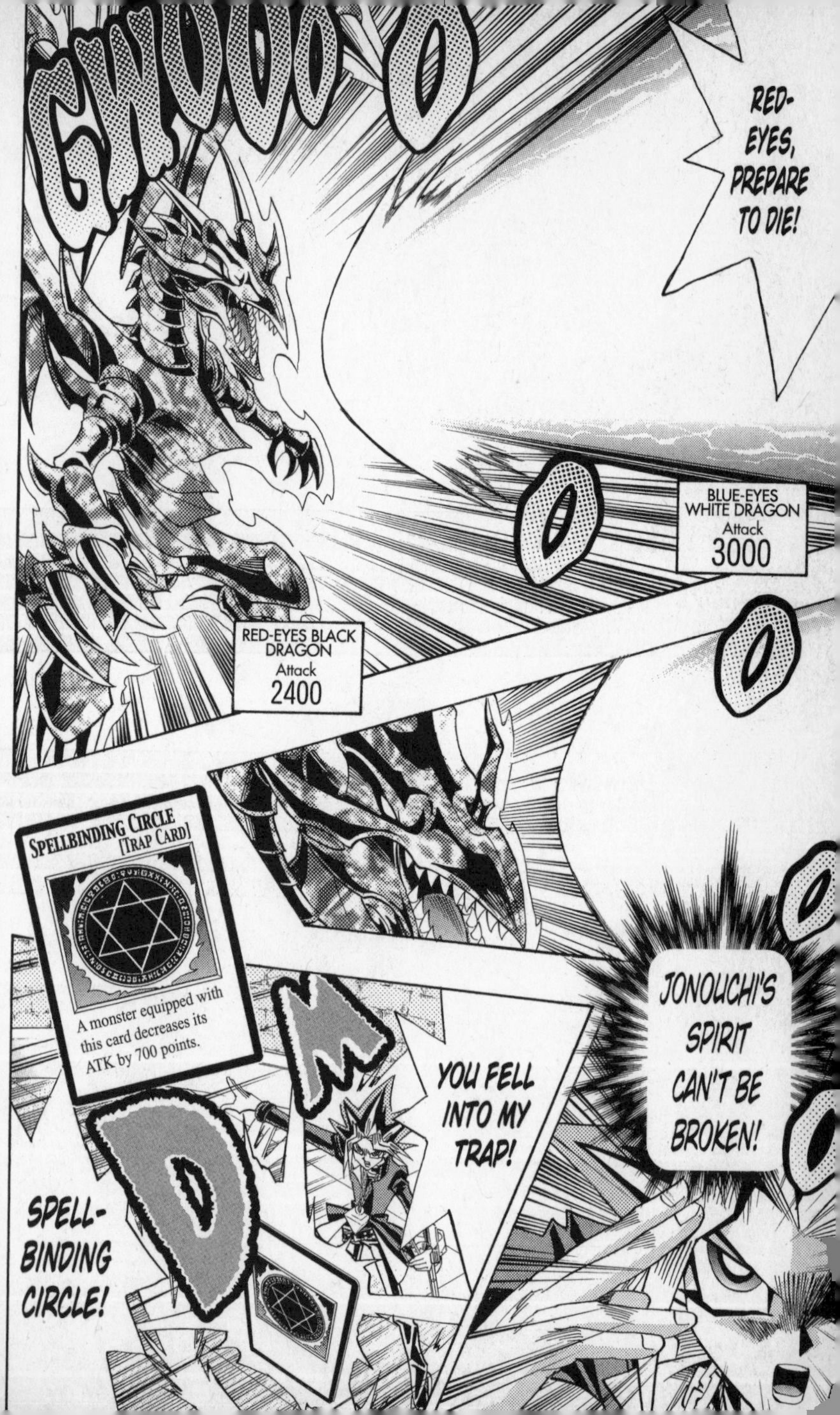
RED-EYES, PREPARE TO DIE!
BLUE-EYES WHITE DRAGON
Attack
3000
RED-EYES BLACK DRAGON
Attack
2400
JONOUCHI'S SPIRIT CAN'T BE BROKEN!
YOU FELL INTO MY TRAP!
SPELLBINDING CIRCLE
[TRAP CARD]
A monster equipped with this card decreases its ATK by 700 points.
SPELL-BINDING CIRCLE!

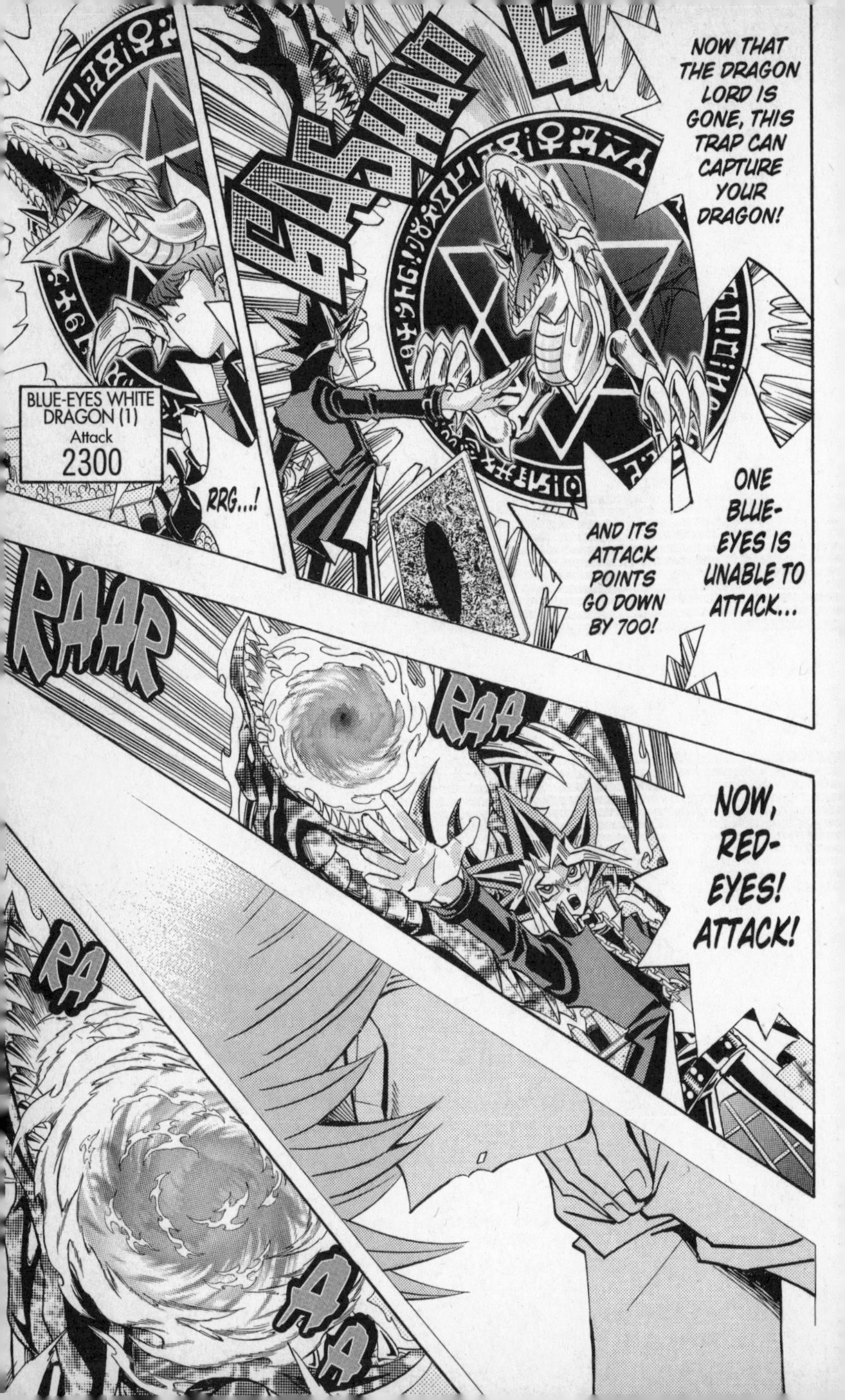
NOW THAT THE DRAGON LORD IS GONE, THIS TRAP CAN CAPTURE YOUR DRAGON!
ONE BLUE-EYES IS UNABLE TO ATTACK...
AND ITS ATTACK POINTS GO DOWN BY 700!
BLUE-EYES WHITE DRAGON (1) Attack 2300
RRG...!
RAAR
RAA
NOW, RED-EYES! ATTACK!
RA
AA

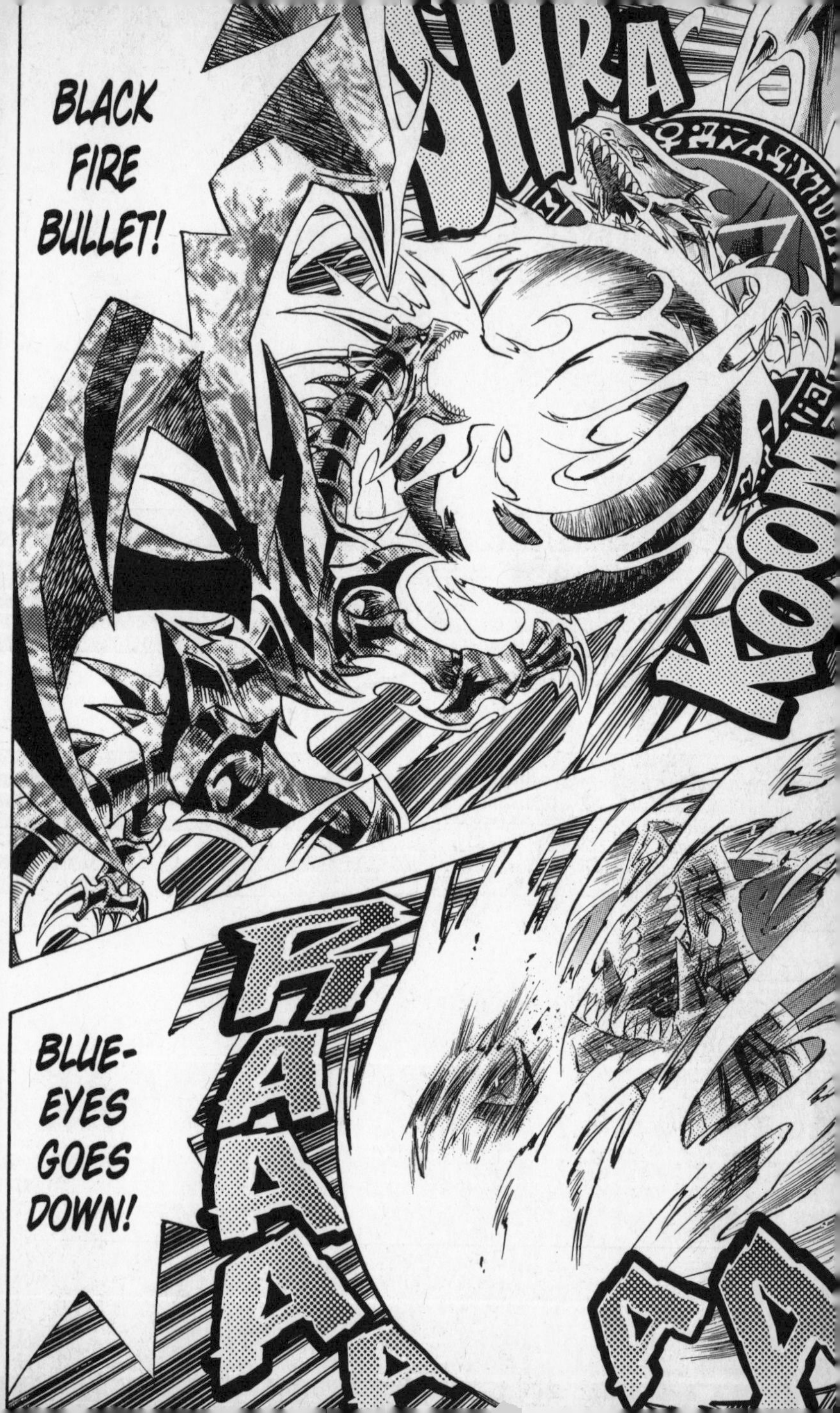
SHRA
BLACK FIRE BULLET!
KOOM
FAA
BLUE-EYES GOES DOWN!

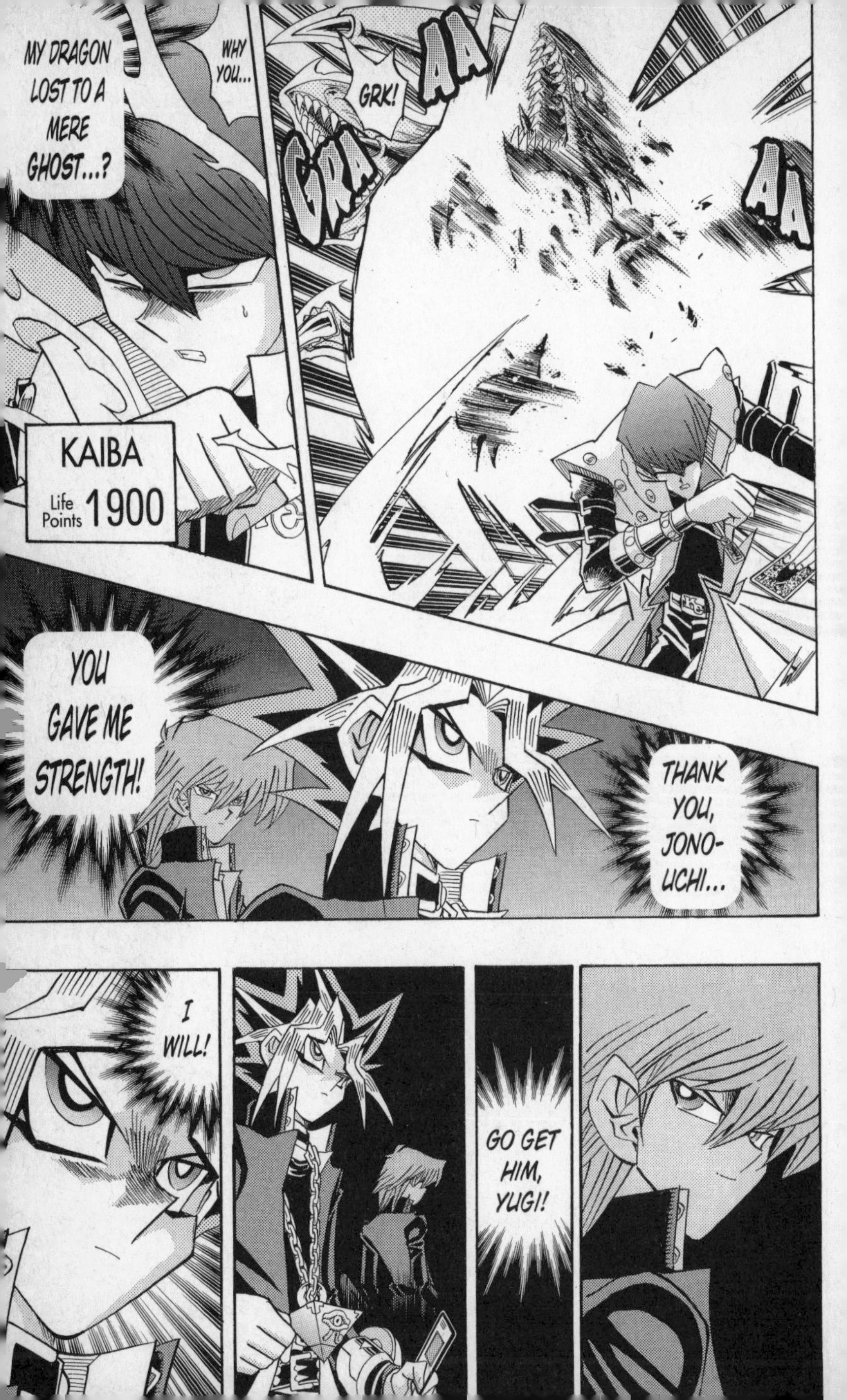
GRK!
GRA
AA
AA
WHY YOU...
MY DRAGON LOST TO A MERE GHOST...?
KAIBA
Life Points 1900
THANK YOU, JONO-UCHI...
YOU GAVE ME STRENGTH!
GO GET HIM, YUGI!
I WILL!

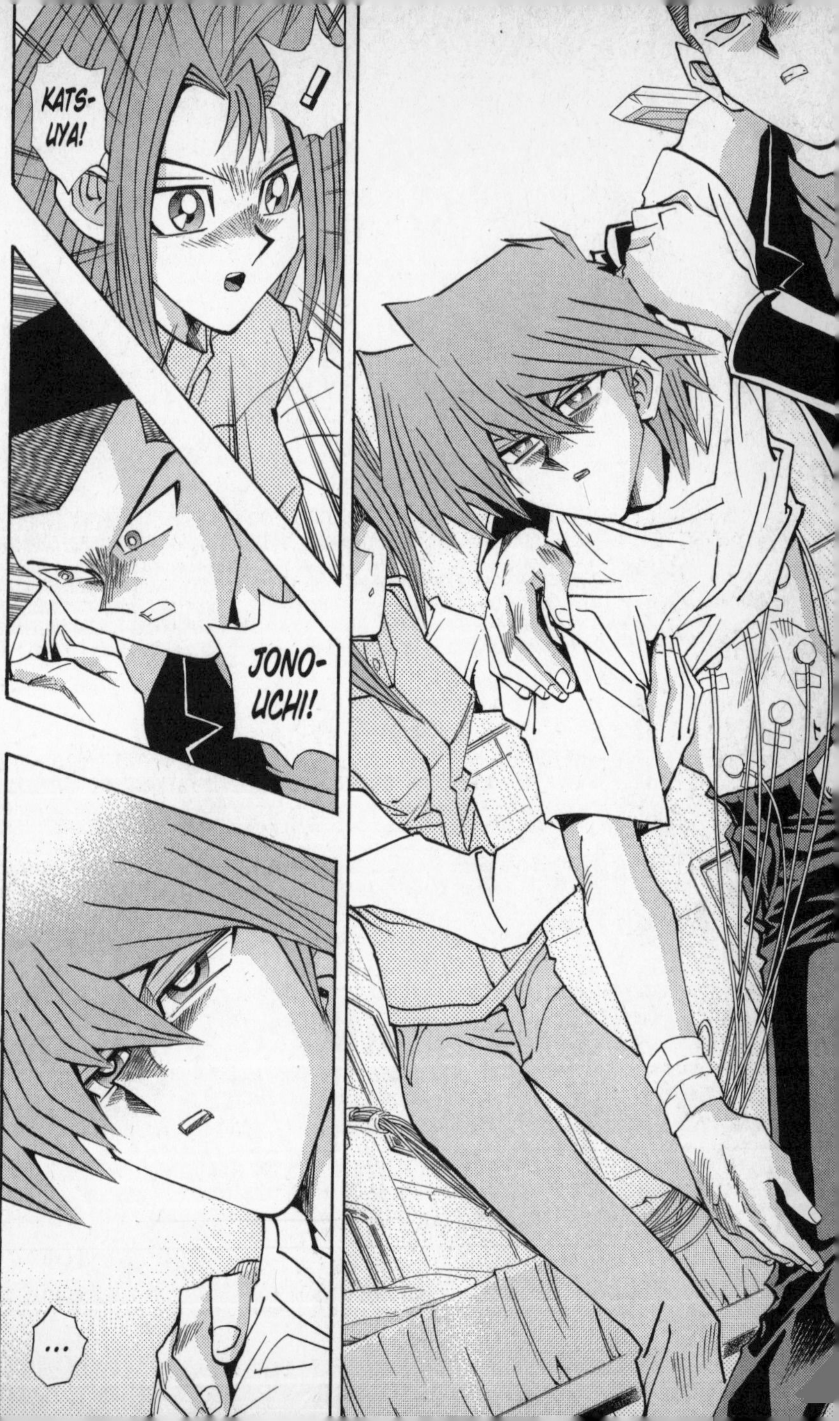
KATS-UYA!
JONO-UCHI!
...

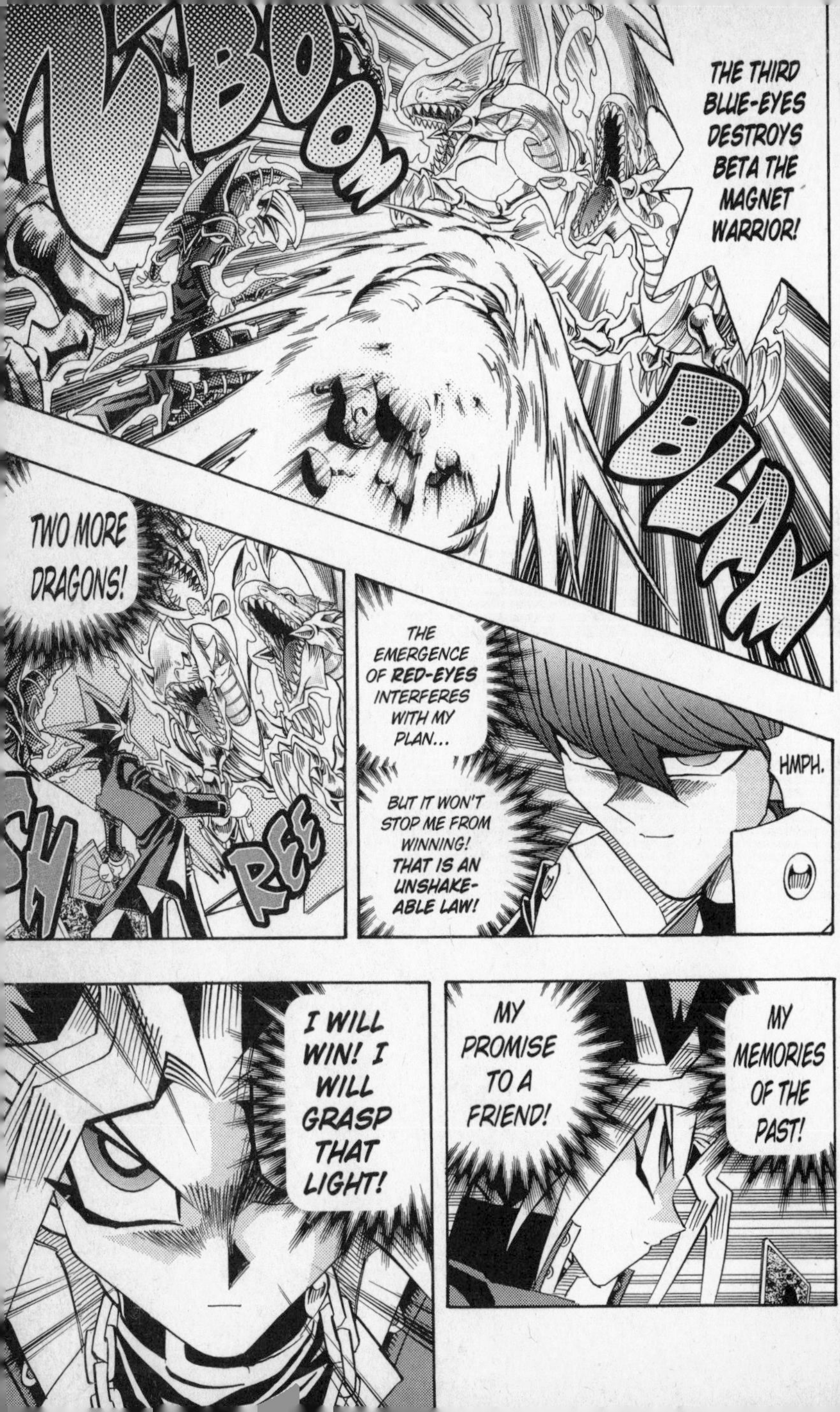
BOOM
THE THIRD BLUE-EYES DESTROYS BETA THE MAGNET WARRIOR!
BLAM
HMPH.
THE EMERGENCE OF RED-EYES INTERFERES WITH MY PLAN...
BUT IT WON'T STOP ME FROM WINNING! THAT IS AN UNSHAKE-ABLE LAW!
TWO MORE DRAGONS!
REE
MY MEMORIES OF THE PAST!
MY PROMISE TO A FRIEND!
I WILL WIN! I WILL GRASP THAT LIGHT!

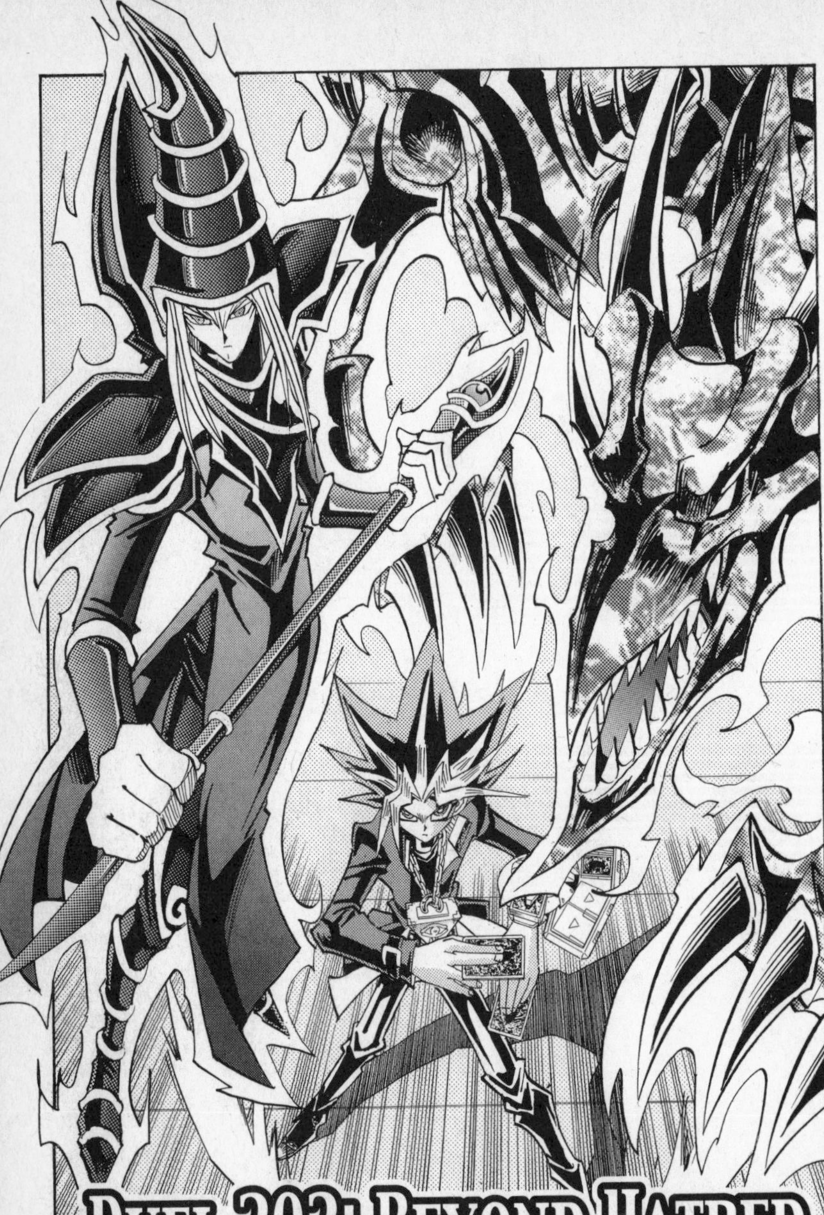
DUEL 202: BEYOND HATRED

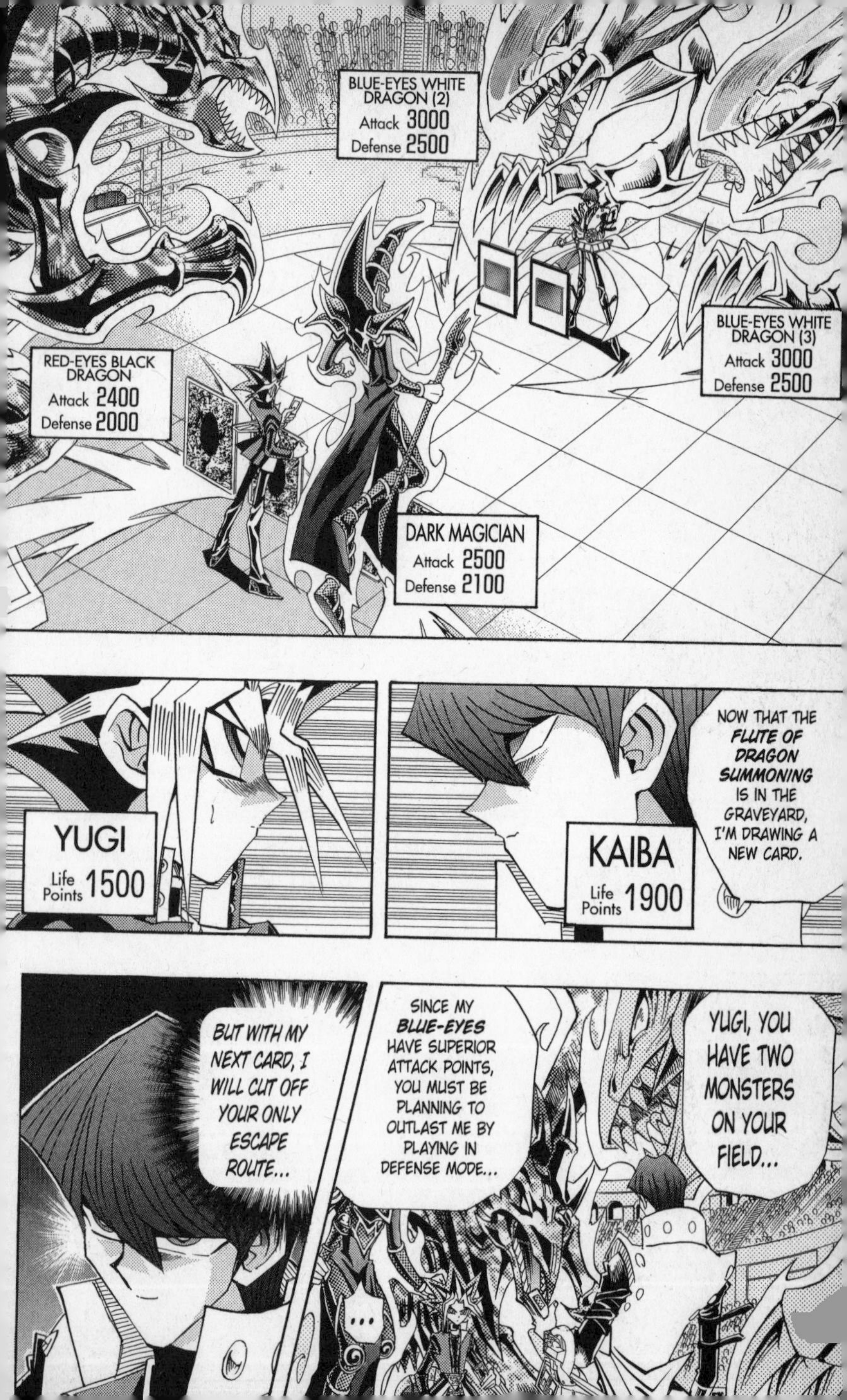

BLUE-EYES WHITE DRAGON (2) Attack 3000 Defense 2500
BLUE-EYES WHITE DRAGON (3) Attack 3000 Defense 2500
RED-EYES BLACK DRAGON Attack 2400 Defense 2000
DARK MAGICIAN Attack 2500 Defense 2100
NOW THAT THE *FLUTE OF DRAGON SUMMONING* IS IN THE GRAVEYARD, I'M DRAWING A NEW CARD.
KAIBA Life Points 1900
YUGI Life Points 1500
YUGI, YOU HAVE TWO MONSTERS ON YOUR FIELD...
SINCE MY *BLUE-EYES* HAVE SUPERIOR ATTACK POINTS, YOU MUST BE PLANNING TO OUTLAST ME BY PLAYING IN DEFENSE MODE...
...
BUT WITH MY NEXT CARD, I WILL CUT OFF YOUR ONLY ESCAPE ROUTE...

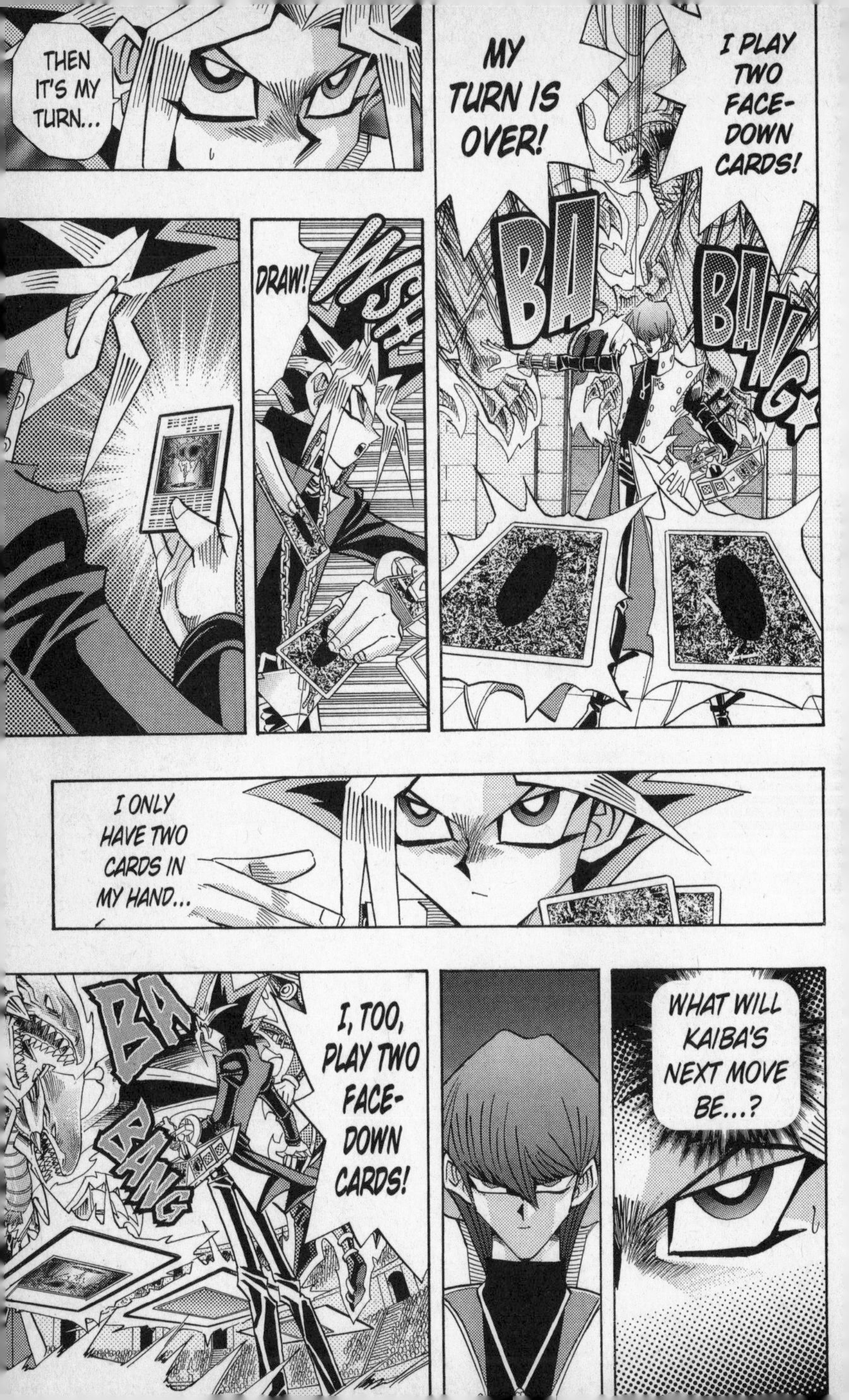
I PLAY TWO FACE-DOWN CARDS!
MY TURN IS OVER!
BA
BANG
THEN IT'S MY TURN...
DRAW!
WSH
I ONLY HAVE TWO CARDS IN MY HAND...
WHAT WILL KAIBA'S NEXT MOVE BE...?
I, TOO, PLAY TWO FACE-DOWN CARDS!
BA
BANG

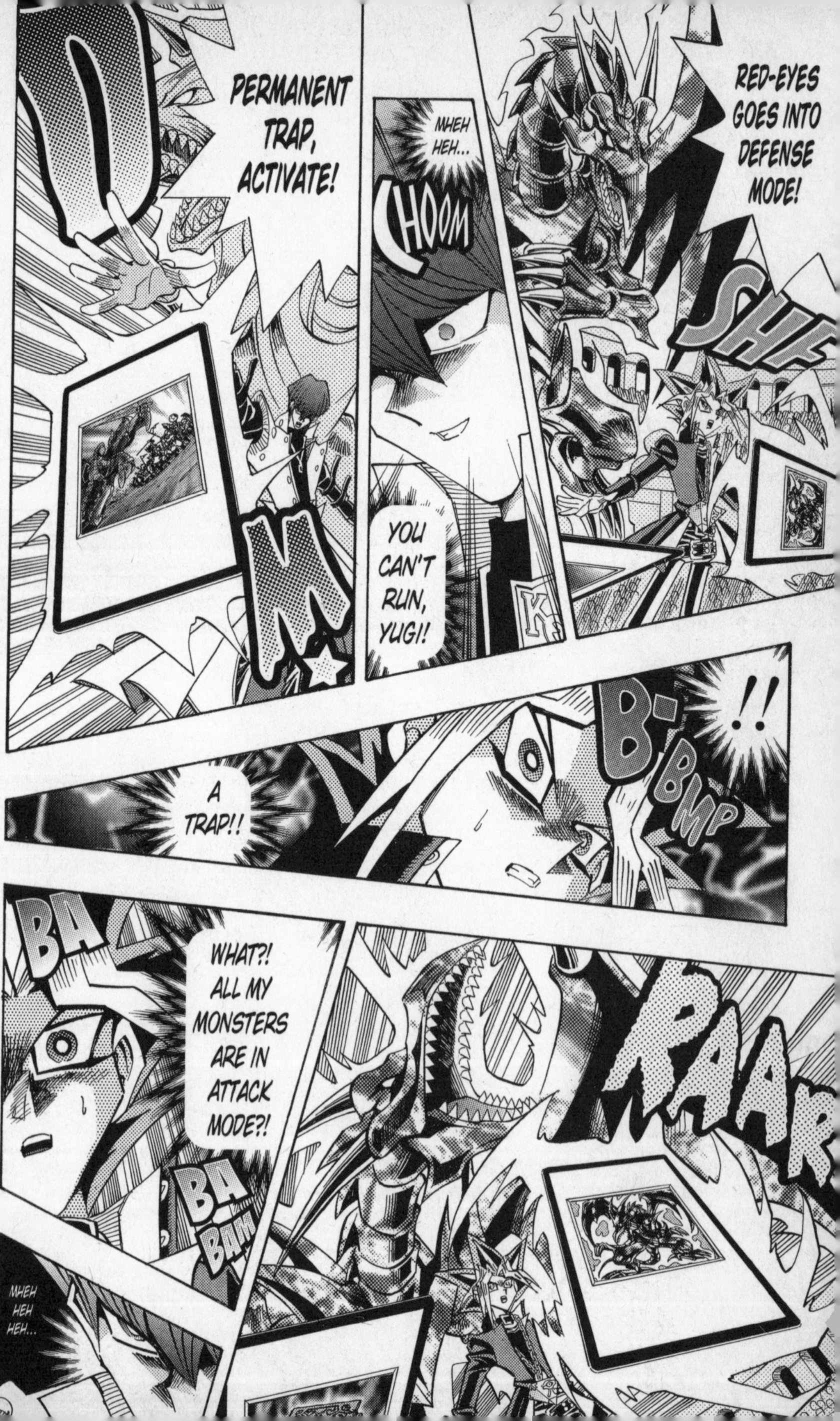

RED-EYES GOES INTO DEFENSE MODE!
SHF
MHEH HEH...
CHOOM
YOU CAN'T RUN, YUGI!
PERMANENT TRAP, ACTIVATE!
M
B-BMP
!!
A TRAP!!
RAAR
BA
WHAT?! ALL MY MONSTERS ARE IN ATTACK MODE?!
BA BAM
MHEH HEH HEH...

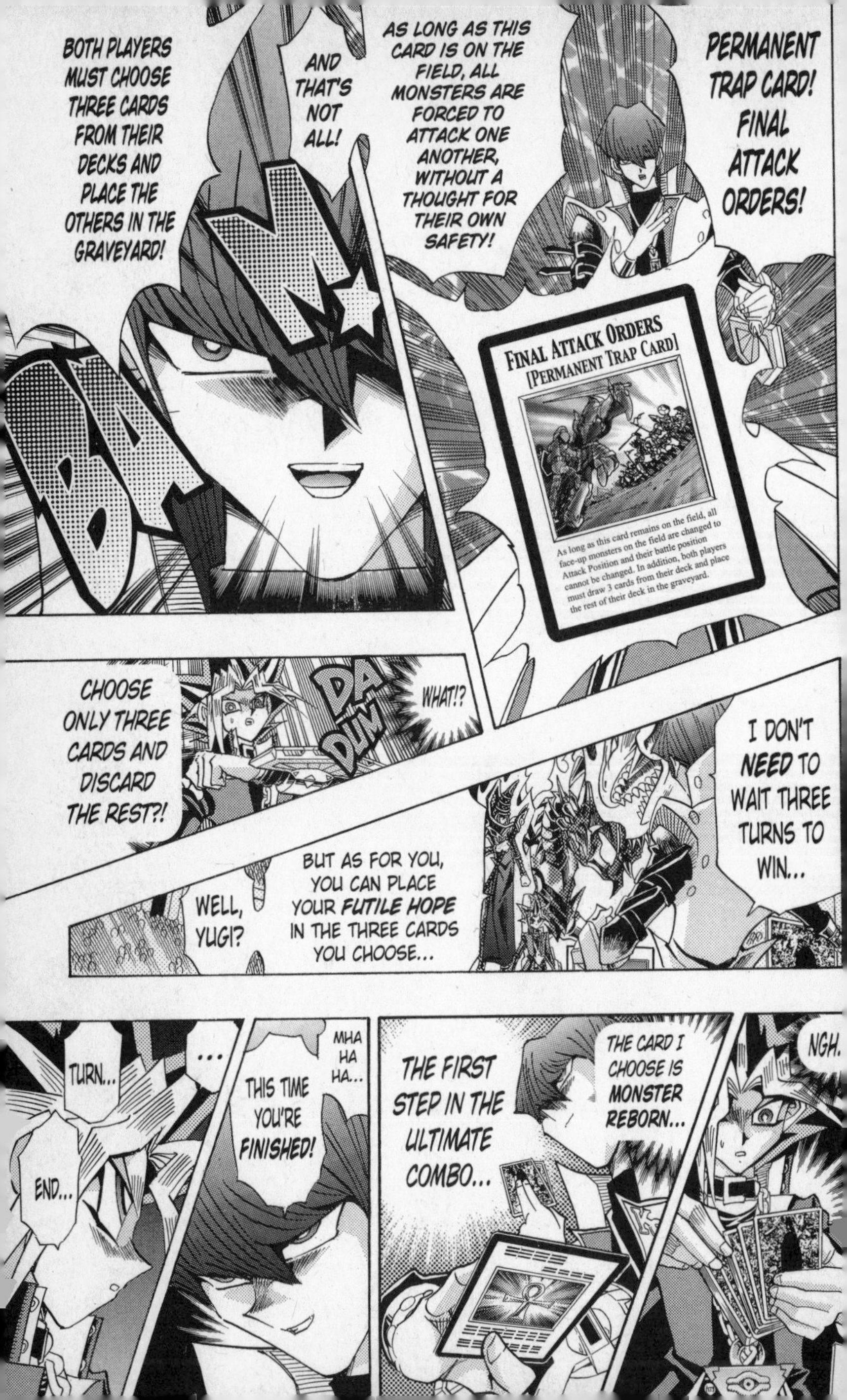
PERMANENT TRAP CARD! FINAL ATTACK ORDERS!
FINAL ATTACK ORDERS
[PERMANENT TRAP CARD]
As long as this card remains on the field, all face-up monsters on the field are changed to Attack Position and their battle position cannot be changed. In addition, both players must draw 3 cards from their deck and place the rest of their deck in the graveyard.
AS LONG AS THIS CARD IS ON THE FIELD, ALL MONSTERS ARE FORCED TO ATTACK ONE ANOTHER, WITHOUT A THOUGHT FOR THEIR OWN SAFETY!
AND THAT'S NOT ALL!
BAM
BOTH PLAYERS MUST CHOOSE THREE CARDS FROM THEIR DECKS AND PLACE THE OTHERS IN THE GRAVEYARD!
WHAT!?
DA DUM
CHOOSE ONLY THREE CARDS AND DISCARD THE REST?!
I DON'T NEED TO WAIT THREE TURNS TO WIN...
BUT AS FOR YOU, YOU CAN PLACE YOUR FUTILE HOPE IN THE THREE CARDS YOU CHOOSE...
WELL, YUGI?
NGH.
THE CARD I CHOOSE IS MONSTER REBORN...
THE FIRST STEP IN THE ULTIMATE COMBO...
MHA HA HA...
THIS TIME YOU'RE FINISHED!
...
TURN...
END...

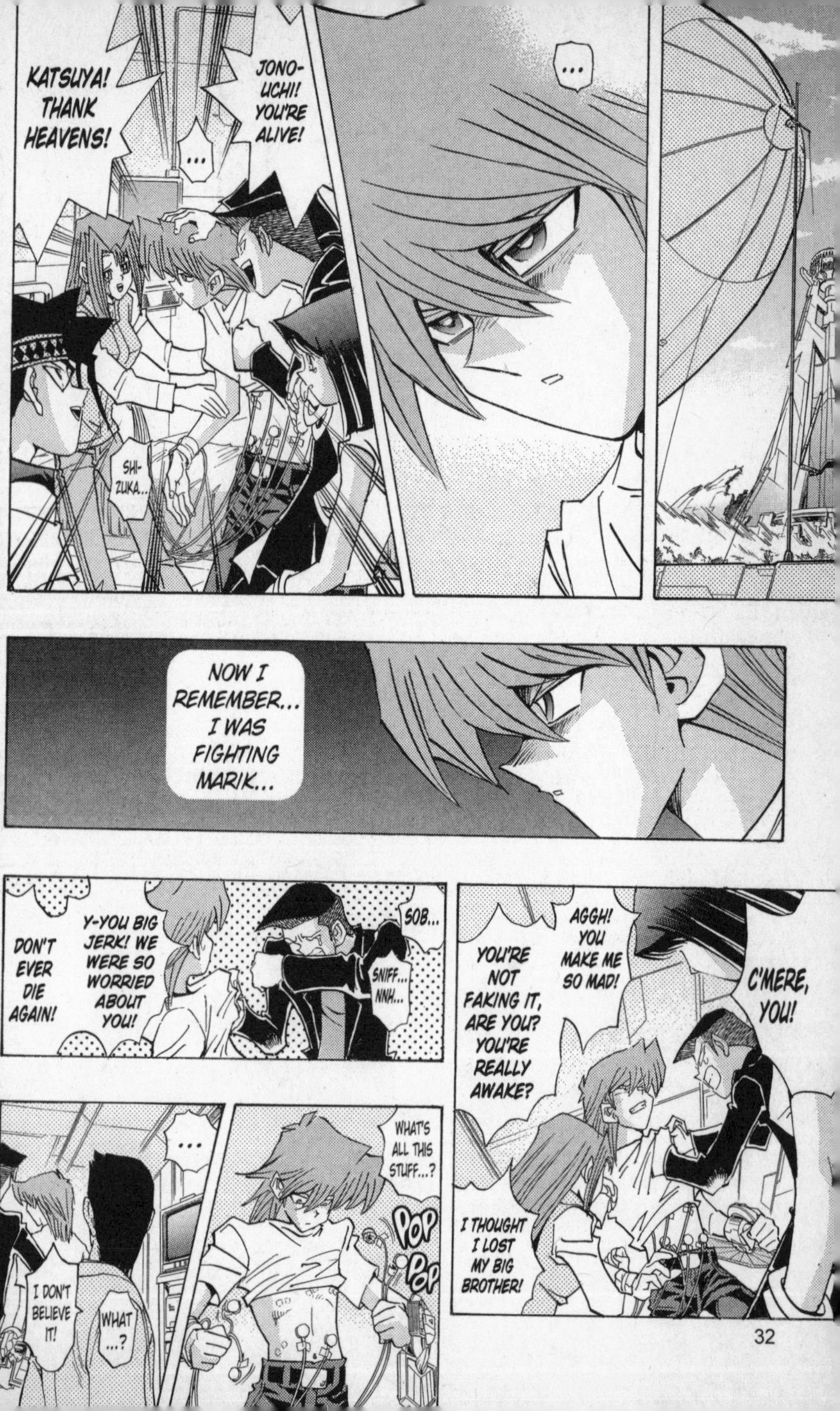
...
JONO-UCHI! YOU'RE ALIVE!
KATSUYA! THANK HEAVENS!
...
SHI-ZUKA...
NOW I REMEMBER... I WAS FIGHTING MARIK...
C'MERE, YOU!
AGGH! YOU MAKE ME SO MAD!
YOU'RE NOT FAKING IT, ARE YOU? YOU'RE REALLY AWAKE?
I THOUGHT I LOST MY BIG BROTHER!
SOB...
SNIFF... NNH...
Y-YOU BIG JERK! WE WERE SO WORRIED ABOUT YOU!
DON'T EVER DIE AGAIN!
WHAT'S ALL THIS STUFF...?
POP
POP
...
WHAT ...?
I DON'T BELIEVE IT!

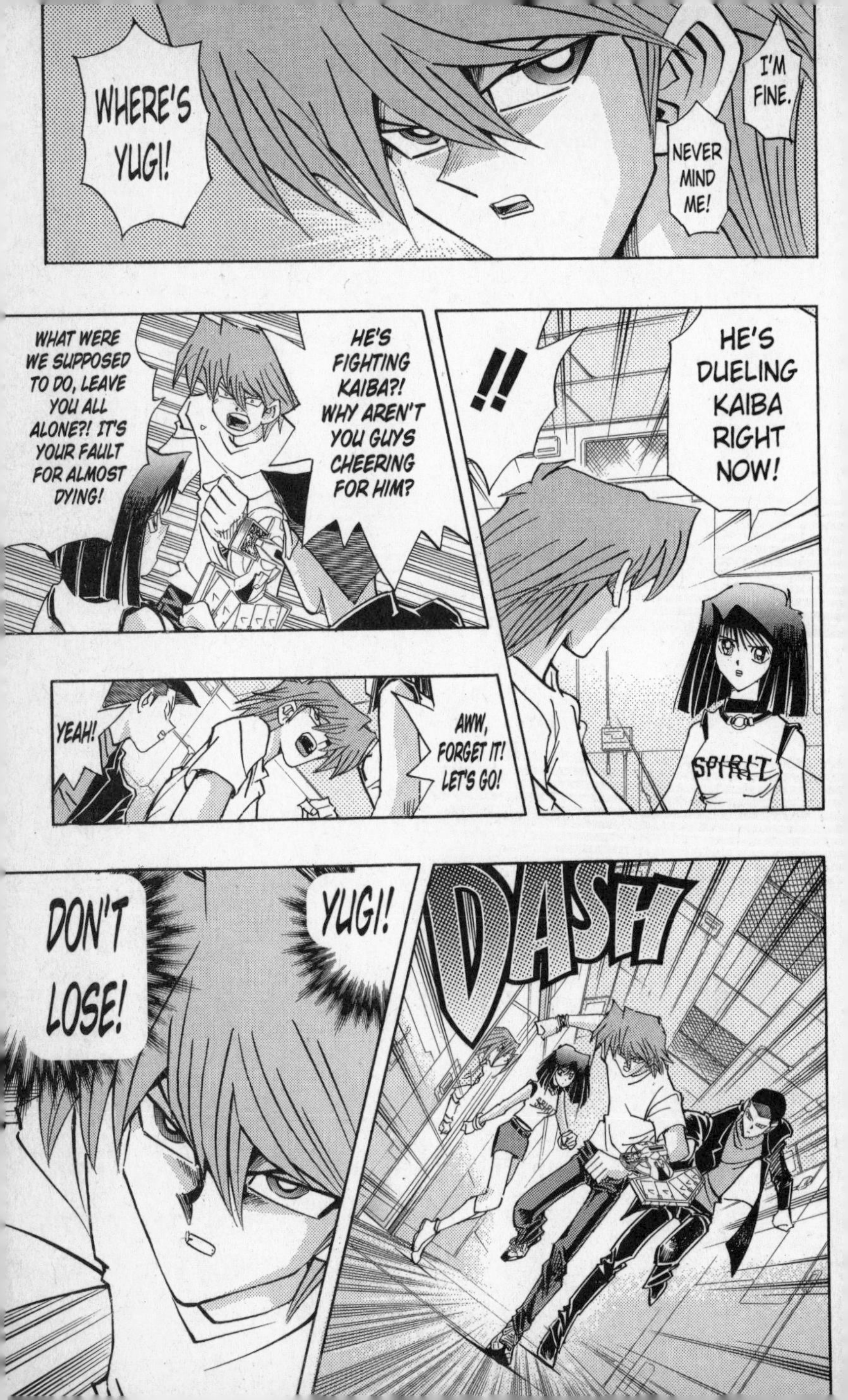
I'M FINE.
NEVER MIND ME!
WHERE'S YUGI!
HE'S DUELING KAIBA RIGHT NOW!
!!
SPIRIT
HE'S FIGHTING KAIBA?! WHY AREN'T YOU GUYS CHEERING FOR HIM?
WHAT WERE WE SUPPOSED TO DO, LEAVE YOU ALL ALONE?! IT'S YOUR FAULT FOR ALMOST DYING!
AWW, FORGET IT! LET'S GO!
YEAH!
DASH
YUGI!
DON'T LOSE!

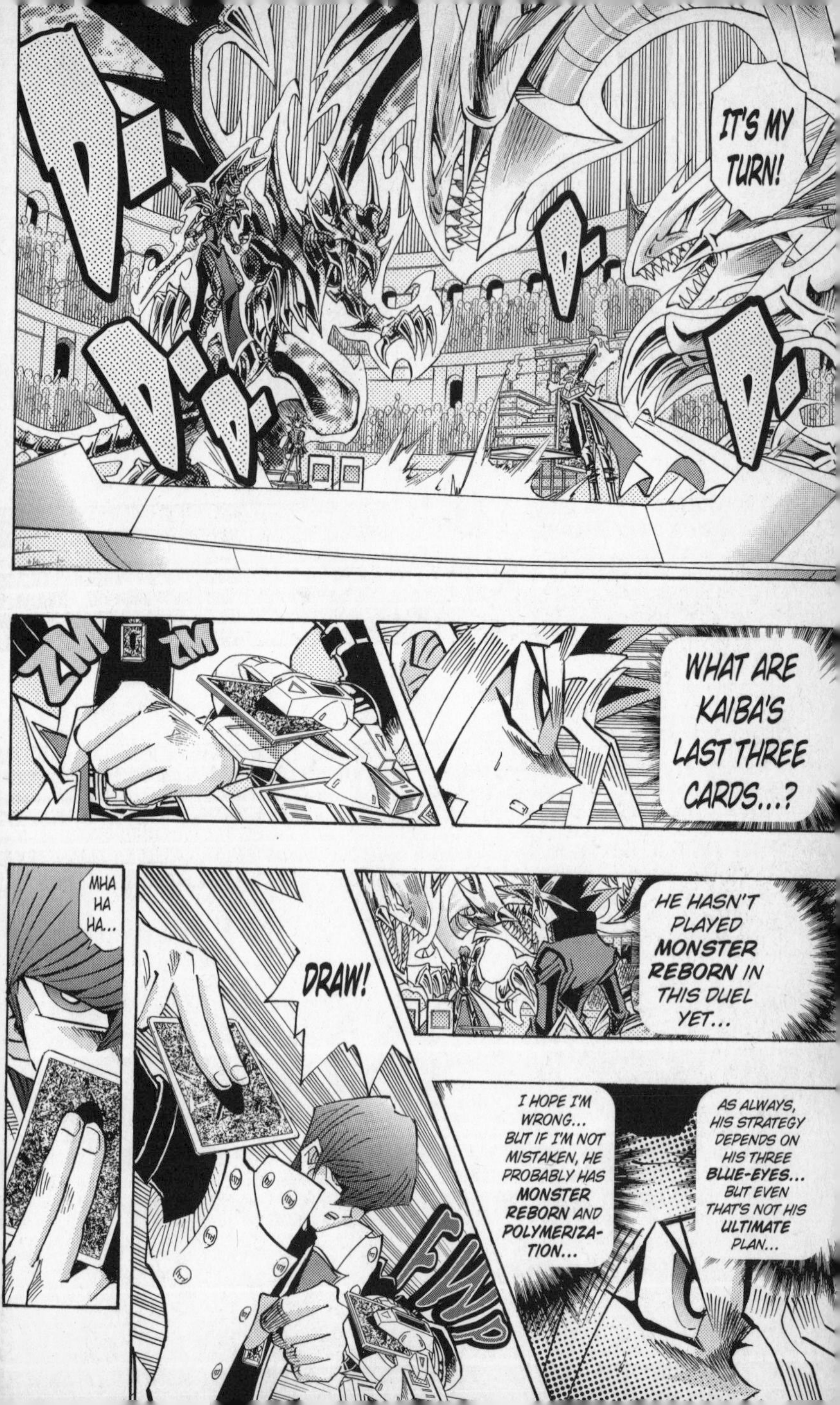
IT'S MY TURN!
WHAT ARE KAIBA'S LAST THREE CARDS...?
ZM
ZM
HE HASN'T PLAYED MONSTER REBORN IN THIS DUEL YET...
AS ALWAYS, HIS STRATEGY DEPENDS ON HIS THREE BLUE-EYES... BUT EVEN THAT'S NOT HIS ULTIMATE PLAN...
I HOPE I'M WRONG... BUT IF I'M NOT MISTAKEN, HE PROBABLY HAS MONSTER REBORN AND POLYMERIZA-TION...
DRAW!
FWMP
MHA HA HA...

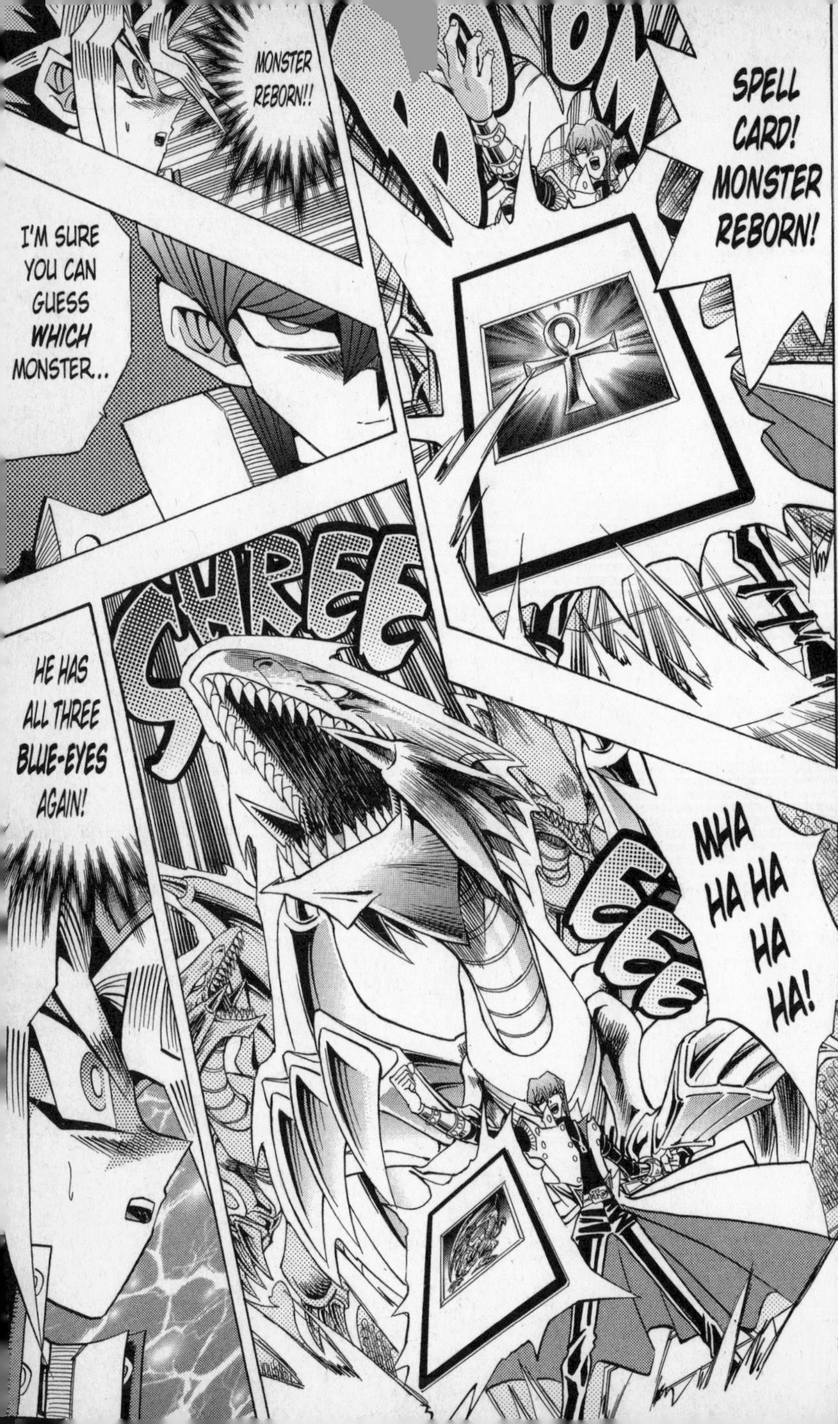
SPELL CARD! MONSTER REBORN!
MONSTER REBORN!!
I'M SURE YOU CAN GUESS WHICH MONSTER...
MHA HA HA HA HA!
SHREE
HE HAS ALL THREE BLUE-EYES AGAIN!

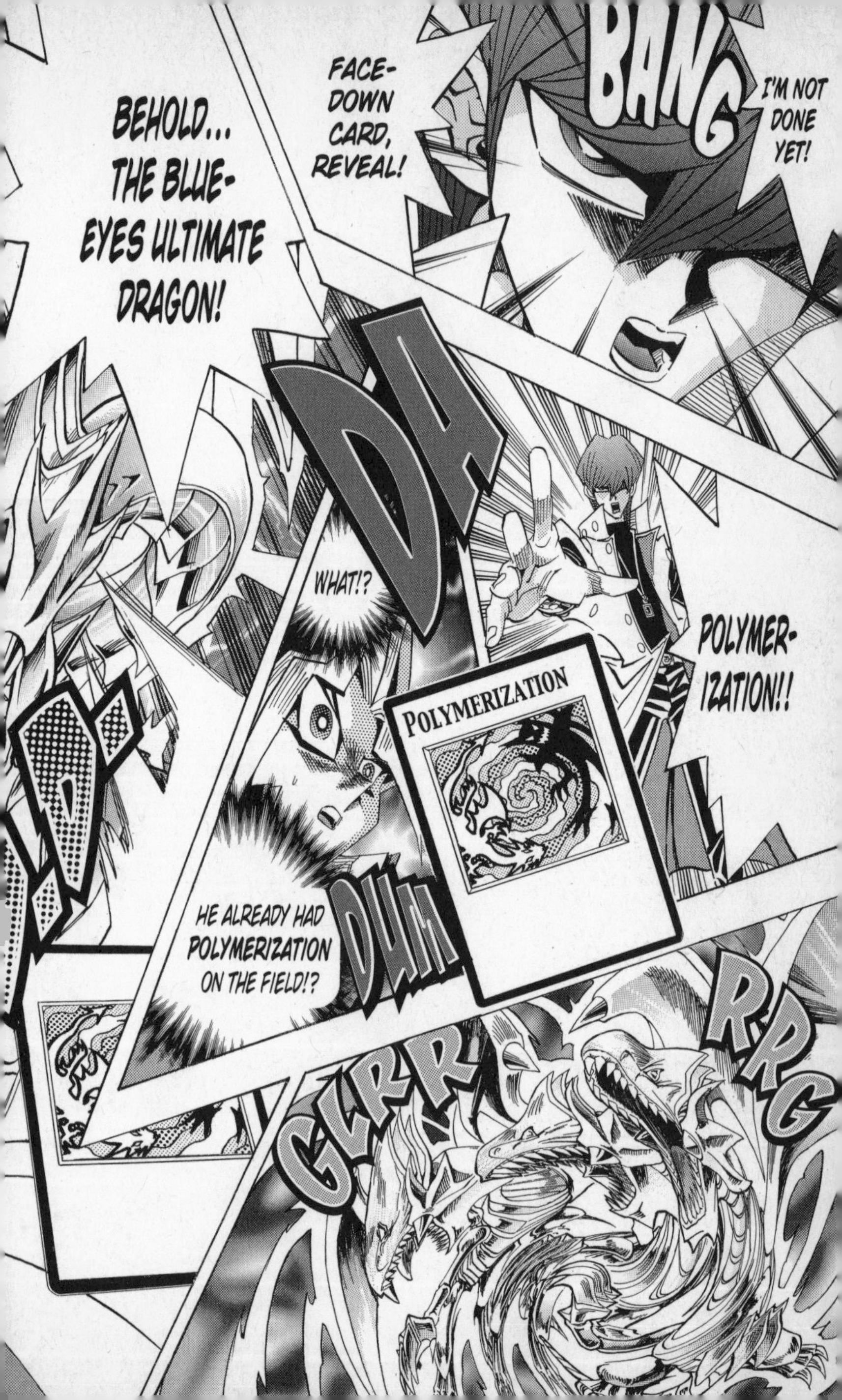
I'M NOT DONE YET!
BANG
FACE-DOWN CARD, REVEAL!
BEHOLD... THE BLUE-EYES ULTIMATE DRAGON!
POLYMER-IZATION!!
DA
POLYMERIZATION
WHAT!?
HE ALREADY HAD POLYMERIZATION ON THE FIELD!?
DUN
RRRG
GLRR

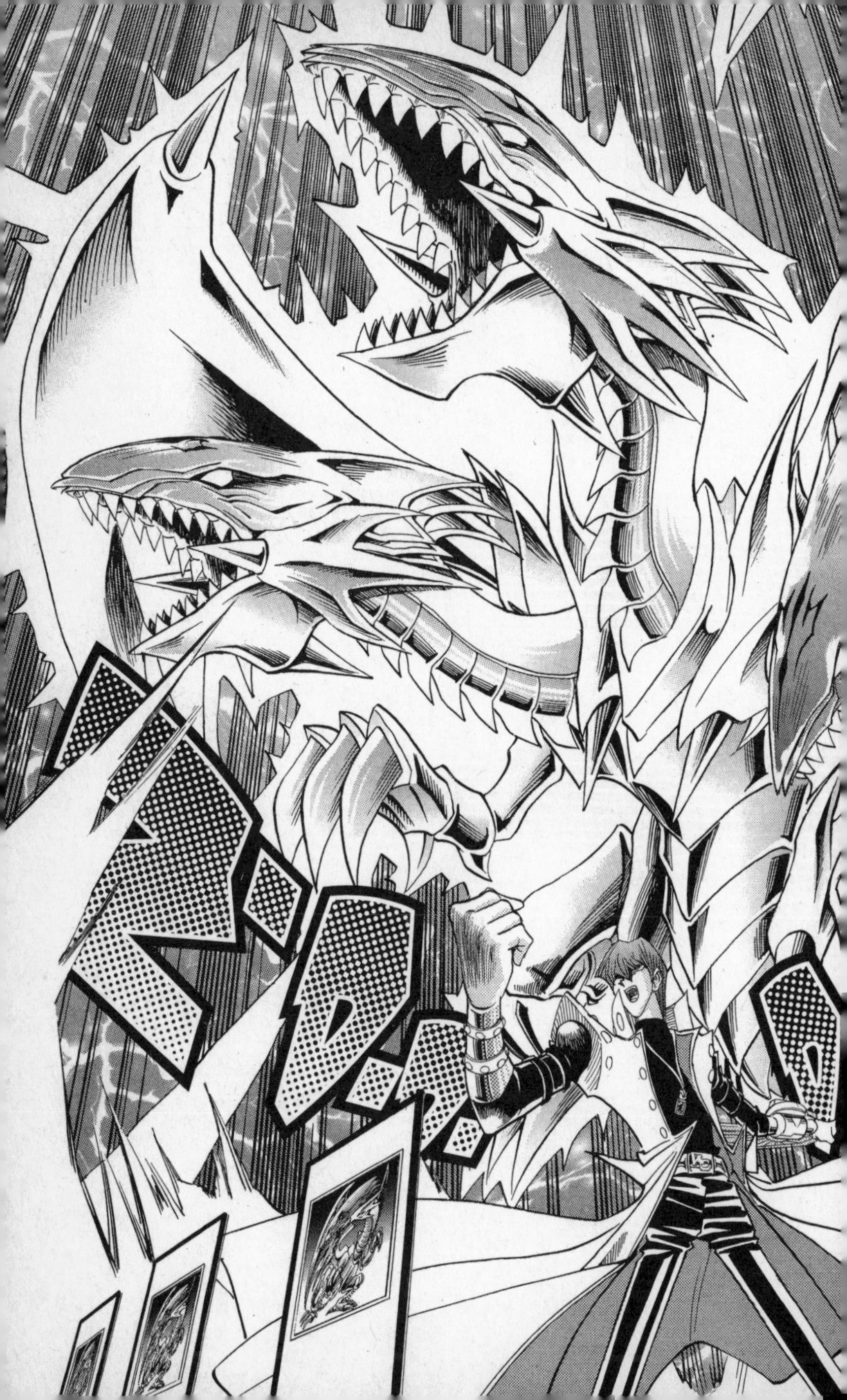

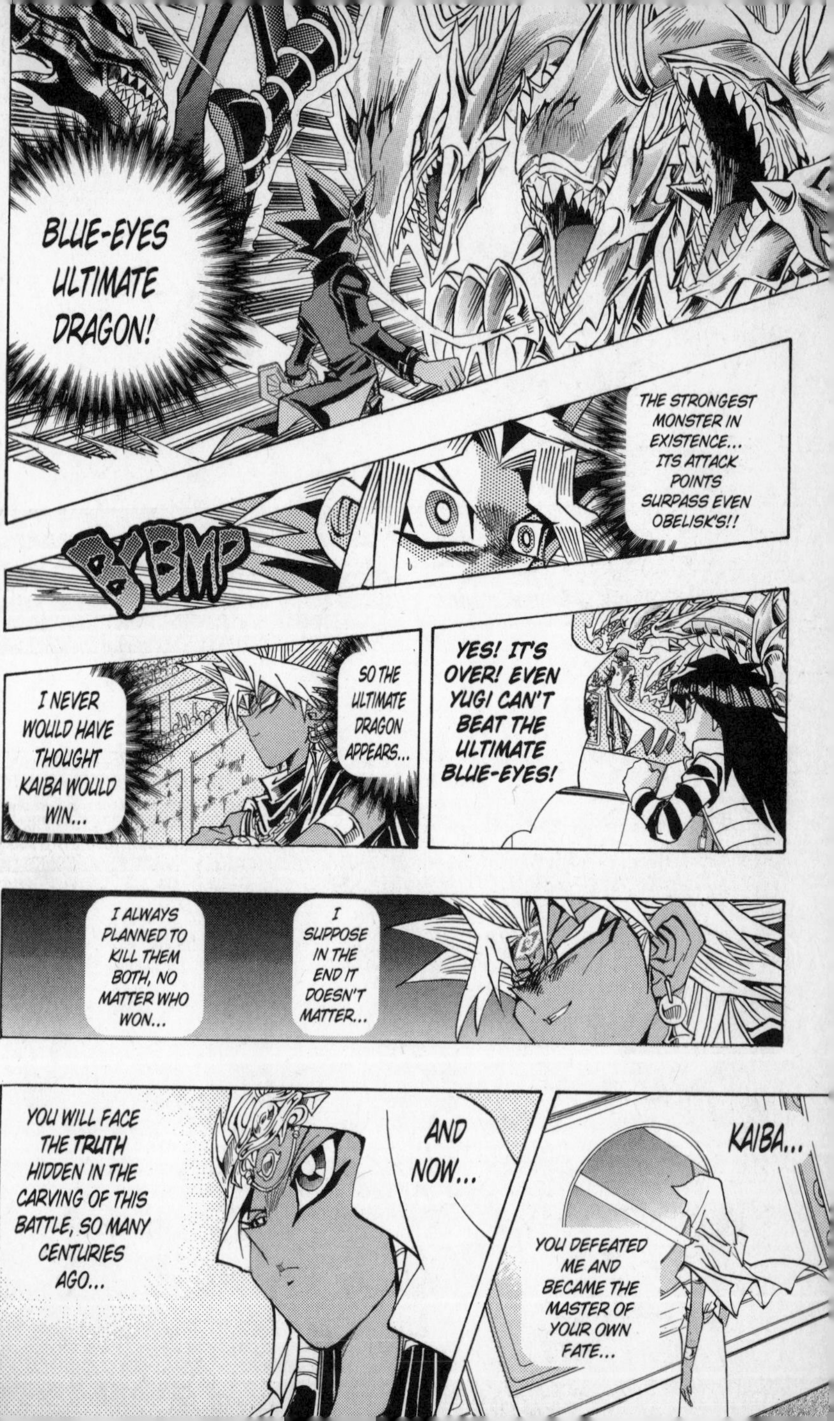
BLUE-EYES ULTIMATE DRAGON!
THE STRONGEST MONSTER IN EXISTENCE... ITS ATTACK POINTS SURPASS EVEN OBELISK'S!!
B'BMP
YES! IT'S OVER! EVEN YUGI CAN'T BEAT THE ULTIMATE BLUE-EYES!
SO THE ULTIMATE DRAGON APPEARS...
I NEVER WOULD HAVE THOUGHT KAIBA WOULD WIN...
I SUPPOSE IN THE END IT DOESN'T MATTER...
I ALWAYS PLANNED TO KILL THEM BOTH, NO MATTER WHO WON...
KAIBA...
YOU DEFEATED ME AND BECAME THE MASTER OF YOUR OWN FATE...
AND NOW...
YOU WILL FACE THE TRUTH HIDDEN IN THE CARVING OF THIS BATTLE, SO MANY CENTURIES AGO...

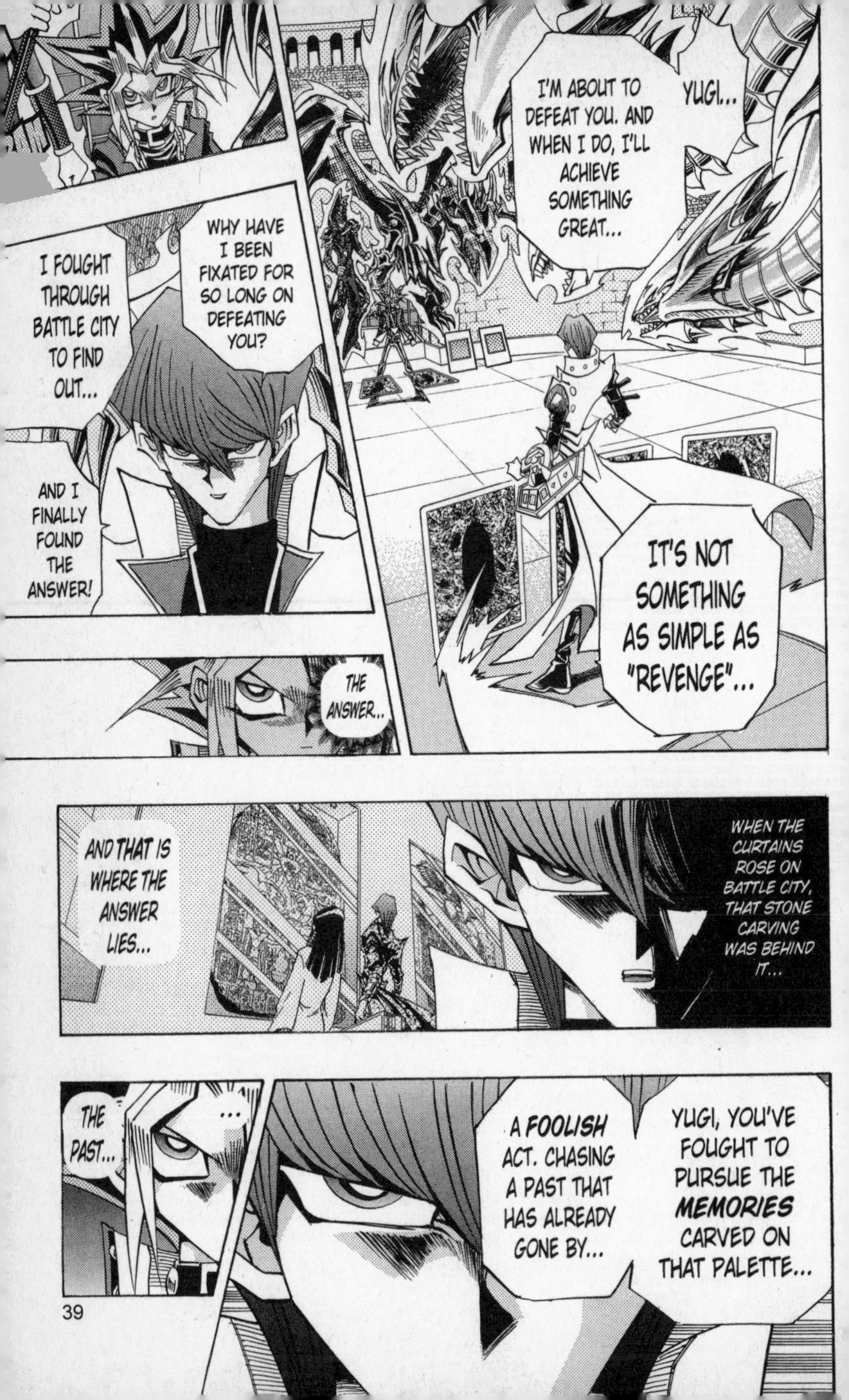
YUGI...
I'M ABOUT TO DEFEAT YOU. AND WHEN I DO, I'LL ACHIEVE SOMETHING GREAT...
IT'S NOT SOMETHING AS SIMPLE AS "REVENGE"...
WHY HAVE I BEEN FIXATED FOR SO LONG ON DEFEATING YOU?
I FOUGHT THROUGH BATTLE CITY TO FIND OUT...
AND I FINALLY FOUND THE ANSWER!
THE ANSWER...
WHEN THE CURTAINS ROSE ON BATTLE CITY, THAT STONE CARVING WAS BEHIND IT...
AND THAT IS WHERE THE ANSWER LIES...
YUGI, YOU'VE FOUGHT TO PURSUE THE MEMORIES CARVED ON THAT PALETTE...
A FOOLISH ACT. CHASING A PAST THAT HAS ALREADY GONE BY...
...
THE PAST...

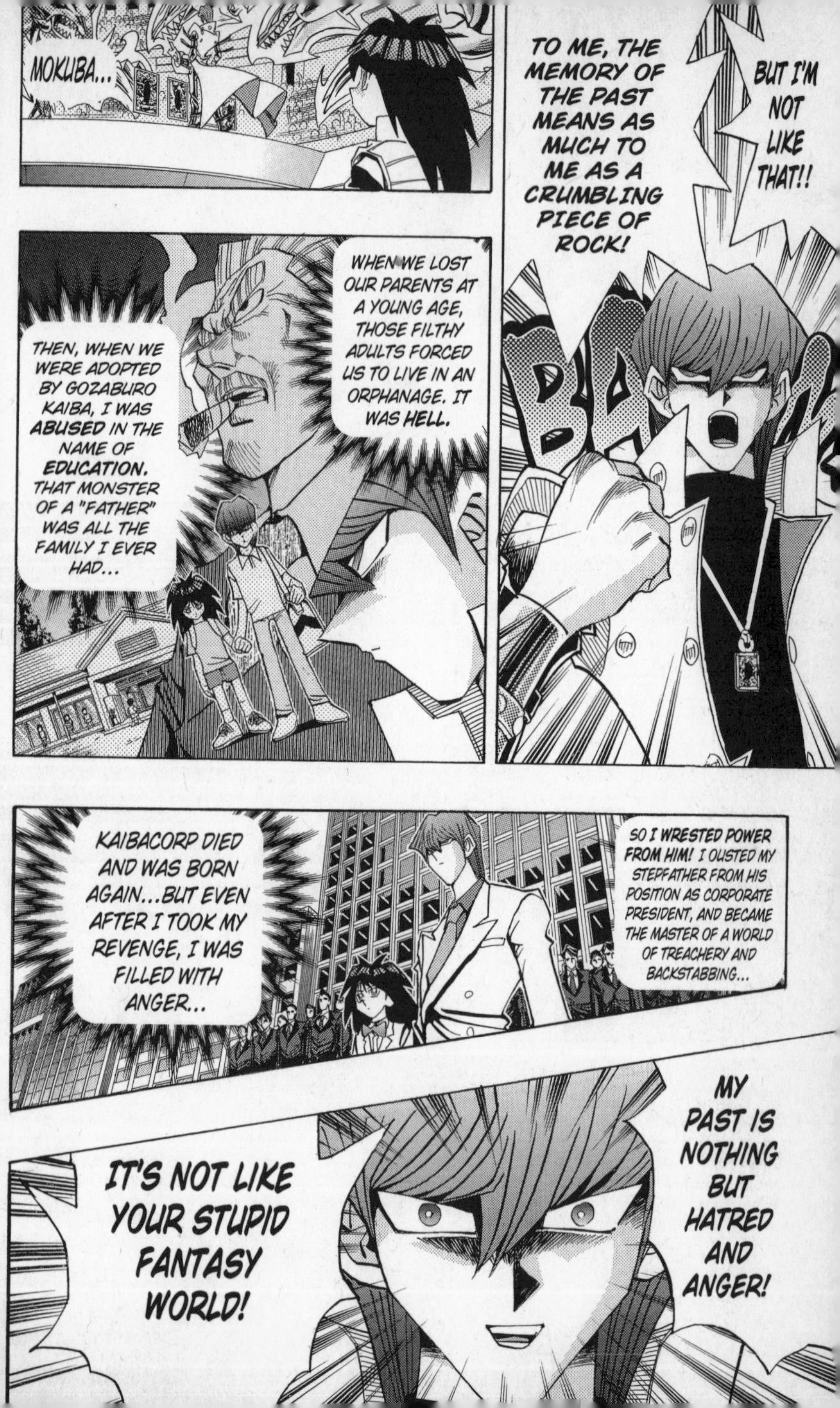
BUT I'M NOT LIKE THAT!!
TO ME, THE MEMORY OF THE PAST MEANS AS MUCH TO ME AS A CRUMBLING PIECE OF ROCK!
MOKUBA...
WHEN WE LOST OUR PARENTS AT A YOUNG AGE, THOSE FILTHY ADULTS FORCED US TO LIVE IN AN ORPHANAGE. IT WAS HELL.
THEN, WHEN WE WERE ADOPTED BY GOZABURO KAIBA, I WAS ABUSED IN THE NAME OF EDUCATION. THAT MONSTER OF A "FATHER" WAS ALL THE FAMILY I EVER HAD...
SO I WRESTED POWER FROM HIM! I OUSTED MY STEPFATHER FROM HIS POSITION AS CORPORATE PRESIDENT, AND BECAME THE MASTER OF A WORLD OF TREACHERY AND BACKSTABBING...
KAIBACORP DIED AND WAS BORN AGAIN...BUT EVEN AFTER I TOOK MY REVENGE, I WAS FILLED WITH ANGER...
MY PAST IS NOTHING BUT HATRED AND ANGER!
IT'S NOT LIKE YOUR STUPID FANTASY WORLD!

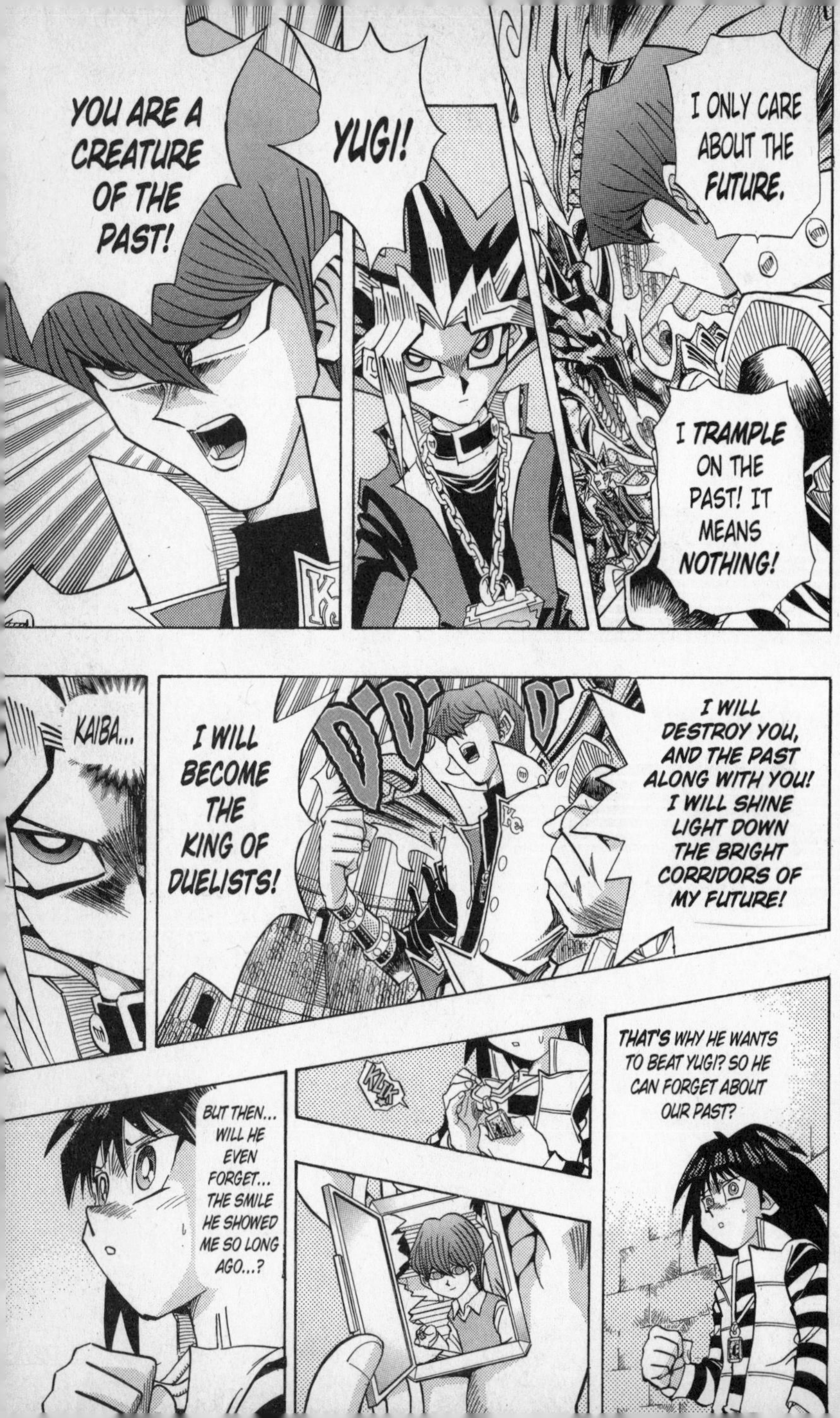

I ONLY CARE ABOUT THE FUTURE.
I TRAMPLE ON THE PAST! IT MEANS NOTHING!
YUGI!
YOU ARE A CREATURE OF THE PAST!
I WILL DESTROY YOU, AND THE PAST ALONG WITH YOU! I WILL SHINE LIGHT DOWN THE BRIGHT CORRIDORS OF MY FUTURE!
I WILL BECOME THE KING OF DUELISTS!
KAIBA...
THAT'S WHY HE WANTS TO BEAT YUGI? SO HE CAN FORGET ABOUT OUR PAST?
KLIK
BUT THEN... WILL HE EVEN FORGET... THE SMILE HE SHOWED ME SO LONG AGO...?

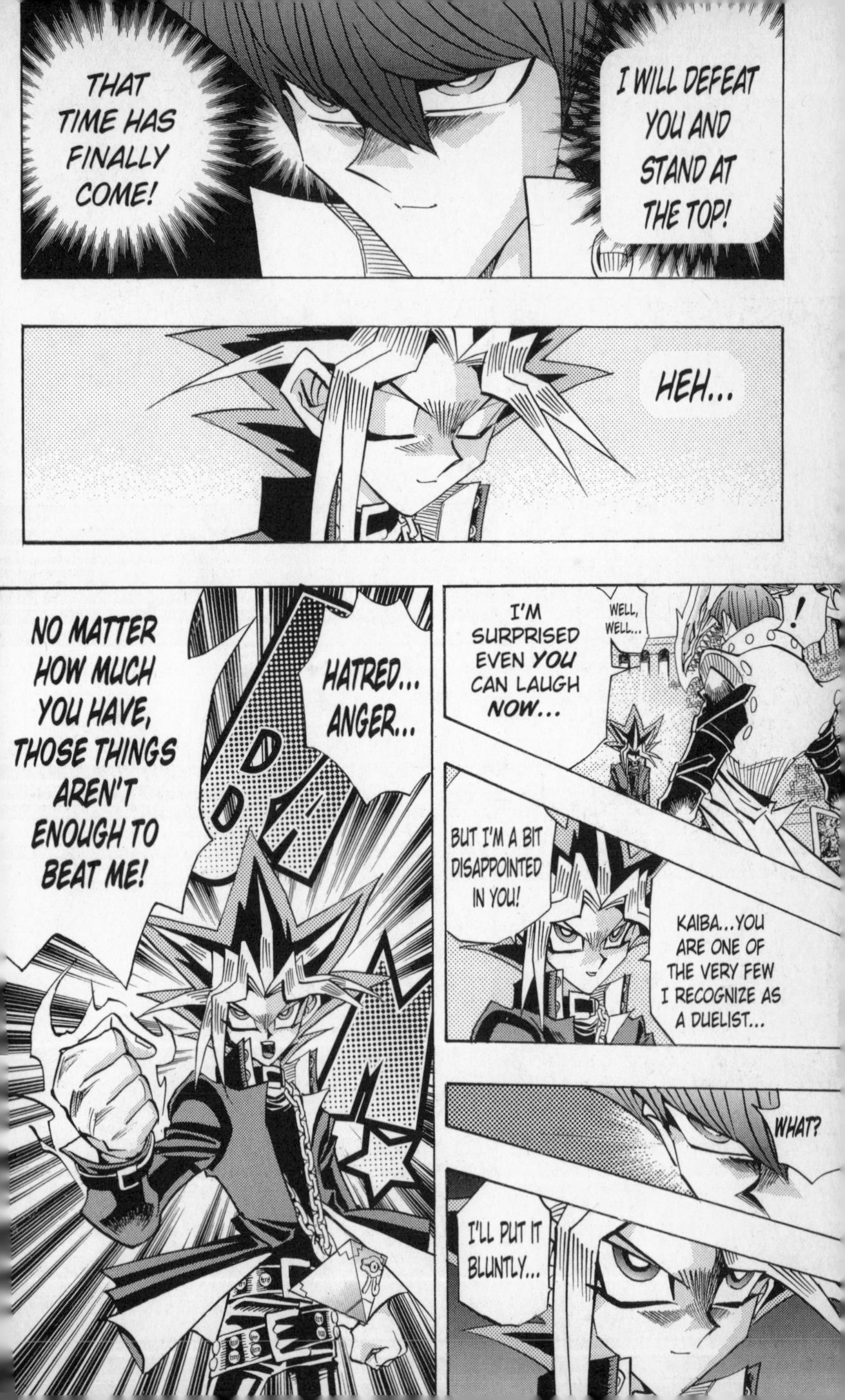
I WILL DEFEAT YOU AND STAND AT THE TOP!
THAT TIME HAS FINALLY COME!
HEH...
WELL, WELL...
I'M SURPRISED EVEN *YOU* CAN LAUGH *NOW*...
!
KAIBA...YOU ARE ONE OF THE VERY FEW I RECOGNIZE AS A DUELIST...
BUT I'M A BIT DISAPPOINTED IN YOU!
WHAT?
I'LL PUT IT BLUNTLY...
HATRED... ANGER...
NO MATTER HOW MUCH YOU HAVE, THOSE THINGS AREN'T ENOUGH TO BEAT ME!

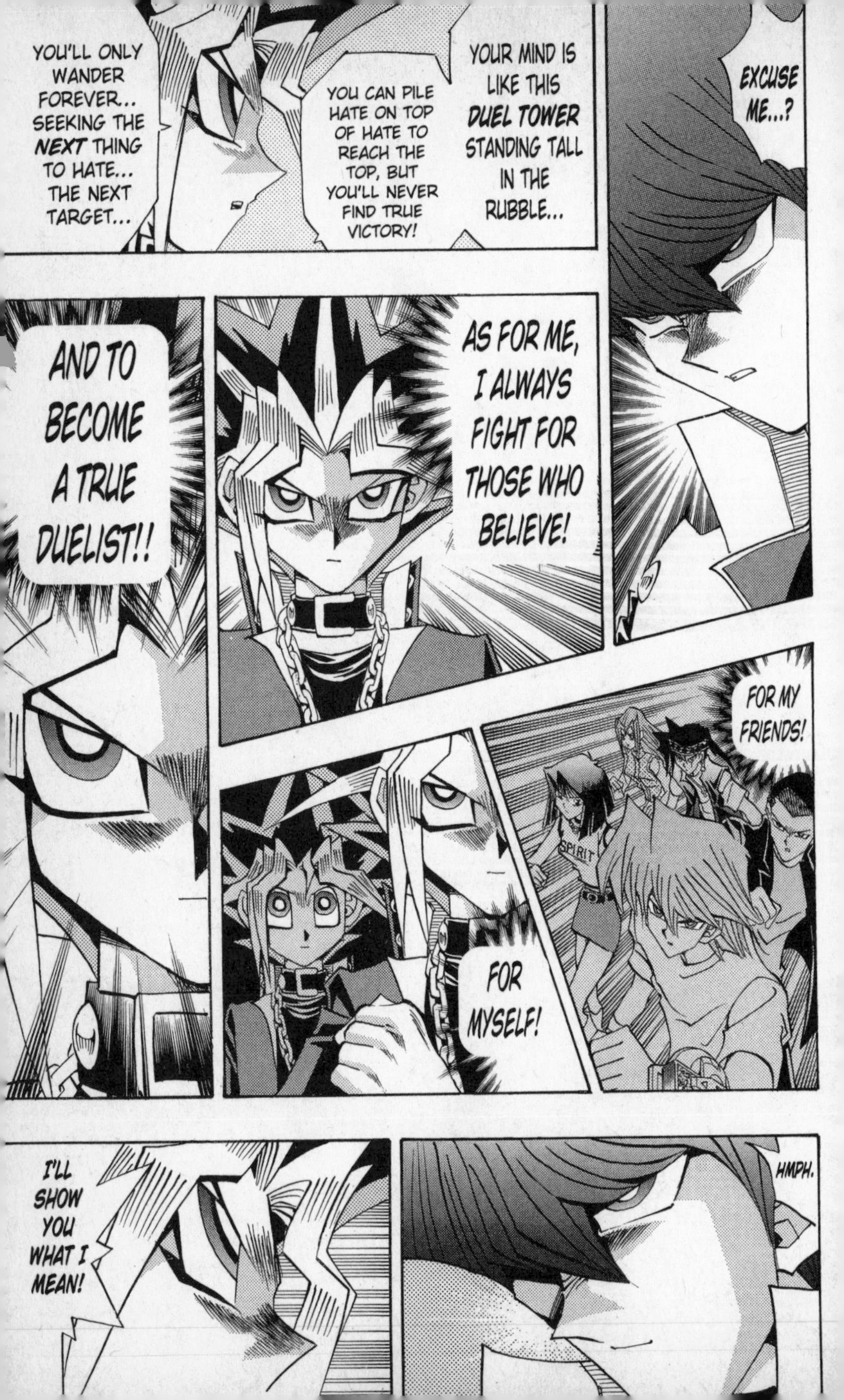
YOUR MIND IS LIKE THIS DUEL TOWER STANDING TALL IN THE RUBBLE...
YOU CAN PILE HATE ON TOP OF HATE TO REACH THE TOP, BUT YOU'LL NEVER FIND TRUE VICTORY!
YOU'LL ONLY WANDER FOREVER... SEEKING THE NEXT THING TO HATE... THE NEXT TARGET...
EXCUSE ME...?
AS FOR ME, I ALWAYS FIGHT FOR THOSE WHO BELIEVE!
FOR MY FRIENDS!
FOR MYSELF!
AND TO BECOME A TRUE DUELIST!!
HMPH.
I'LL SHOW YOU WHAT I MEAN!

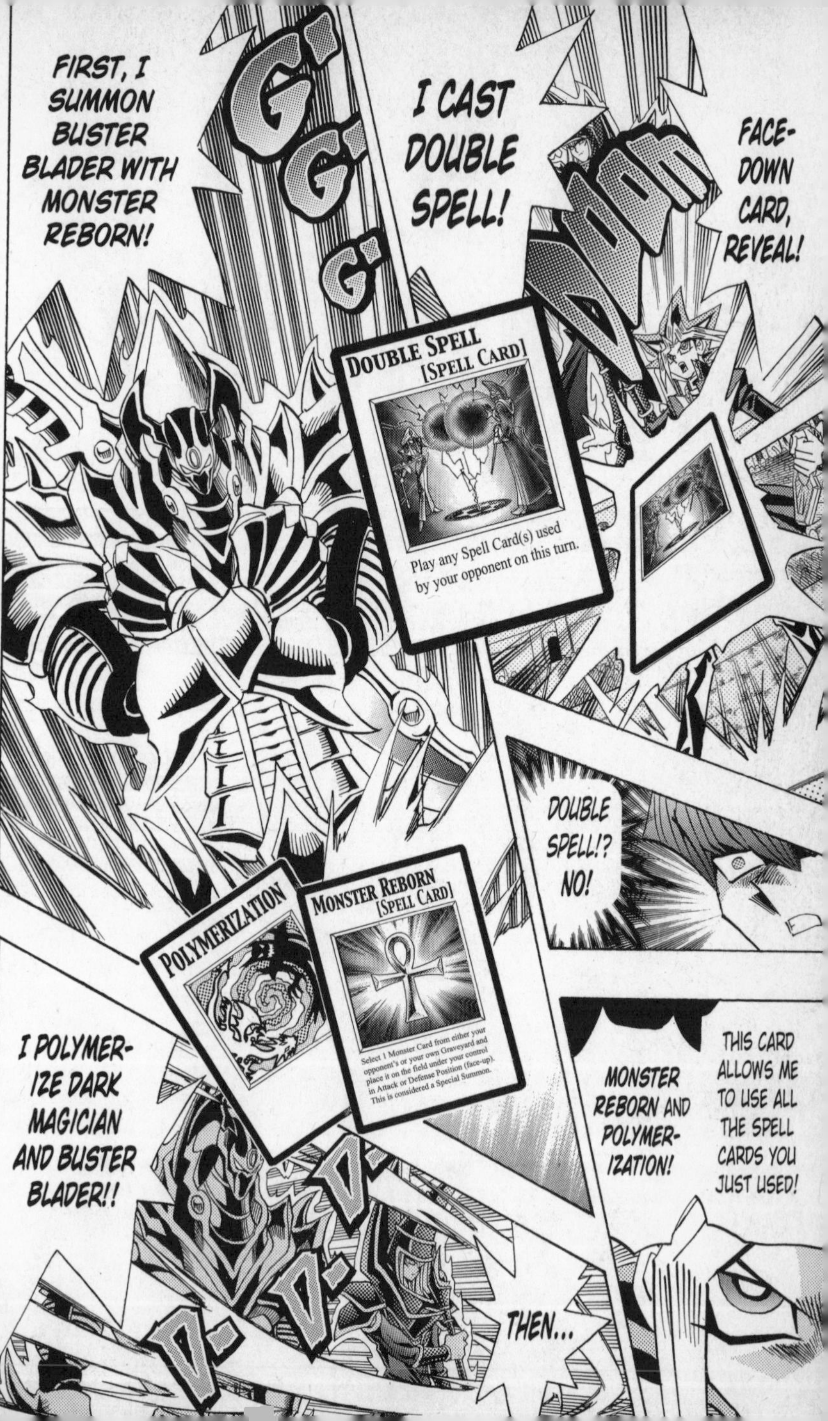
FACE-DOWN CARD, REVEAL!
I CAST DOUBLE SPELL!
DOUBLE SPELL [SPELL CARD]
Play any Spell Card(s) used by your opponent on this turn.
DOUBLE SPELL!? NO!
THIS CARD ALLOWS ME TO USE ALL THE SPELL CARDS YOU JUST USED!
MONSTER REBORN AND POLYMERIZATION!
THEN...
FIRST, I SUMMON BUSTER BLADER WITH MONSTER REBORN!
MONSTER REBORN [SPELL CARD]
Select 1 Monster Card from either your opponent's or your own Graveyard and place it on the field under your control in Attack or Defense Position (face-up). This is considered a Special Summon.
POLYMERIZATION
I POLYMERIZE DARK MAGICIAN AND BUSTER BLADER!!

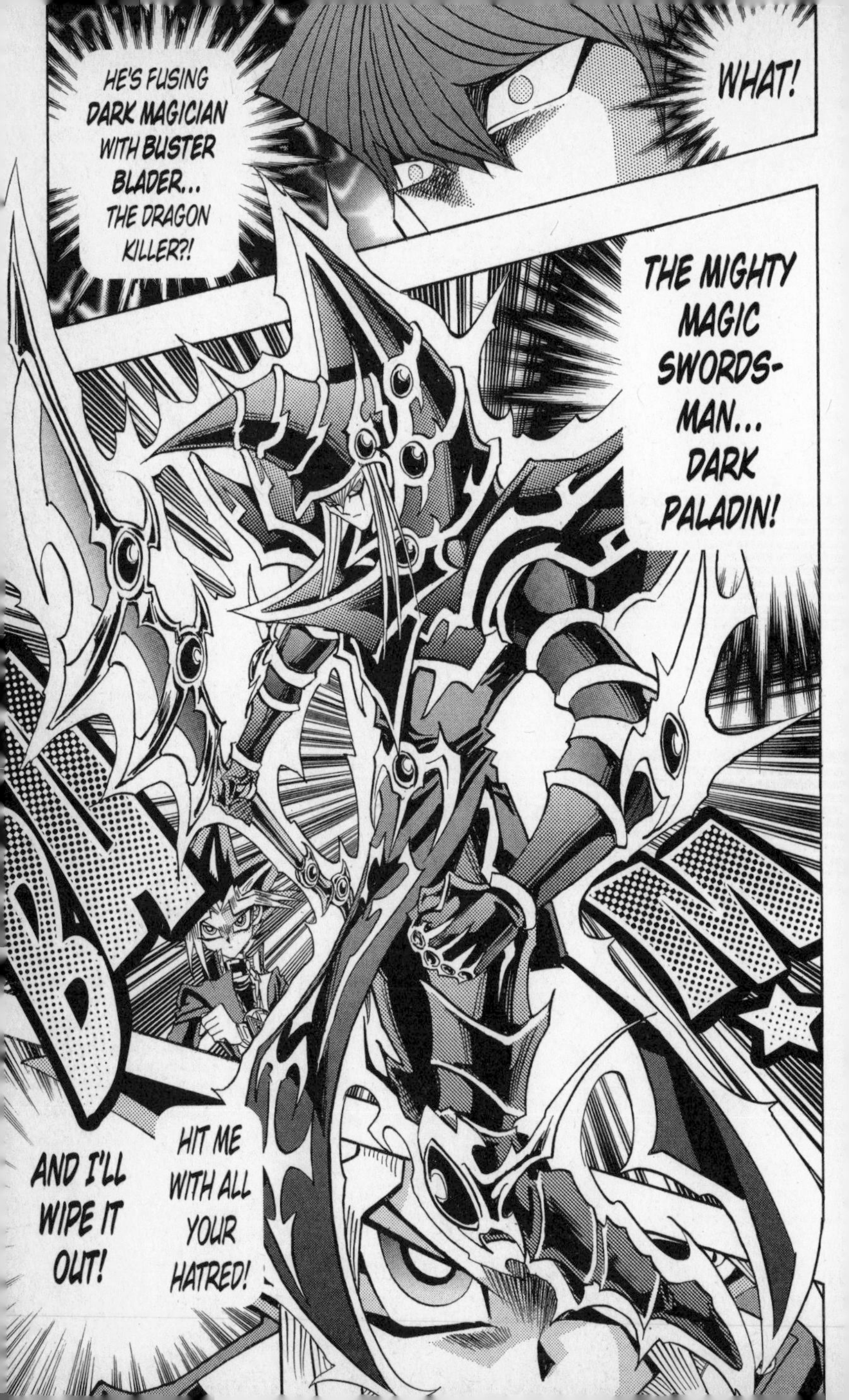
WHAT!
HE'S FUSING DARK MAGICIAN WITH BUSTER BLADER... THE DRAGON KILLER?!
THE MIGHTY MAGIC SWORDS-MAN... DARK PALADIN!
HIT ME WITH ALL YOUR HATRED!
AND I'LL WIPE IT OUT!

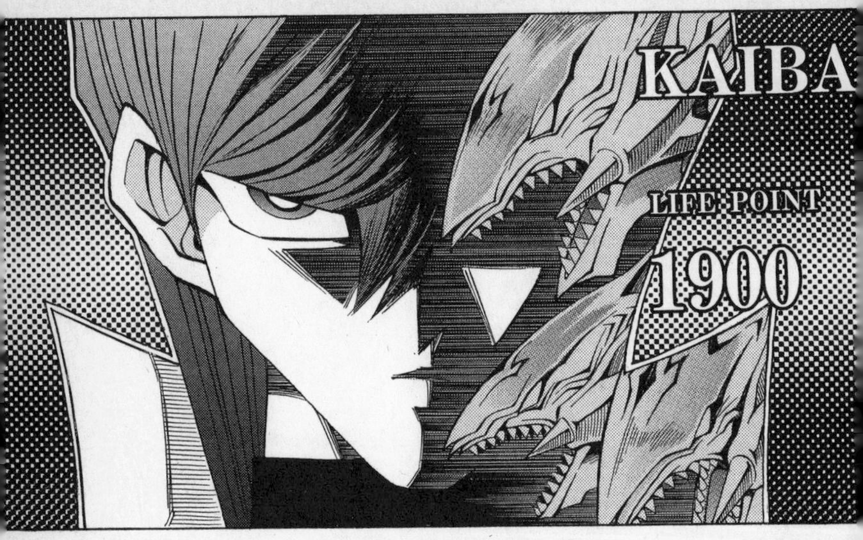
KAIBA
LIFE POINT
1900

Duel 203: As a Friend

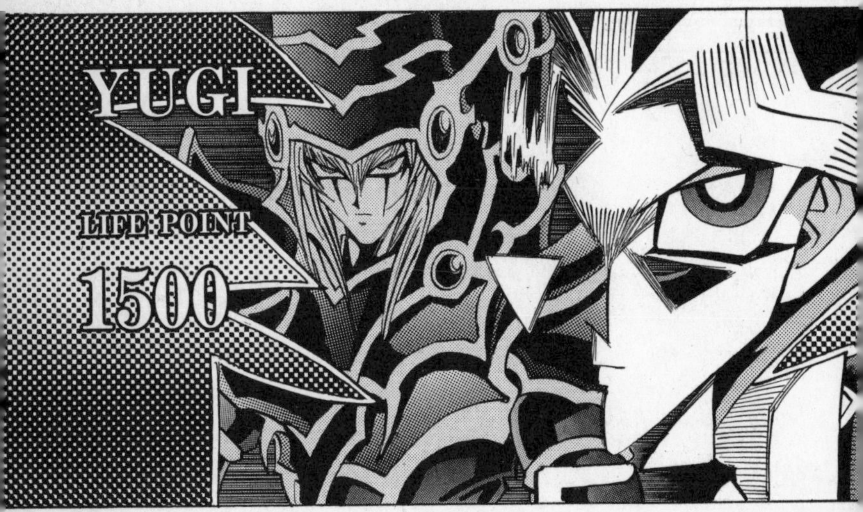
YUGI
LIFE POINT
1500

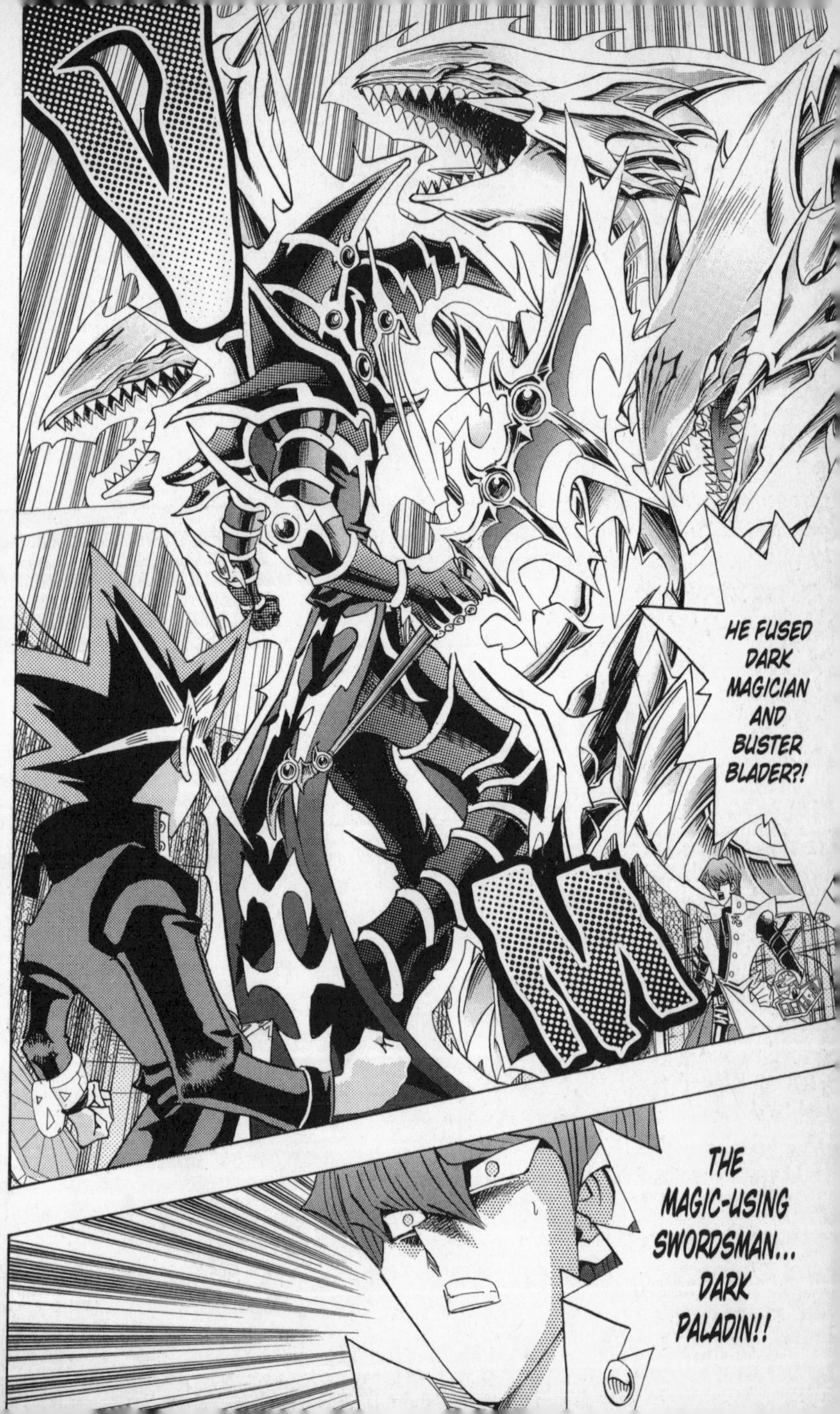
HE FUSED DARK MAGICIAN AND BUSTER BLADER?!
THE MAGIC-USING SWORDSMAN... DARK PALADIN!!

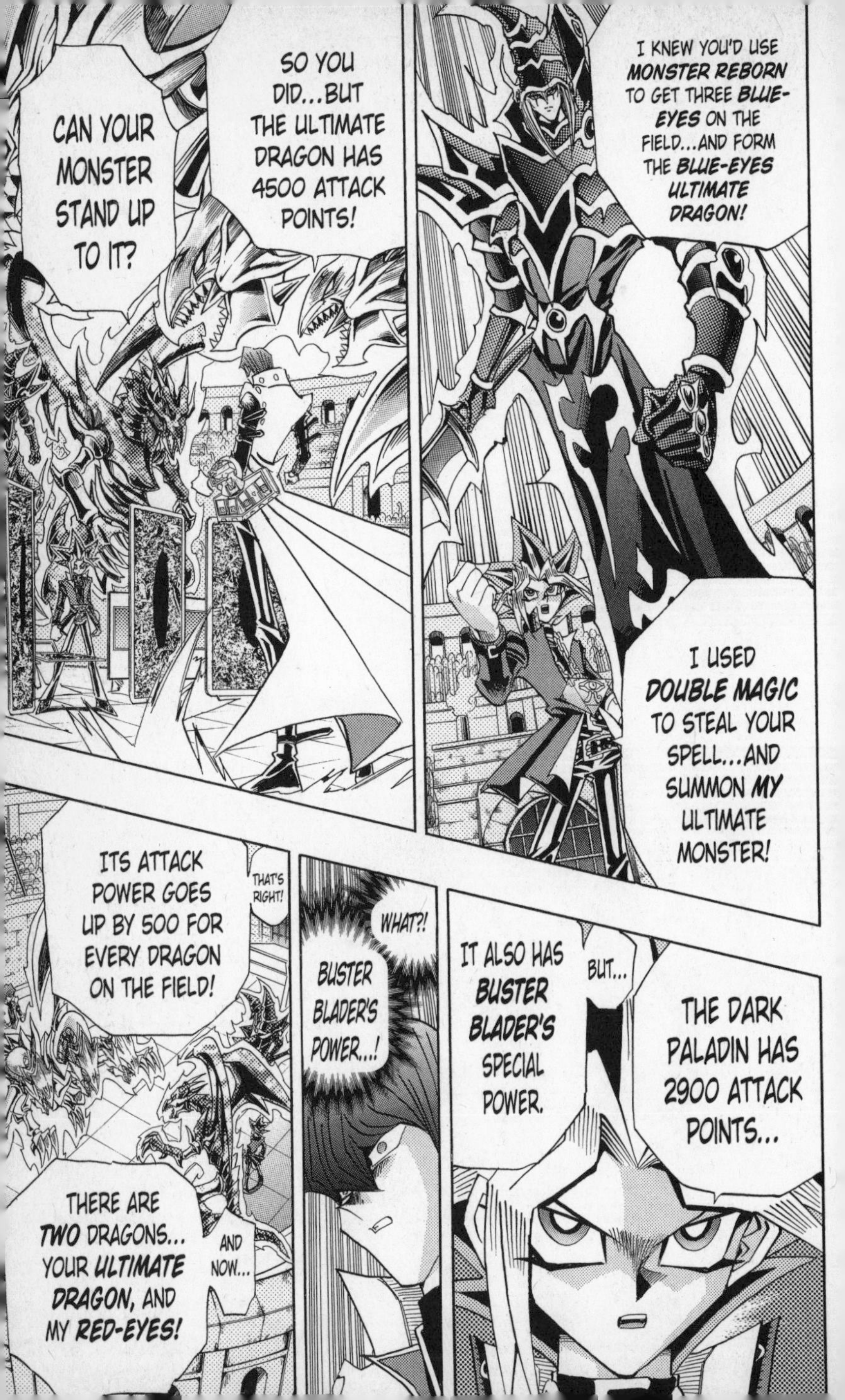
I KNEW YOU'D USE MONSTER REBORN TO GET THREE BLUE-EYES ON THE FIELD...AND FORM THE BLUE-EYES ULTIMATE DRAGON!
I USED DOUBLE MAGIC TO STEAL YOUR SPELL...AND SUMMON MY ULTIMATE MONSTER!
SO YOU DID...BUT THE ULTIMATE DRAGON HAS 4500 ATTACK POINTS!
CAN YOUR MONSTER STAND UP TO IT?
THE DARK PALADIN HAS 2900 ATTACK POINTS...
BUT...
IT ALSO HAS BUSTER BLADER'S SPECIAL POWER.
WHAT?!
BUSTER BLADER'S POWER...!
THAT'S RIGHT!
ITS ATTACK POWER GOES UP BY 500 FOR EVERY DRAGON ON THE FIELD!
AND NOW...
THERE ARE TWO DRAGONS... YOUR ULTIMATE DRAGON, AND MY RED-EYES!

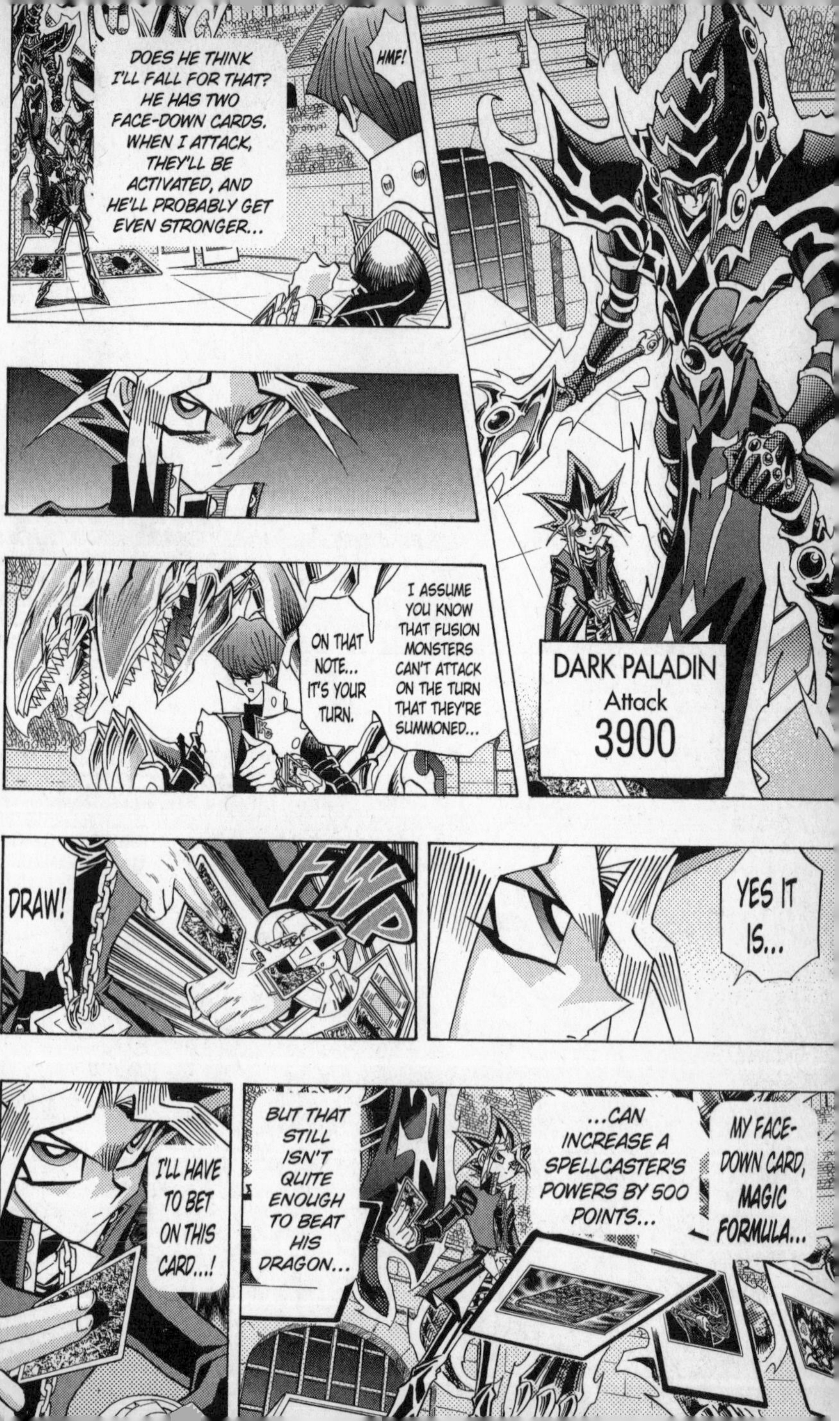
DARK PALADIN Attack 3900
HMF!
DOES HE THINK I'LL FALL FOR THAT? HE HAS TWO FACE-DOWN CARDS. WHEN I ATTACK, THEY'LL BE ACTIVATED, AND HE'LL PROBABLY GET EVEN STRONGER...
I ASSUME YOU KNOW THAT FUSION MONSTERS CAN'T ATTACK ON THE TURN THAT THEY'RE SUMMONED...
ON THAT NOTE... IT'S YOUR TURN.
YES IT IS...
FWP
DRAW!
MY FACE-DOWN CARD, MAGIC FORMULA...
...CAN INCREASE A SPELLCASTER'S POWERS BY 500 POINTS...
BUT THAT STILL ISN'T QUITE ENOUGH TO BEAT HIS DRAGON...
I'LL HAVE TO BET ON THIS CARD...!

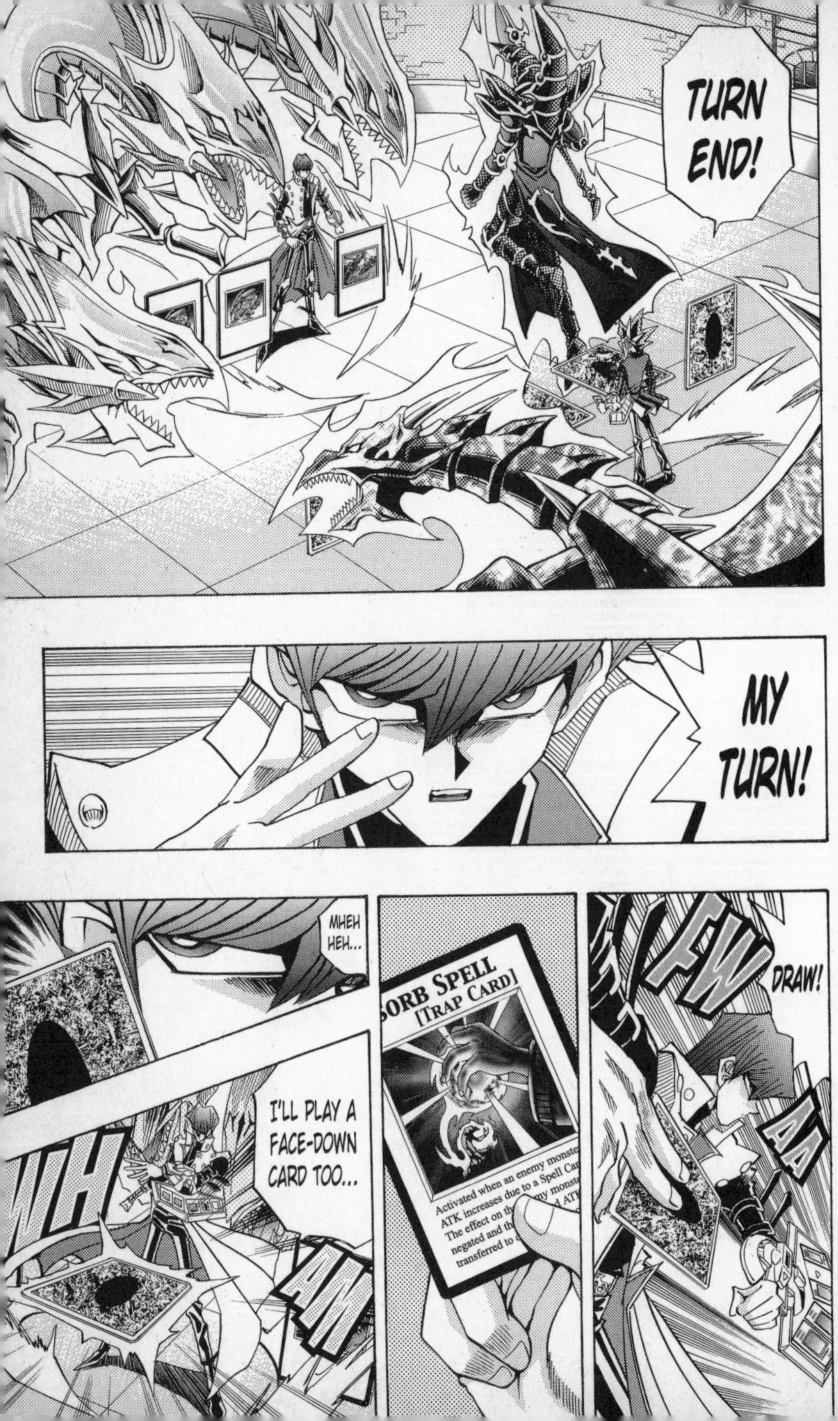
TURN END!
MY TURN!
FW
DRAW!
AA
SORB SPELL
[TRAP CARD]
Activated when an enemy monste
ATK increases due to a Spell Car
The effect on th
my monste
negated and th
ATK
transferred to
MHEH HEH...
I'LL PLAY A FACE-DOWN CARD TOO...
WH
AM

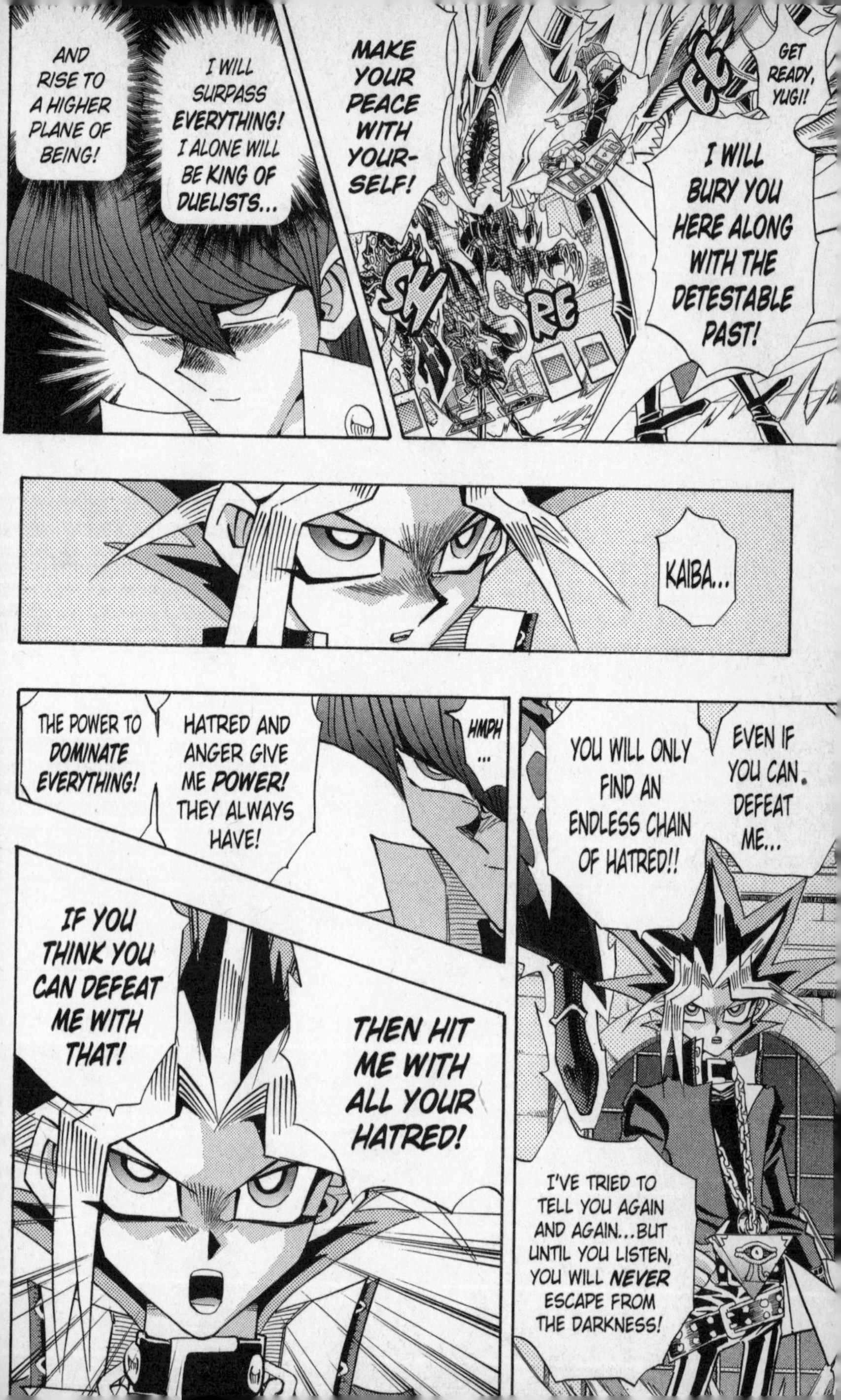
GET READY, YUGI!!
I WILL BURY YOU HERE ALONG WITH THE DETESTABLE PAST!
SH
RE
MAKE YOUR PEACE WITH YOUR-SELF!
I WILL SURPASS EVERYTHING! I ALONE WILL BE KING OF DUELISTS...
AND RISE TO A HIGHER PLANE OF BEING!
KAIBA...
EVEN IF YOU CAN DEFEAT ME...
YOU WILL ONLY FIND AN ENDLESS CHAIN OF HATRED!!
I'VE TRIED TO TELL YOU AGAIN AND AGAIN...BUT UNTIL YOU LISTEN, YOU WILL NEVER ESCAPE FROM THE DARKNESS!
HMPH...
HATRED AND ANGER GIVE ME POWER! THEY ALWAYS HAVE!
THE POWER TO DOMINATE EVERYTHING!
THEN HIT ME WITH ALL YOUR HATRED!
IF YOU THINK YOU CAN DEFEAT ME WITH THAT!

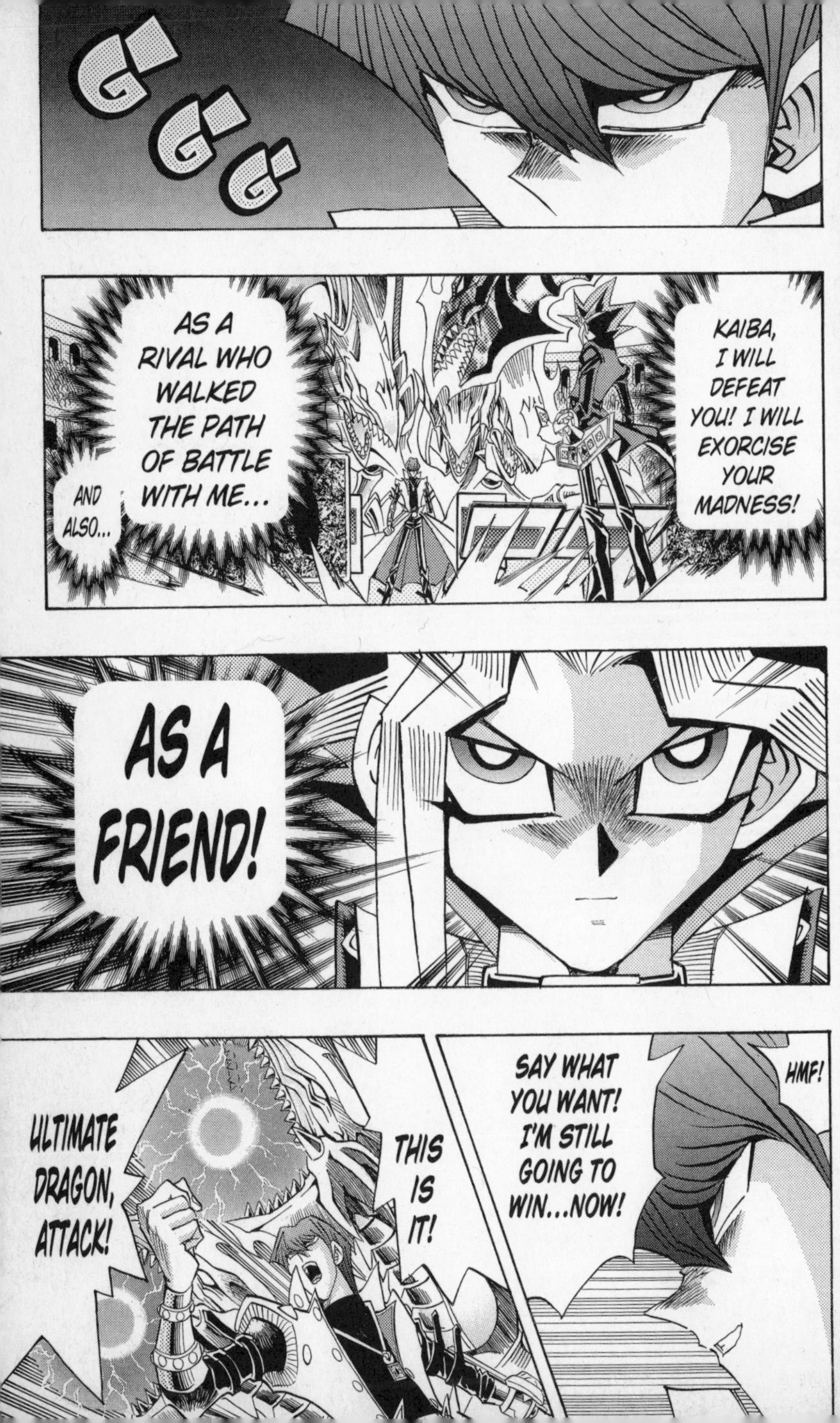
GGG
KAIBA, I WILL DEFEAT YOU! I WILL EXORCISE YOUR MADNESS!
AS A RIVAL WHO WALKED THE PATH OF BATTLE WITH ME...
AND ALSO...
AS A FRIEND!
HMF!
SAY WHAT YOU WANT! I'M STILL GOING TO WIN...NOW!
THIS IS IT!
ULTIMATE DRAGON, ATTACK!

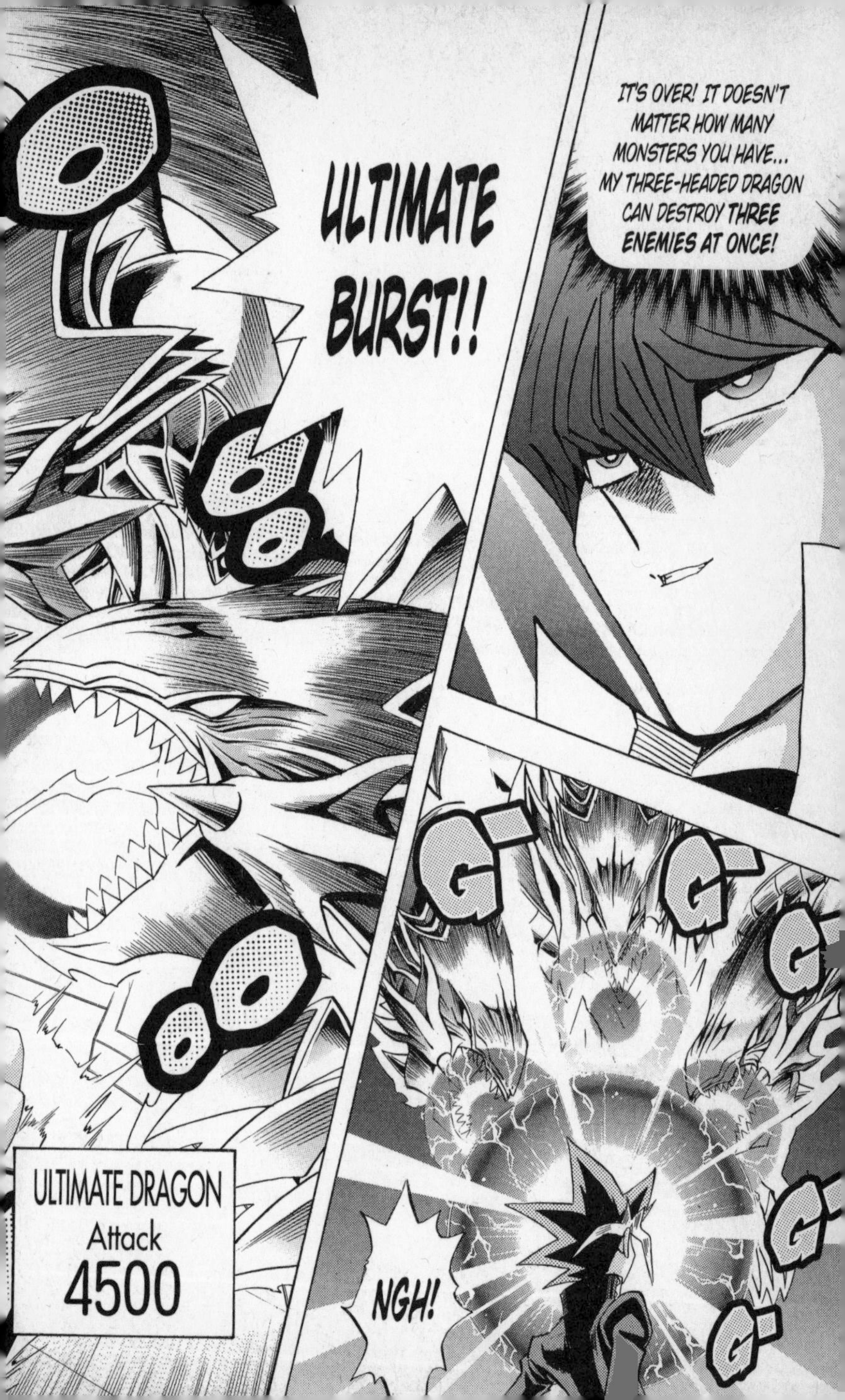
IT'S OVER! IT DOESN'T MATTER HOW MANY MONSTERS YOU HAVE... MY THREE-HEADED DRAGON CAN DESTROY THREE ENEMIES AT ONCE!
G G G
G G
NGH!
ULTIMATE BURST!!
OOO
OOO
ULTIMATE DRAGON
Attack
4500

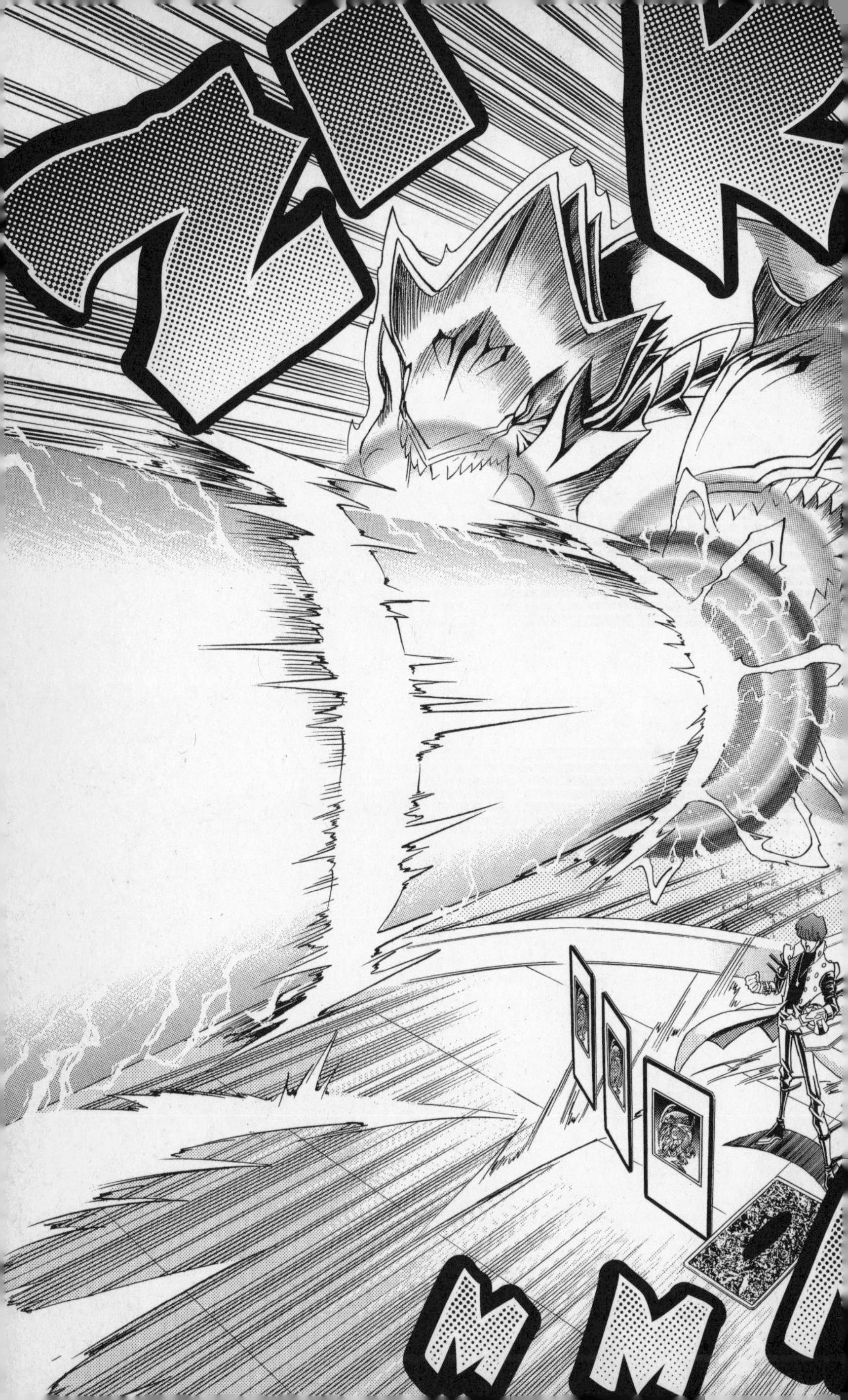

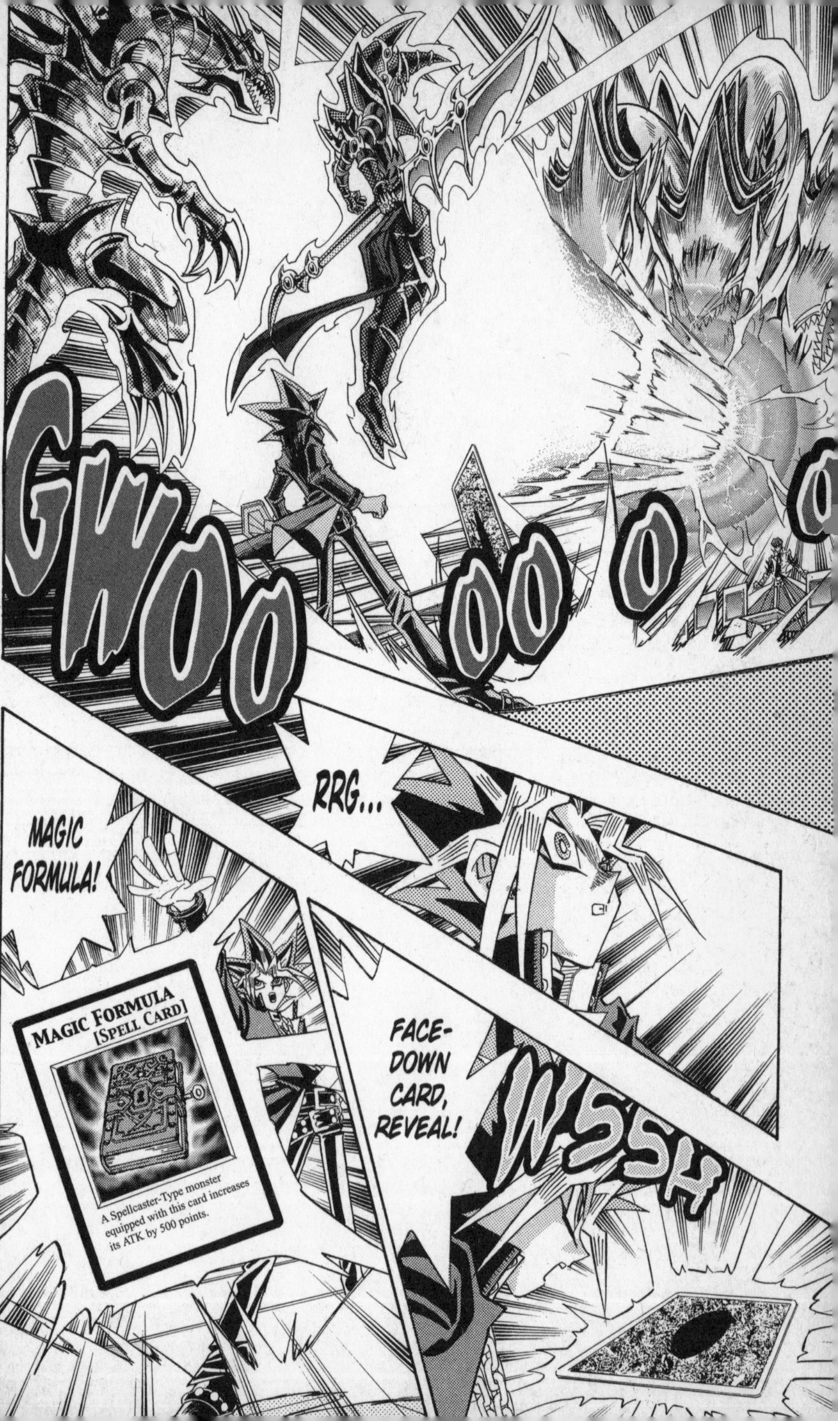
GHOOOOOOO
RRG...
FACE-DOWN CARD, REVEAL!
WSSH
MAGIC FORMULA!
MAGIC FORMULA
[SPELL CARD]
A Spellcaster-Type monster equipped with this card increases its ATK by 500 points.

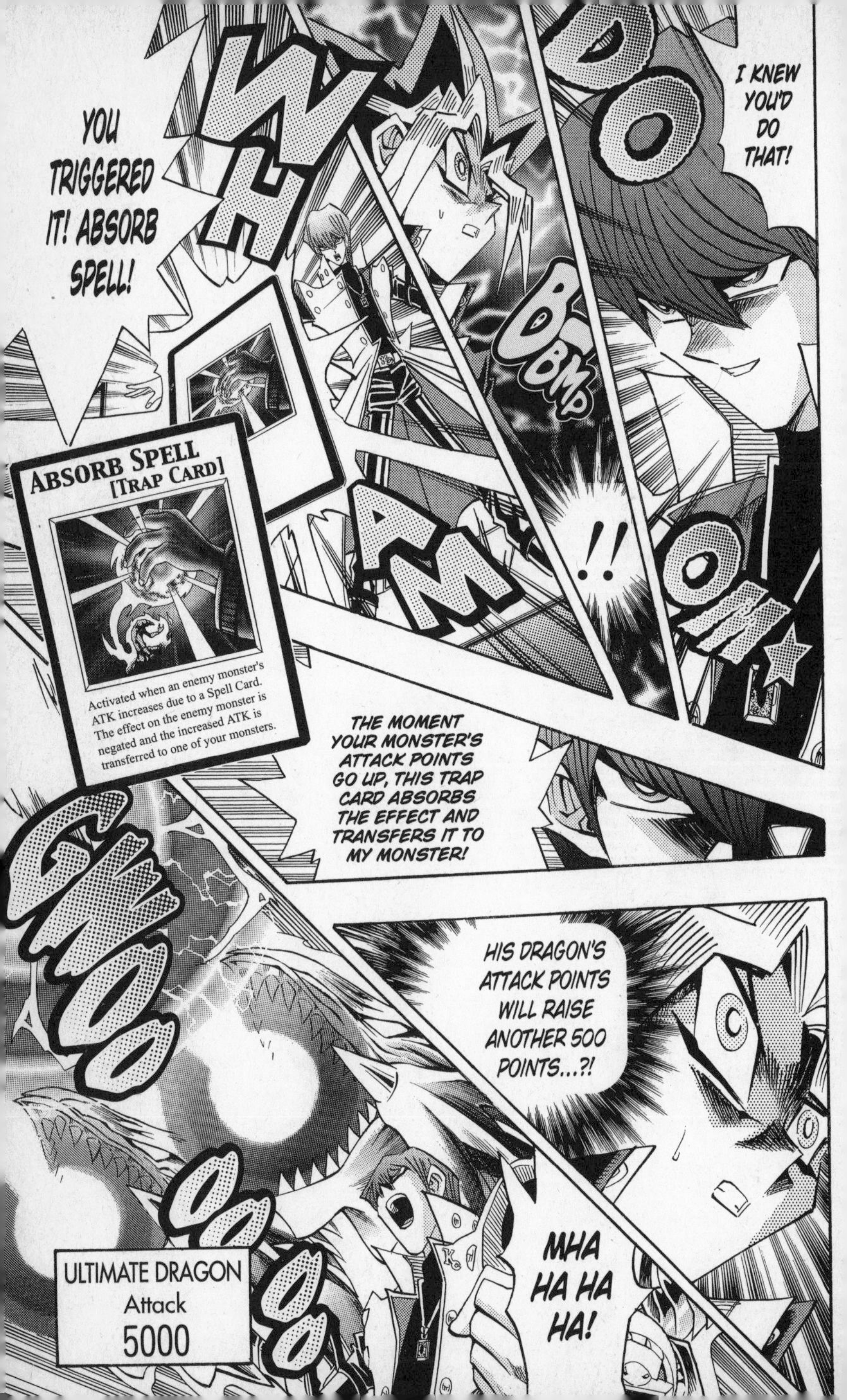
I KNEW YOU'D DO THAT!
YOU TRIGGERED IT! ABSORB SPELL!
!!
ABSORB SPELL [TRAP CARD]
Activated when an enemy monster's ATK increases due to a Spell Card. The effect on the enemy monster is negated and the increased ATK is transferred to one of your monsters.
THE MOMENT YOUR MONSTER'S ATTACK POINTS GO UP, THIS TRAP CARD ABSORBS THE EFFECT AND TRANSFERS IT TO MY MONSTER!
HIS DRAGON'S ATTACK POINTS WILL RAISE ANOTHER 500 POINTS...?!
MHA HA HA HA!
ULTIMATE DRAGON
Attack
5000

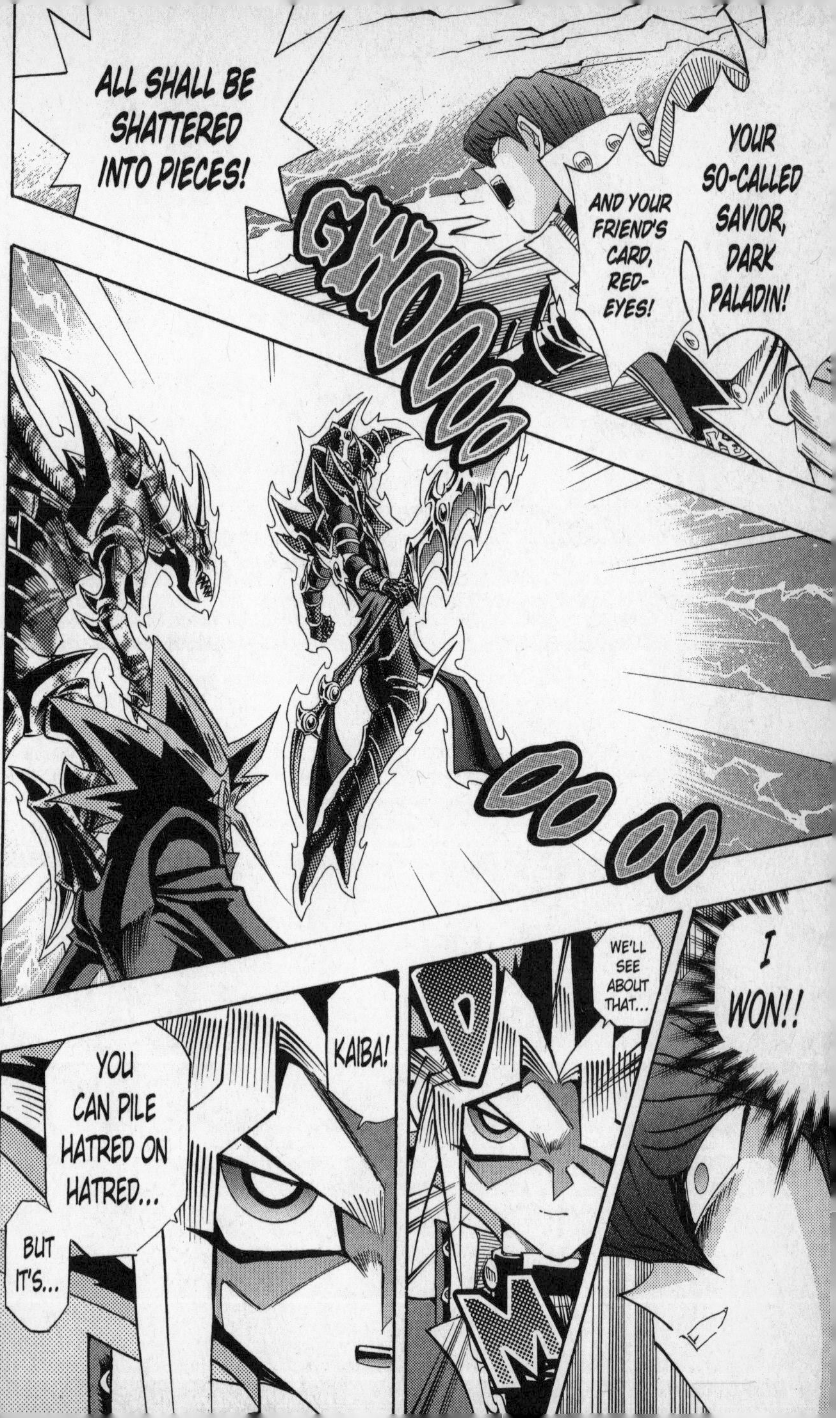
YOUR SO-CALLED SAVIOR, DARK PALADIN!
AND YOUR FRIEND'S CARD, RED-EYES!
ALL SHALL BE SHATTERED INTO PIECES!
GHOOOOOO
OO OO
I WON!!
WE'LL SEE ABOUT THAT...
KAIBA!
YOU CAN PILE HATRED ON HATRED...
BUT IT'S...

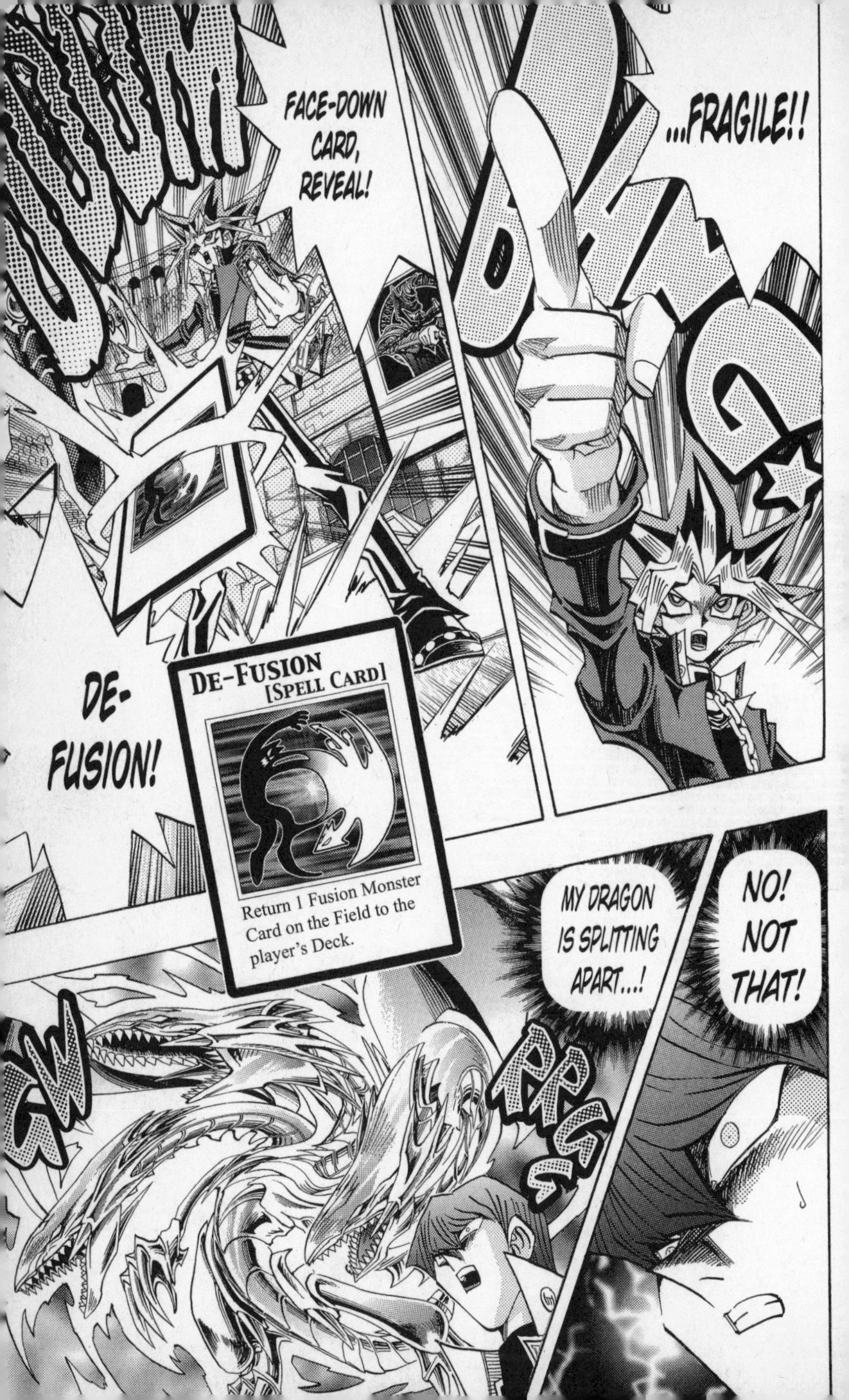
...FRAGILE!!
FACE-DOWN CARD, REVEAL!
DE-FUSION!
DE-FUSION
[SPELL CARD]
Return 1 Fusion Monster Card on the Field to the player's Deck.
NO! NOT THAT!
MY DRAGON IS SPLITTING APART...!

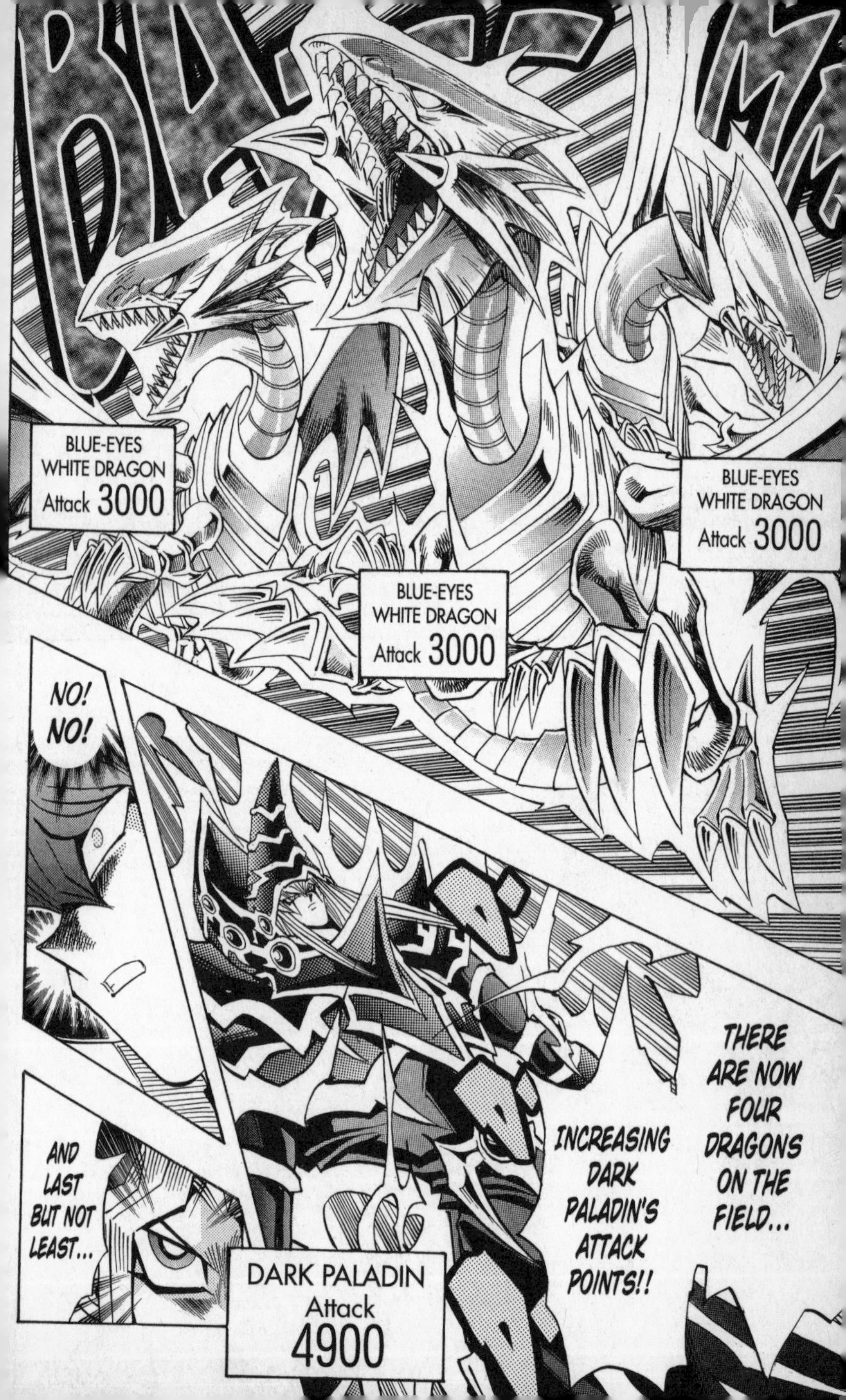
BLUE-EYES WHITE DRAGON Attack 3000
BLUE-EYES WHITE DRAGON Attack 3000
BLUE-EYES WHITE DRAGON Attack 3000
THERE ARE NOW FOUR DRAGONS ON THE FIELD...
INCREASING DARK PALADIN'S ATTACK POINTS!!
DARK PALADIN Attack 4900
NO! NO!
AND LAST BUT NOT LEAST...

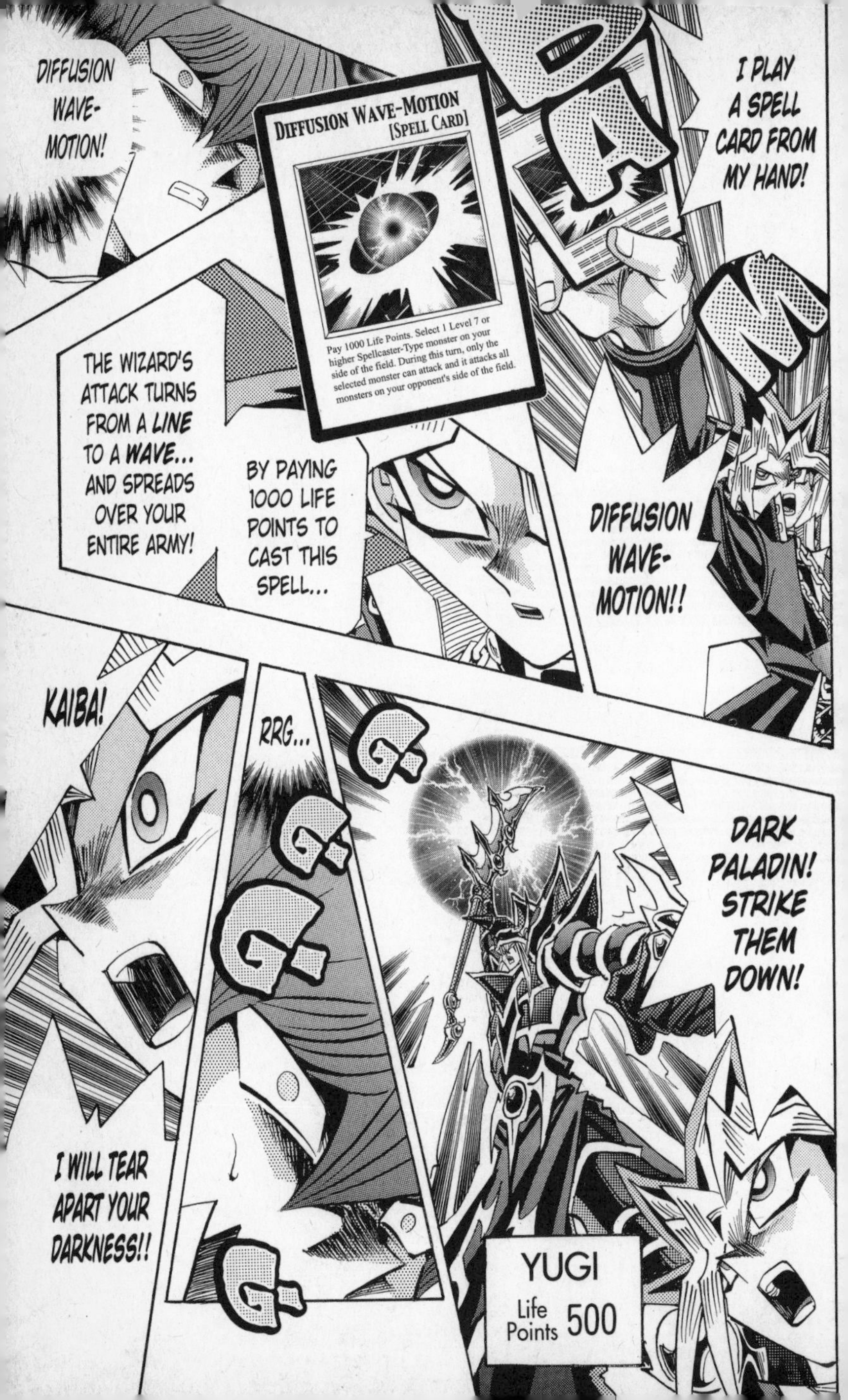
I PLAY A SPELL CARD FROM MY HAND!
DIFFUSION WAVE-MOTION [SPELL CARD]
Pay 1000 Life Points. Select 1 Level 7 or higher Spellcaster-Type monster on your side of the field. During this turn, only the selected monster can attack and it attacks all monsters on your opponent's side of the field.
DIFFUSION WAVE-MOTION!
DIFFUSION WAVE-MOTION!!
BY PAYING 1000 LIFE POINTS TO CAST THIS SPELL...
THE WIZARD'S ATTACK TURNS FROM A LINE TO A WAVE... AND SPREADS OVER YOUR ENTIRE ARMY!
DARK PALADIN! STRIKE THEM DOWN!
YUGI Life Points 500
G
G
G
RRG...
G
KAIBA!
I WILL TEAR APART YOUR DARKNESS!!

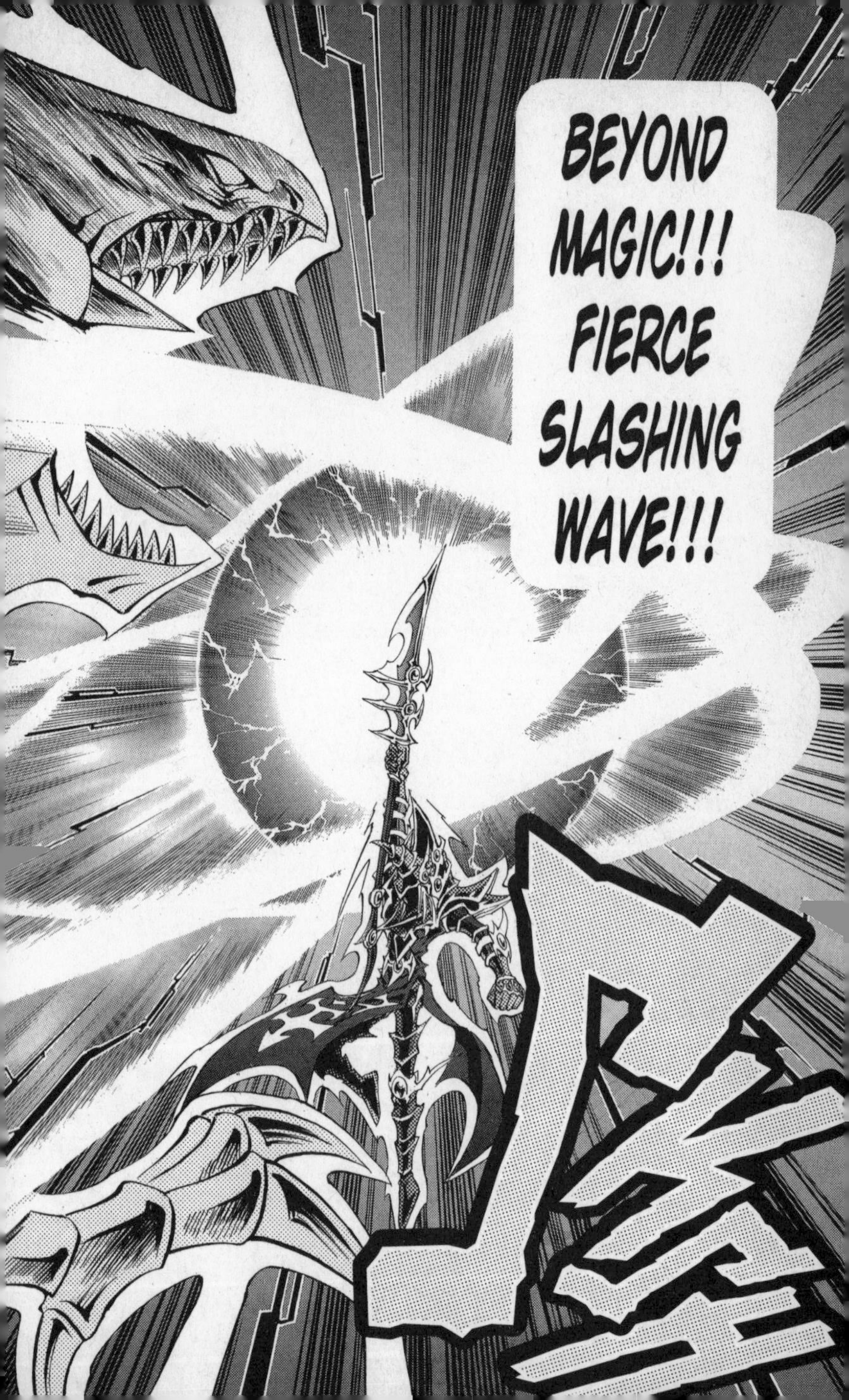
BEYOND MAGIC!!! FIERCE SLASHING WAVE!!!

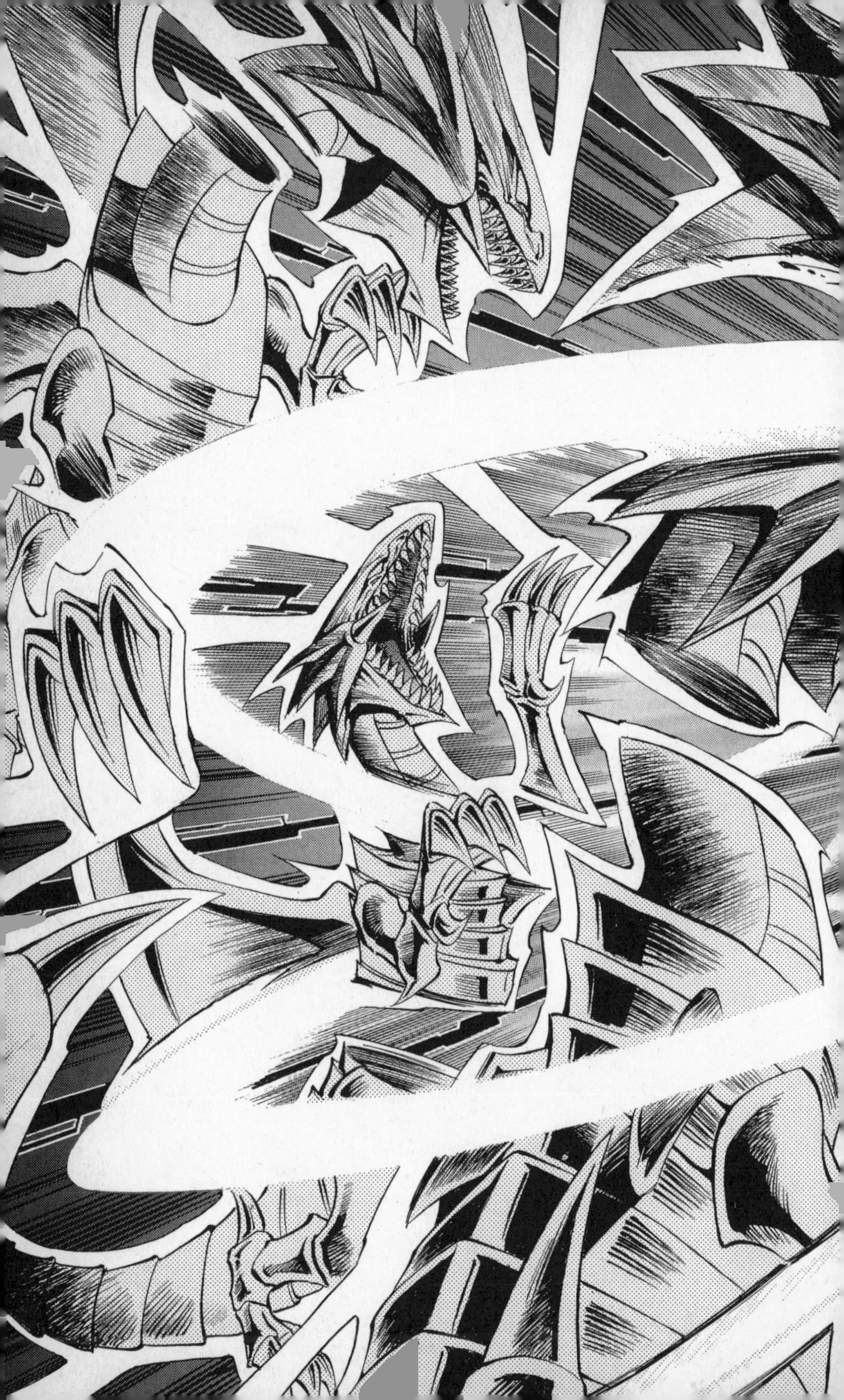

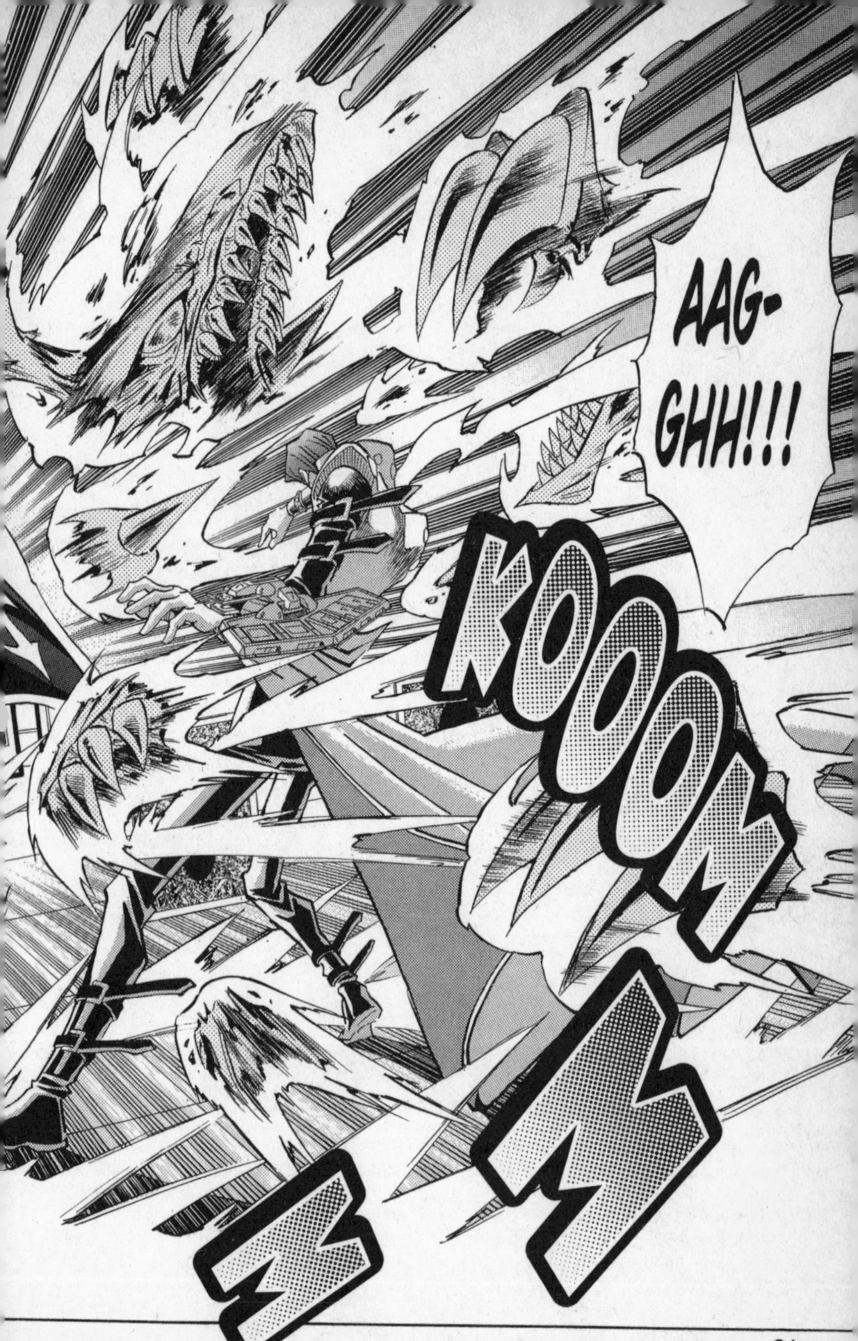
AAG-
GHH!!!
KOOOOM
MM

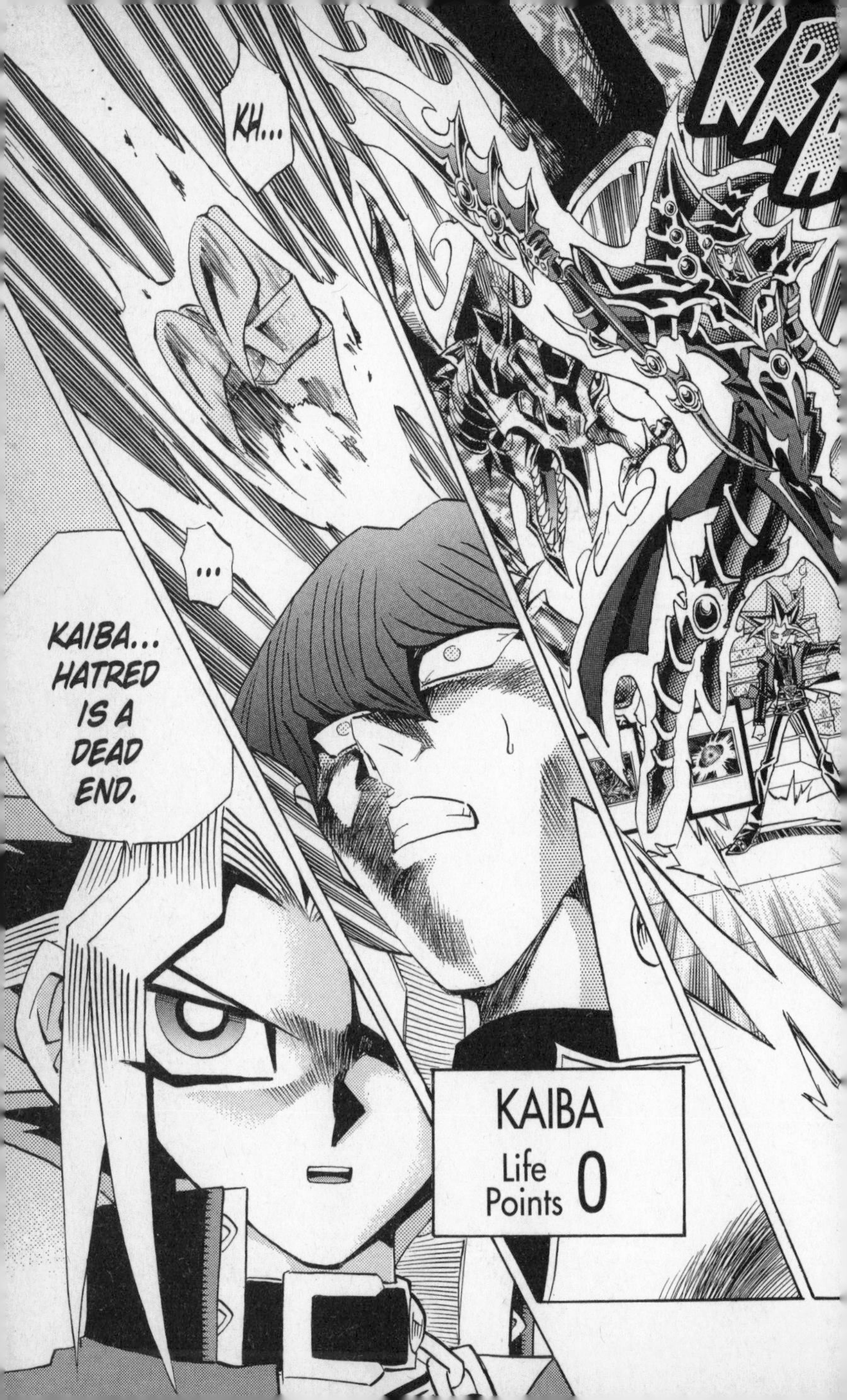
KH...
...
KAIBA... HATRED IS A DEAD END.
KAIBA
Life Points 0

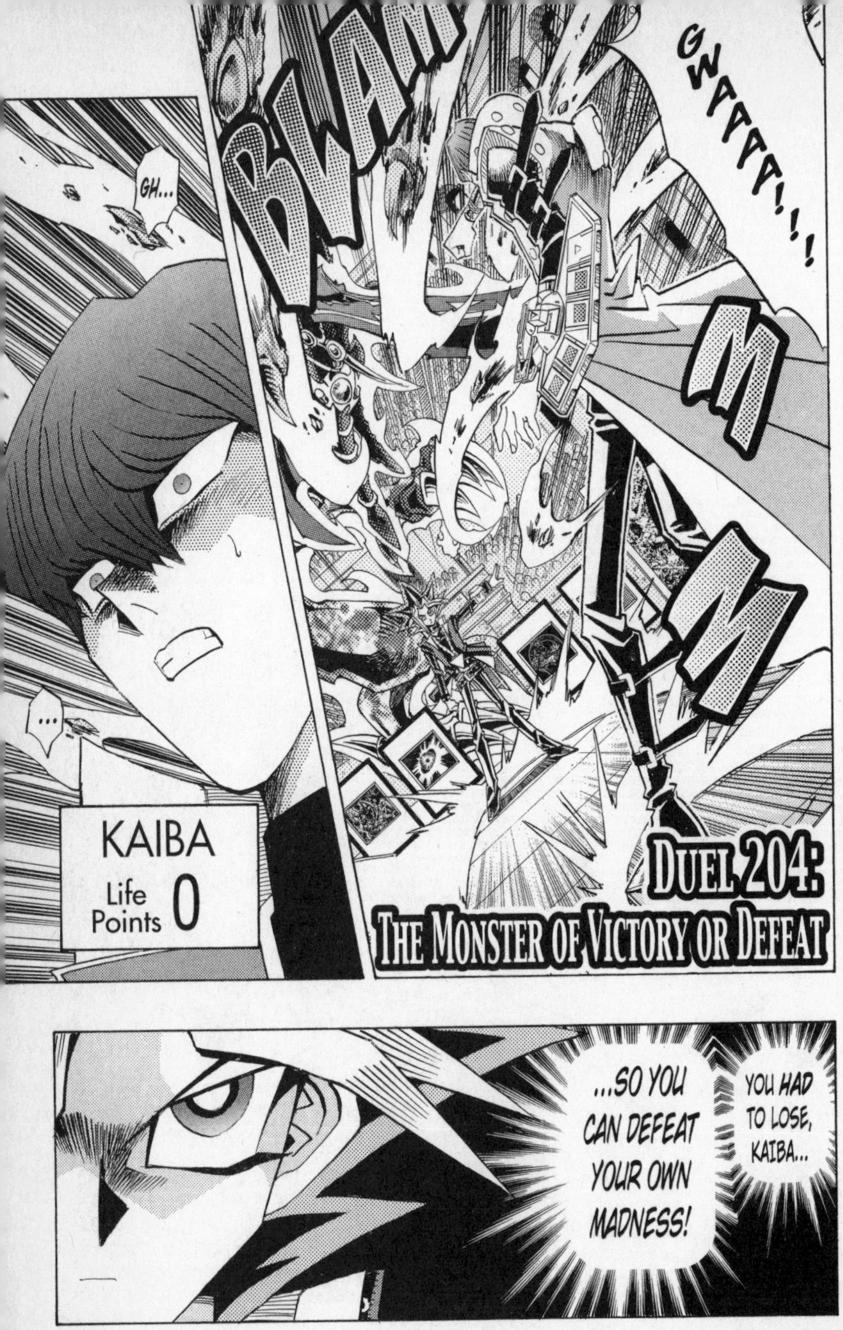
BLAM
GWAAAAA!!!
M
M
DUEL 204:
THE MONSTER OF VICTORY OR DEFEAT
GH...
...
KAIBA
Life Points 0
YOU HAD TO LOSE, KAIBA...
...SO YOU CAN DEFEAT YOUR OWN MADNESS!

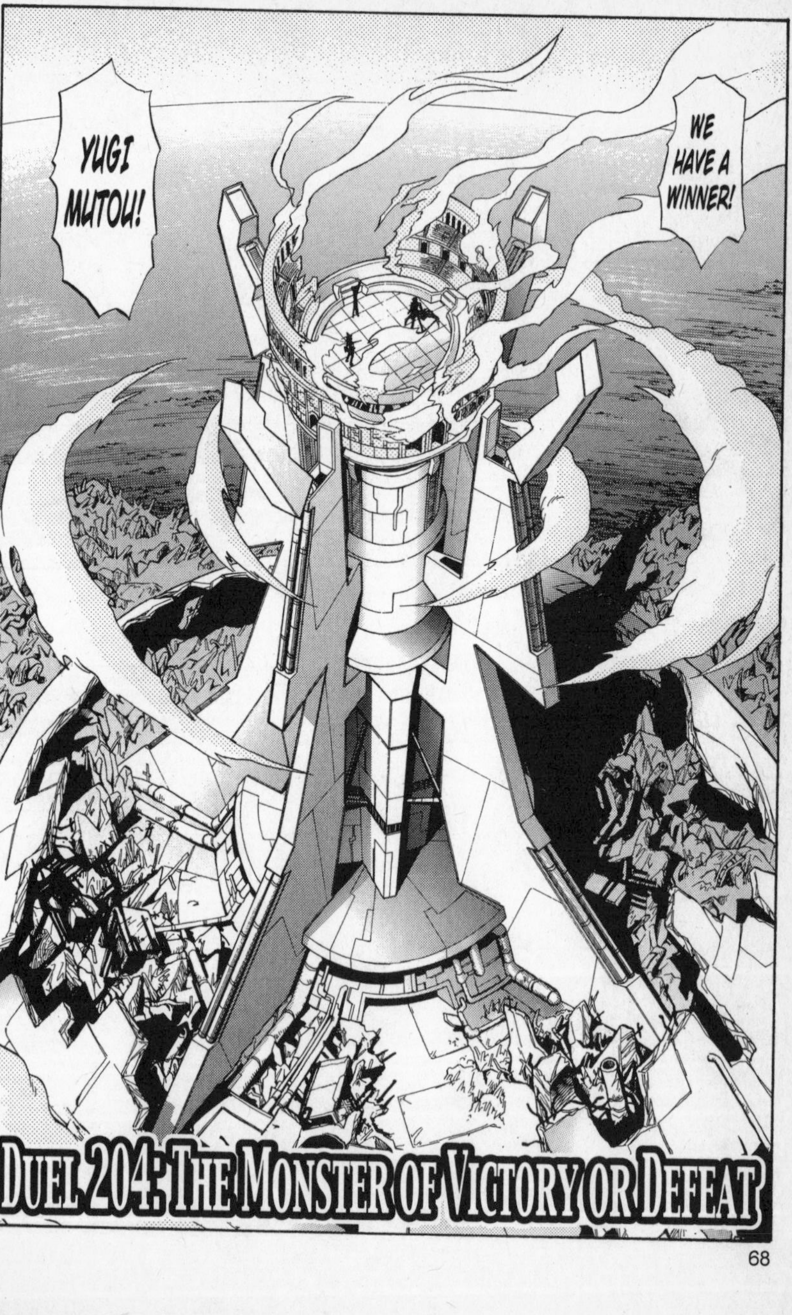
WE HAVE A WINNER!
YUGI MUTOU!
DUEL 204: THE MONSTER OF VICTORY OR DEFEAT

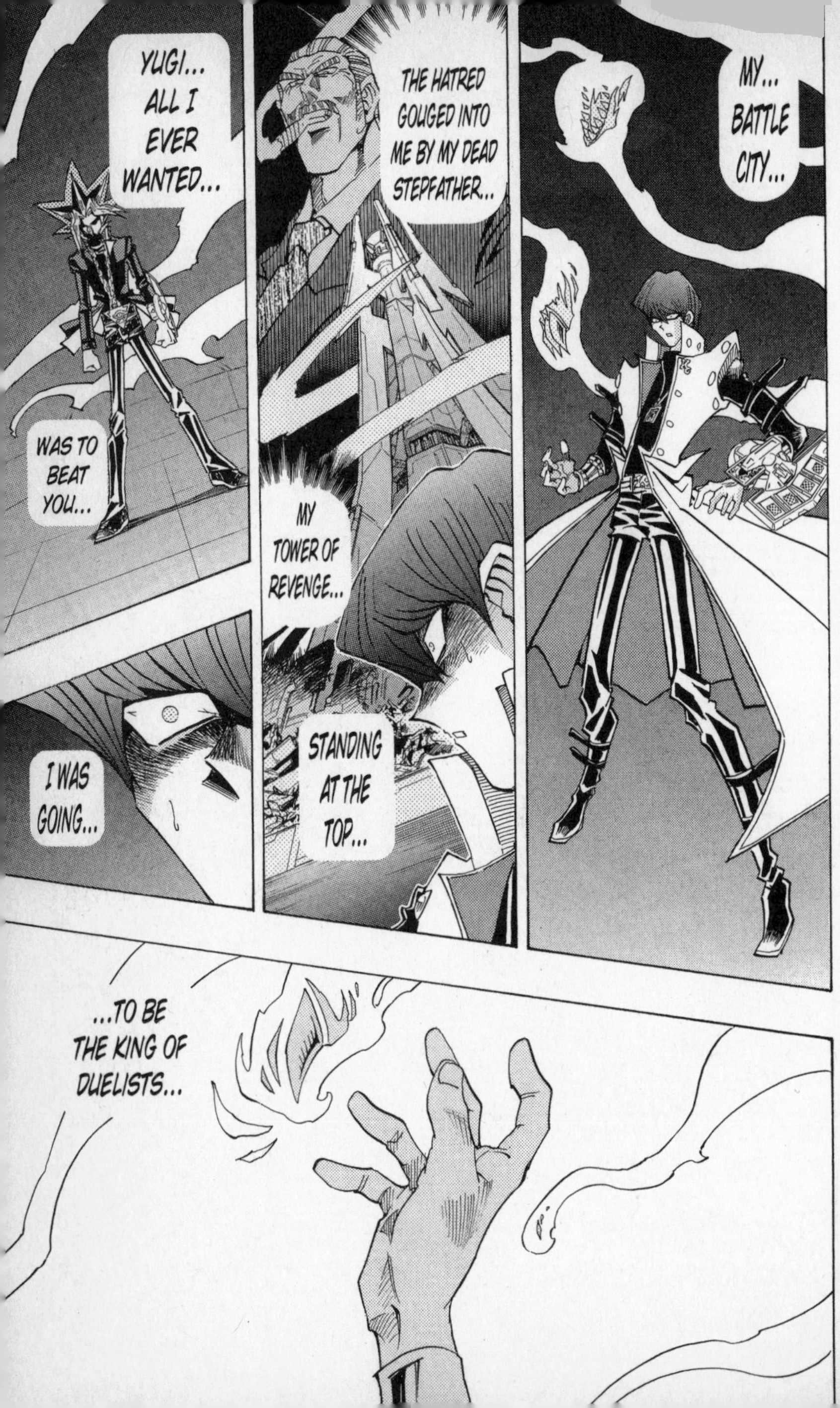
MY... BATTLE CITY...
THE HATRED GOUGED INTO ME BY MY DEAD STEPFATHER...
MY TOWER OF REVENGE...
STANDING AT THE TOP...
YUGI... ALL I EVER WANTED...
WAS TO BEAT YOU...
I WAS GOING...
...TO BE THE KING OF DUELISTS...

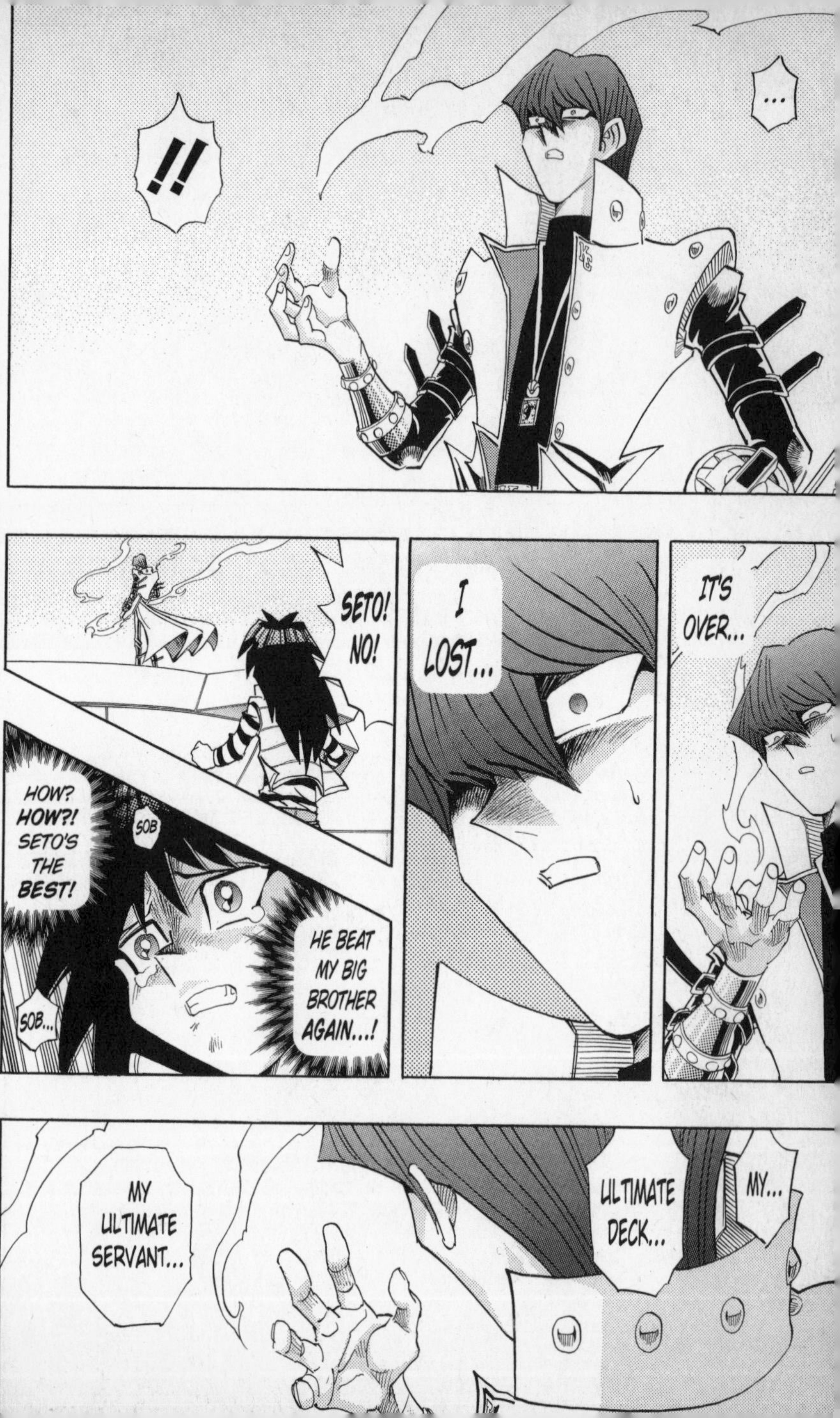
...
!!
IT'S OVER...
I LOST...
SETO! NO!
HOW? HOW?! SETO'S THE BEST!
SOB
HE BEAT MY BIG BROTHER AGAIN...!
SOB...
MY...
ULTIMATE DECK...
MY ULTIMATE SERVANT...

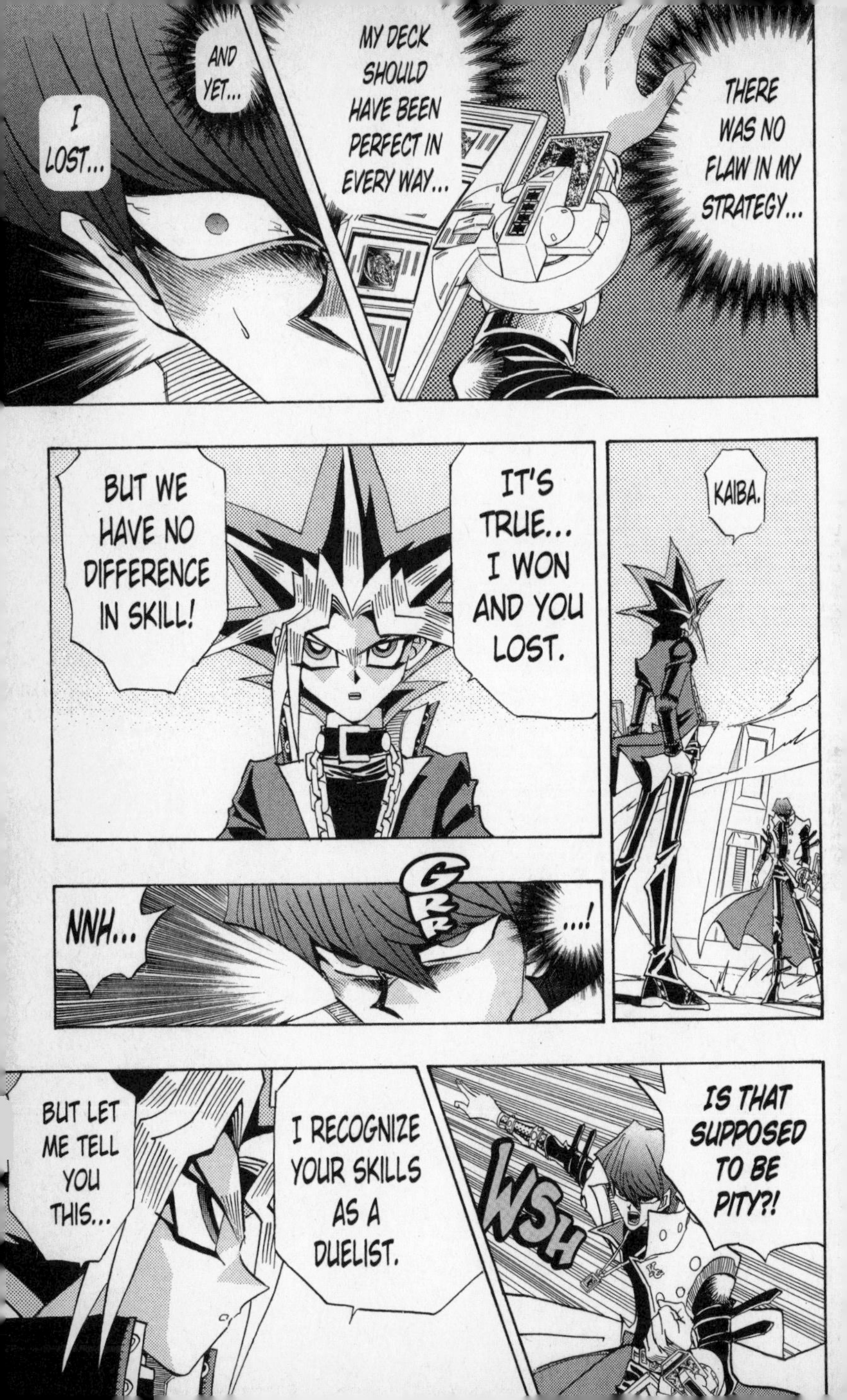
THERE WAS NO FLAW IN MY STRATEGY...
MY DECK SHOULD HAVE BEEN PERFECT IN EVERY WAY...
AND YET...
I LOST...
KAIBA.
IT'S TRUE... I WON AND YOU LOST.
BUT WE HAVE NO DIFFERENCE IN SKILL!
...!
GRR
NNH...
IS THAT SUPPOSED TO BE PITY?!
WSH
I RECOGNIZE YOUR SKILLS AS A DUELIST.
BUT LET ME TELL YOU THIS...

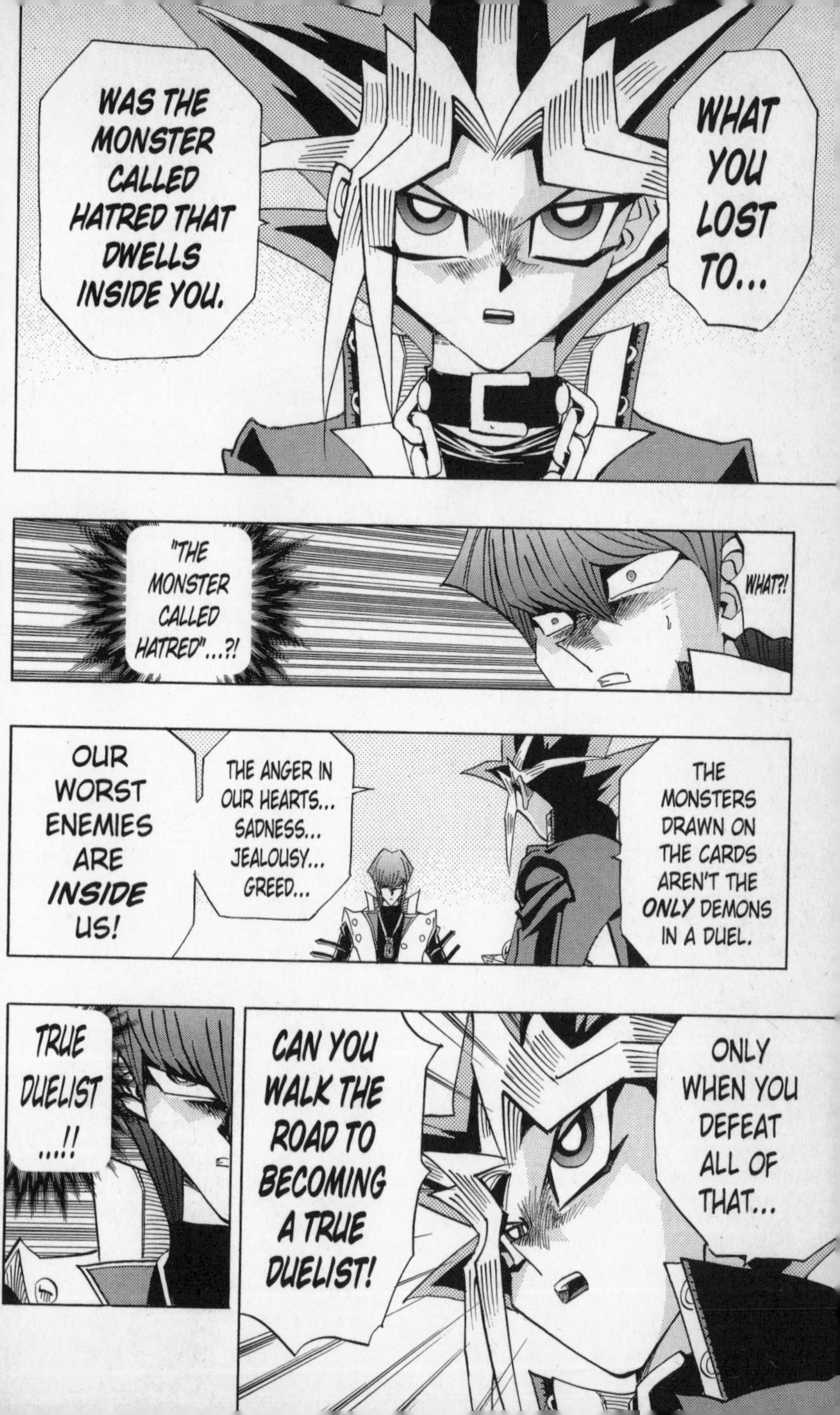
WHAT YOU LOST TO...
WAS THE MONSTER CALLED HATRED THAT DWELLS INSIDE YOU.
WHAT?!
"THE MONSTER CALLED HATRED"...?!
THE MONSTERS DRAWN ON THE CARDS AREN'T THE *ONLY* DEMONS IN A DUEL.
THE ANGER IN OUR HEARTS... SADNESS... JEALOUSY... GREED...
OUR WORST ENEMIES ARE *INSIDE* US!
ONLY WHEN YOU DEFEAT ALL OF THAT...
CAN YOU WALK THE ROAD TO BECOMING A TRUE DUELIST!
TRUE DUELIST ...!!

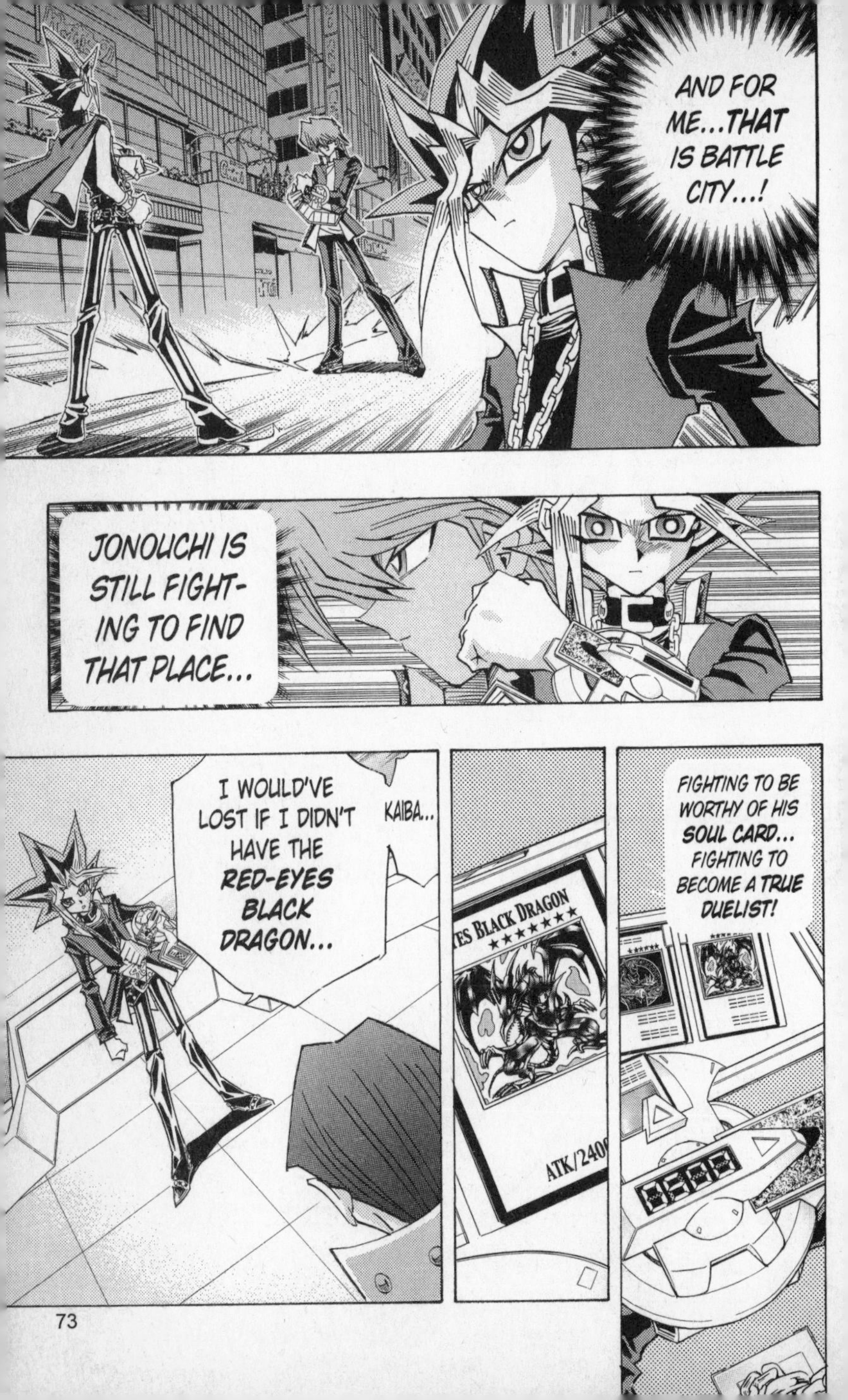
AND FOR ME...THAT IS BATTLE CITY...!
JONOUCHI IS STILL FIGHTING TO FIND THAT PLACE...
FIGHTING TO BE WORTHY OF HIS SOUL CARD... FIGHTING TO BECOME A TRUE DUELIST!
KAIBA...
I WOULD'VE LOST IF I DIDN'T HAVE THE RED-EYES BLACK DRAGON...

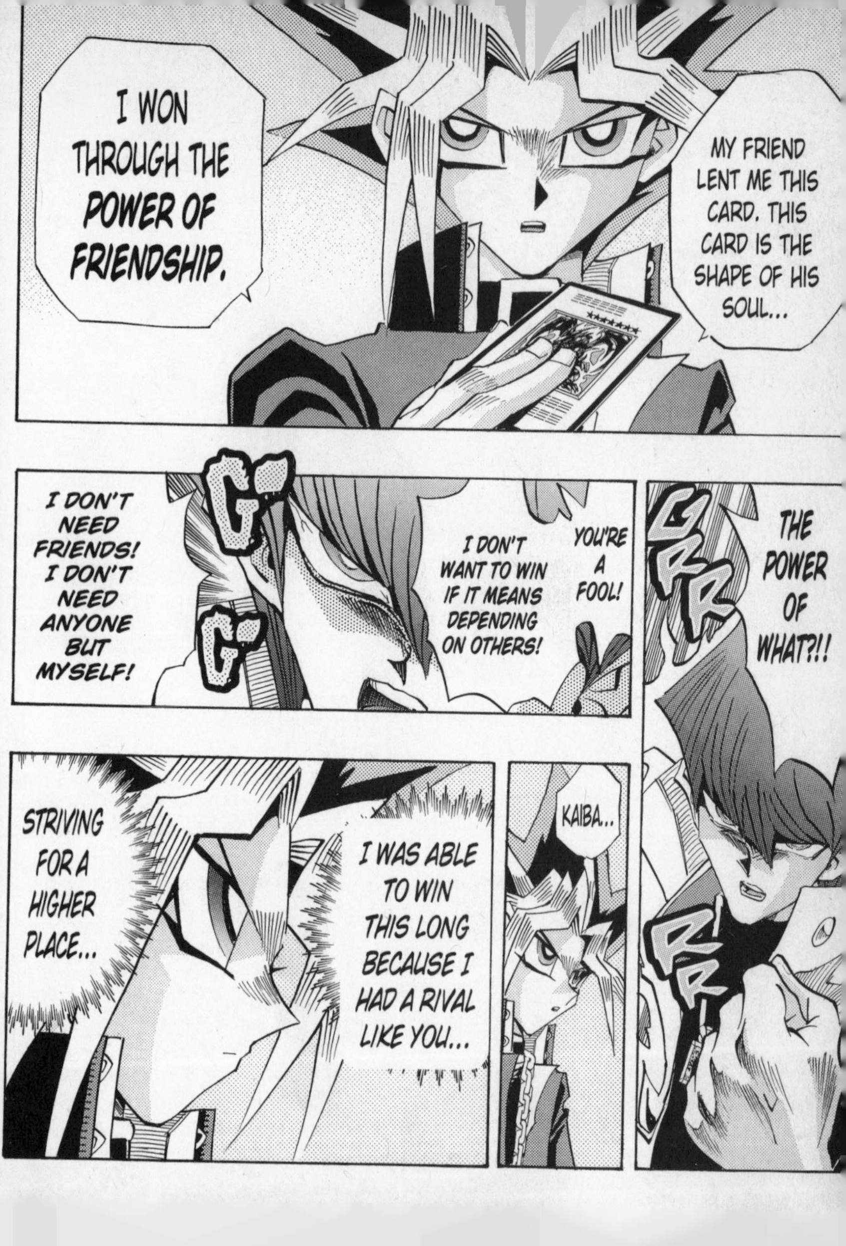
MY FRIEND LENT ME THIS CARD. THIS CARD IS THE SHAPE OF HIS SOUL...
I WON THROUGH THE POWER OF FRIENDSHIP.
GRR
THE POWER OF WHAT?!!
RR
YOU'RE A FOOL!
I DON'T WANT TO WIN IF IT MEANS DEPENDING ON OTHERS!
G
I DON'T NEED FRIENDS! I DON'T NEED ANYONE BUT MYSELF!
G
KAIBA...
I WAS ABLE TO WIN THIS LONG BECAUSE I HAD A RIVAL LIKE YOU...
STRIVING FOR A HIGHER PLACE...

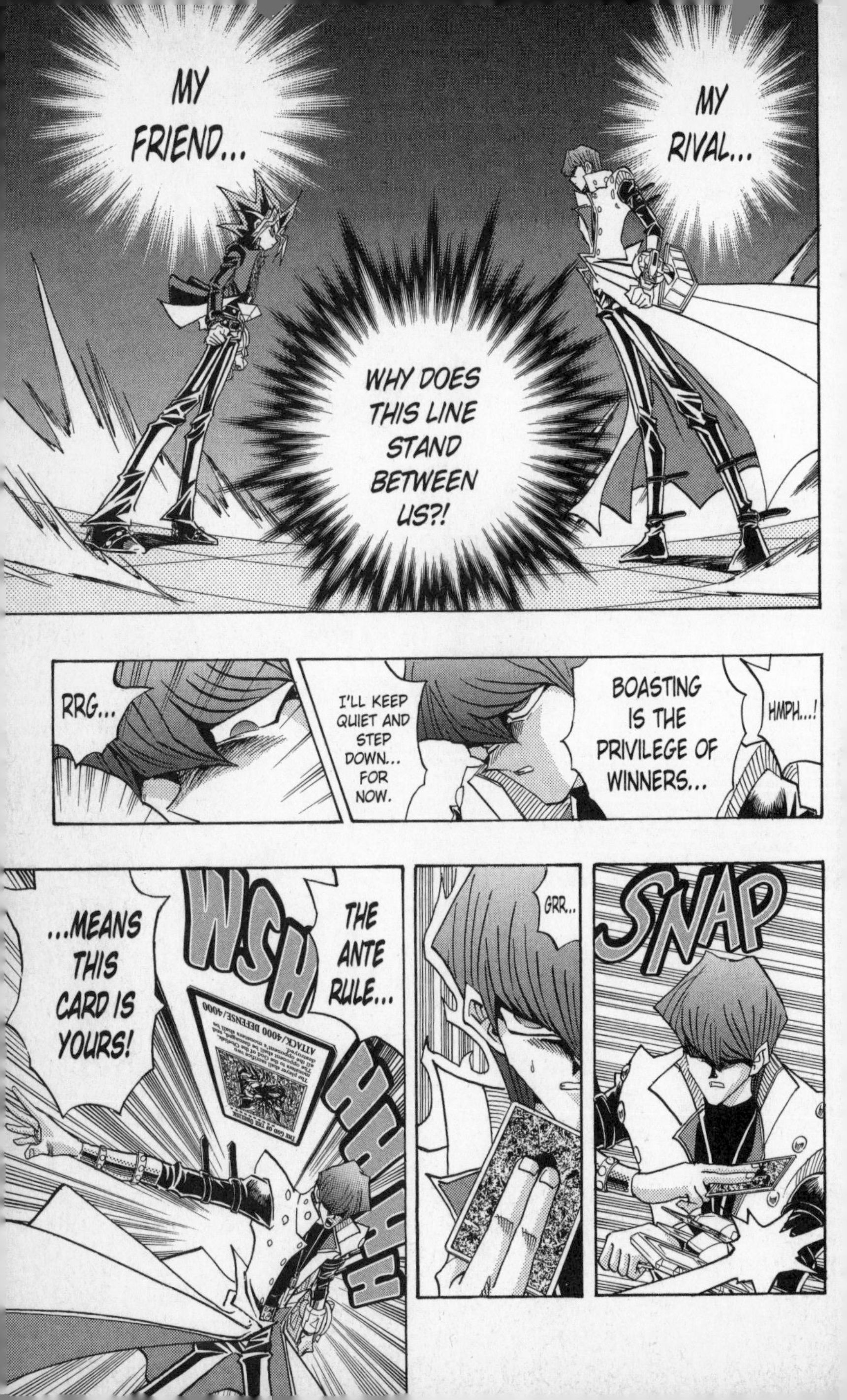
MY RIVAL...
MY FRIEND...
WHY DOES THIS LINE STAND BETWEEN US?!
HMPH...!
BOASTING IS THE PRIVILEGE OF WINNERS...
I'LL KEEP QUIET AND STEP DOWN... FOR NOW.
RRG...
SNAP
GRR...
THE ANTE RULE...
WSH
...MEANS THIS CARD IS YOURS!

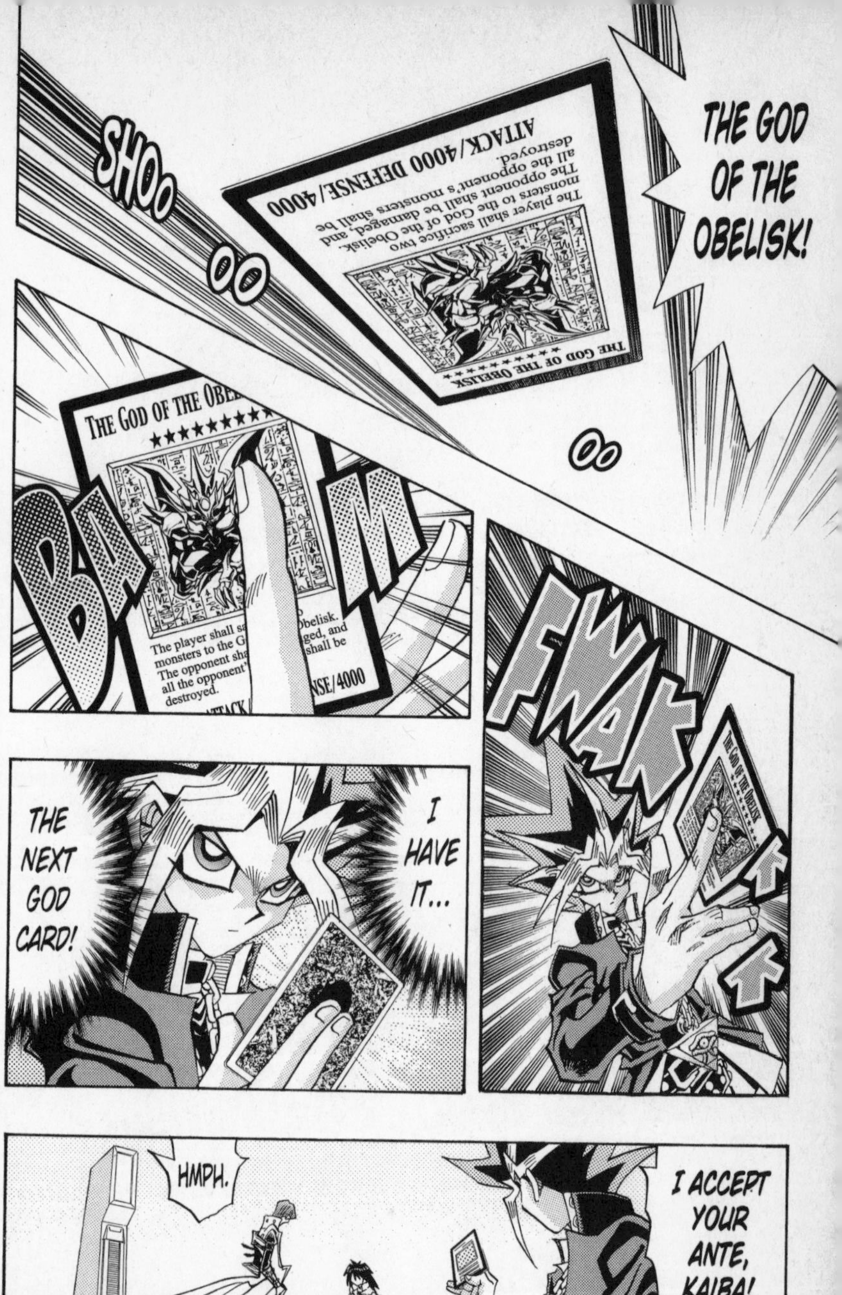
THE GOD OF THE OBELISK!
THE GOD OF THE OBELISK
The player shall sacrifice two monsters to the God of the Obelisk. The opponent shall be damaged, and all the opponent's monsters shall be destroyed.
ATTACK/4000 DEFENSE/4000
SHOOOOOO
FWAK
THE GOD OF THE OBELISK
BAM
I HAVE IT...
THE NEXT GOD CARD!
I ACCEPT YOUR ANTE, KAIBA!
HMPH.

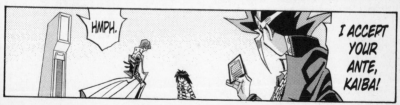

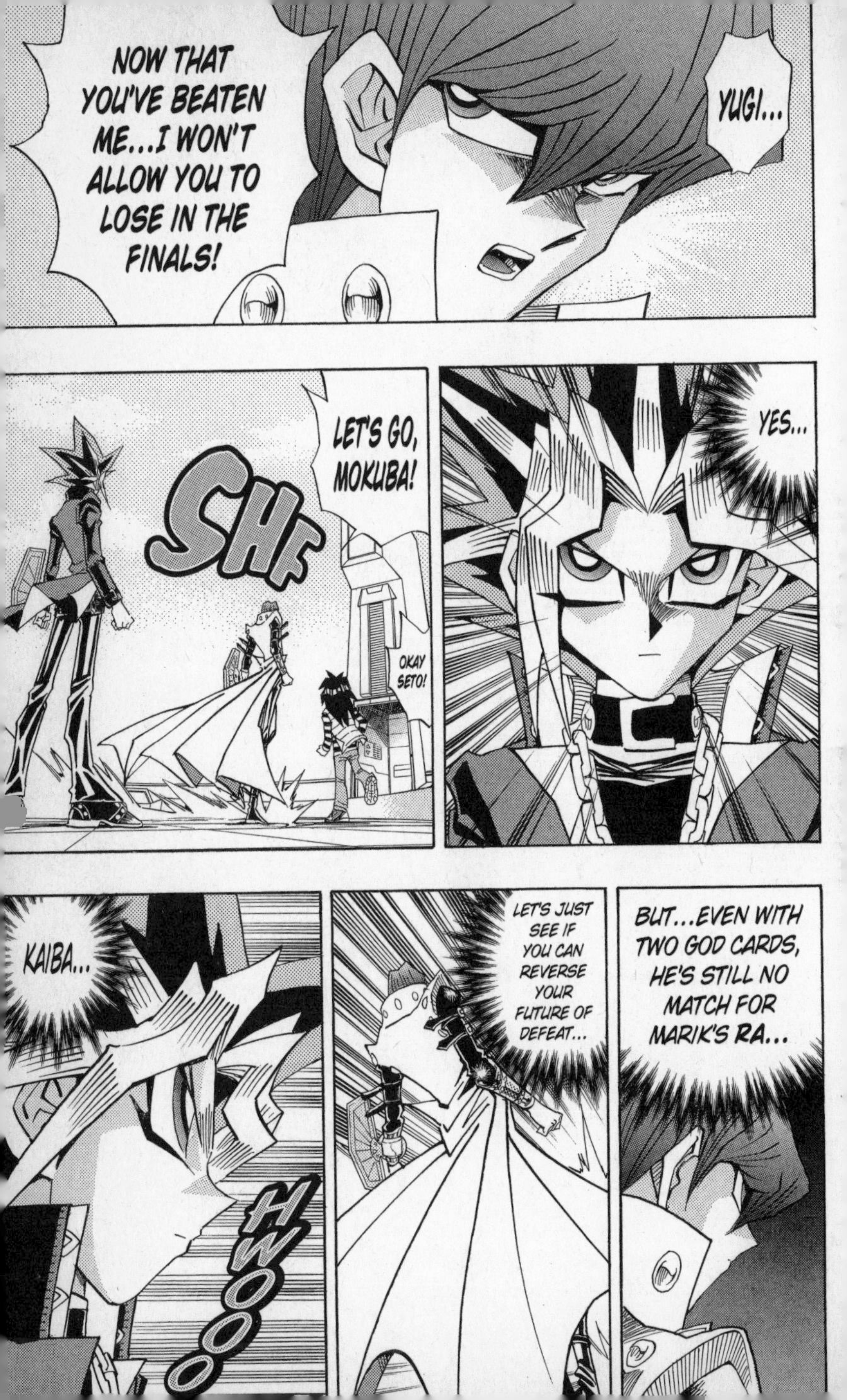
YUGI...
NOW THAT YOU'VE BEATEN ME...I WON'T ALLOW YOU TO LOSE IN THE FINALS!
YES...
LET'S GO, MOKUBA!
SHF
OKAY SETO!
BUT...EVEN WITH TWO GOD CARDS, HE'S STILL NO MATCH FOR MARIK'S RA...
LET'S JUST SEE IF YOU CAN REVERSE YOUR FUTURE OF DEFEAT...
KAIBA...
HWOOOO

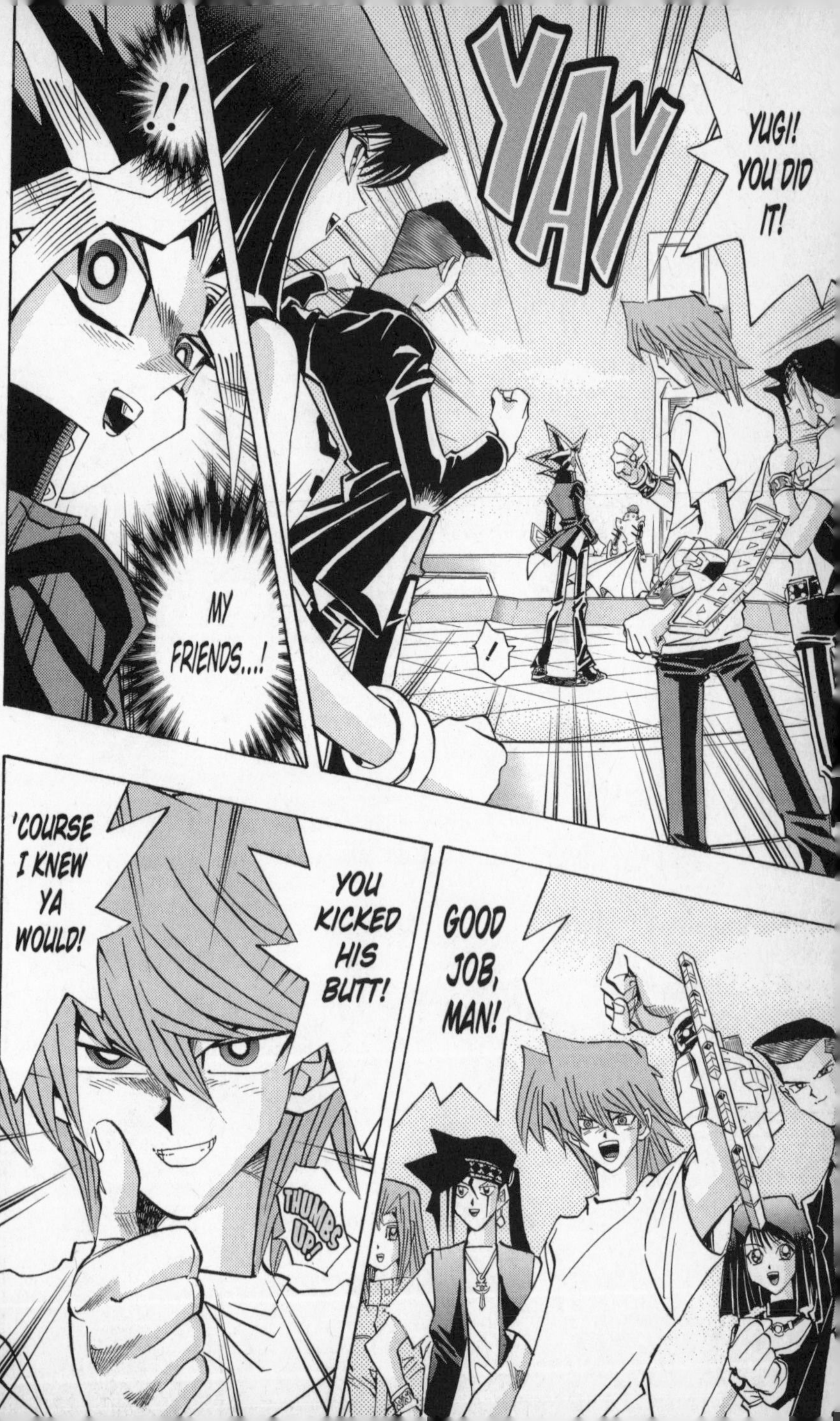
YAY
YUGI! YOU DID IT!
!
!!
MY FRIENDS...!
GOOD JOB, MAN!
YOU KICKED HIS BUTT!
'COURSE I KNEW YA WOULD!
THUMBS UP!

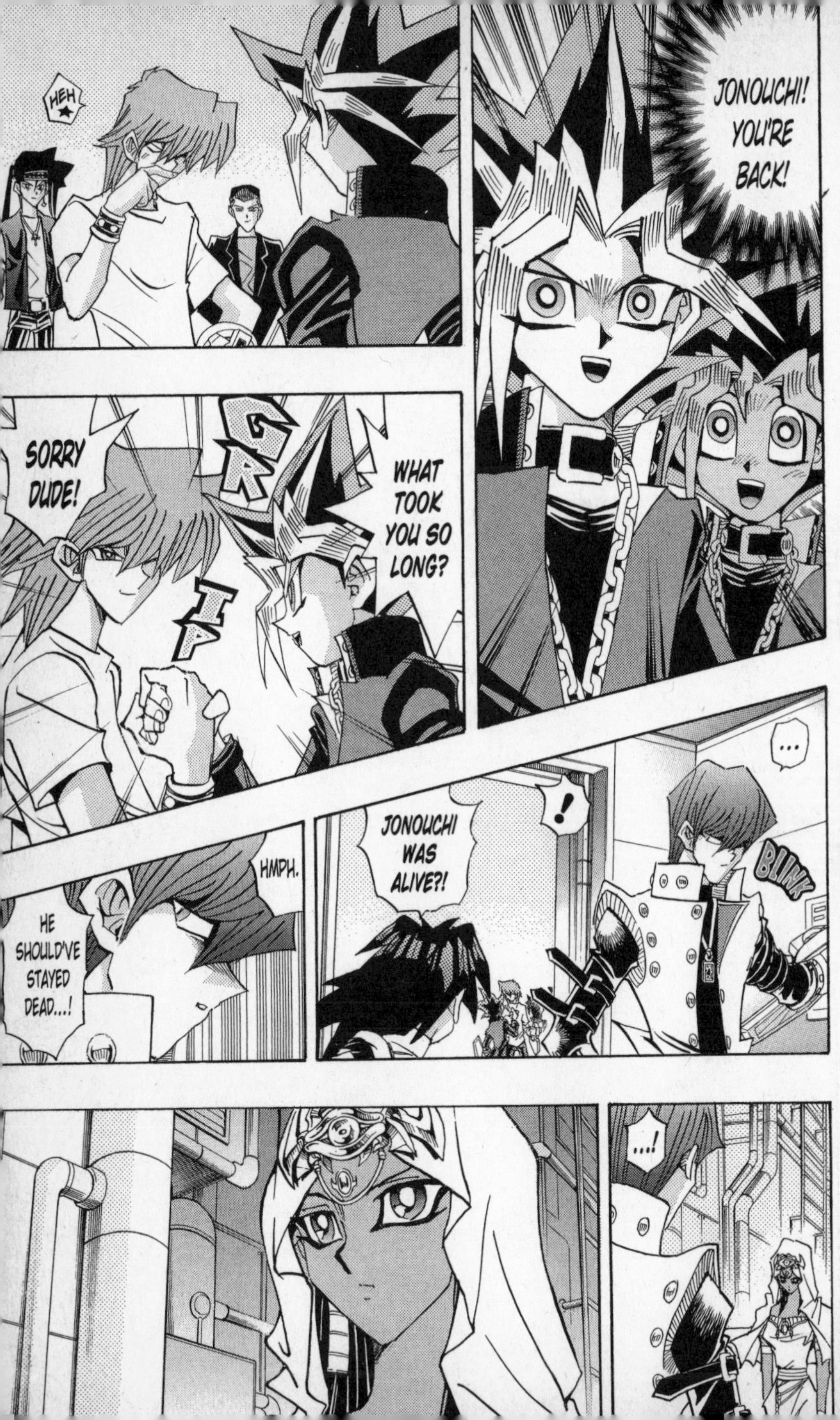
JONOUCHI! YOU'RE BACK!
HEH ★
WHAT TOOK YOU SO LONG?
GRIP
SORRY DUDE!
...
!
BLINK
JONOUCHI WAS ALIVE?!
HMPH.
HE SHOULD'VE STAYED DEAD...!
...!

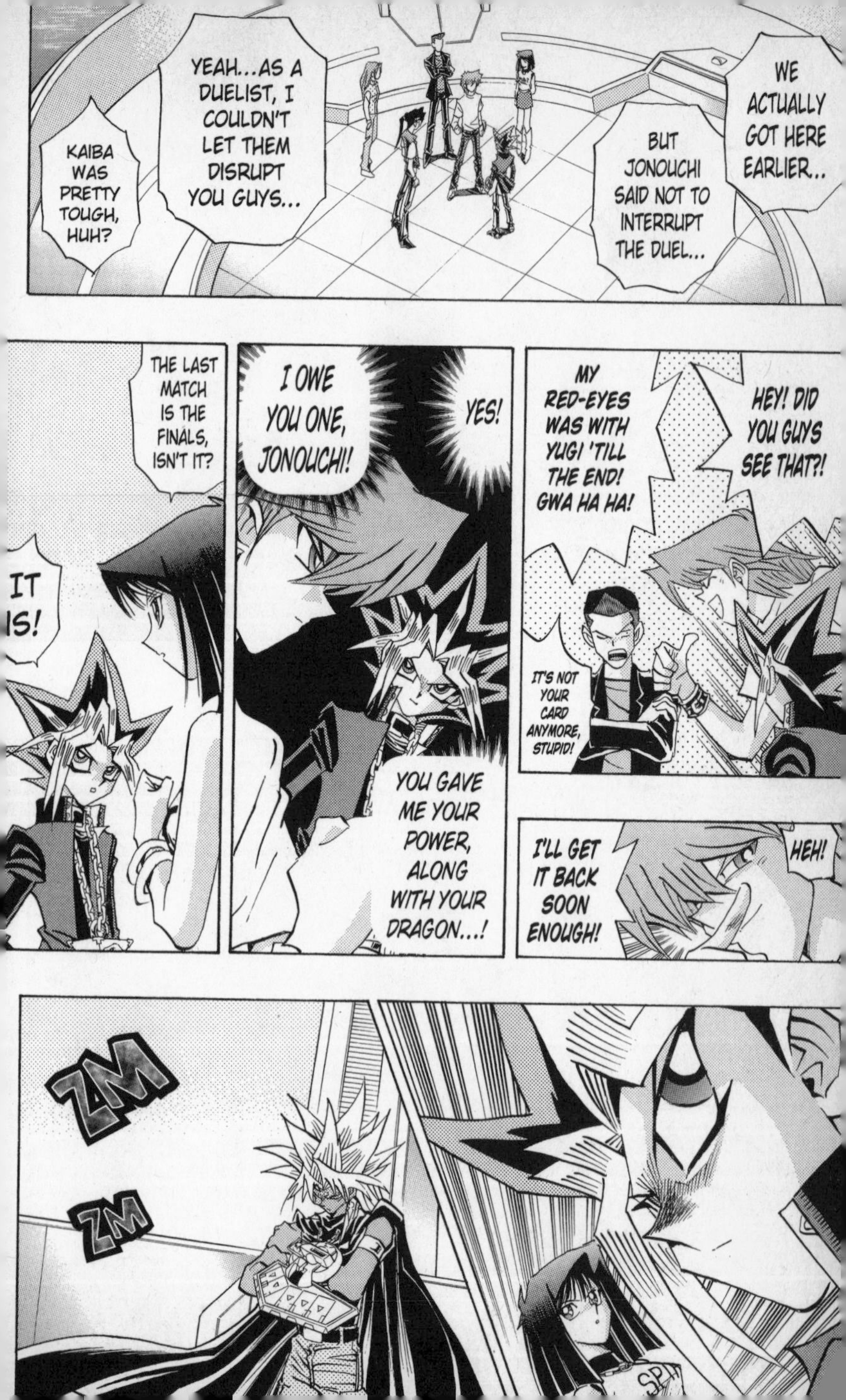
WE ACTUALLY GOT HERE EARLIER...
BUT JONOUCHI SAID NOT TO INTERRUPT THE DUEL...
YEAH...AS A DUELIST, I COULDN'T LET THEM DISRUPT YOU GUYS...
KAIBA WAS PRETTY TOUGH, HUH?
HEY! DID YOU GUYS SEE THAT?!
MY RED-EYES WAS WITH YUGI 'TILL THE END! GWA HA HA!
IT'S NOT YOUR CARD ANYMORE, STUPID!
HEH!
I'LL GET IT BACK SOON ENOUGH!
I OWE YOU ONE, JONOUCHI!
YES!
YOU GAVE ME YOUR POWER, ALONG WITH YOUR DRAGON...!
THE LAST MATCH IS THE FINALS, ISN'T IT?
IT S!
ZM
ZM

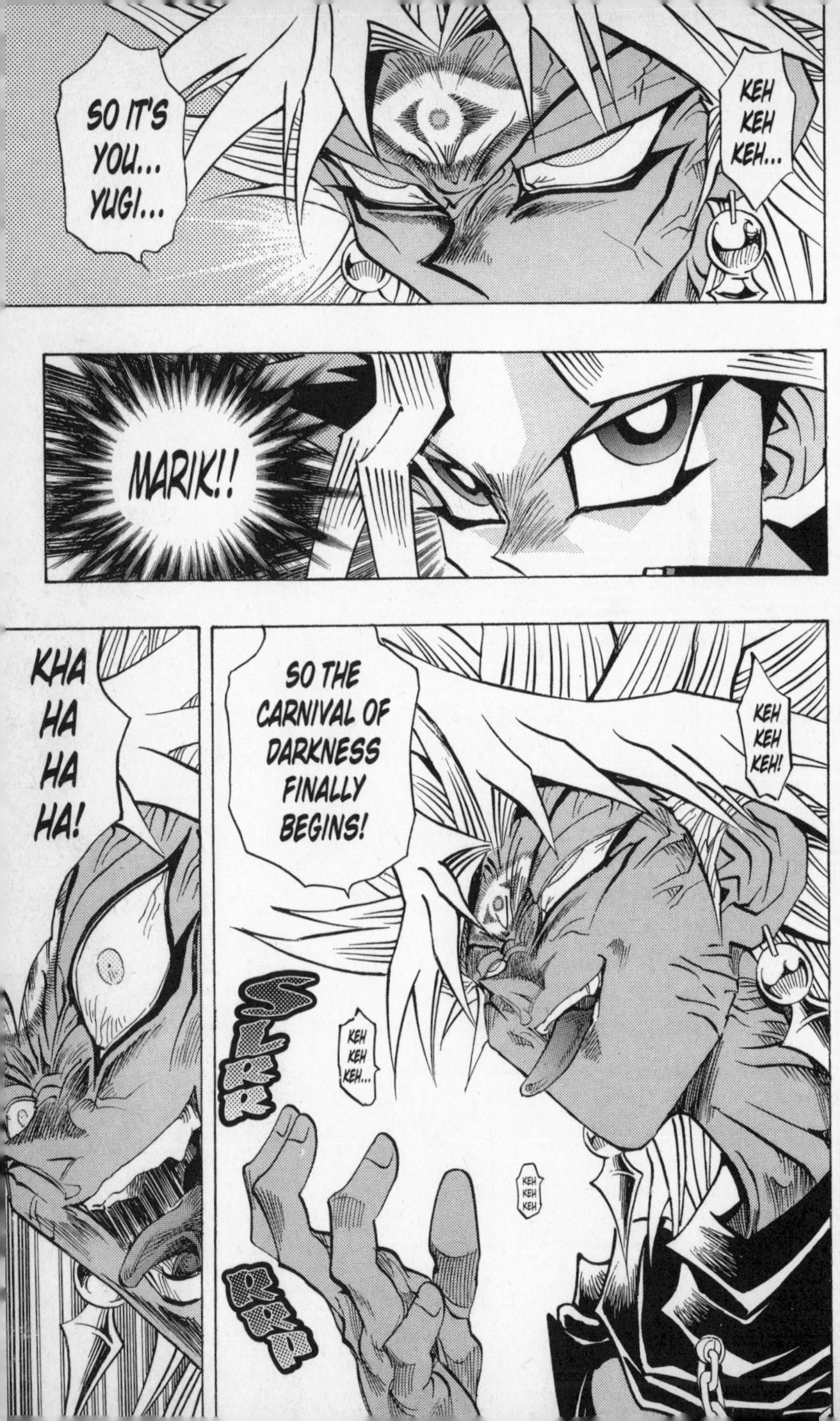
KEH KEH KEH...
SO IT'S YOU... YUGI...
MARIK!!
KEH KEH KEH!
SO THE CARNIVAL OF DARKNESS FINALLY BEGINS!
KEH KEH KEH...
SLRR
RRP
KEH KEH KEH
KHA HA HA HA!

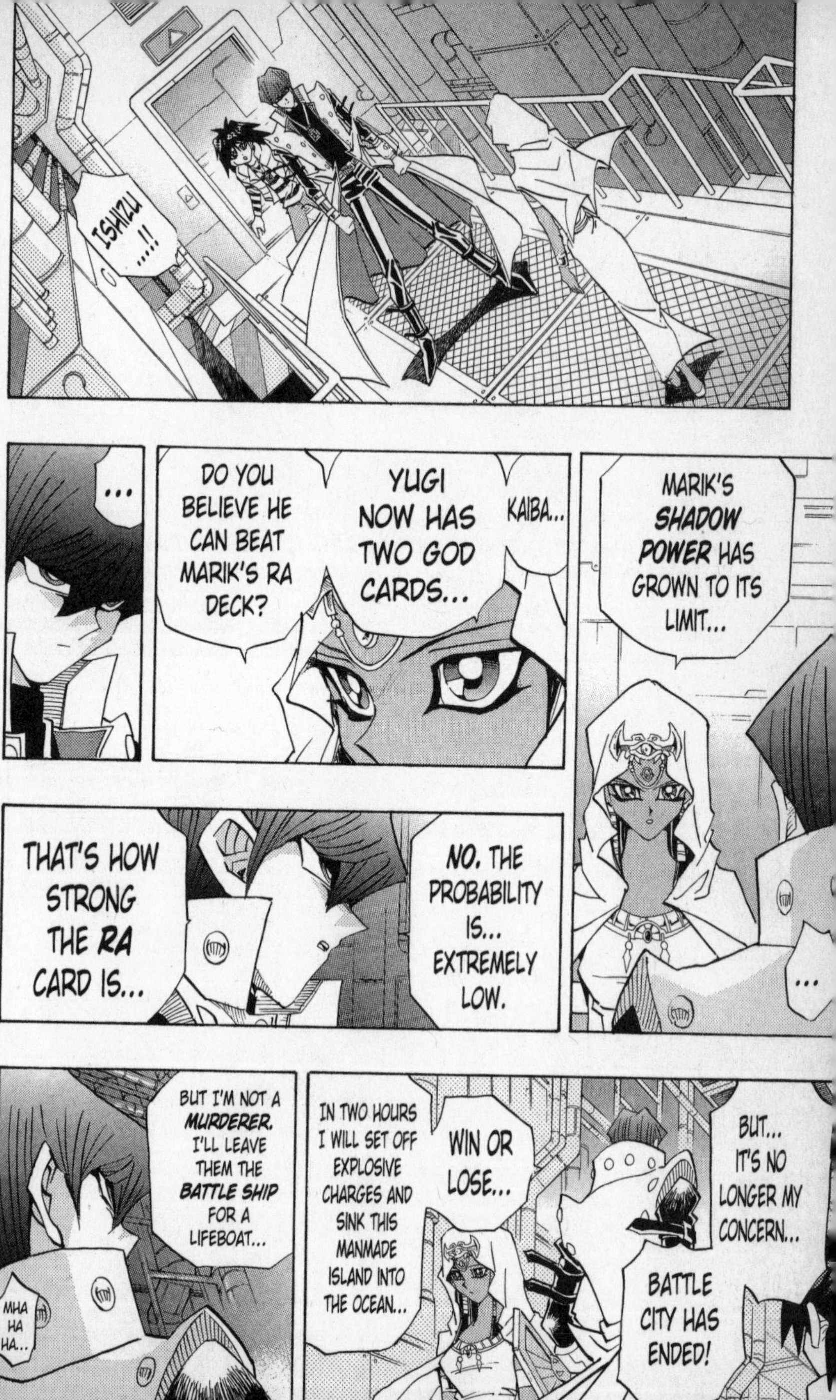
ISHIZU ...!!
MARIK'S SHADOW POWER HAS GROWN TO ITS LIMIT...
...
KAIBA...
YUGI NOW HAS TWO GOD CARDS...
DO YOU BELIEVE HE CAN BEAT MARIK'S RA DECK?
...
NO. THE PROBABILITY IS... EXTREMELY LOW.
THAT'S HOW STRONG THE RA CARD IS...
BUT... IT'S NO LONGER MY CONCERN...
WIN OR LOSE...
IN TWO HOURS I WILL SET OFF EXPLOSIVE CHARGES AND SINK THIS MANMADE ISLAND INTO THE OCEAN...
BATTLE CITY HAS ENDED!
BUT I'M NOT A MURDERER. I'LL LEAVE THEM THE BATTLE SHIP FOR A LIFEBOAT...
MHA HA HA...

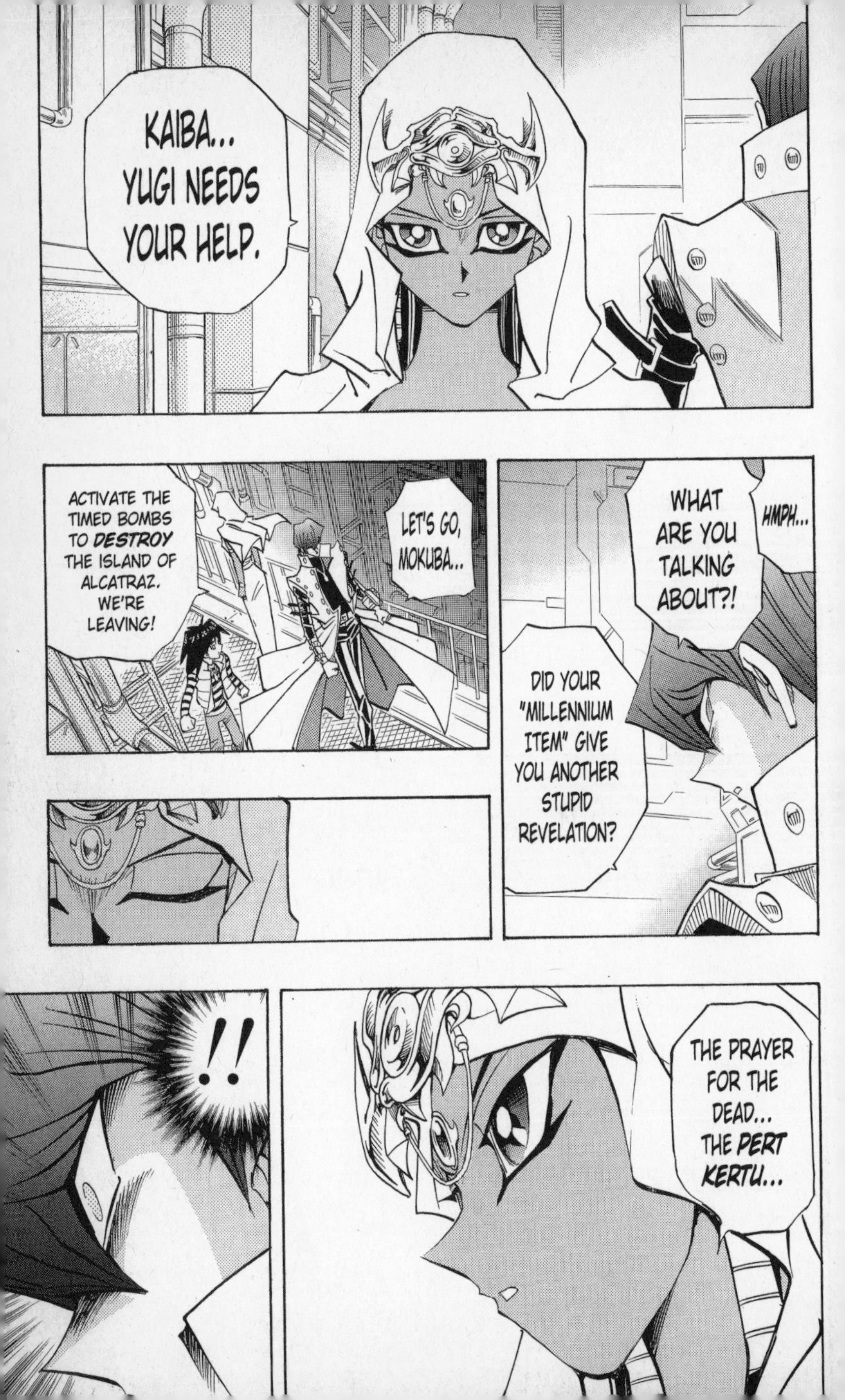
KAIBA... YUGI NEEDS YOUR HELP.
HMPH...
WHAT ARE YOU TALKING ABOUT?!
DID YOUR "MILLENNIUM ITEM" GIVE YOU ANOTHER STUPID REVELATION?
LET'S GO, MOKUBA...
ACTIVATE THE TIMED BOMBS TO DESTROY THE ISLAND OF ALCATRAZ. WE'RE LEAVING!
THE PRAYER FOR THE DEAD... THE PERT KERTU...
!!

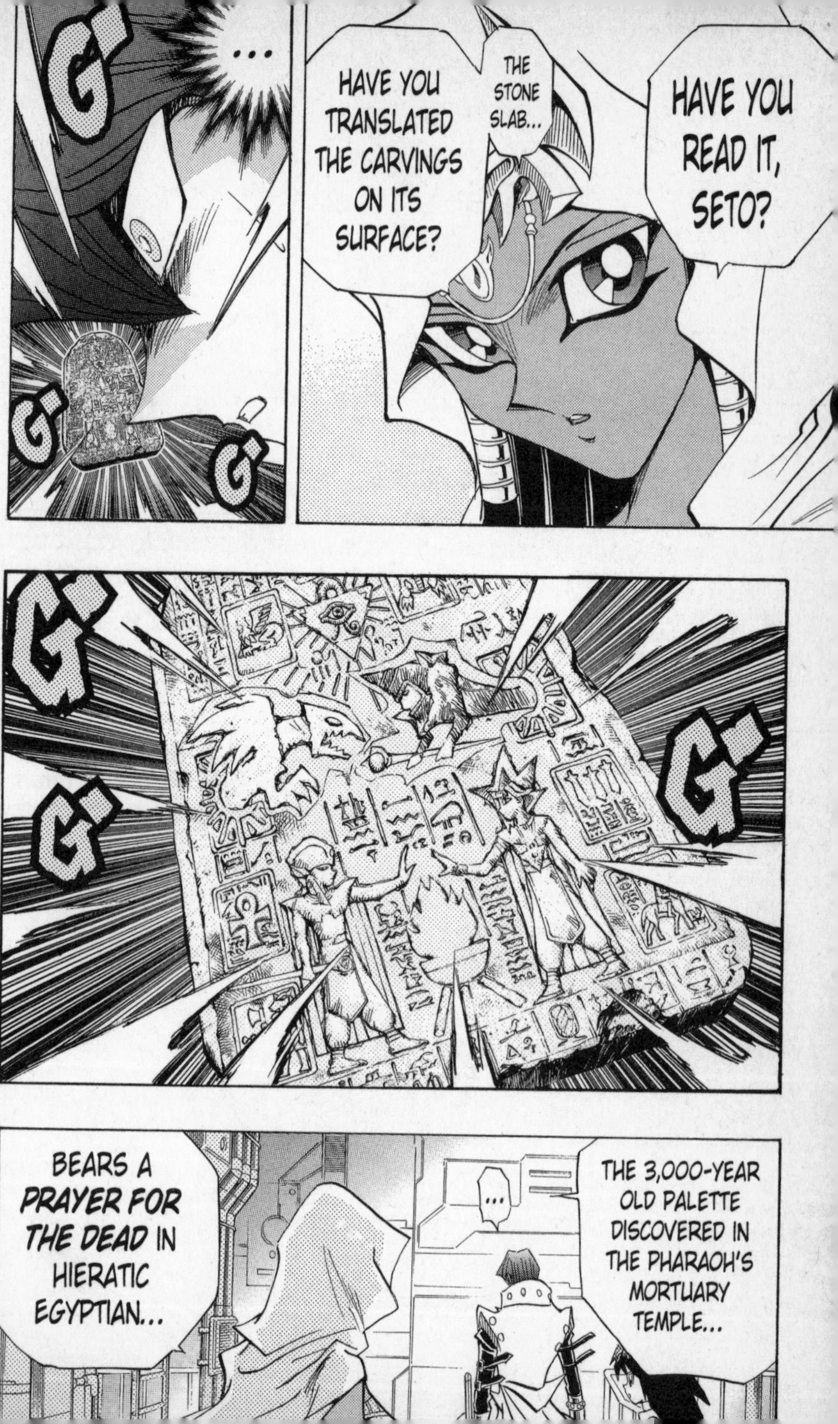
HAVE YOU READ IT, SETO?
THE STONE SLAB...
HAVE YOU TRANSLATED THE CARVINGS ON ITS SURFACE?
...
G
G
G
G
G
G
THE 3,000-YEAR OLD PALETTE DISCOVERED IN THE PHARAOH'S MORTUARY TEMPLE...
...
BEARS A *PRAYER FOR THE DEAD* IN HIERATIC EGYPTIAN...

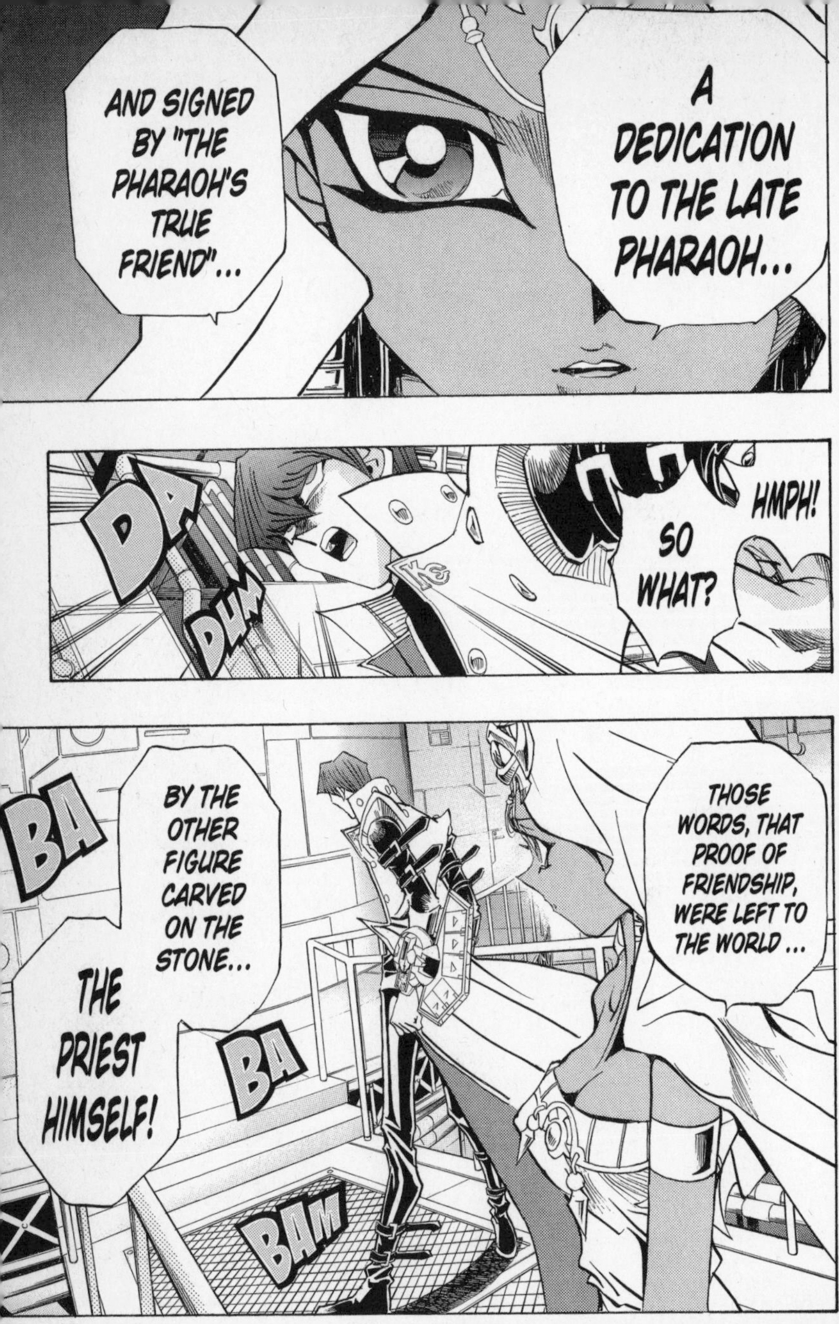
A DEDICATION TO THE LATE PHARAOH...
AND SIGNED BY "THE PHARAOH'S TRUE FRIEND"...
HMPH! SO WHAT?
DA DUM
THOSE WORDS, THAT PROOF OF FRIENDSHIP, WERE LEFT TO THE WORLD ...
BY THE OTHER FIGURE CARVED ON THE STONE...
BA
THE PRIEST HIMSELF!
BA
BAM

DUEL 205: THE ENTRUSTED CARD

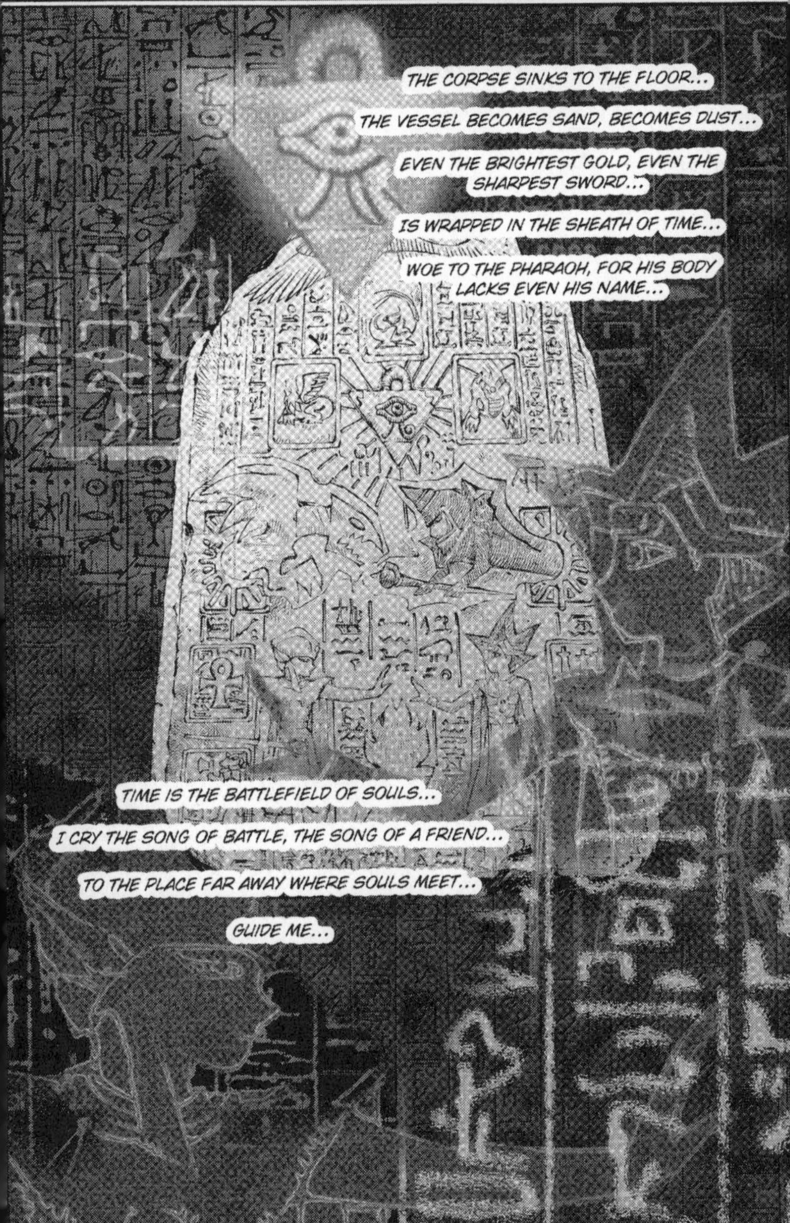
THE CORPSE SINKS TO THE FLOOR...
THE VESSEL BECOMES SAND, BECOMES DUST...
EVEN THE BRIGHTEST GOLD, EVEN THE SHARPEST SWORD...
IS WRAPPED IN THE SHEATH OF TIME...
WOE TO THE PHARAOH, FOR HIS BODY LACKS EVEN HIS NAME...
TIME IS THE BATTLEFIELD OF SOULS...
I CRY THE SONG OF BATTLE, THE SONG OF A FRIEND...
TO THE PLACE FAR AWAY WHERE SOULS MEET...
GUIDE ME...

DUEL 205: THE ENTRUSTED CARD

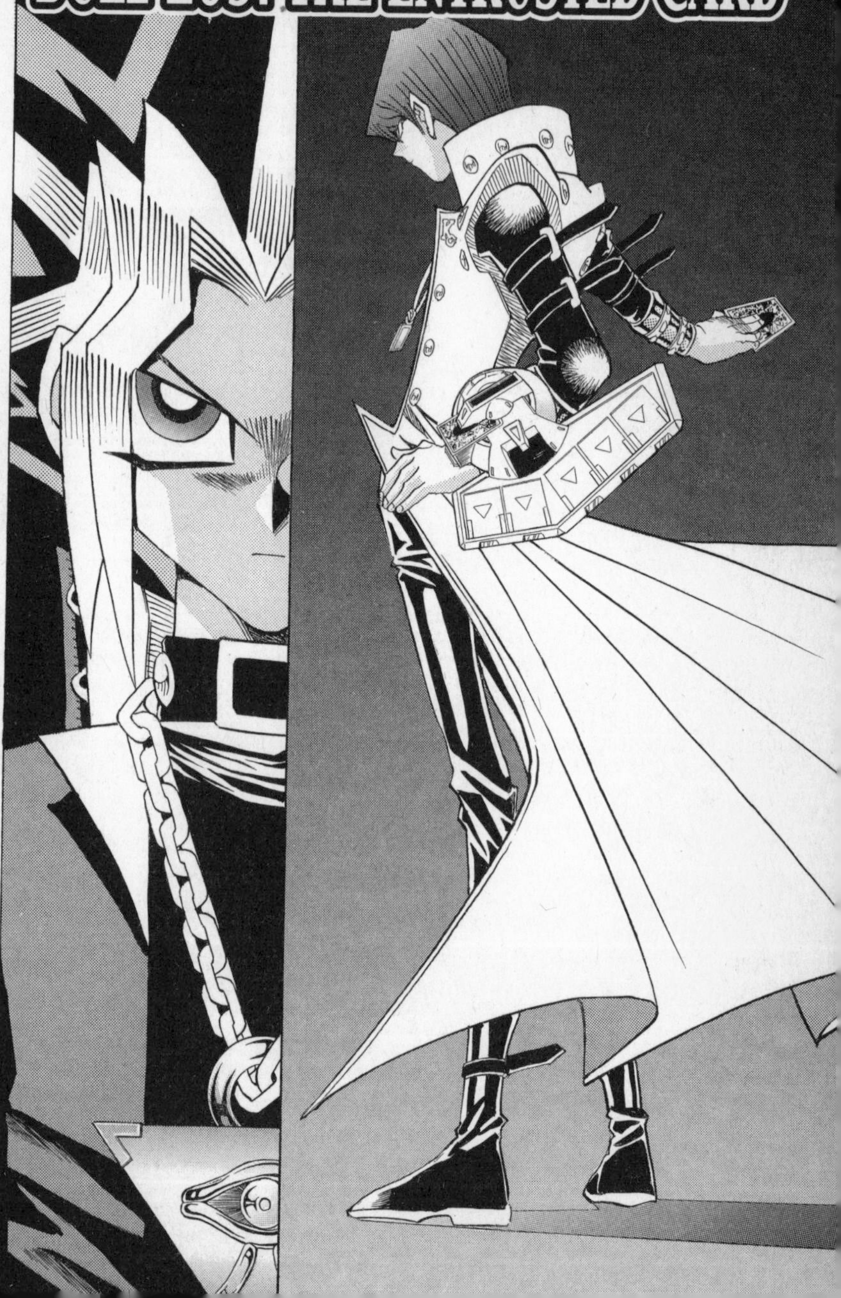

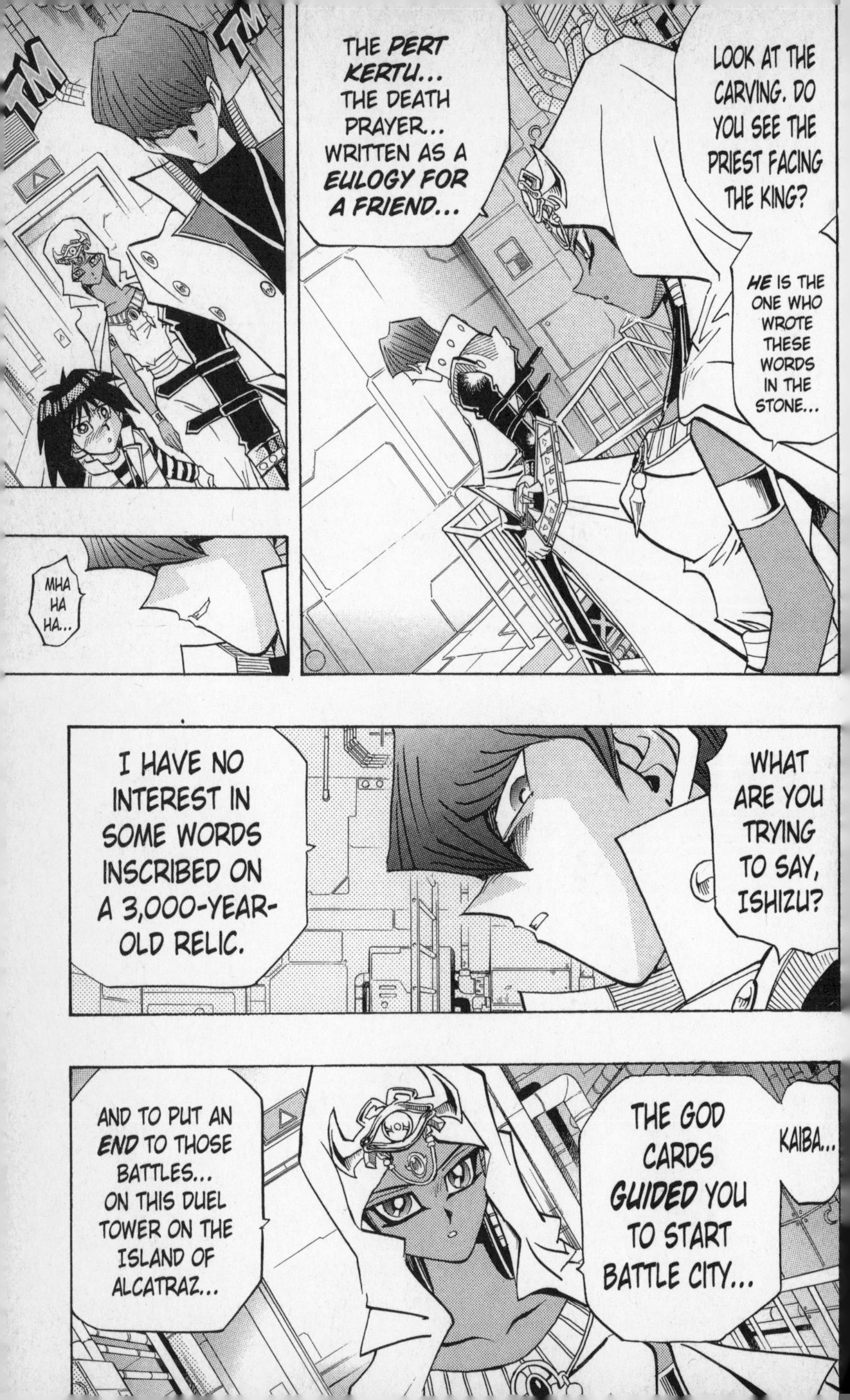
LOOK AT THE CARVING. DO YOU SEE THE PRIEST FACING THE KING?
HE IS THE ONE WHO WROTE THESE WORDS IN THE STONE...
THE PERT KERTU... THE DEATH PRAYER... WRITTEN AS A EULOGY FOR A FRIEND...
TM
TM
MHA HA HA...
WHAT ARE YOU TRYING TO SAY, ISHIZU?
I HAVE NO INTEREST IN SOME WORDS INSCRIBED ON A 3,000-YEAR-OLD RELIC.
KAIBA...
THE GOD CARDS GUIDED YOU TO START BATTLE CITY...
AND TO PUT AN END TO THOSE BATTLES... ON THIS DUEL TOWER ON THE ISLAND OF ALCATRAZ...

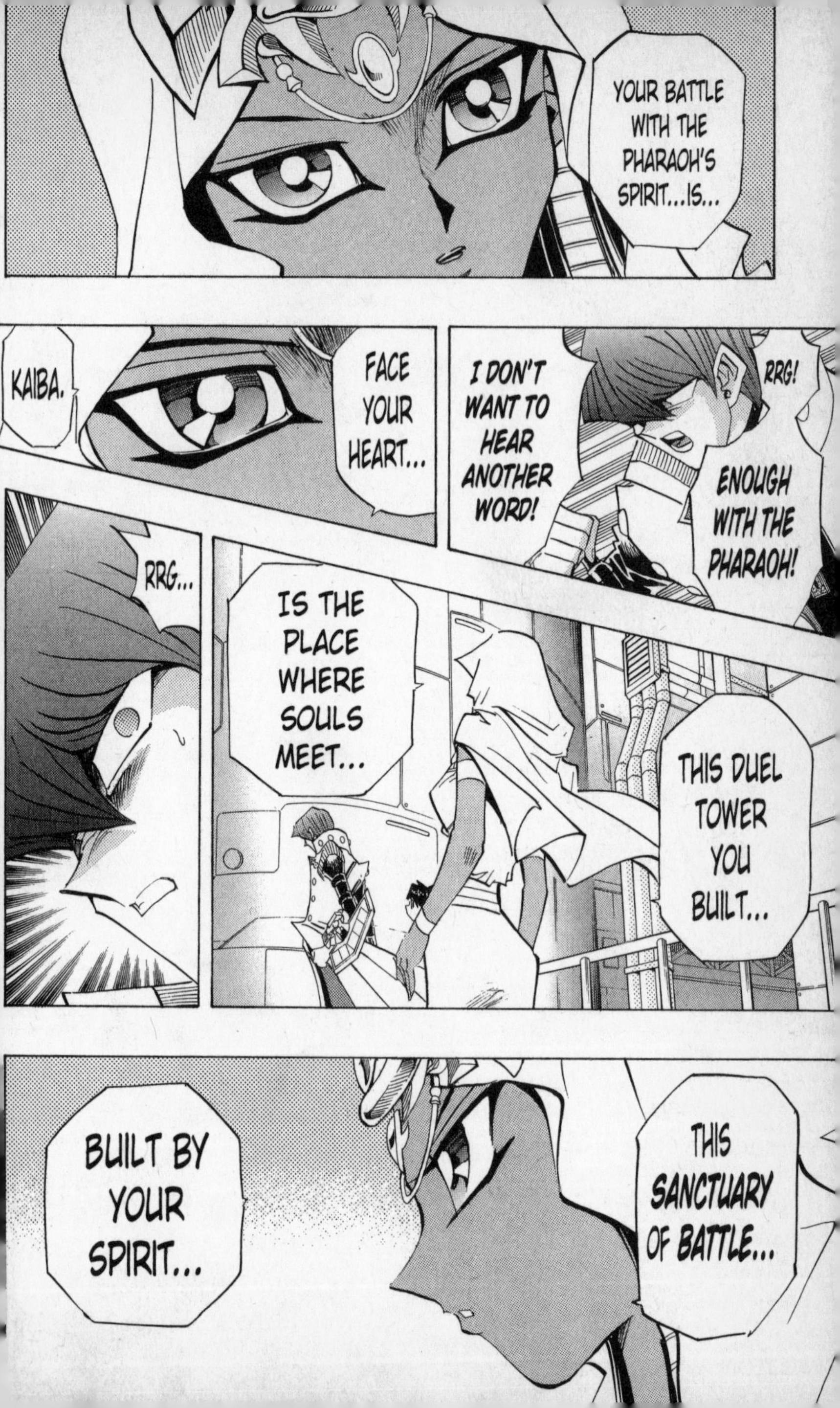
YOUR BATTLE WITH THE PHARAOH'S SPIRIT...IS...
RRG!
ENOUGH WITH THE PHARAOH!
I DON'T WANT TO HEAR ANOTHER WORD!
FACE YOUR HEART...
KAIBA.
THIS DUEL TOWER YOU BUILT...
IS THE PLACE WHERE SOULS MEET...
RRG...
THIS SANCTUARY OF BATTLE...
BUILT BY YOUR SPIRIT...

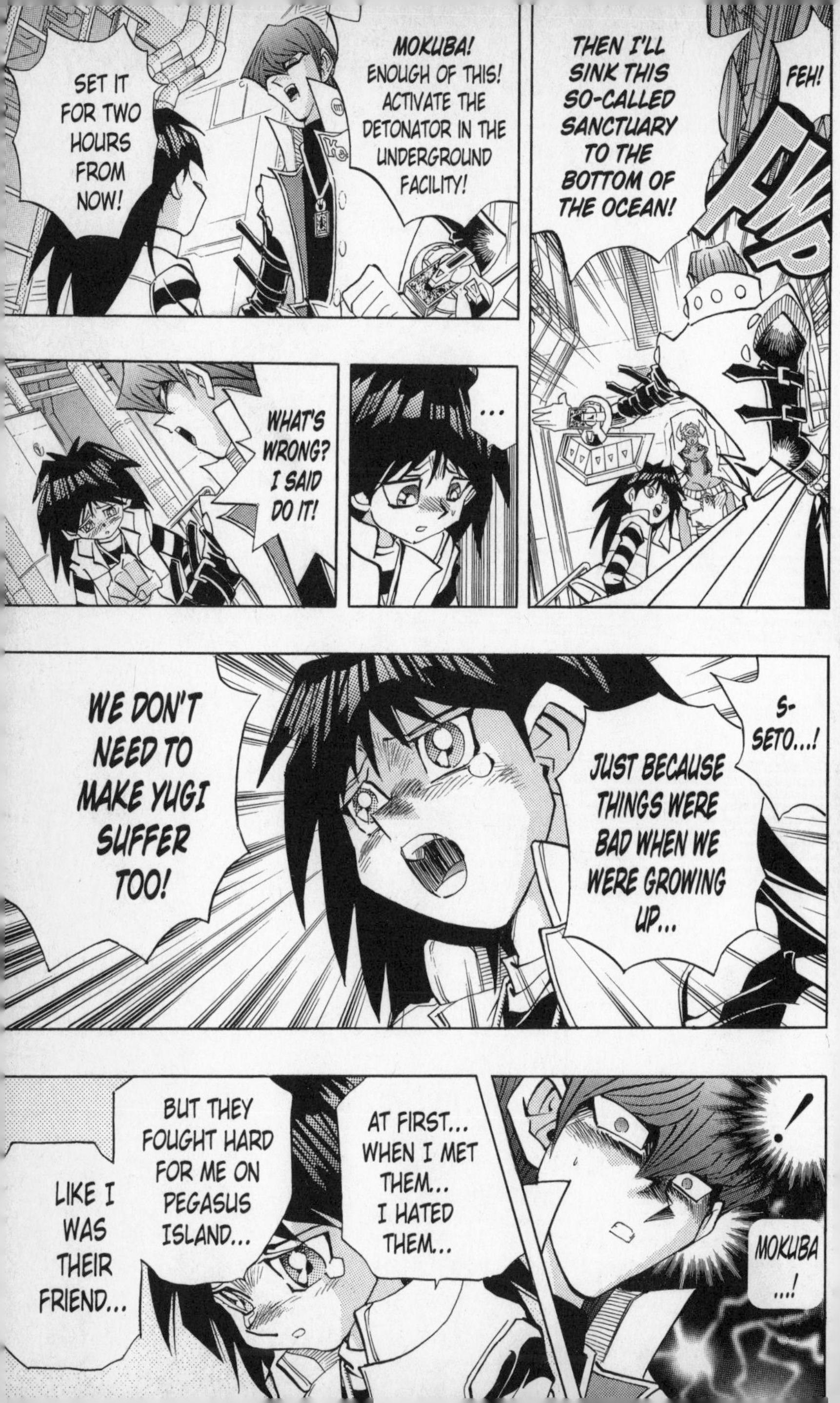
FEH!
FWP
THEN I'LL SINK THIS SO-CALLED SANCTUARY TO THE BOTTOM OF THE OCEAN!
MOKUBA! ENOUGH OF THIS! ACTIVATE THE DETONATOR IN THE UNDERGROUND FACILITY!
SET IT FOR TWO HOURS FROM NOW!
...
WHAT'S WRONG? I SAID DO IT!
S-SETO...!
JUST BECAUSE THINGS WERE BAD WHEN WE WERE GROWING UP...
WE DON'T NEED TO MAKE YUGI SUFFER TOO!
!
MOKUBA...!
AT FIRST... WHEN I MET THEM... I HATED THEM...
BUT THEY FOUGHT HARD FOR ME ON PEGASUS ISLAND...
LIKE I WAS THEIR FRIEND...

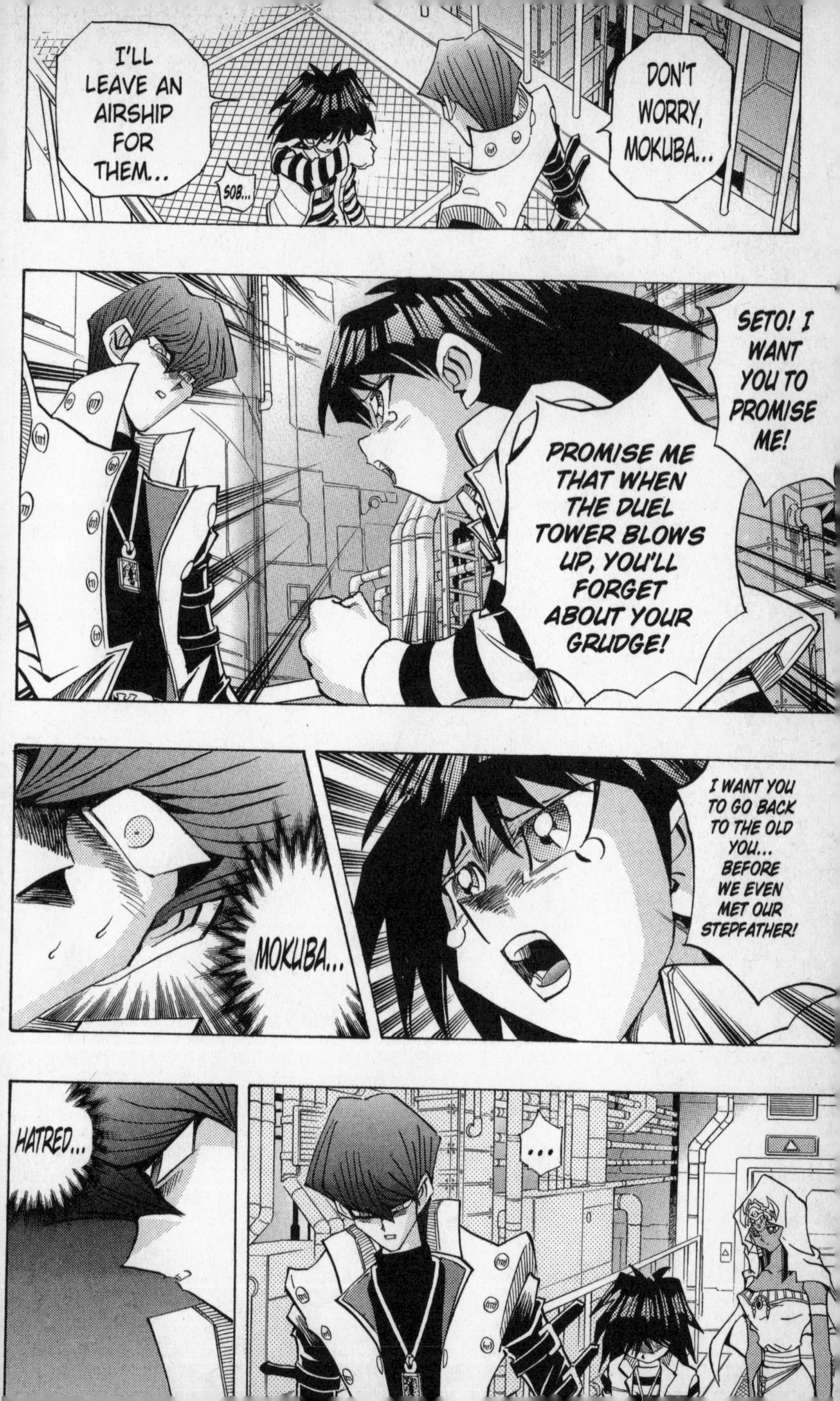
DON'T WORRY, MOKUBA...
I'LL LEAVE AN AIRSHIP FOR THEM...
SOB...
SETO! I WANT YOU TO PROMISE ME!
PROMISE ME THAT WHEN THE DUEL TOWER BLOWS UP, YOU'LL FORGET ABOUT YOUR GRUDGE!
I WANT YOU TO GO BACK TO THE OLD YOU... BEFORE WE EVEN MET OUR STEPFATHER!
MOKUBA...
...
HATRED...

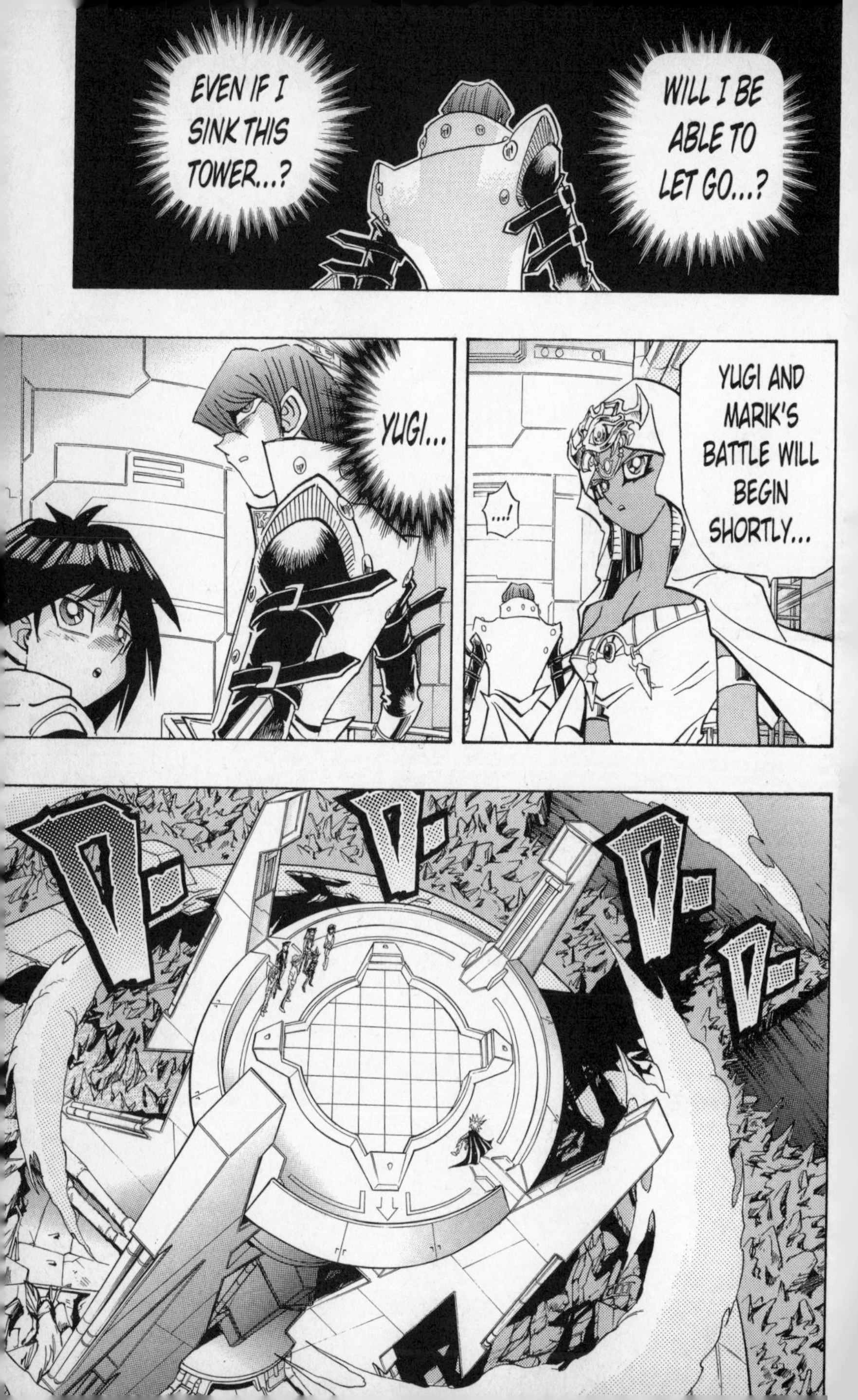
WILL I BE ABLE TO LET GO...?
EVEN IF I SINK THIS TOWER...?
YUGI AND MARIK'S BATTLE WILL BEGIN SHORTLY...
...!
YUGI...

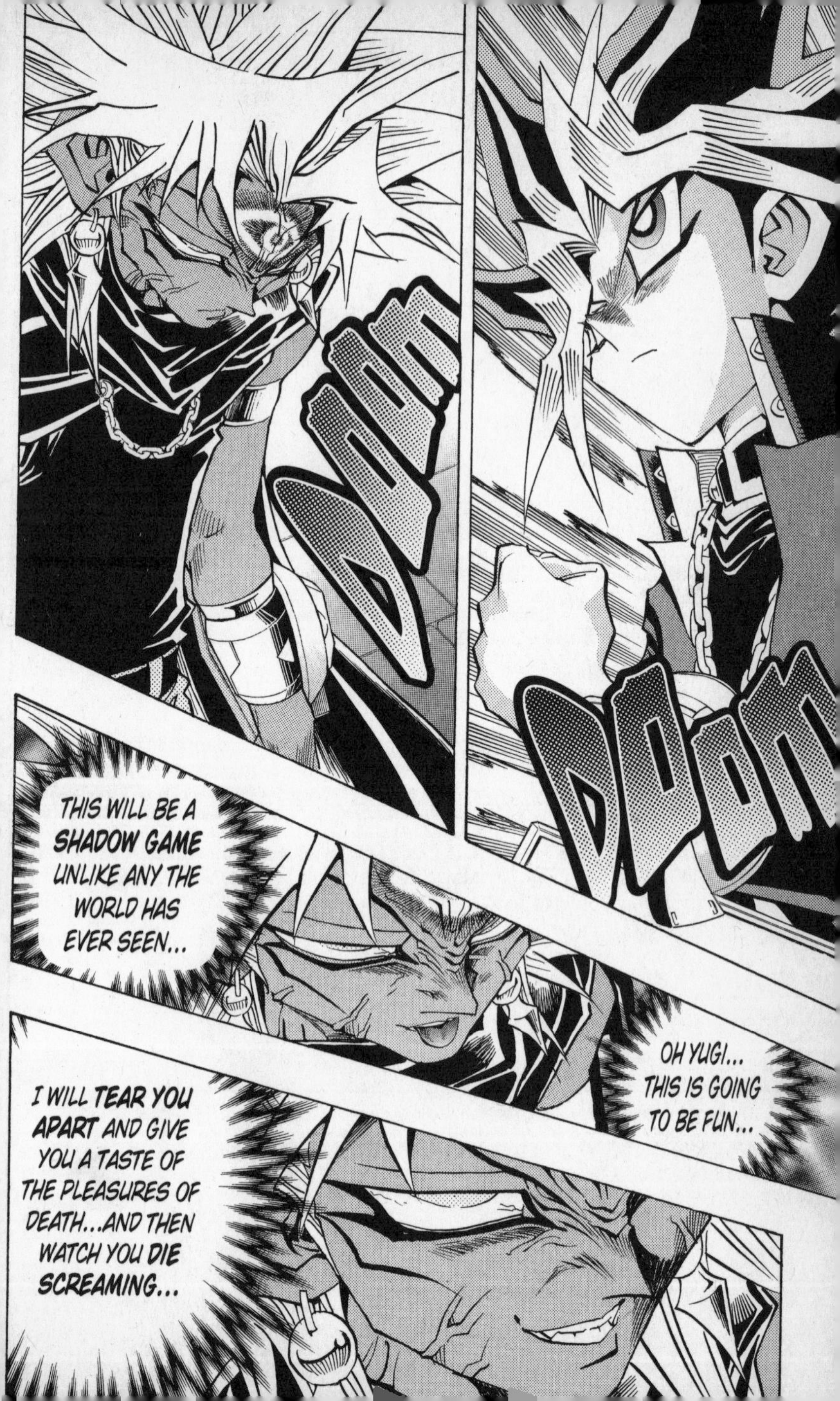
DOOM
DOOM
THIS WILL BE A SHADOW GAME UNLIKE ANY THE WORLD HAS EVER SEEN...
OH YUGI... THIS IS GOING TO BE FUN...
I WILL TEAR YOU APART AND GIVE YOU A TASTE OF THE PLEASURES OF DEATH...AND THEN WATCH YOU DIE SCREAMING...

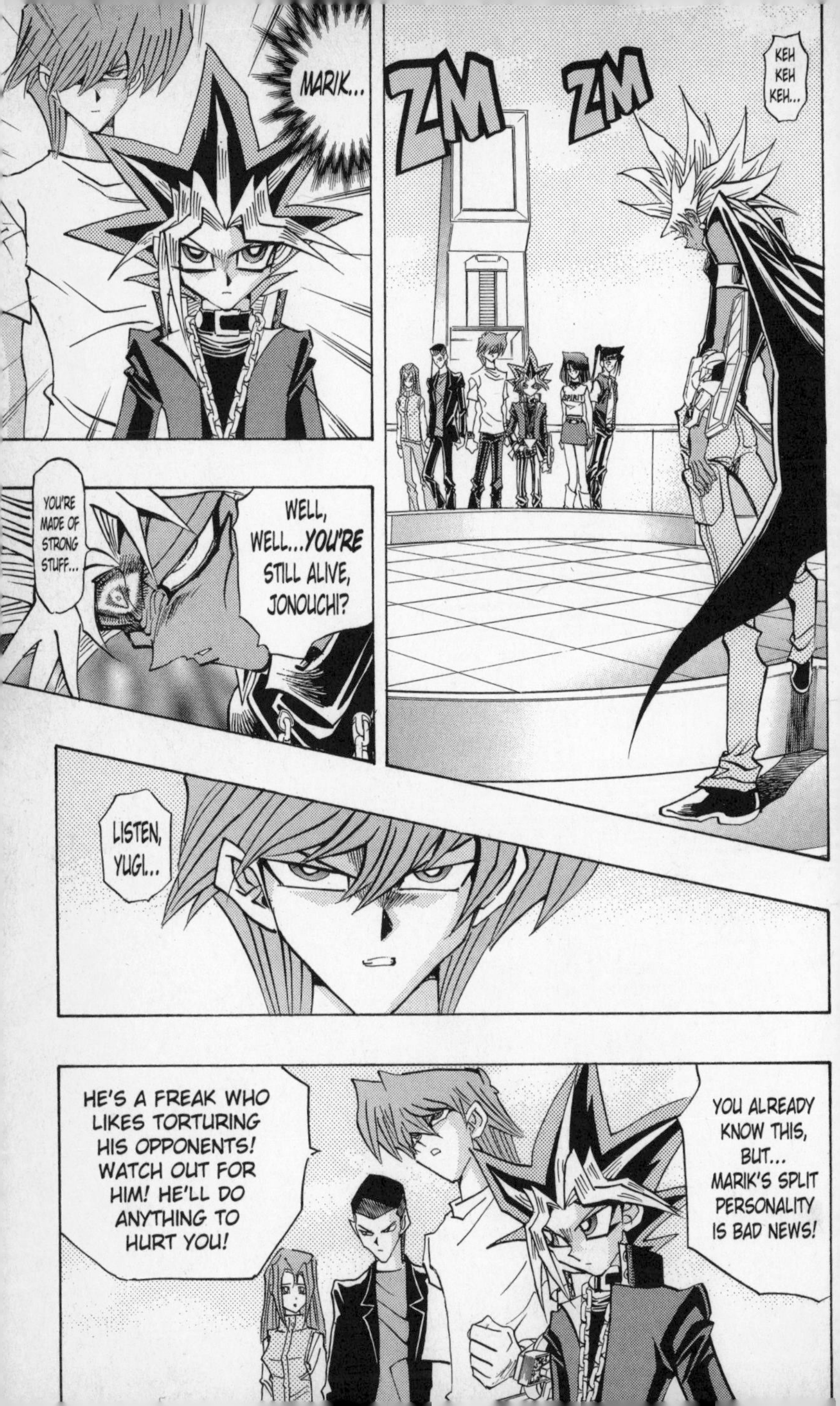
KEH KEH KEH...
ZM
ZM
MARIK...
WELL, WELL...*YOU'RE* STILL ALIVE, JONOUCHI?
YOU'RE MADE OF STRONG STUFF...
LISTEN, YUGI...
YOU ALREADY KNOW THIS, BUT... MARIK'S SPLIT PERSONALITY IS BAD NEWS!
HE'S A FREAK WHO LIKES TORTURING HIS OPPONENTS! WATCH OUT FOR HIM! HE'LL DO ANYTHING TO HURT YOU!

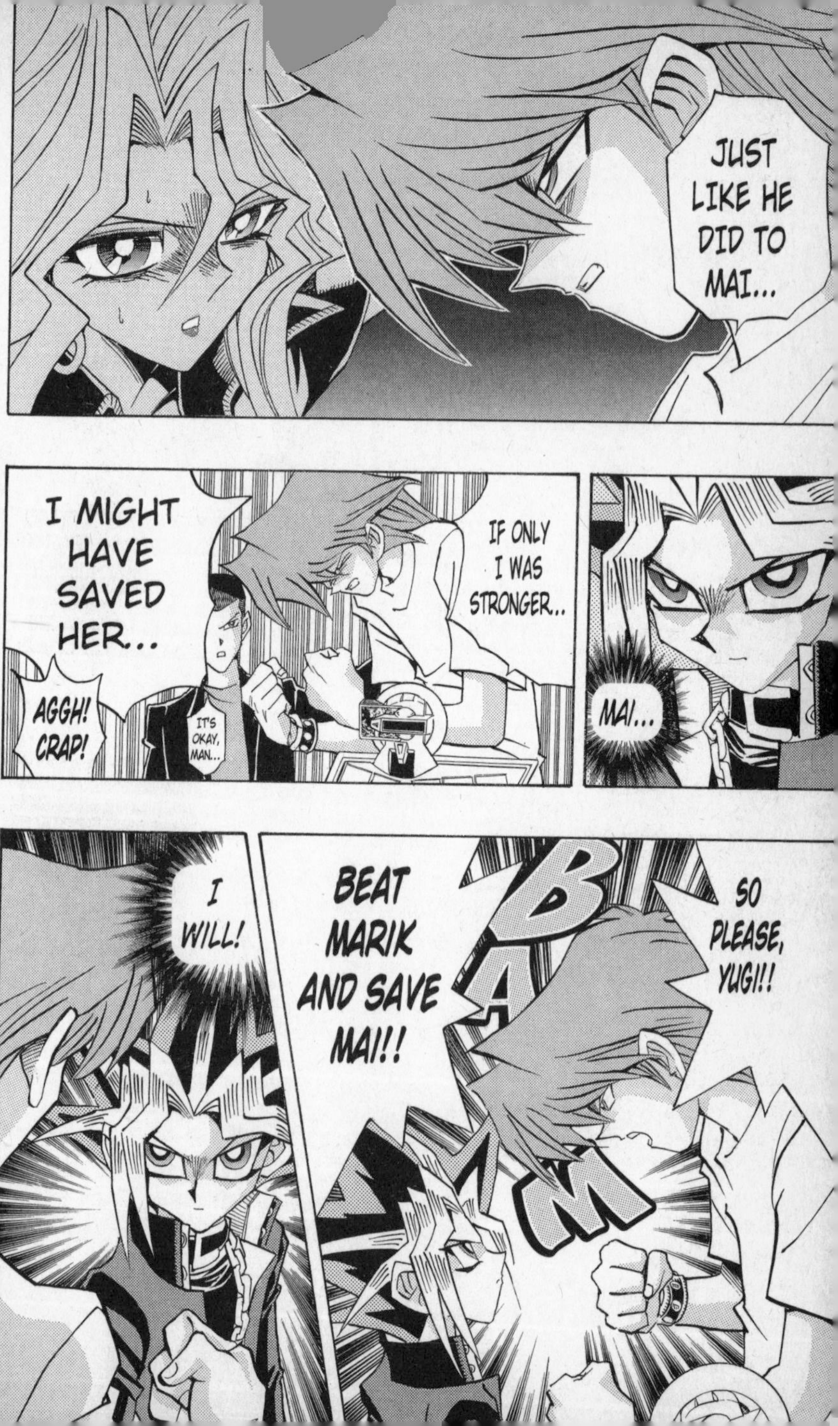
JUST LIKE HE DID TO MAI...
MAI...
IF ONLY I WAS STRONGER...
I MIGHT HAVE SAVED HER...
IT'S OKAY, MAN...
AGGH! CRAP!
SO PLEASE, YUGI!!
BAM
BEAT MARIK AND SAVE MAI!!
I WILL!

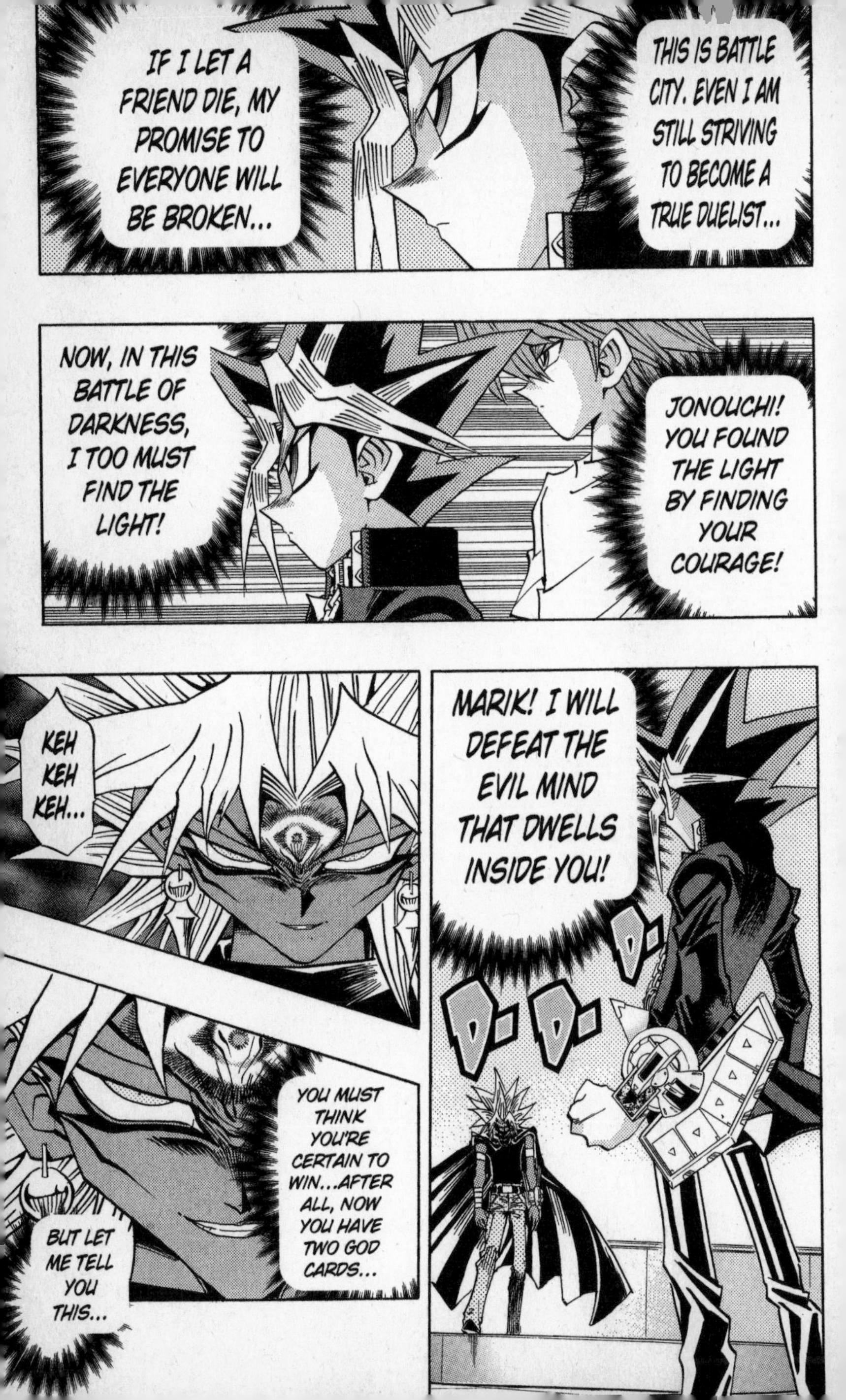
THIS IS BATTLE CITY. EVEN I AM STILL STRIVING TO BECOME A TRUE DUELIST...
IF I LET A FRIEND DIE, MY PROMISE TO EVERYONE WILL BE BROKEN...
JONOUCHI! YOU FOUND THE LIGHT BY FINDING YOUR COURAGE!
NOW, IN THIS BATTLE OF DARKNESS, I TOO MUST FIND THE LIGHT!
MARIK! I WILL DEFEAT THE EVIL MIND THAT DWELLS INSIDE YOU!
D D D
KEH KEH KEH...
YOU MUST THINK YOU'RE CERTAIN TO WIN...AFTER ALL, NOW YOU HAVE TWO GOD CARDS...
BUT LET ME TELL YOU THIS...

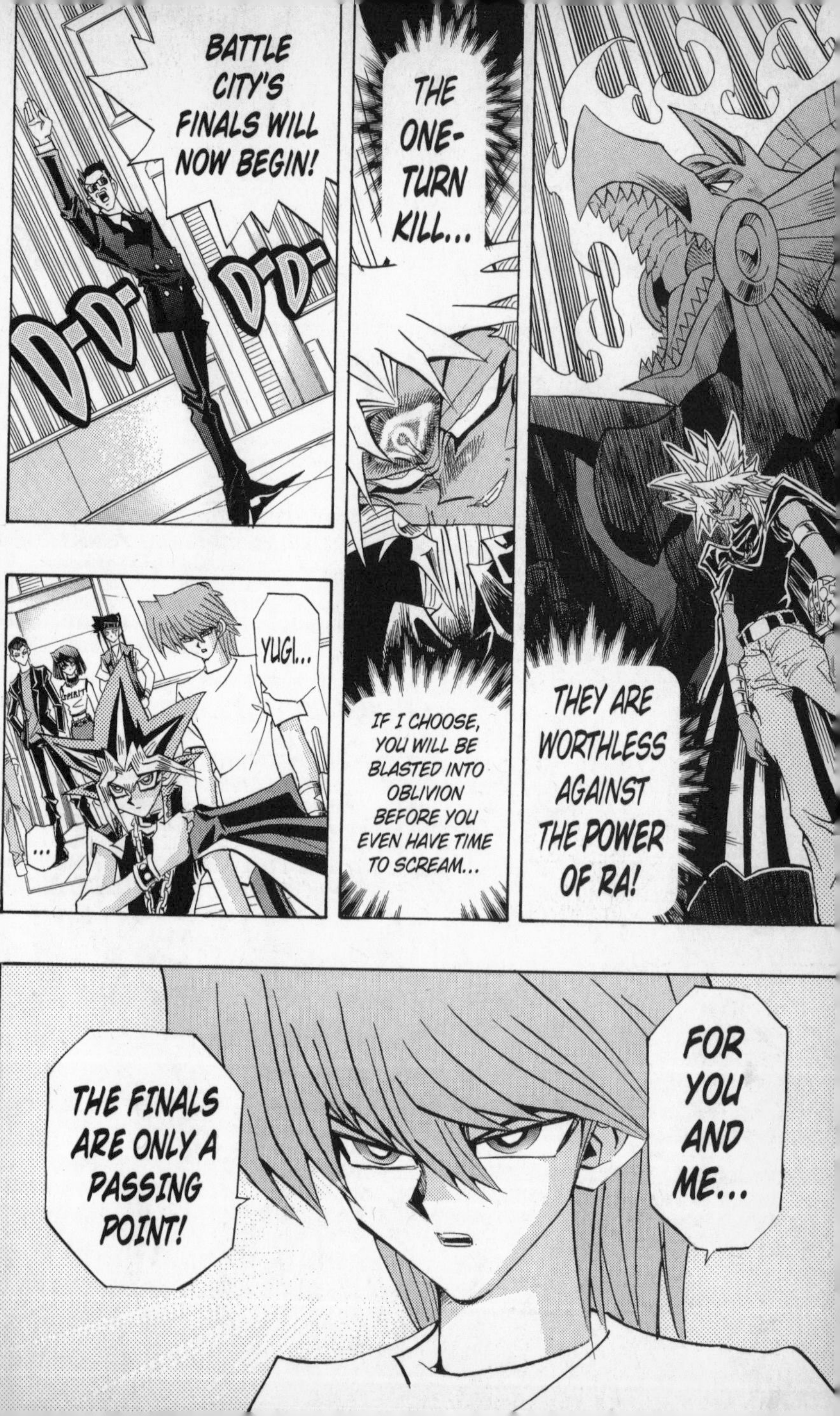
THEY ARE WORTHLESS AGAINST THE POWER OF RA!
THE ONE-TURN KILL...
IF I CHOOSE, YOU WILL BE BLASTED INTO OBLIVION BEFORE YOU EVEN HAVE TIME TO SCREAM...
BATTLE CITY'S FINALS WILL NOW BEGIN!
D-D-
D-D-
YUGI...
...
FOR YOU AND ME...
THE FINALS ARE ONLY A PASSING POINT!

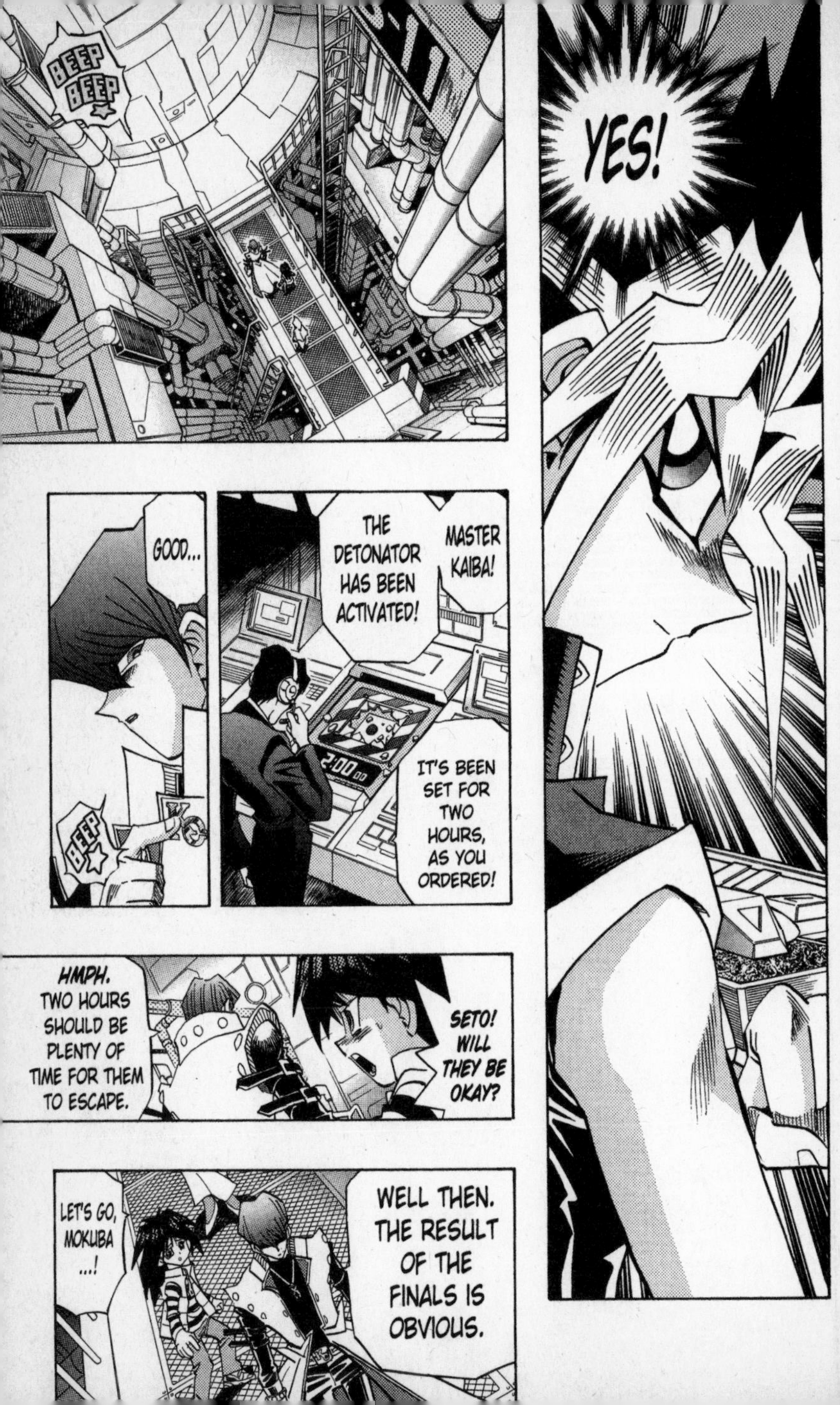
YES!
BEEP BEEP
MASTER KAIBA!
THE DETONATOR HAS BEEN ACTIVATED!
IT'S BEEN SET FOR TWO HOURS, AS YOU ORDERED!
GOOD...
BEEP
SETO! WILL THEY BE OKAY?
HMPH. TWO HOURS SHOULD BE PLENTY OF TIME FOR THEM TO ESCAPE.
WELL THEN. THE RESULT OF THE FINALS IS OBVIOUS.
LET'S GO, MOKUBA ...!

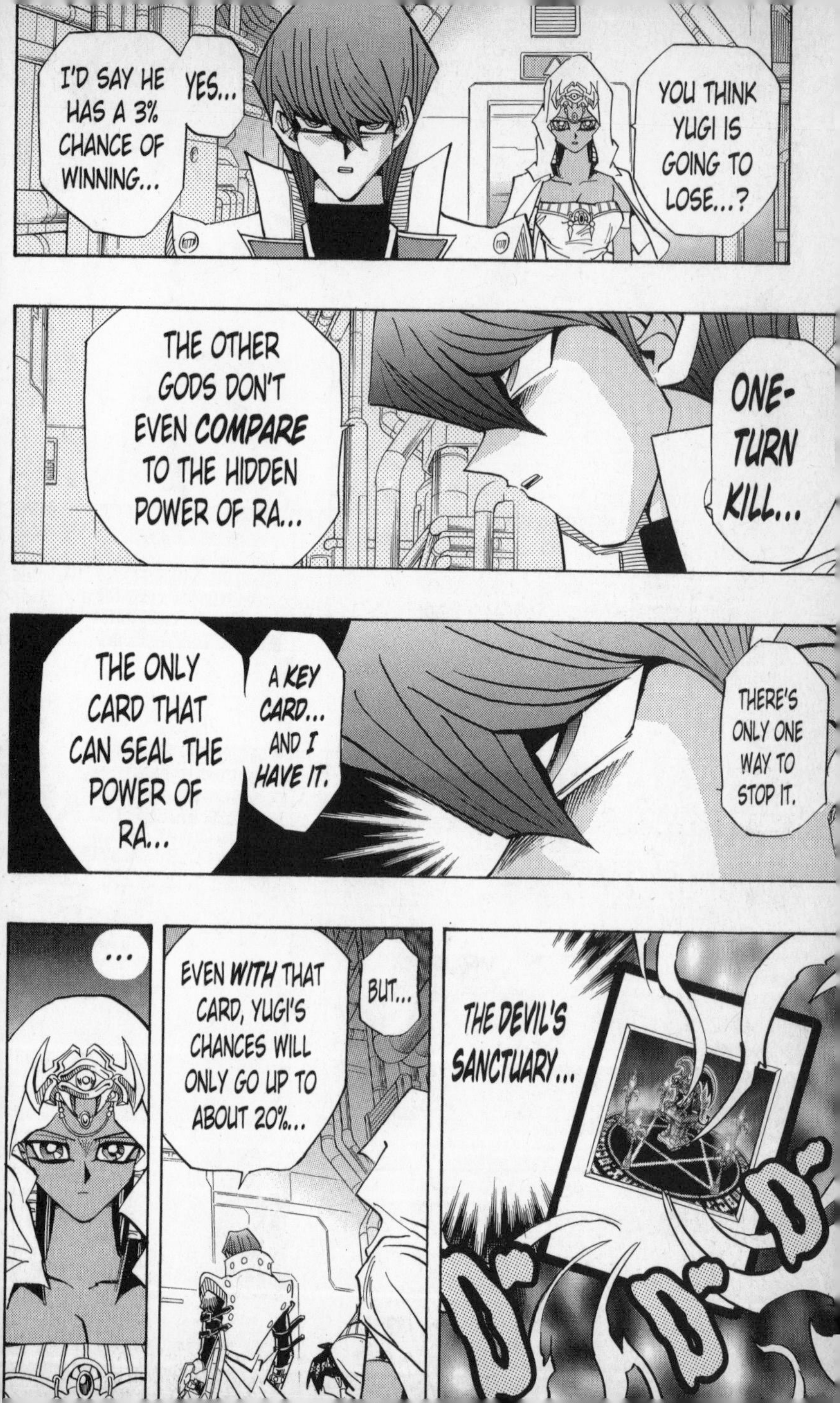
YOU THINK YUGI IS GOING TO LOSE...?
YES...
I'D SAY HE HAS A 3% CHANCE OF WINNING...
ONE-TURN KILL...
THE OTHER GODS DON'T EVEN *COMPARE* TO THE HIDDEN POWER OF RA...
THERE'S ONLY ONE WAY TO STOP IT.
A *KEY CARD*... AND I *HAVE IT*.
THE ONLY CARD THAT CAN SEAL THE POWER OF RA...
THE DEVIL'S SANCTUARY...
BUT...
EVEN *WITH* THAT CARD, YUGI'S CHANCES WILL ONLY GO UP TO ABOUT 20%...
...

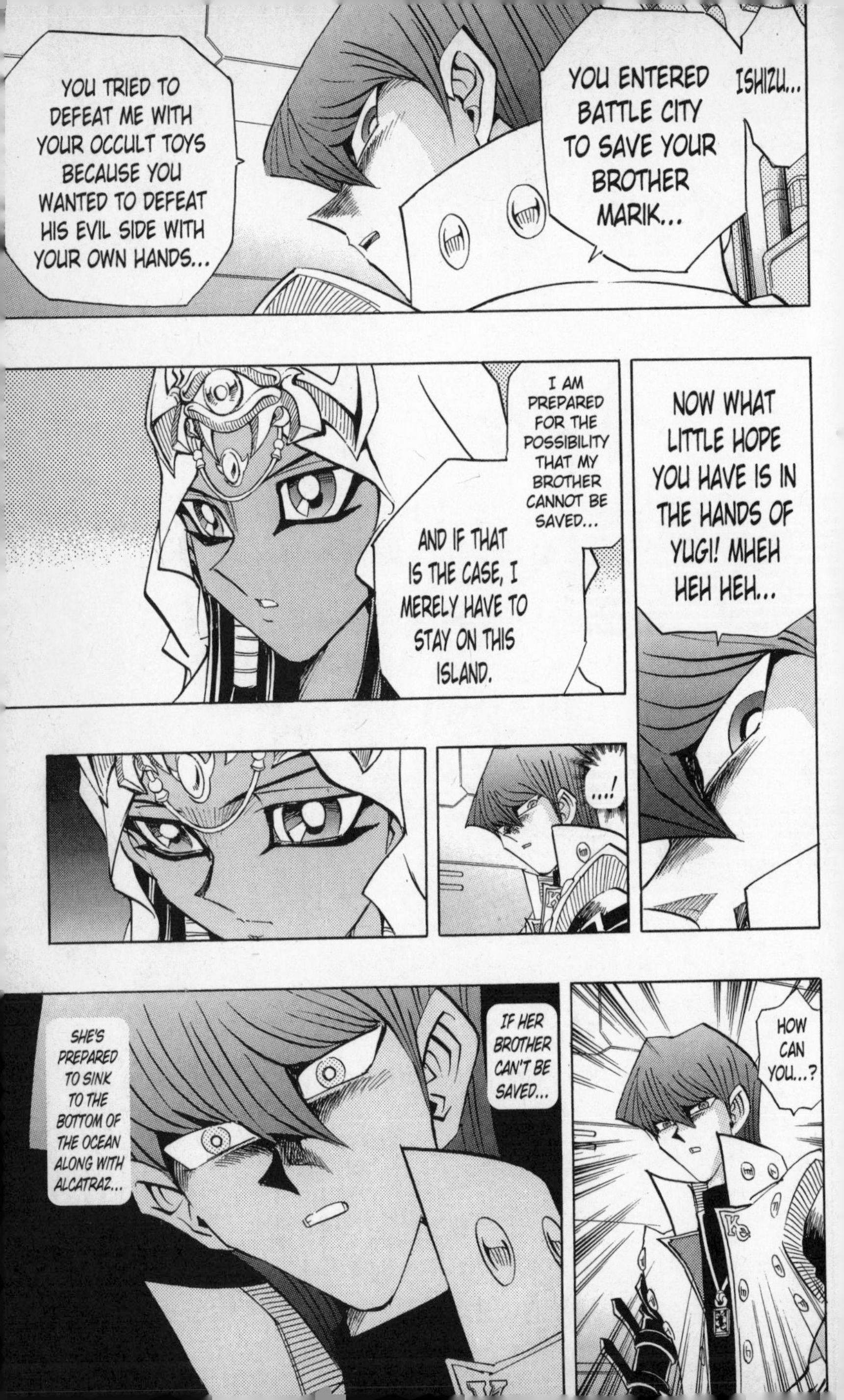
ISHIZU...
YOU ENTERED BATTLE CITY TO SAVE YOUR BROTHER MARIK...
YOU TRIED TO DEFEAT ME WITH YOUR OCCULT TOYS BECAUSE YOU WANTED TO DEFEAT HIS EVIL SIDE WITH YOUR OWN HANDS...
NOW WHAT LITTLE HOPE YOU HAVE IS IN THE HANDS OF YUGI! MHEH HEH HEH...
I AM PREPARED FOR THE POSSIBILITY THAT MY BROTHER CANNOT BE SAVED...
AND IF THAT IS THE CASE, I MERELY HAVE TO STAY ON THIS ISLAND.
...!
HOW CAN YOU...?
IF HER BROTHER CAN'T BE SAVED...
SHE'S PREPARED TO SINK TO THE BOTTOM OF THE OCEAN ALONG WITH ALCATRAZ...

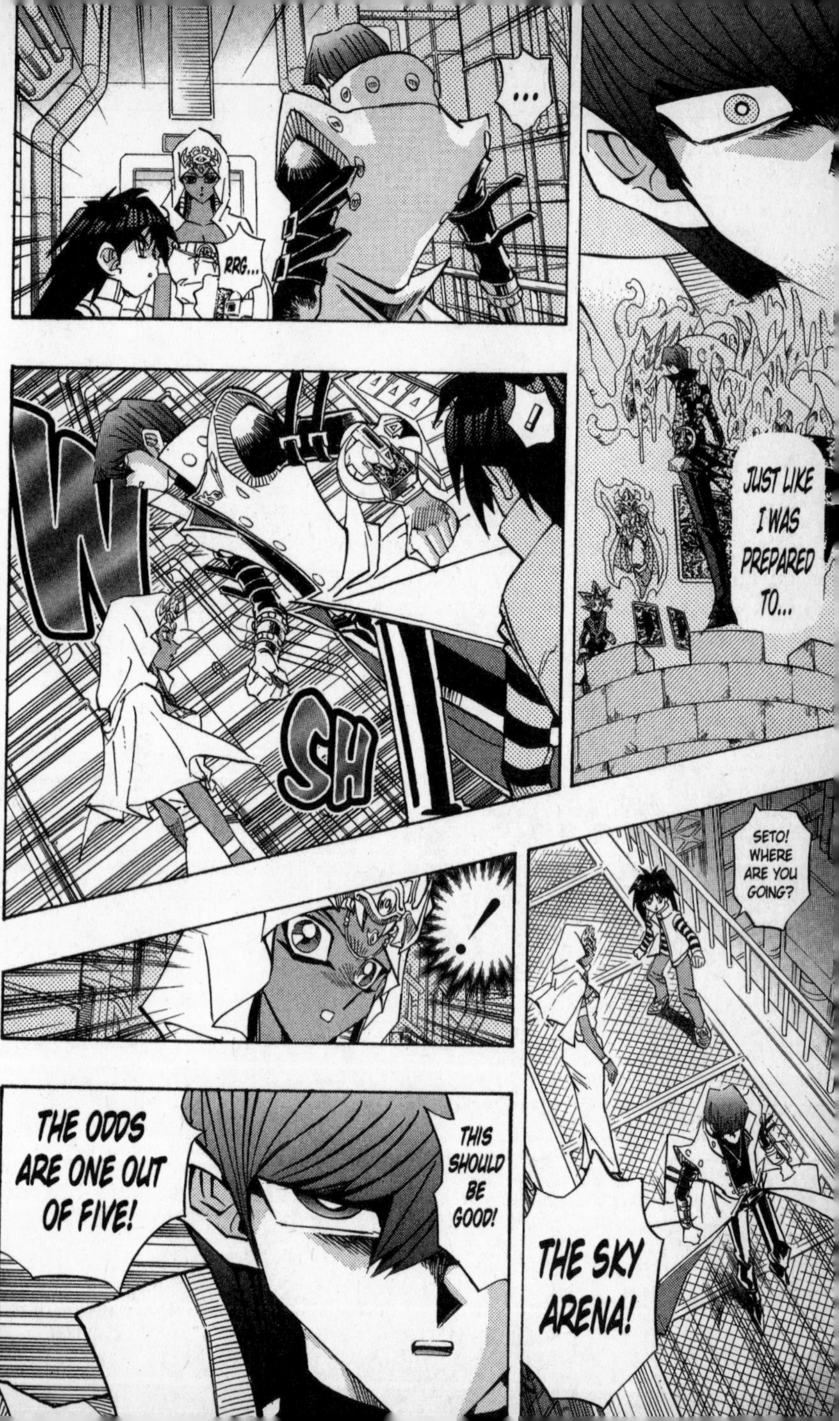
JUST LIKE I WAS PREPARED TO...
...
RRG...
!
W
SH
SETO! WHERE ARE YOU GOING?
THE SKY ARENA!
!
THIS SHOULD BE GOOD!
THE ODDS ARE ONE OUT OF FIVE!

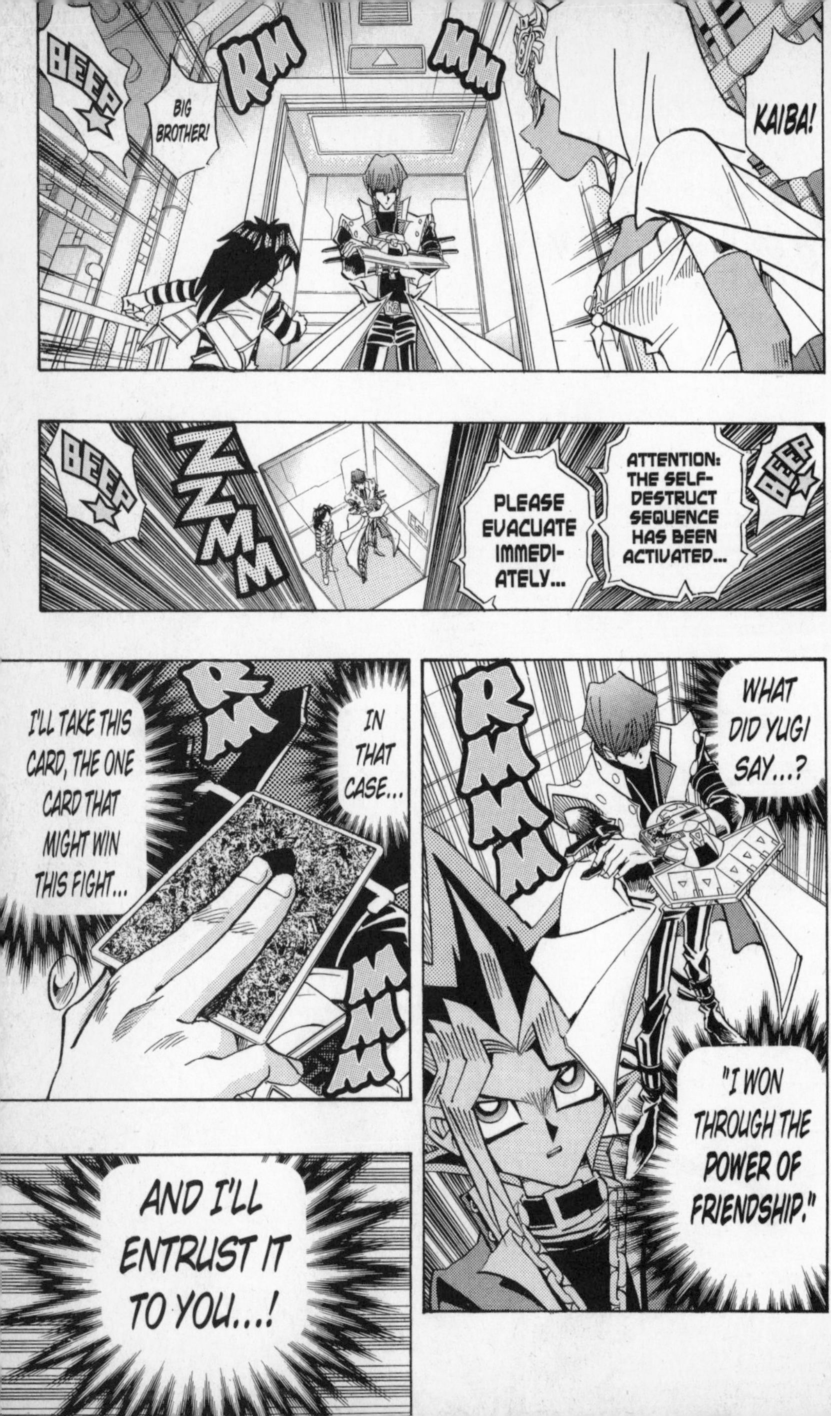
KAIBA!
MM
RM
BIG BROTHER!
BEEP
BEEP
ATTENTION: THE SELF-DESTRUCT SEQUENCE HAS BEEN ACTIVATED...
PLEASE EVACUATE IMMEDI-ATELY...
ZNMM
BEEP
WHAT DID YUGI SAY...?
RMMMM
"I WON THROUGH THE POWER OF FRIENDSHIP."
IN THAT CASE...
RM
I'LL TAKE THIS CARD, THE ONE CARD THAT MIGHT WIN THIS FIGHT...
MMMM
AND I'LL ENTRUST IT TO YOU...!

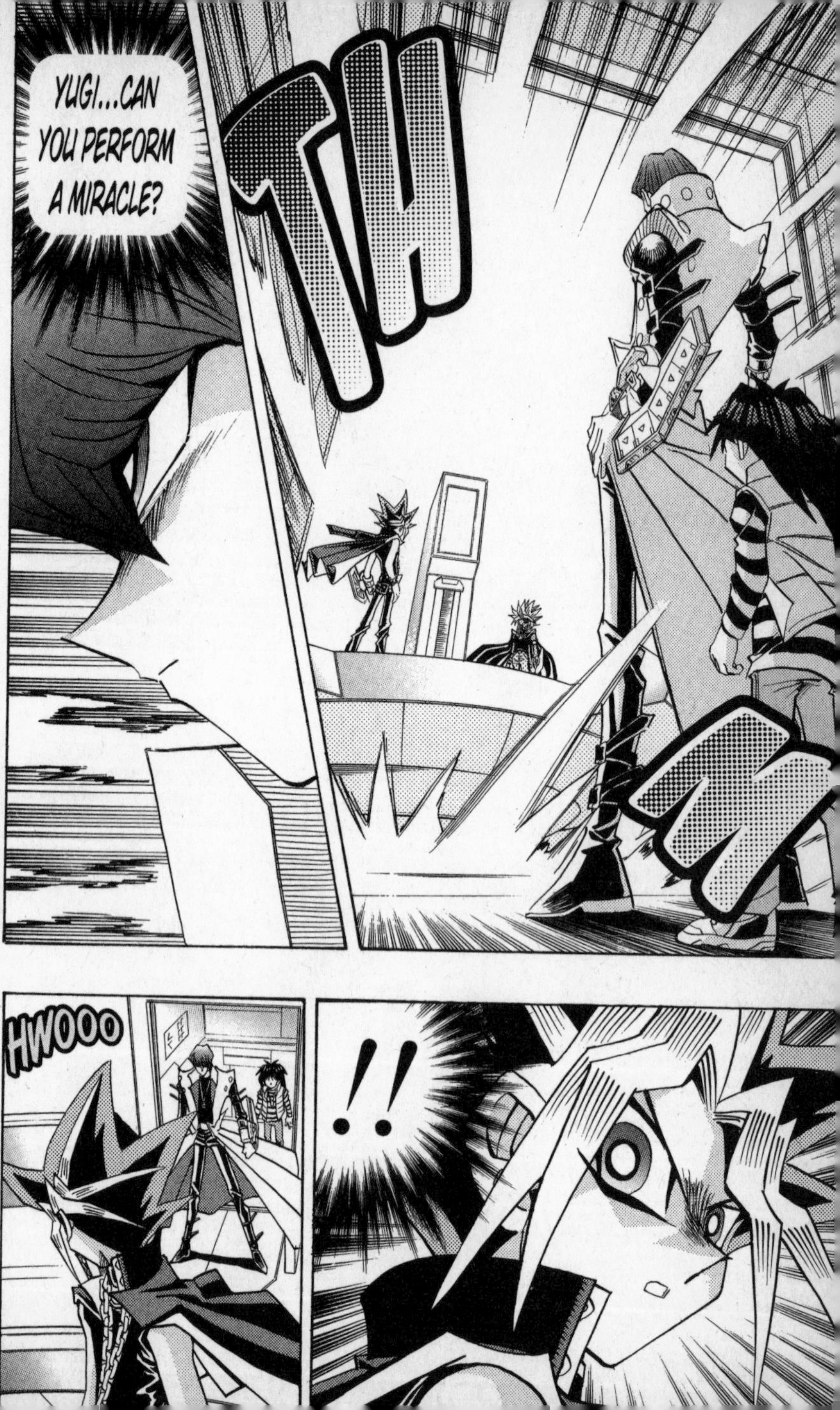
TH
YUGI...CAN YOU PERFORM A MIRACLE?
!!
HWOOO

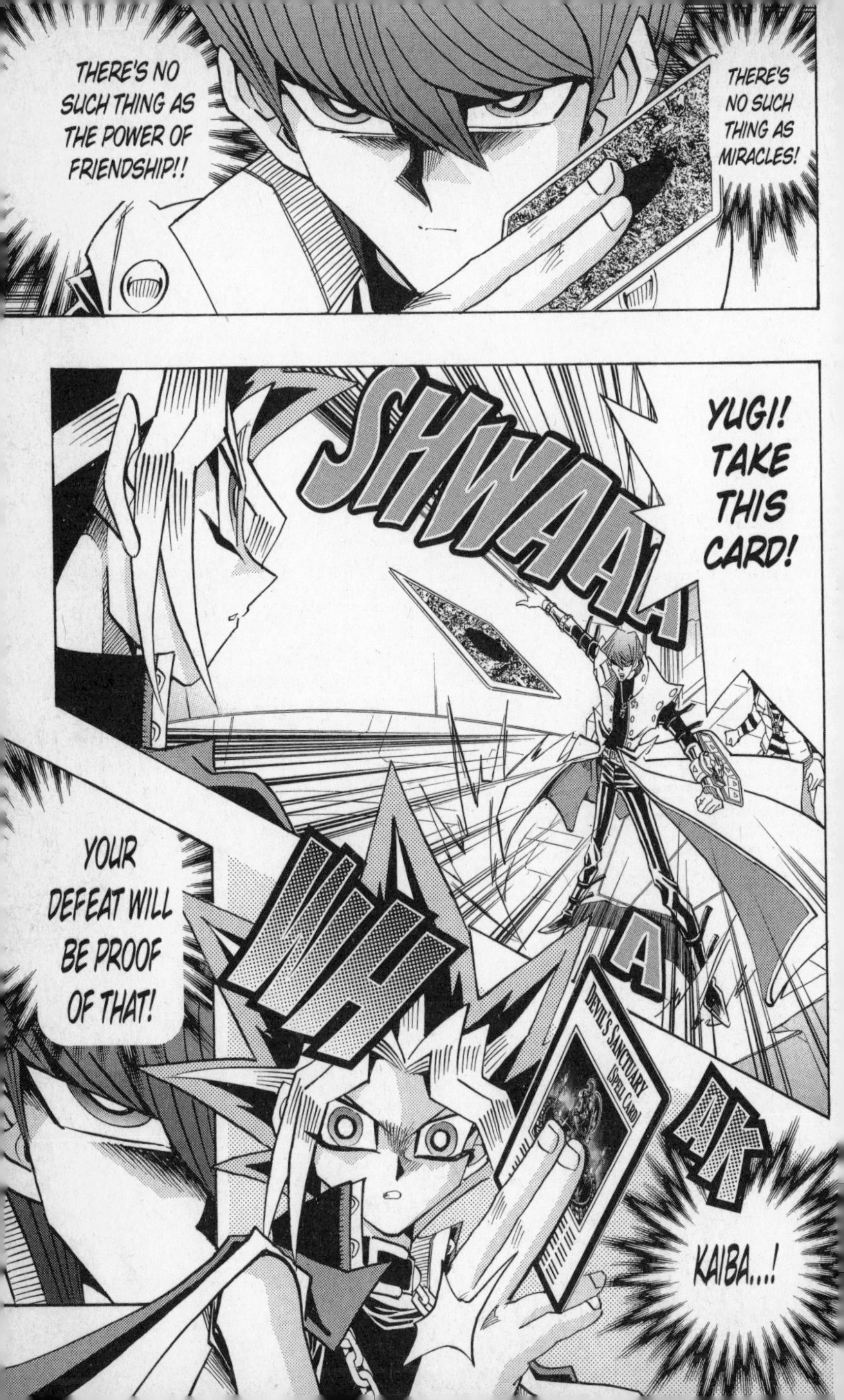
THERE'S NO SUCH THING AS MIRACLES!
THERE'S NO SUCH THING AS THE POWER OF FRIENDSHIP!!
YUGI! TAKE THIS CARD!
SHWAAA
YOUR DEFEAT WILL BE PROOF OF THAT!
WHA
A
AK
DEVIL'S SANCTUARY
[SPELL CARD]
KAIBA...!

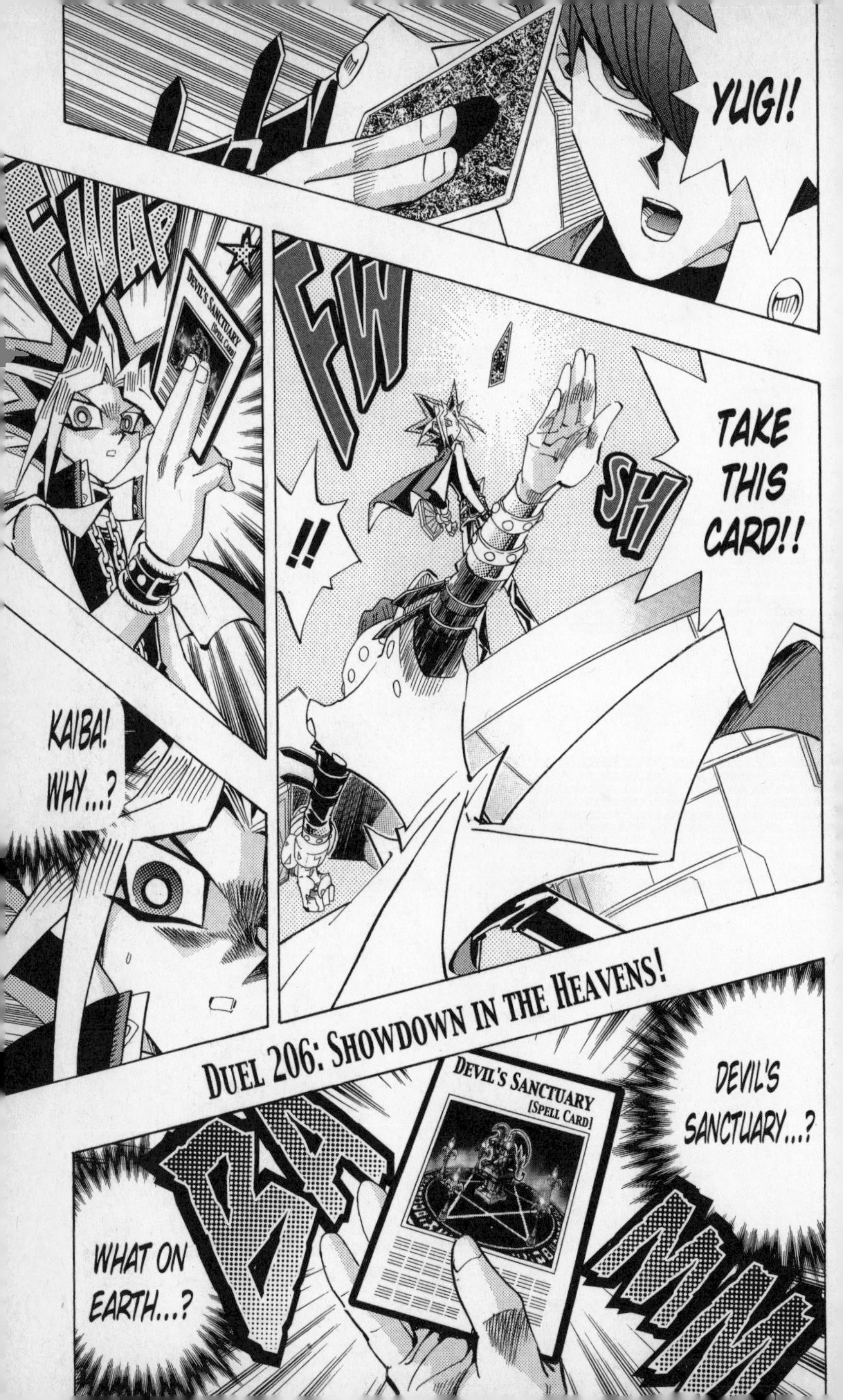
YUGI!
FWAP
FW
SH
TAKE THIS CARD!!
!!
DEVIL'S SANCTUARY [SPELL CARD]
KAIBA! WHY...?
Duel 206: Showdown in the Heavens!
DEVIL'S SANCTUARY...?
DEVIL'S SANCTUARY [SPELL CARD]
WHAT ON EARTH...?

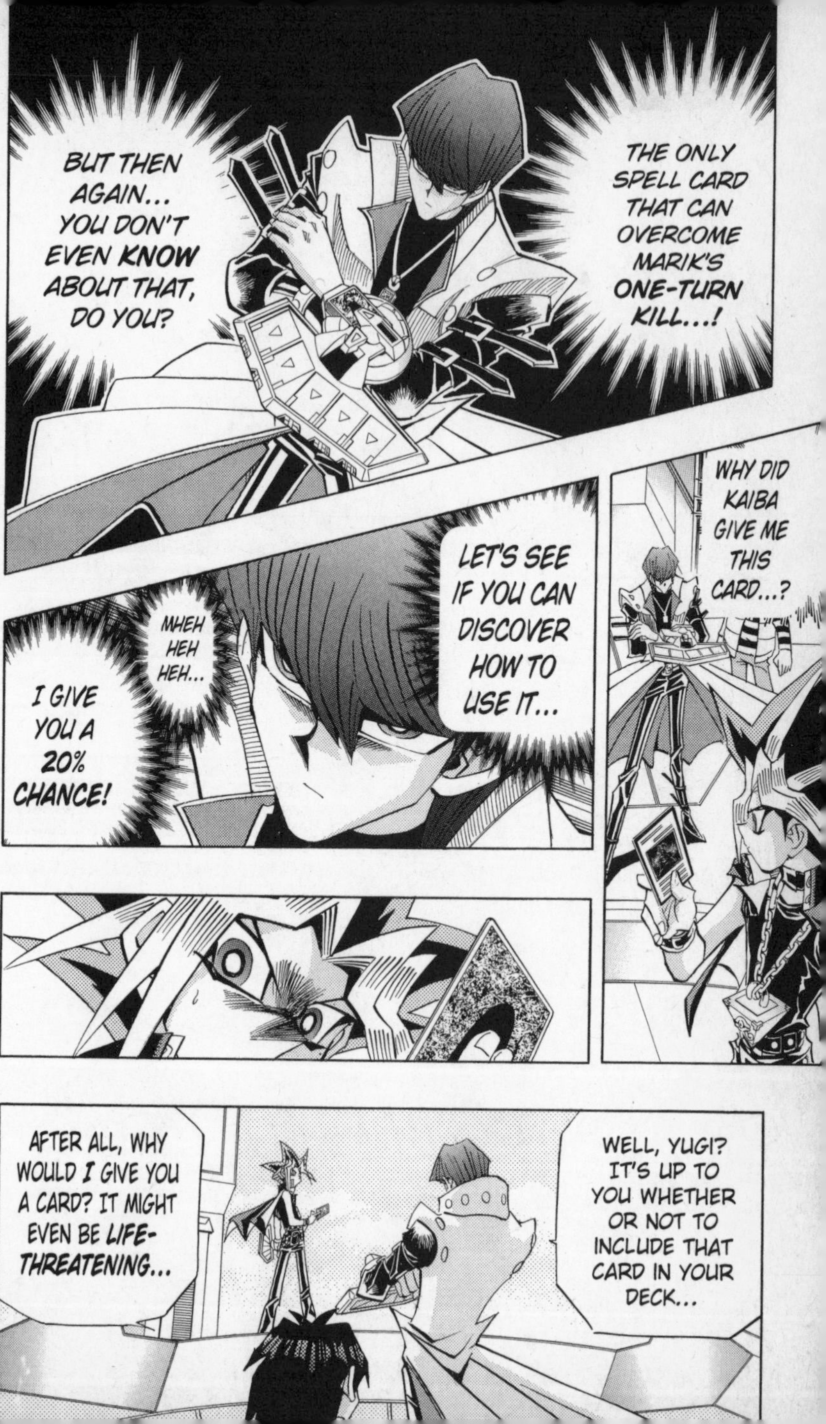
THE ONLY SPELL CARD THAT CAN OVERCOME MARIK'S ONE-TURN KILL...!
BUT THEN AGAIN... YOU DON'T EVEN KNOW ABOUT THAT, DO YOU?
WHY DID KAIBA GIVE ME THIS CARD...?
LET'S SEE IF YOU CAN DISCOVER HOW TO USE IT...
MHEH HEH HEH...
I GIVE YOU A 20% CHANCE!
WELL, YUGI? IT'S UP TO YOU WHETHER OR NOT TO INCLUDE THAT CARD IN YOUR DECK...
AFTER ALL, WHY WOULD I GIVE YOU A CARD? IT MIGHT EVEN BE LIFE-THREATENING...

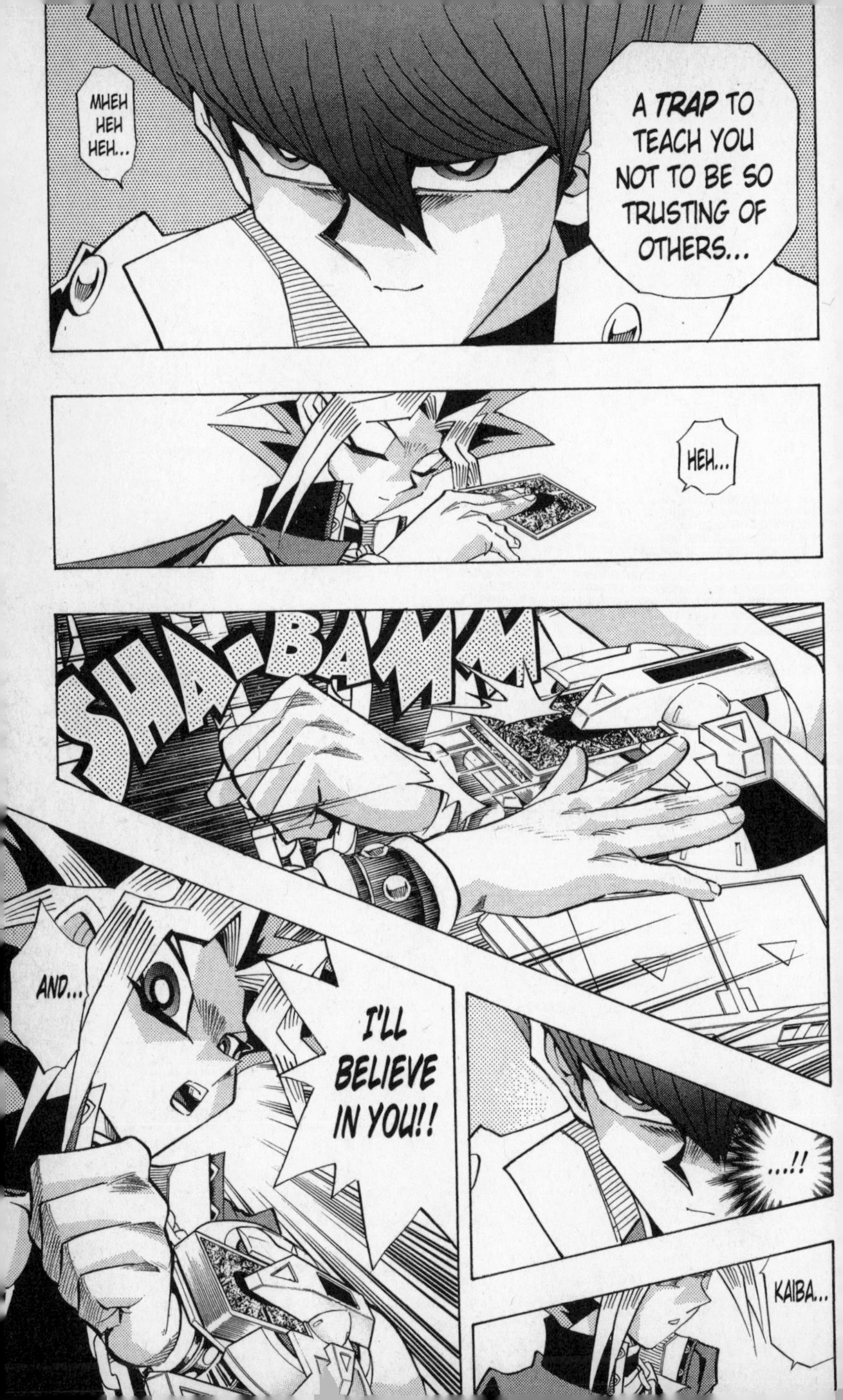
A TRAP TO TEACH YOU NOT TO BE SO TRUSTING OF OTHERS...
MHEH HEH HEH...
HEH...
SHA-BAMM
AND...
I'LL BELIEVE IN YOU!!
...!!
KAIBA...

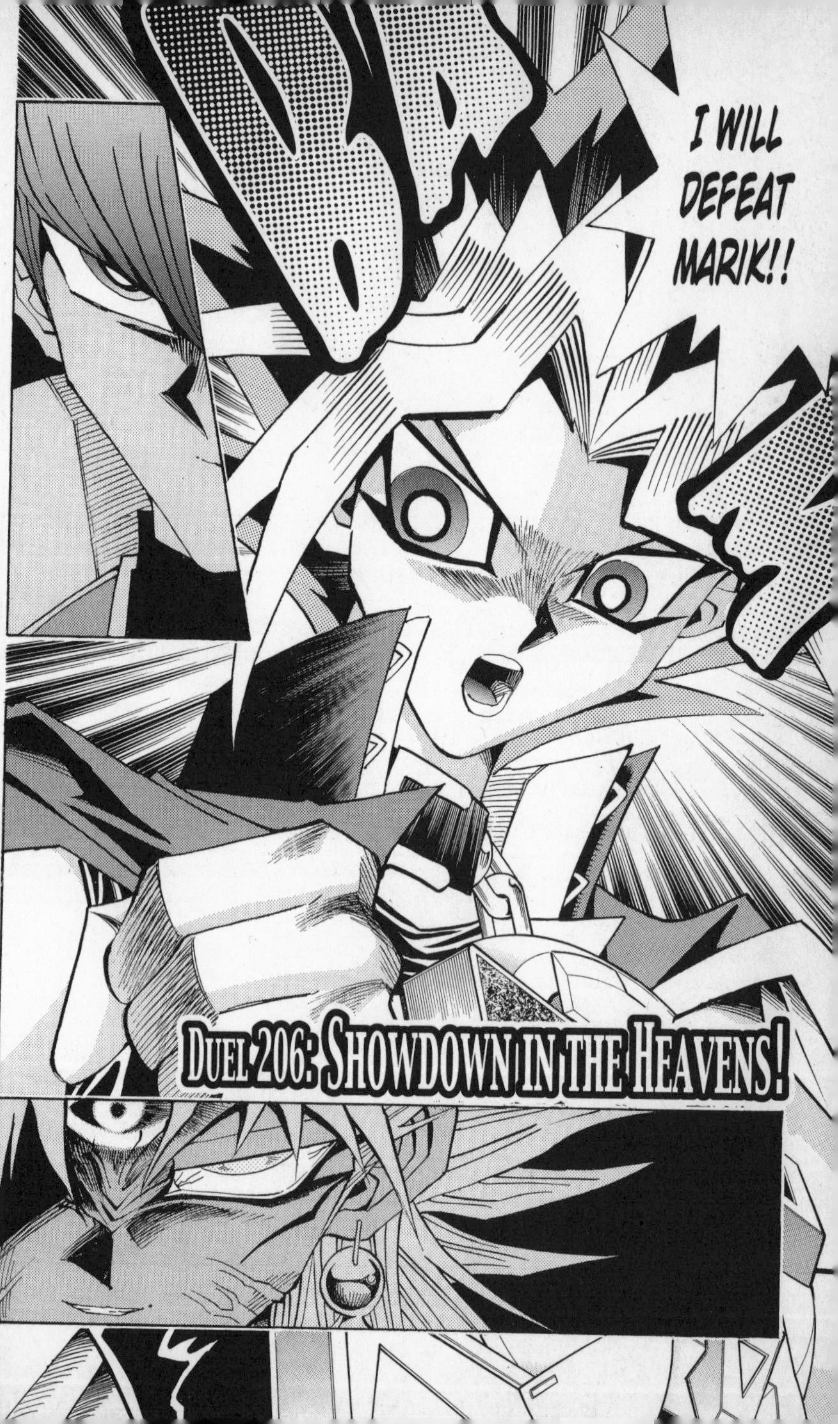
I WILL DEFEAT MARIK!!
Duel 206: Showdown in the Heavens!

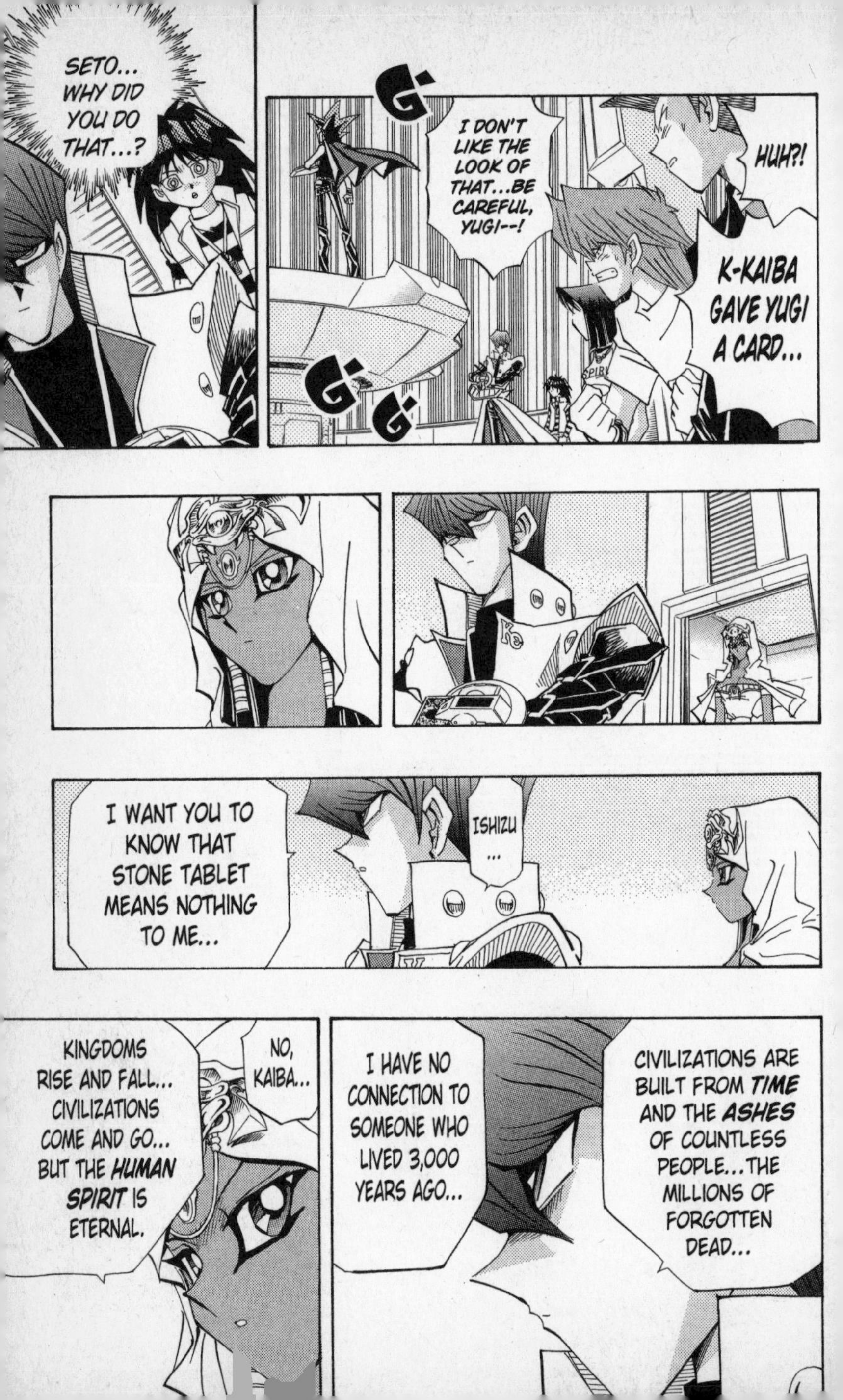
HUH?!
K-KAIBA GAVE YUGI A CARD...
I DON'T LIKE THE LOOK OF THAT...BE CAREFUL, YUGI--!
G
G
G
SETO... WHY DID YOU DO THAT...?
ISHIZU ...
I WANT YOU TO KNOW THAT STONE TABLET MEANS NOTHING TO ME...
CIVILIZATIONS ARE BUILT FROM *TIME* AND THE *ASHES* OF COUNTLESS PEOPLE...THE MILLIONS OF FORGOTTEN DEAD...
I HAVE NO CONNECTION TO SOMEONE WHO LIVED 3,000 YEARS AGO...
NO, KAIBA...
KINGDOMS RISE AND FALL... CIVILIZATIONS COME AND GO... BUT THE *HUMAN SPIRIT* IS ETERNAL.

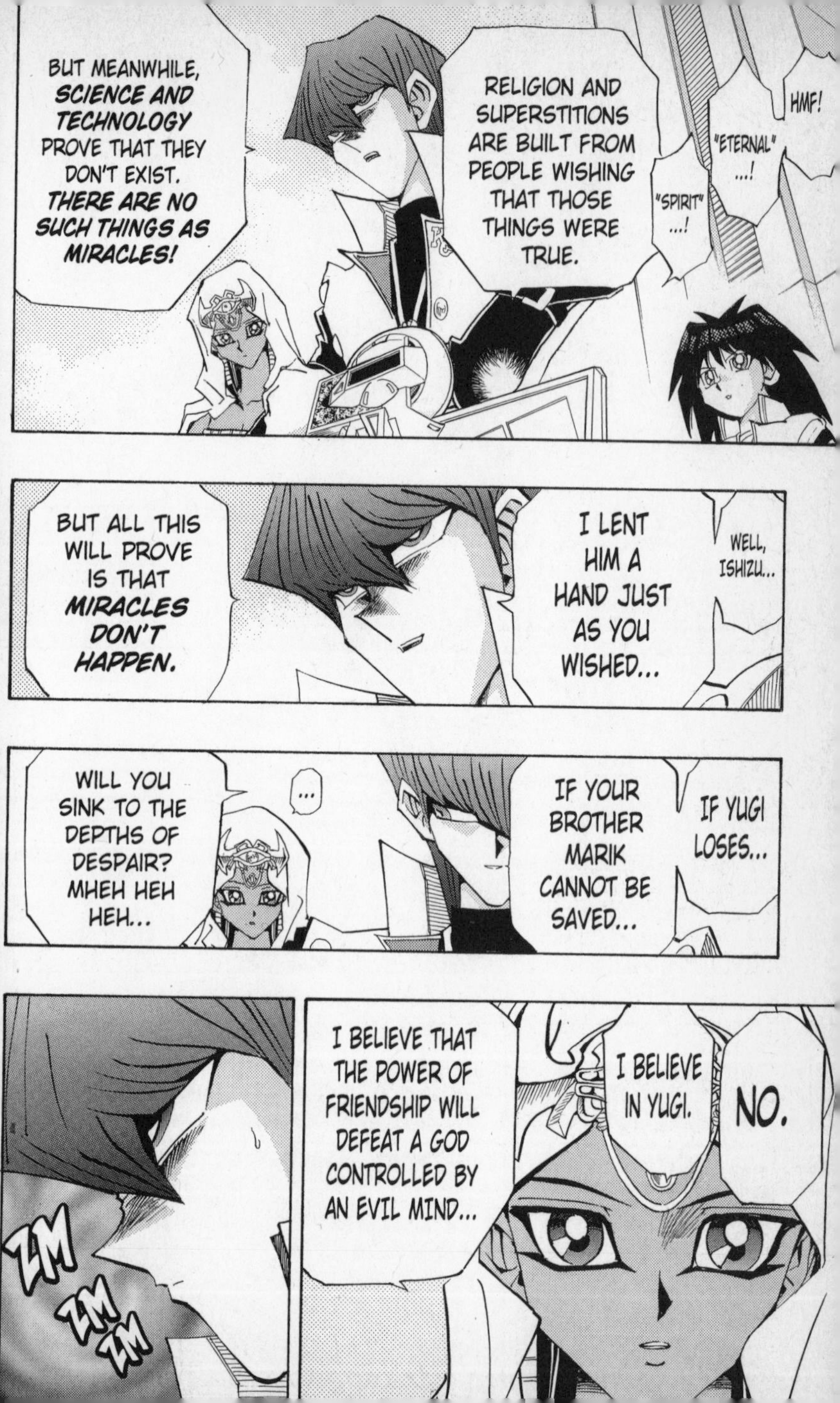
HMF!
"ETERNAL" ...!
"SPIRIT" ...!
RELIGION AND SUPERSTITIONS ARE BUILT FROM PEOPLE WISHING THAT THOSE THINGS WERE TRUE.
BUT MEANWHILE, SCIENCE AND TECHNOLOGY PROVE THAT THEY DON'T EXIST. THERE ARE NO SUCH THINGS AS MIRACLES!
WELL, ISHIZU...
I LENT HIM A HAND JUST AS YOU WISHED...
BUT ALL THIS WILL PROVE IS THAT MIRACLES DON'T HAPPEN.
IF YUGI LOSES...
IF YOUR BROTHER MARIK CANNOT BE SAVED...
...
WILL YOU SINK TO THE DEPTHS OF DESPAIR? MHEH HEH HEH...
NO.
I BELIEVE IN YUGI.
I BELIEVE THAT THE POWER OF FRIENDSHIP WILL DEFEAT A GOD CONTROLLED BY AN EVIL MIND...
ZM ZM ZM

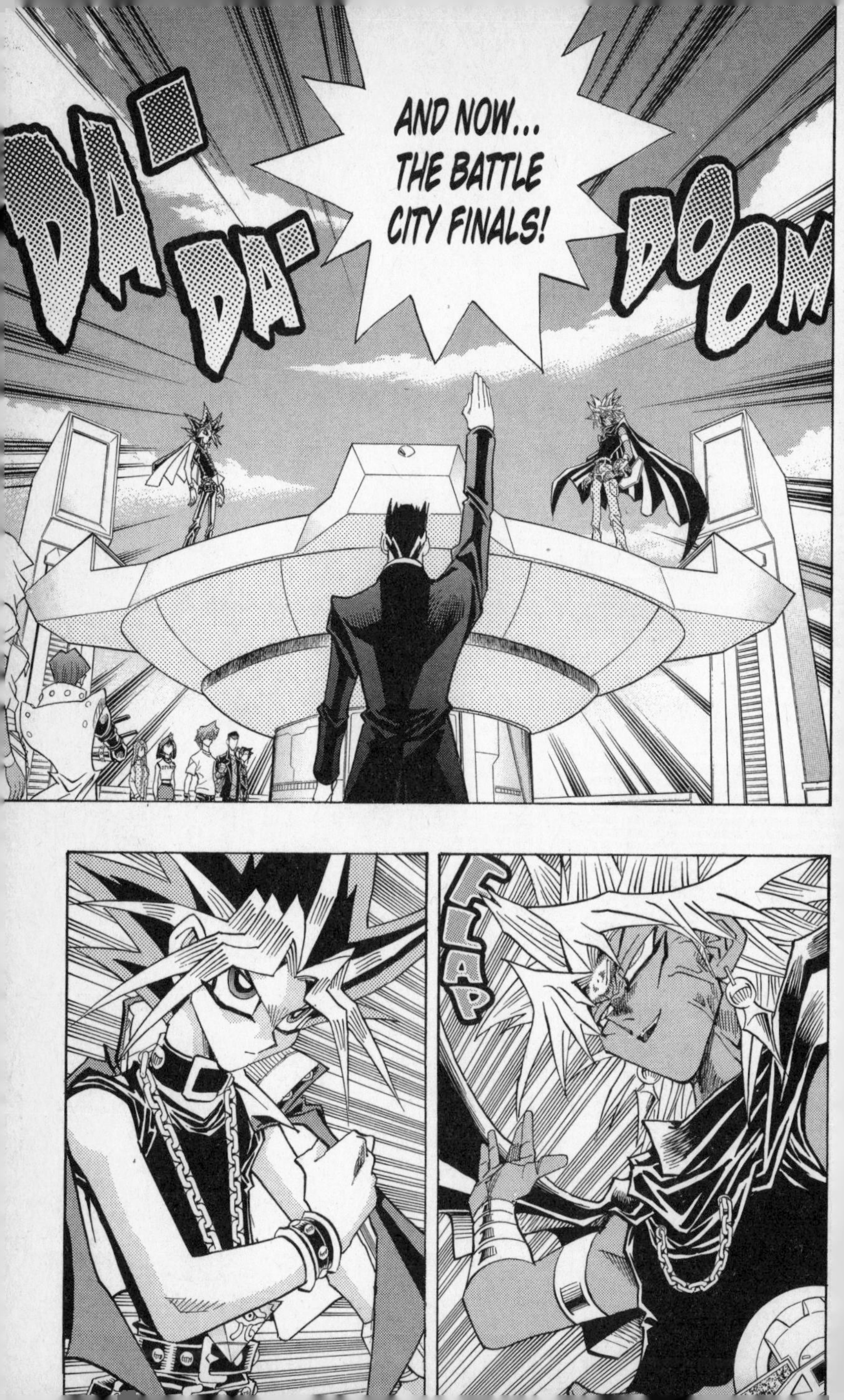
AND NOW... THE BATTLE CITY FINALS!
DA DA DOOM
FLAP

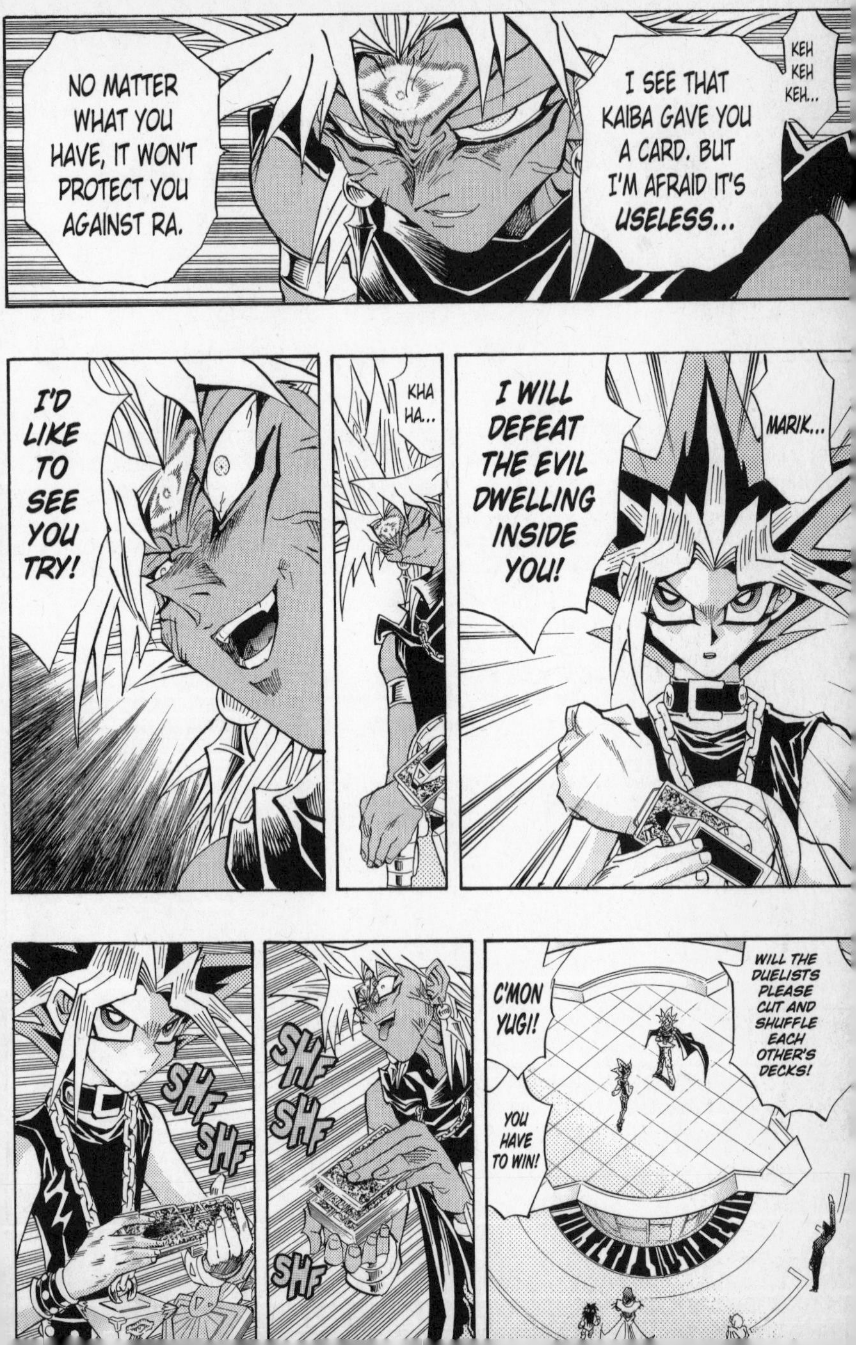
KEH KEH KEH...
I SEE THAT KAIBA GAVE YOU A CARD. BUT I'M AFRAID IT'S USELESS...
NO MATTER WHAT YOU HAVE, IT WON'T PROTECT YOU AGAINST RA.
MARIK...
I WILL DEFEAT THE EVIL DWELLING INSIDE YOU!
KHA HA...
I'D LIKE TO SEE YOU TRY!
WILL THE DUELISTS PLEASE CUT AND SHUFFLE EACH OTHER'S DECKS!
C'MON YUGI!
YOU HAVE TO WIN!
SHF SHF SHF
SHF SHF

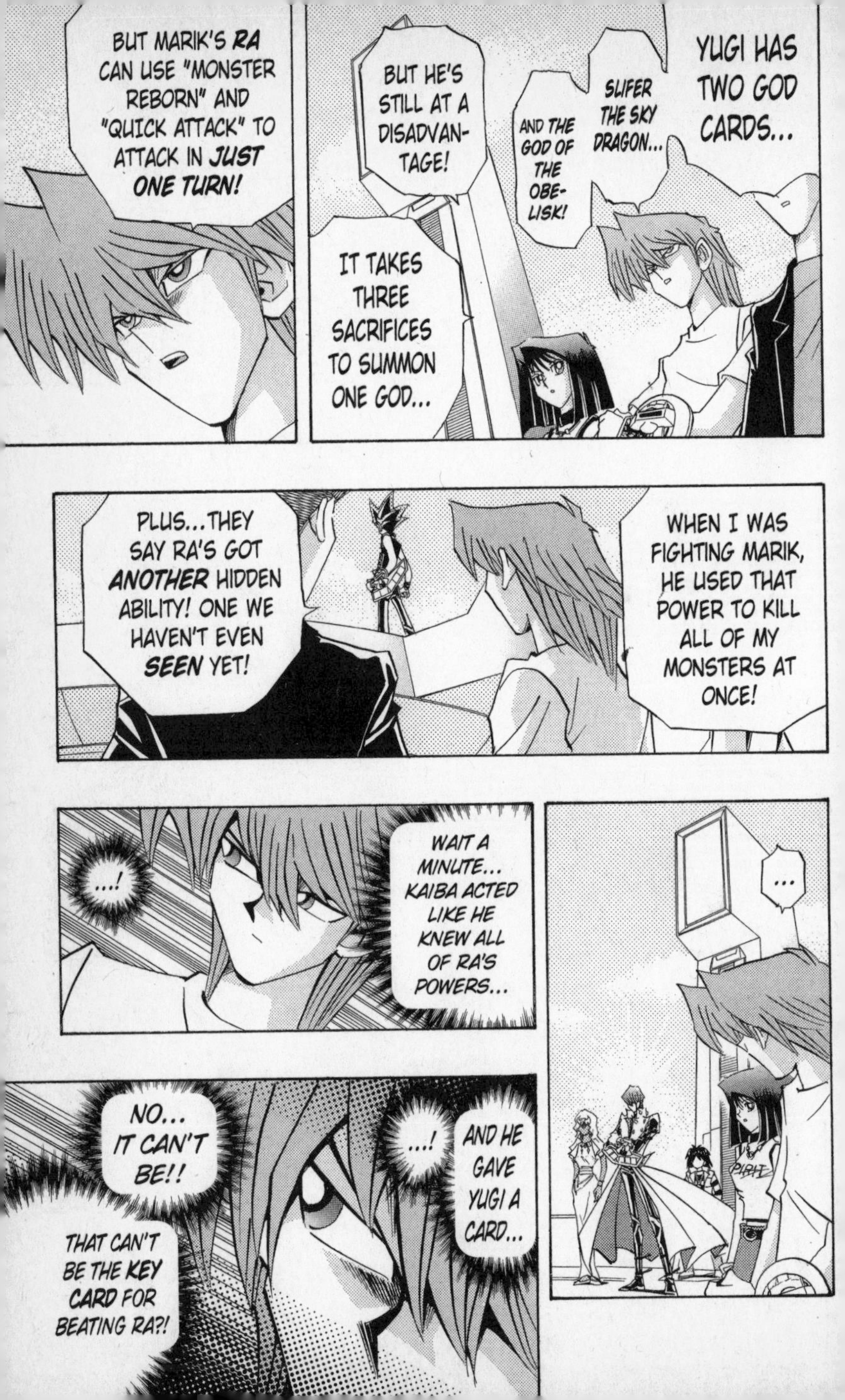
YUGI HAS TWO GOD CARDS...
SLIFER THE SKY DRAGON...
AND THE GOD OF THE OBELISK!
BUT HE'S STILL AT A DISADVANTAGE!
IT TAKES THREE SACRIFICES TO SUMMON ONE GOD...
BUT MARIK'S RA CAN USE "MONSTER REBORN" AND "QUICK ATTACK" TO ATTACK IN JUST ONE TURN!
WHEN I WAS FIGHTING MARIK, HE USED THAT POWER TO KILL ALL OF MY MONSTERS AT ONCE!
PLUS...THEY SAY RA'S GOT ANOTHER HIDDEN ABILITY! ONE WE HAVEN'T EVEN SEEN YET!
...
WAIT A MINUTE... KAIBA ACTED LIKE HE KNEW ALL OF RA'S POWERS...
....!
AND HE GAVE YUGI A CARD...
...!
NO... IT CAN'T BE!!
THAT CAN'T BE THE KEY CARD FOR BEATING RA?!

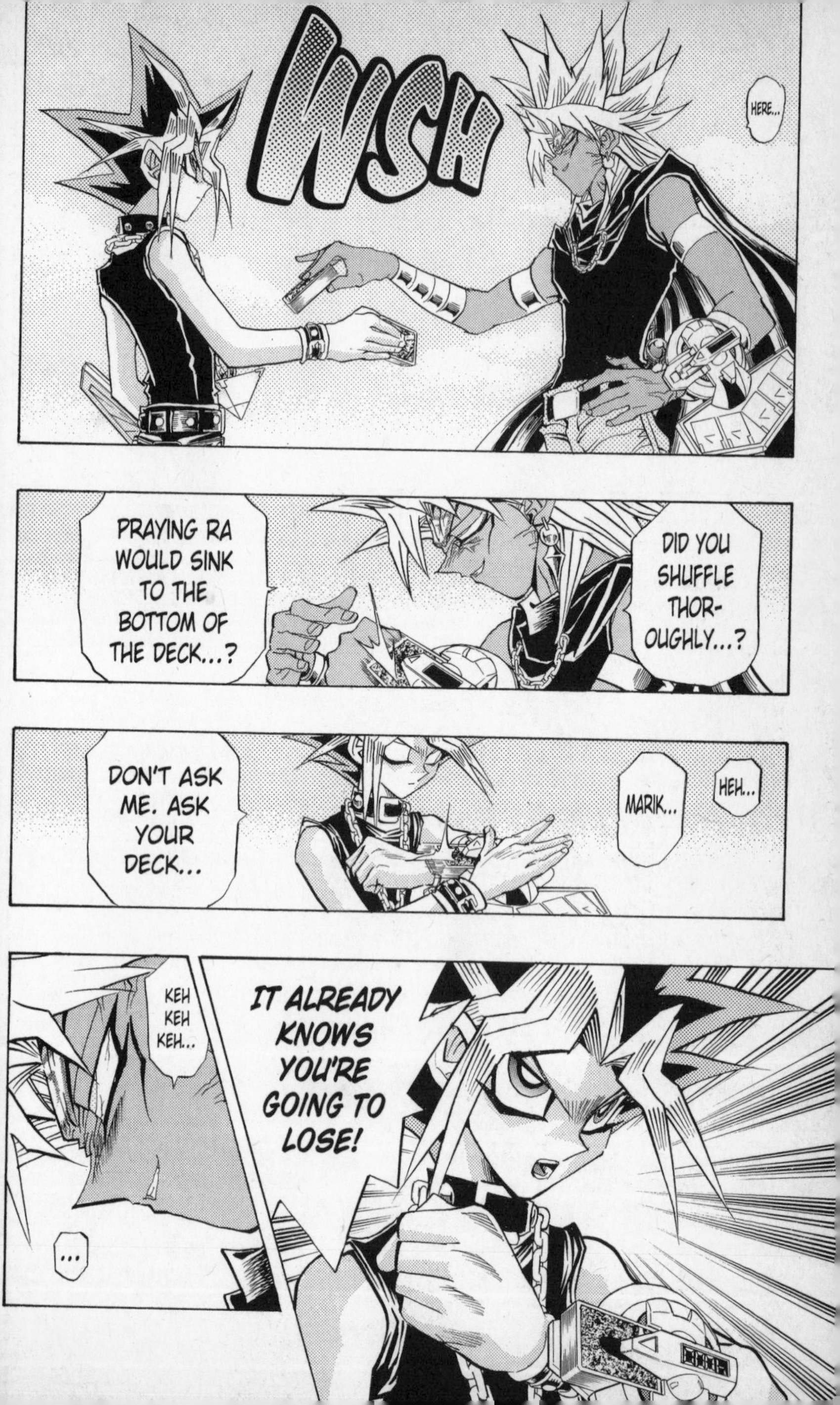
HERE...
WSH
DID YOU SHUFFLE THOR-OUGHLY...?
PRAYING RA WOULD SINK TO THE BOTTOM OF THE DECK...?
HEH...
MARIK...
DON'T ASK ME. ASK YOUR DECK...
IT ALREADY KNOWS YOU'RE GOING TO LOSE!
KEH KEH KEH...
...

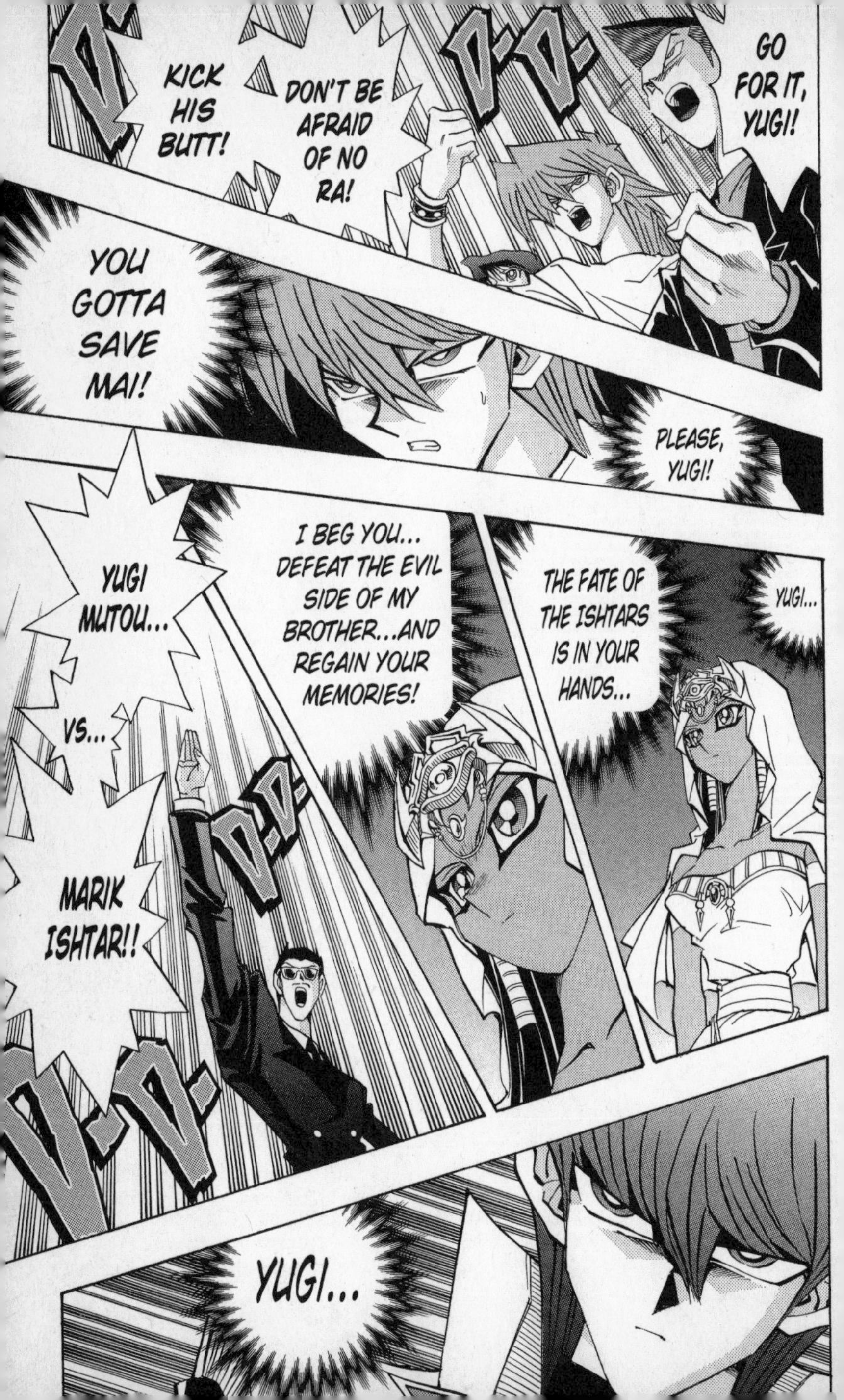
GO FOR IT, YUGI!
D-D-
DON'T BE AFRAID OF NO RA!
KICK HIS BUTT!
YOU GOTTA SAVE MAI!
PLEASE, YUGI!
YUGI...
THE FATE OF THE ISHTARS IS IN YOUR HANDS...
I BEG YOU... DEFEAT THE EVIL SIDE OF MY BROTHER...AND REGAIN YOUR MEMORIES!
YUGI MUTOU...
VS...
D-D-
MARIK ISHTAR!!
D-D-
YUGI...

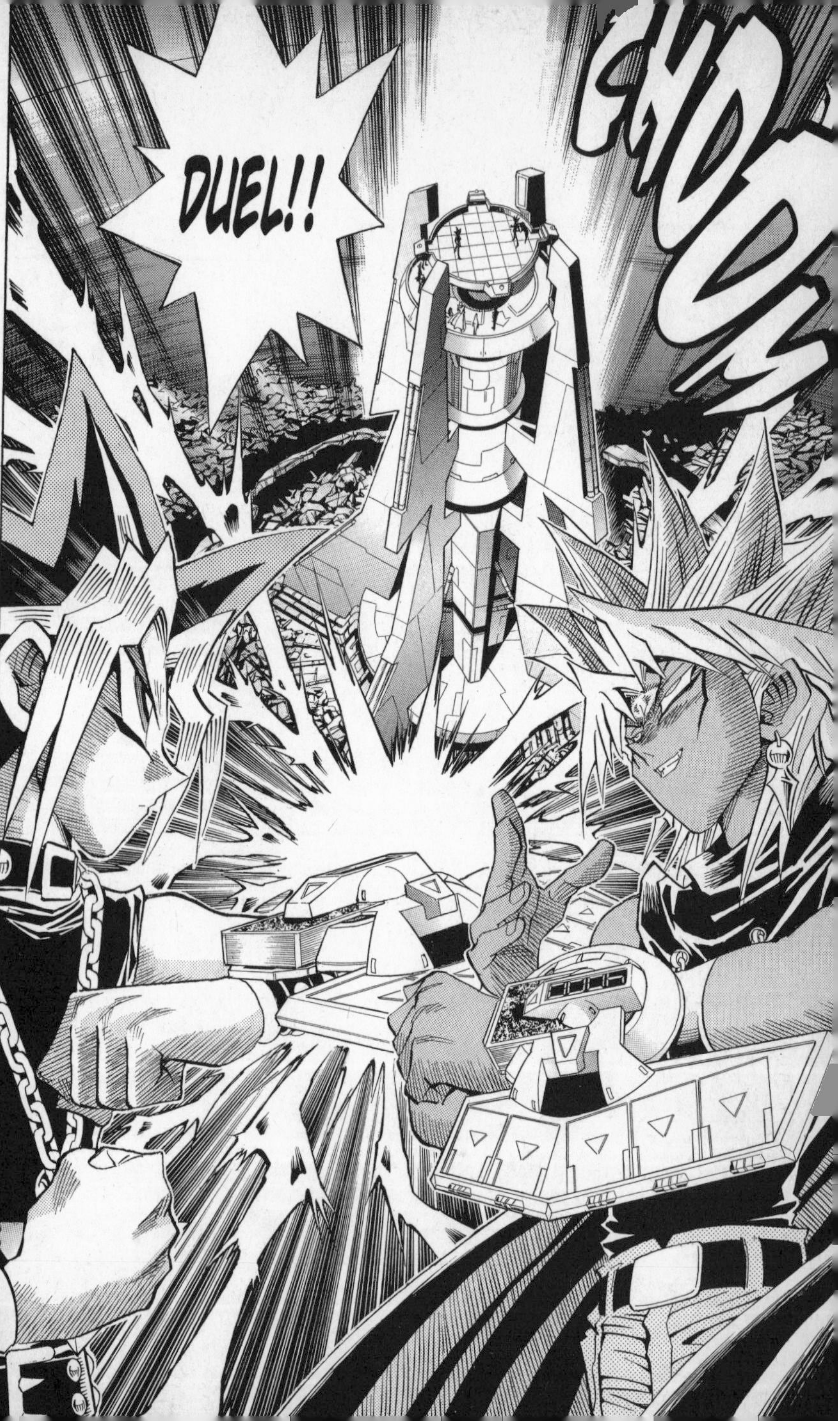
CHOOM
DUEL!!

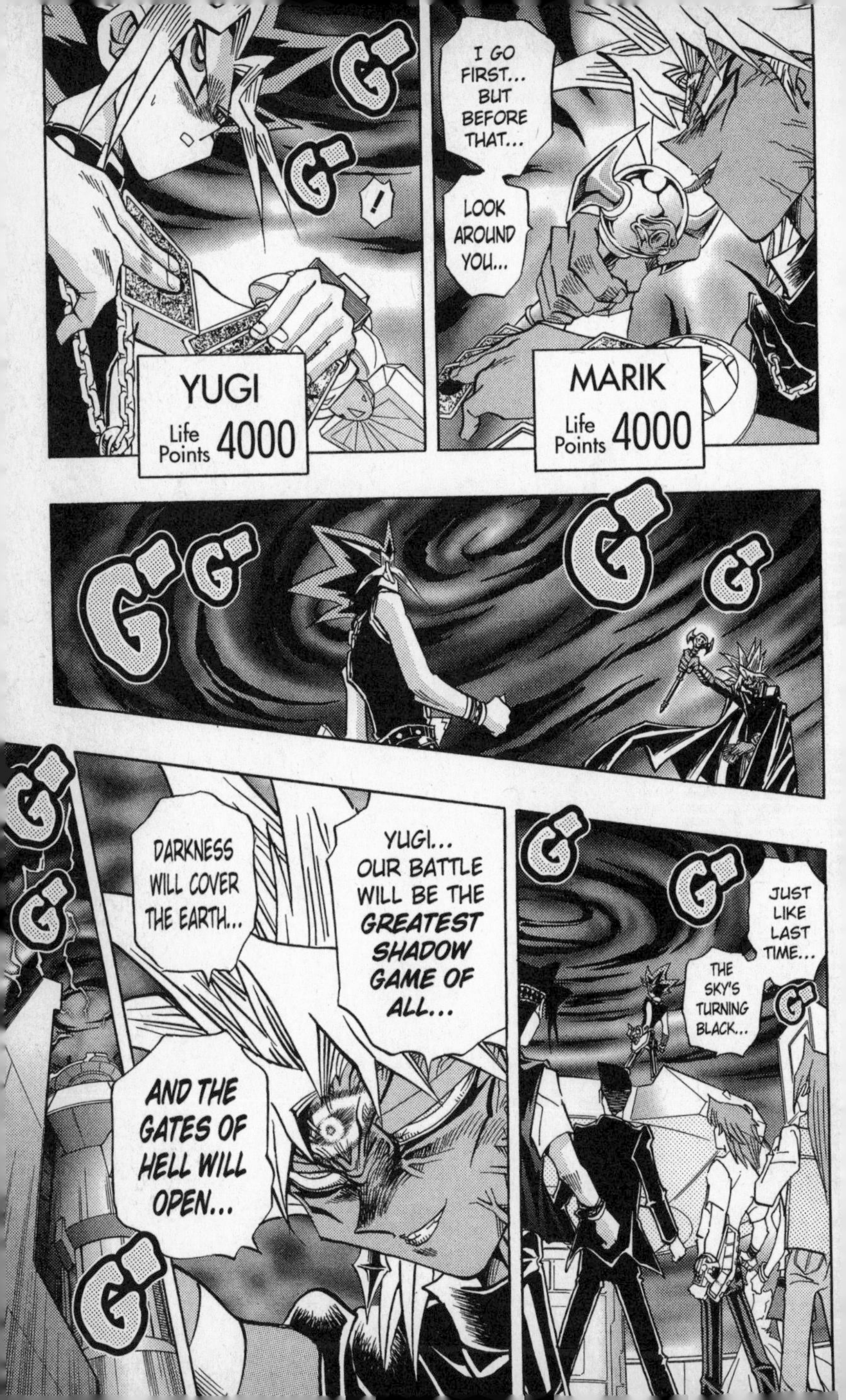
I GO FIRST... BUT BEFORE THAT...
LOOK AROUND YOU...
MARIK
Life Points 4000
G
G
!
YUGI
Life Points 4000
G
G
G
G
JUST LIKE LAST TIME...
THE SKY'S TURNING BLACK...
YUGI... OUR BATTLE WILL BE THE GREATEST SHADOW GAME OF ALL...
DARKNESS WILL COVER THE EARTH...
AND THE GATES OF HELL WILL OPEN...

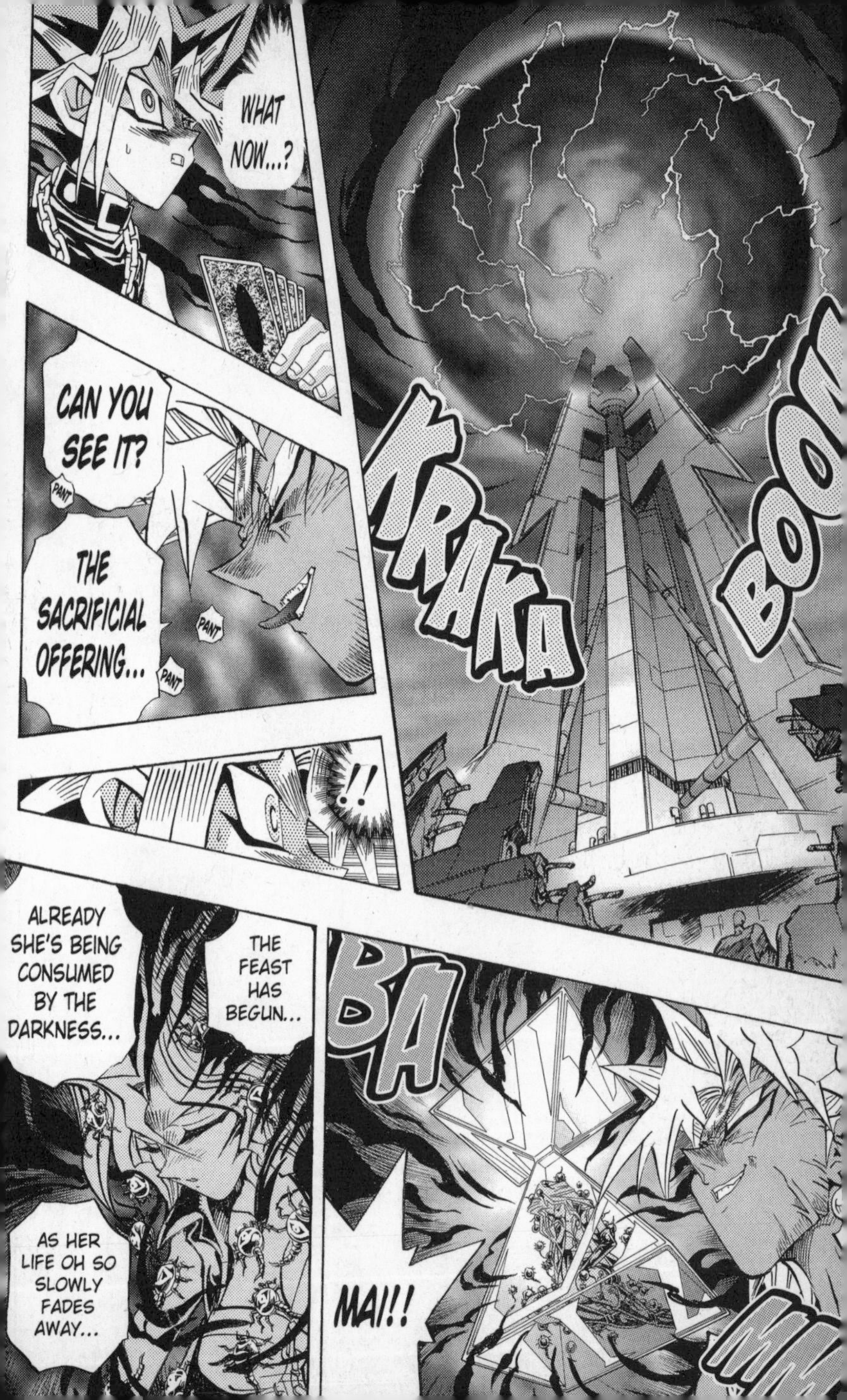
KRAKA
BOO
WHAT NOW...?
CAN YOU SEE IT?
PANT
THE SACRIFICIAL OFFERING...
PANT
PANT
!!
BA
MAI!!
THE FEAST HAS BEGUN...
ALREADY SHE'S BEING CONSUMED BY THE DARKNESS...
AS HER LIFE OH SO SLOWLY FADES AWAY...

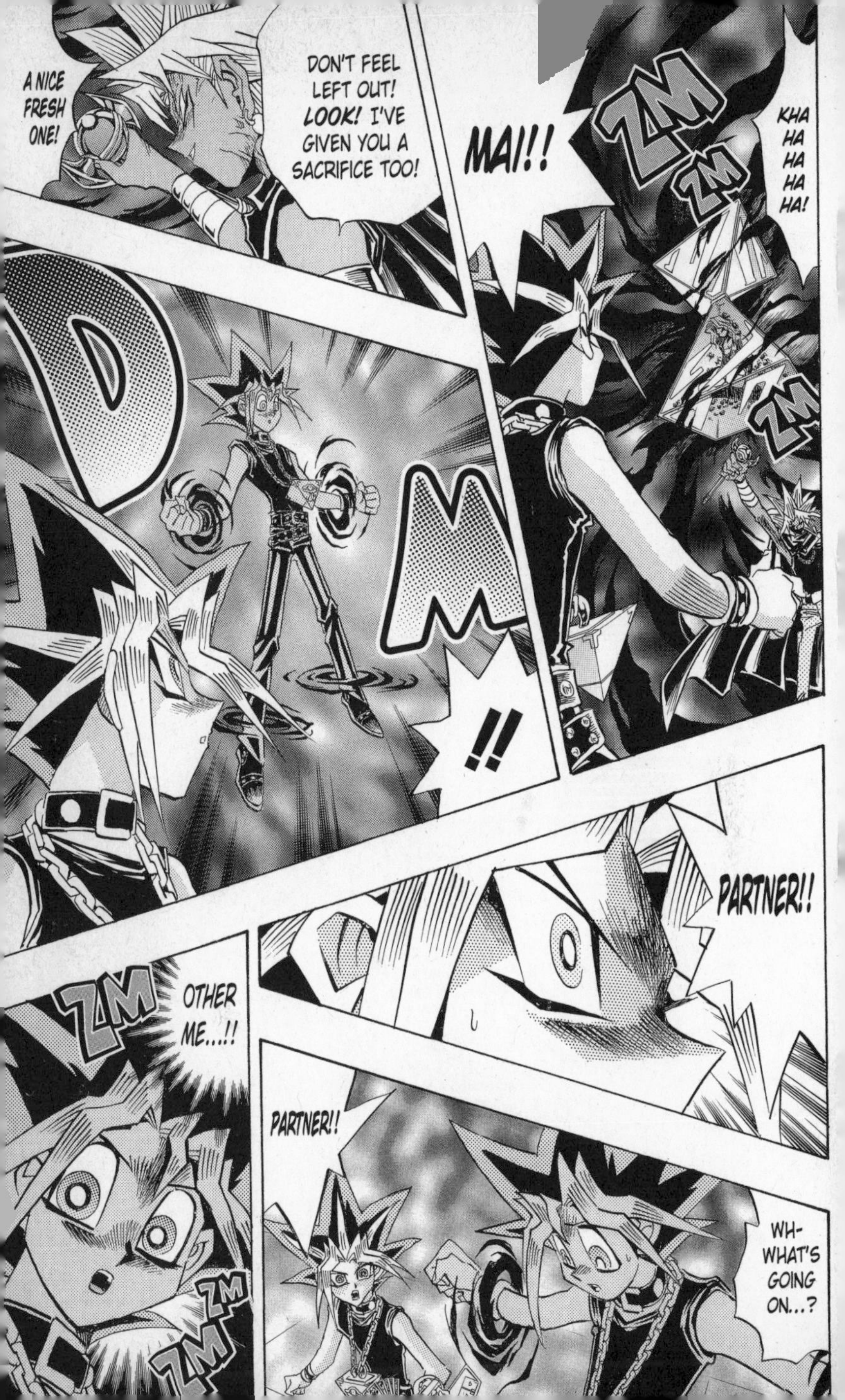
KHA HA HA HA HA!
ZM ZM
MAI!!
ZM
DON'T FEEL LEFT OUT! LOOK! I'VE GIVEN YOU A SACRIFICE TOO!
A NICE FRESH ONE!
DOM
!!
PARTNER!!
PARTNER!!
WH- WHAT'S GOING ON...?
OTHER ME...!!
ZM
ZM ZM

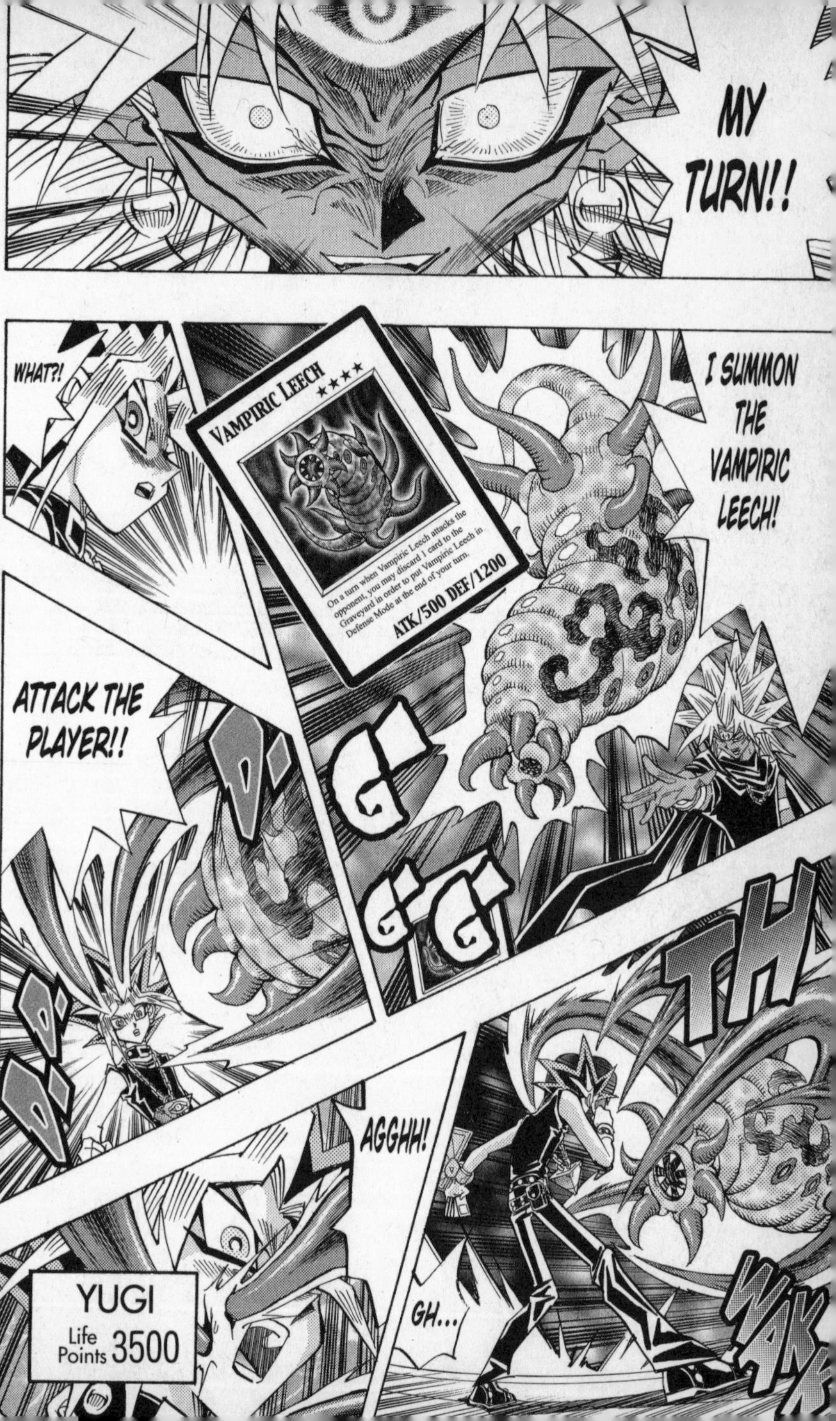
MY TURN!!
I SUMMON THE VAMPIRIC LEECH!
WHAT?!
VAMPIRIC LEECH ★★★★
On a turn when Vampiric Leech attacks the opponent, you may discard 1 card to the Graveyard in order to put Vampiric Leech in Defense Mode at the end of your turn.
ATK/500 DEF/1200
G
G G
ATTACK THE PLAYER!!
TH
WAK
GH...
AGGHH!
YUGI
Life Points 3500

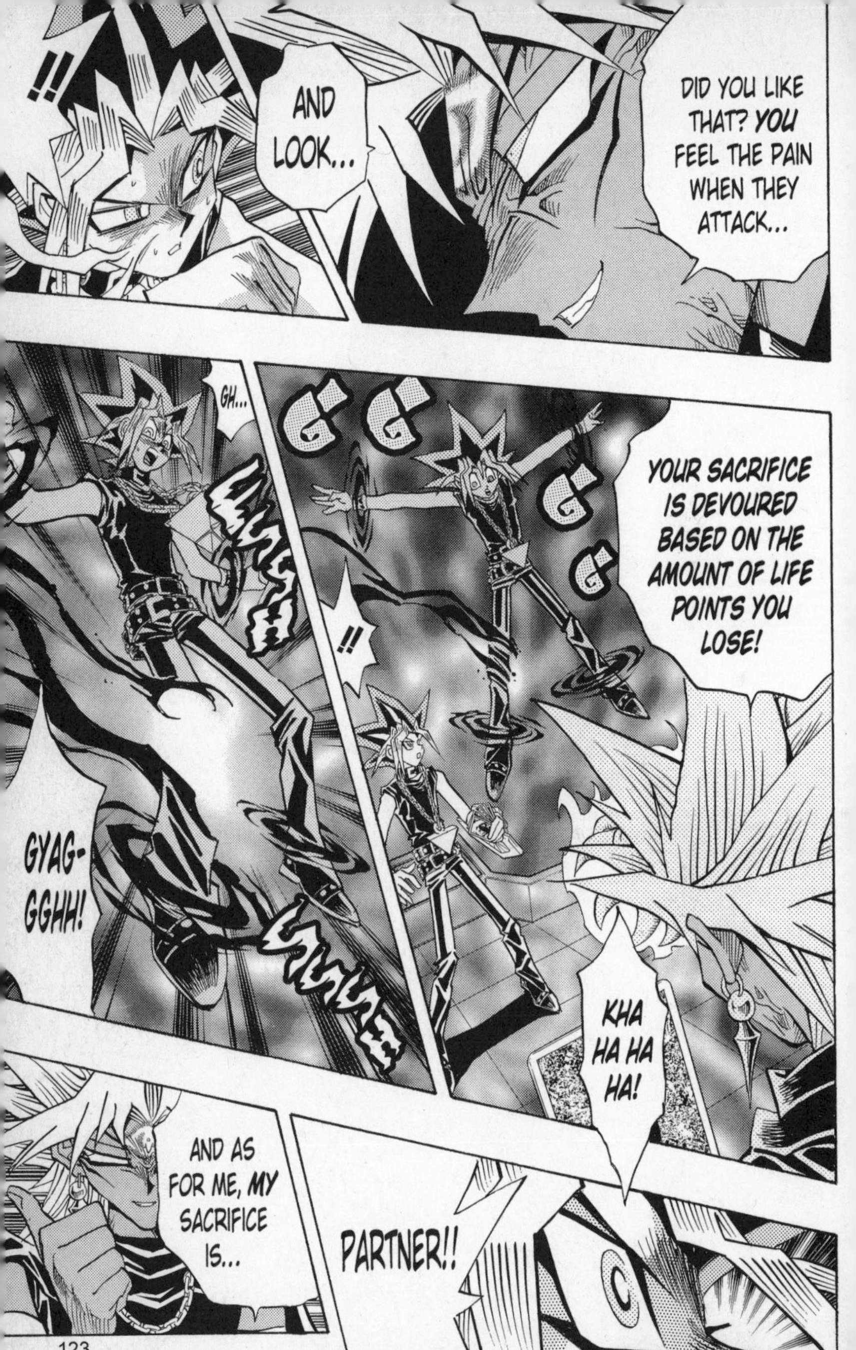
DID YOU LIKE THAT? YOU FEEL THE PAIN WHEN THEY ATTACK...
AND LOOK...
!!
YOUR SACRIFICE IS DEVOURED BASED ON THE AMOUNT OF LIFE POINTS YOU LOSE!
!!
GH...
GYAG-GGHH!
KHA HA HA HA!
PARTNER!!
AND AS FOR ME, MY SACRIFICE IS...

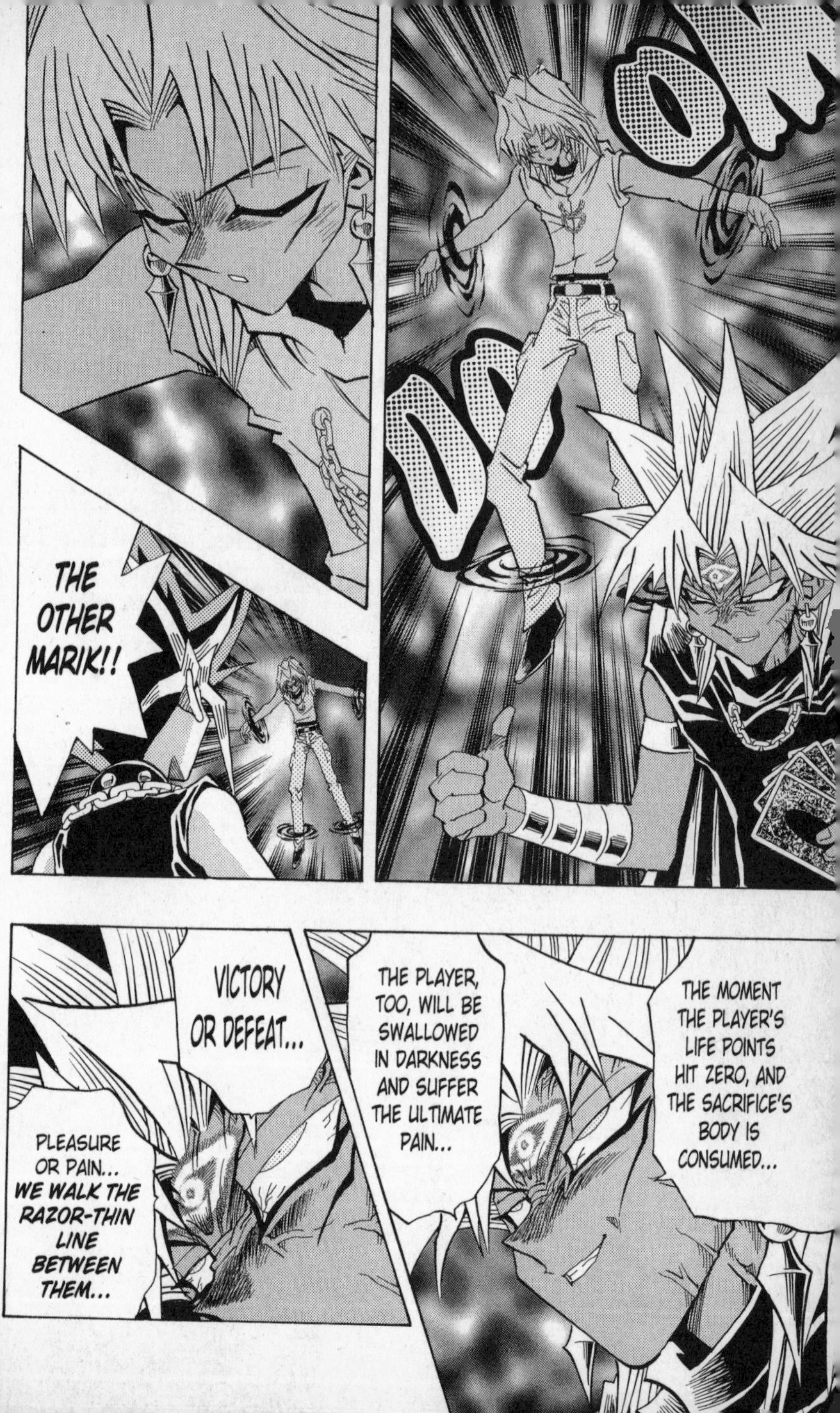
THE OTHER MARIK!!
THE MOMENT THE PLAYER'S LIFE POINTS HIT ZERO, AND THE SACRIFICE'S BODY IS CONSUMED...
THE PLAYER, TOO, WILL BE SWALLOWED IN DARKNESS AND SUFFER THE ULTIMATE PAIN...
VICTORY OR DEFEAT...
PLEASURE OR PAIN... ***WE WALK THE RAZOR-THIN LINE BETWEEN THEM...***

READ THIS WAY

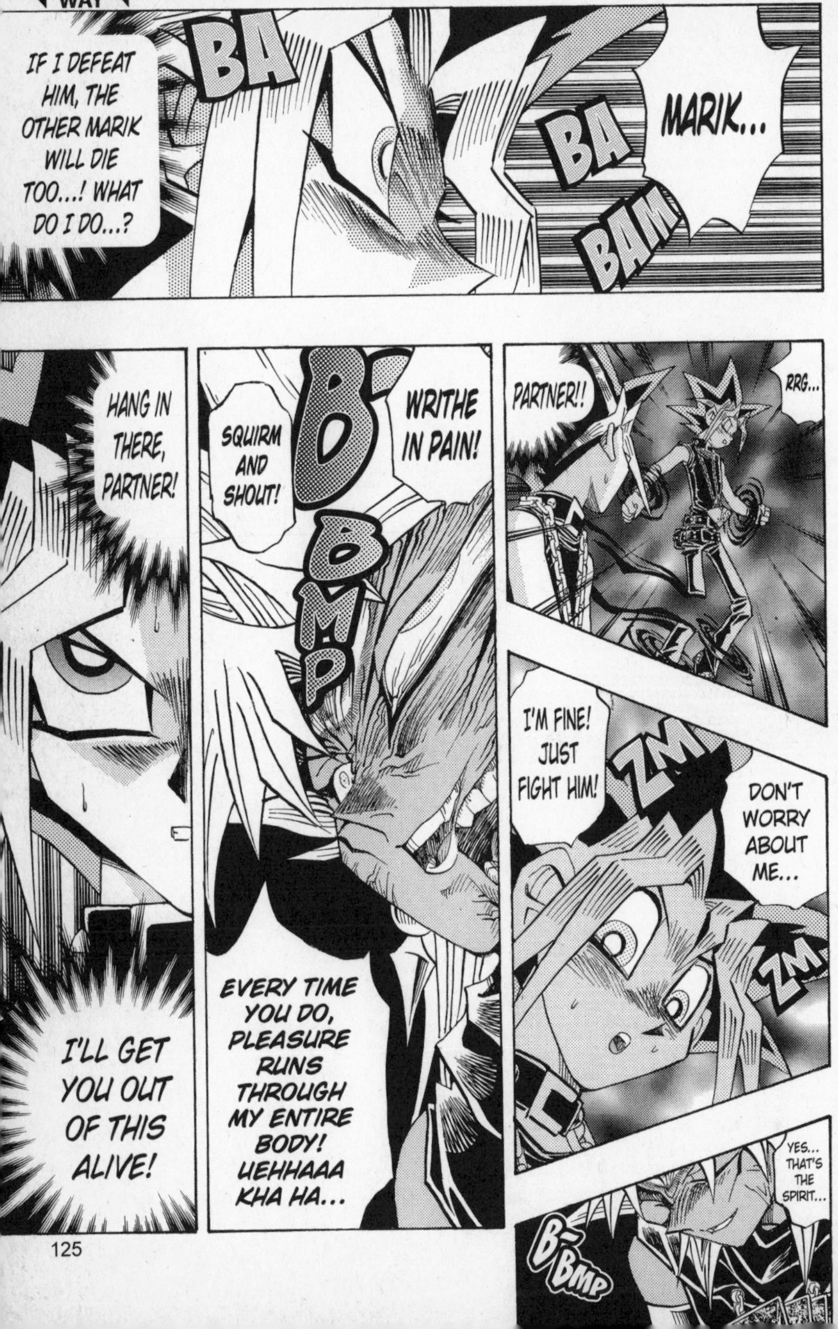

MARIK...
BA BA BAM
BA
IF I DEFEAT HIM, THE OTHER MARIK WILL DIE TOO...! WHAT DO I DO...?
RRG...
PARTNER!!
DON'T WORRY ABOUT ME...
ZM
I'M FINE! JUST FIGHT HIM!
ZM
YES... THAT'S THE SPIRIT...
B-BMP
WRITHE IN PAIN!
B-BMP
SQUIRM AND SHOUT!
EVERY TIME YOU DO, PLEASURE RUNS THROUGH MY ENTIRE BODY! UEHHAAA KHA HA...
HANG IN THERE, PARTNER!
I'LL GET YOU OUT OF THIS ALIVE!

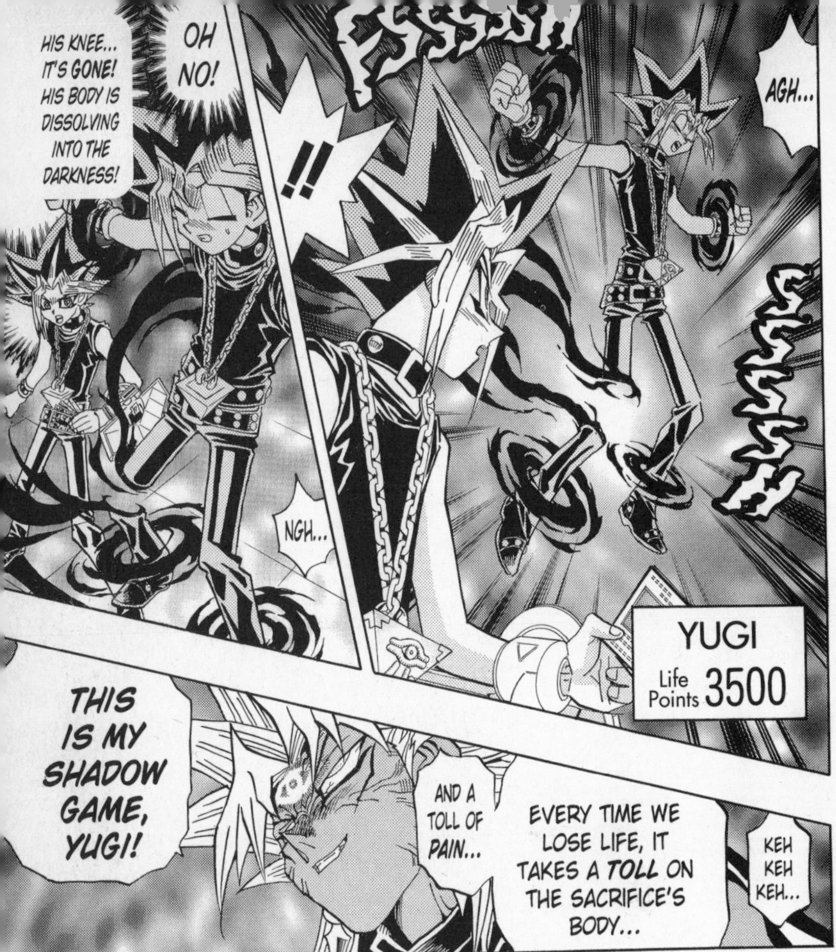
AGH...
FSSSSH!!
!!
OH NO!
HIS KNEE... IT'S GONE! HIS BODY IS DISSOLVING INTO THE DARKNESS!
NGH...
YUGI Life Points 3500
KEH KEH KEH...
EVERY TIME WE LOSE LIFE, IT TAKES A TOLL ON THE SACRIFICE'S BODY...
AND A TOLL OF PAIN...
THIS IS MY SHADOW GAME, YUGI!

Duel 207: The Quick Attack Trap

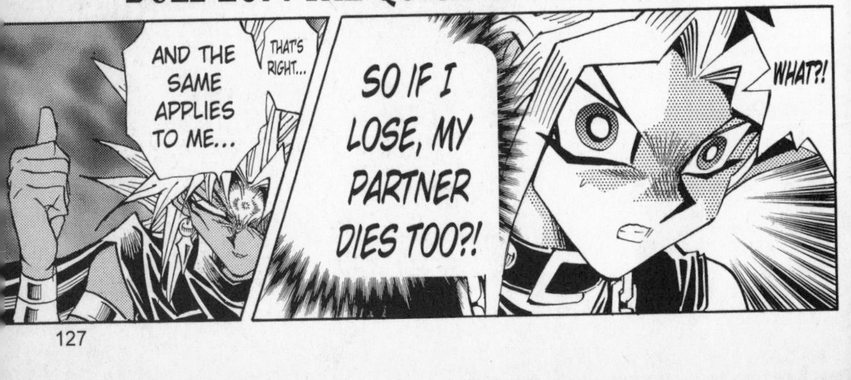
WHAT?!
SO IF I LOSE, MY PARTNER DIES TOO?!
THAT'S RIGHT...
AND THE SAME APPLIES TO ME...

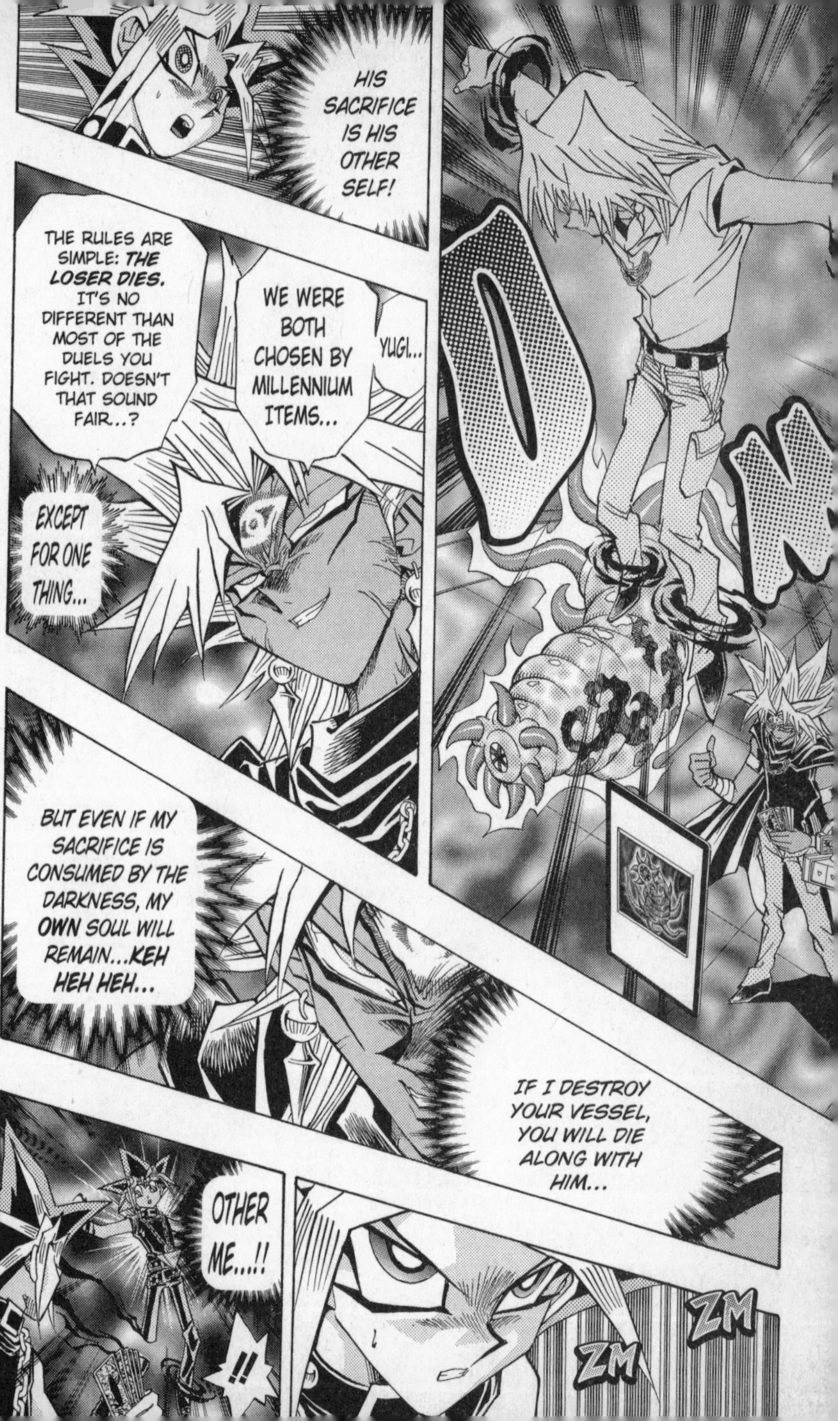

HIS SACRIFICE IS HIS OTHER SELF!
YUGI...
WE WERE BOTH CHOSEN BY MILLENNIUM ITEMS...
THE RULES ARE SIMPLE: ***THE LOSER DIES.*** IT'S NO DIFFERENT THAN MOST OF THE DUELS YOU FIGHT. DOESN'T THAT SOUND FAIR...?
EXCEPT FOR ONE THING...
BUT EVEN IF MY SACRIFICE IS CONSUMED BY THE DARKNESS, MY **OWN** SOUL WILL REMAIN...**KEH HEH HEH...**
IF I DESTROY YOUR VESSEL, YOU WILL DIE ALONG WITH HIM...
ZM
ZM
OTHER ME...!!
!!

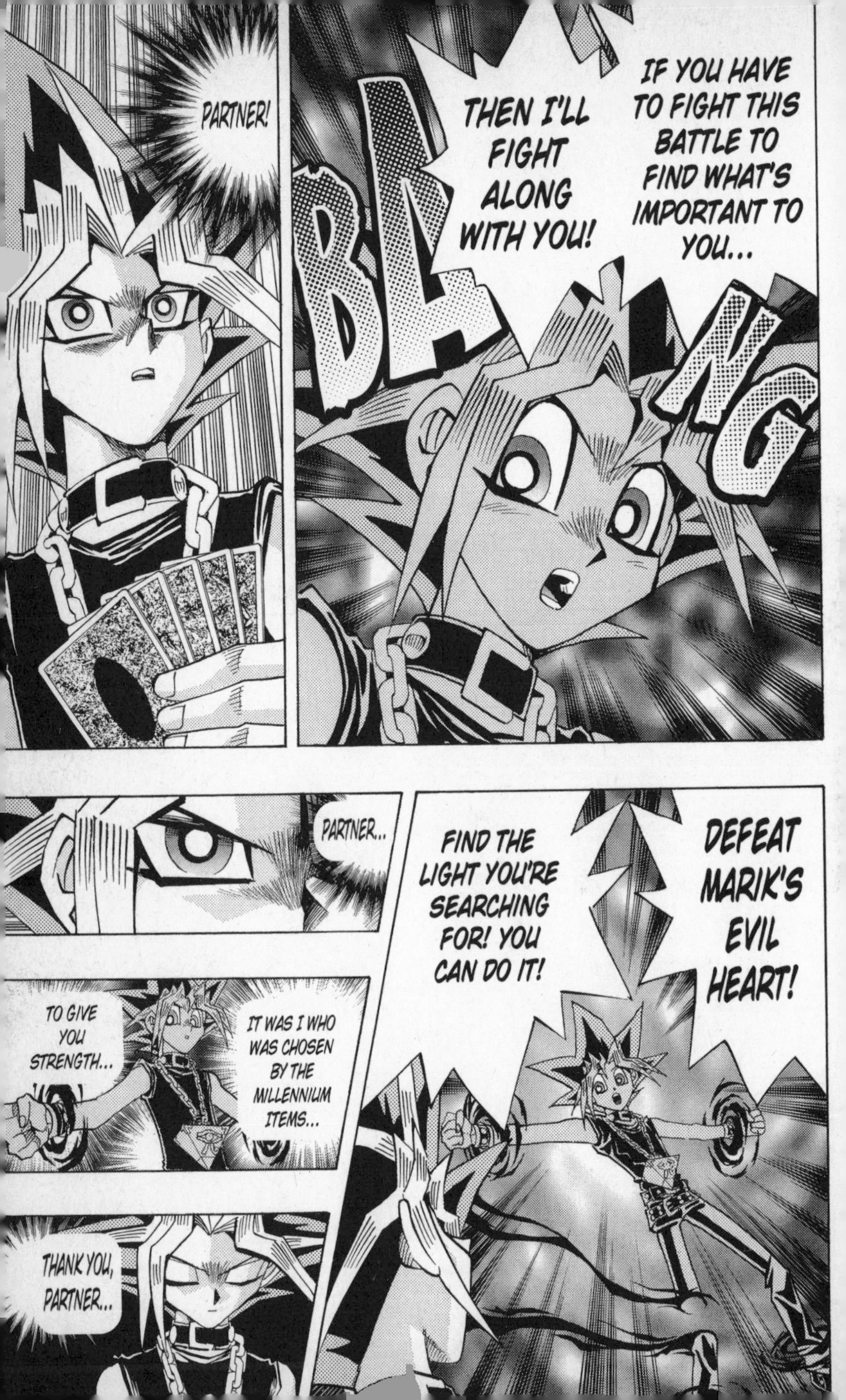
IF YOU HAVE TO FIGHT THIS BATTLE TO FIND WHAT'S IMPORTANT TO YOU...
THEN I'LL FIGHT ALONG WITH YOU!
PARTNER!
DEFEAT MARIK'S EVIL HEART!
FIND THE LIGHT YOU'RE SEARCHING FOR! YOU CAN DO IT!
PARTNER...
IT WAS I WHO WAS CHOSEN BY THE MILLENNIUM ITEMS...
TO GIVE YOU STRENGTH...
THANK YOU, PARTNER...

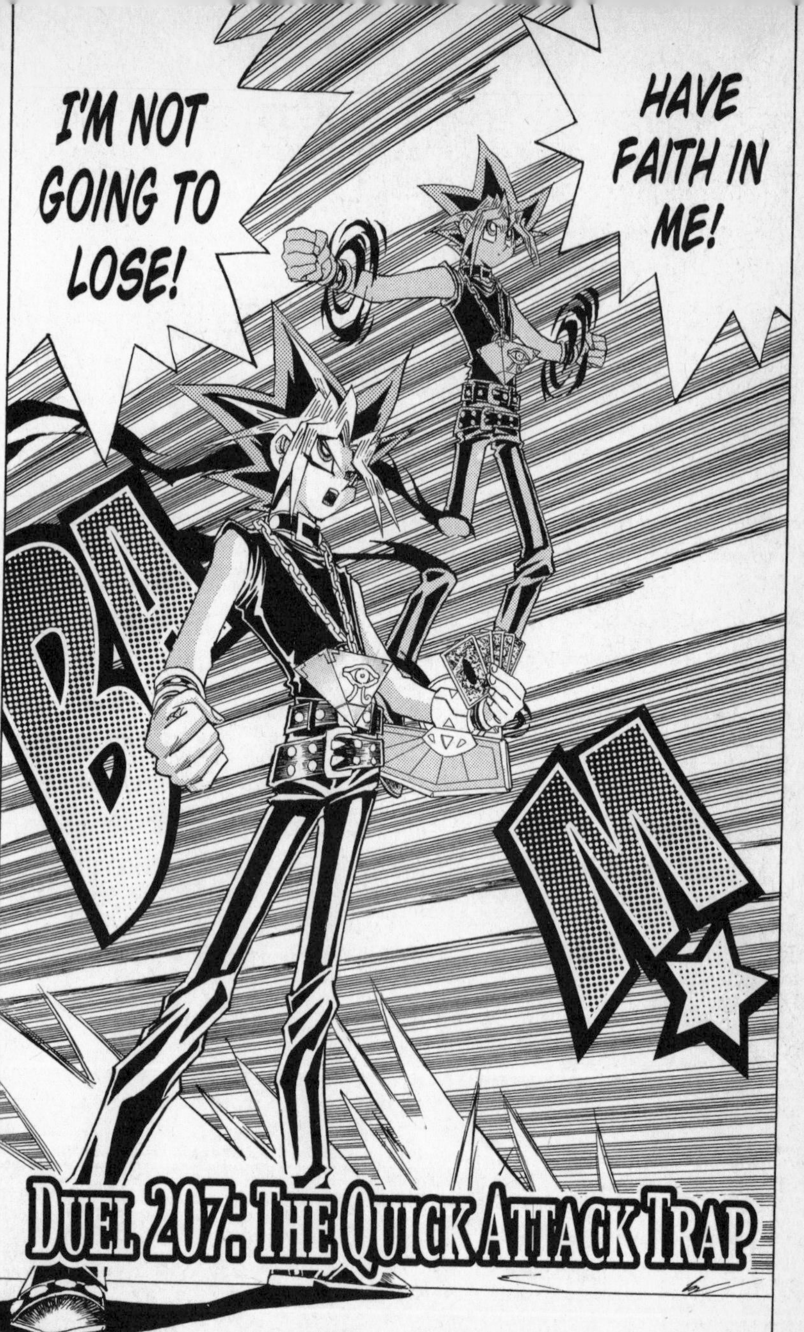
HAVE FAITH IN ME!
I'M NOT GOING TO LOSE!
BAM☆

Duel 207: The Quick Attack Trap

READ THIS WAY

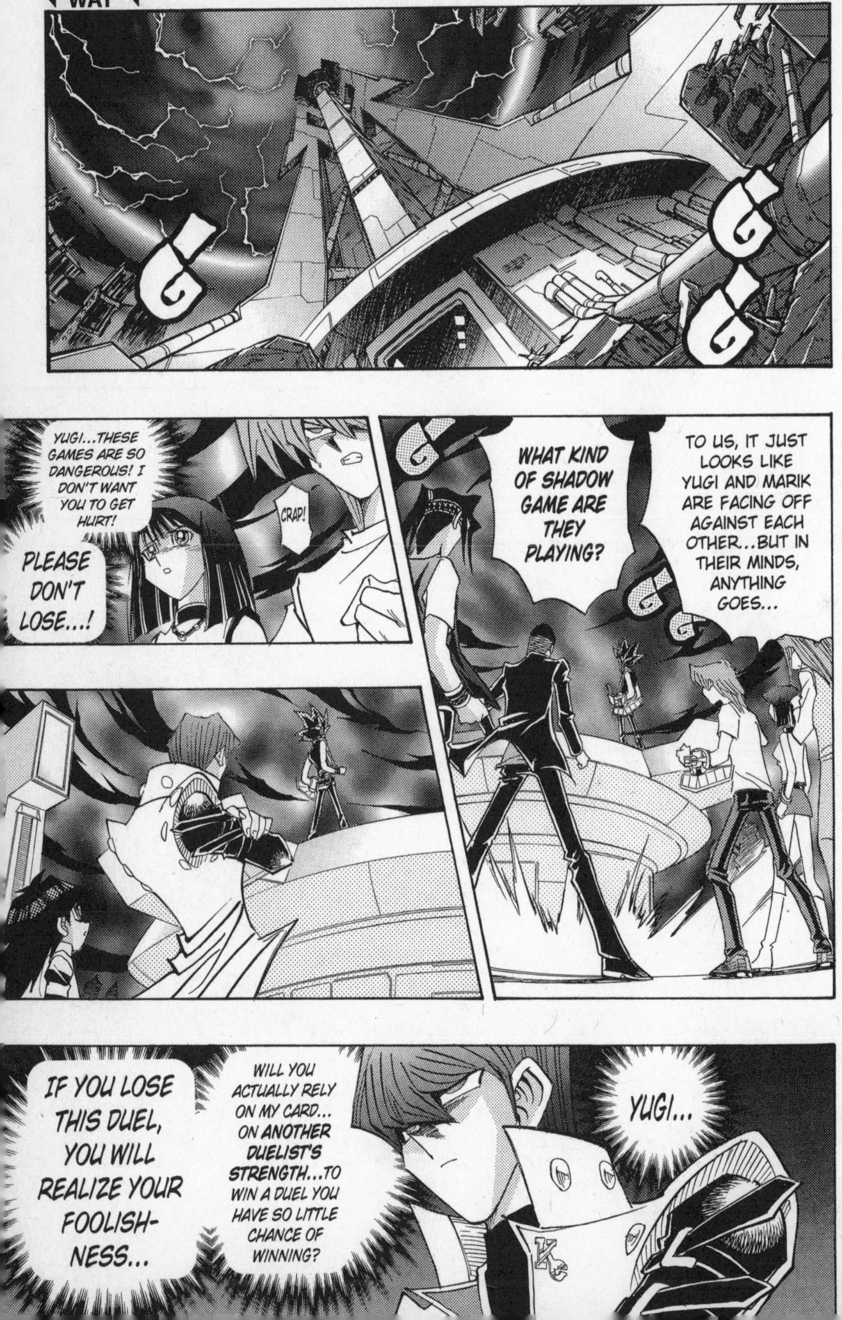
G
G
G
WHAT KIND OF SHADOW GAME ARE THEY PLAYING?
TO US, IT JUST LOOKS LIKE YUGI AND MARIK ARE FACING OFF AGAINST EACH OTHER...BUT IN THEIR MINDS, ANYTHING GOES...
G
G
G
CRAP!
YUGI...THESE GAMES ARE SO DANGEROUS! I DON'T WANT YOU TO GET HURT!
PLEASE DON'T LOSE...!
YUGI...
WILL YOU ACTUALLY RELY ON MY CARD... ON ANOTHER DUELIST'S STRENGTH...TO WIN A DUEL YOU HAVE SO LITTLE CHANCE OF WINNING?
IF YOU LOSE THIS DUEL, YOU WILL REALIZE YOUR FOOLISH-NESS...

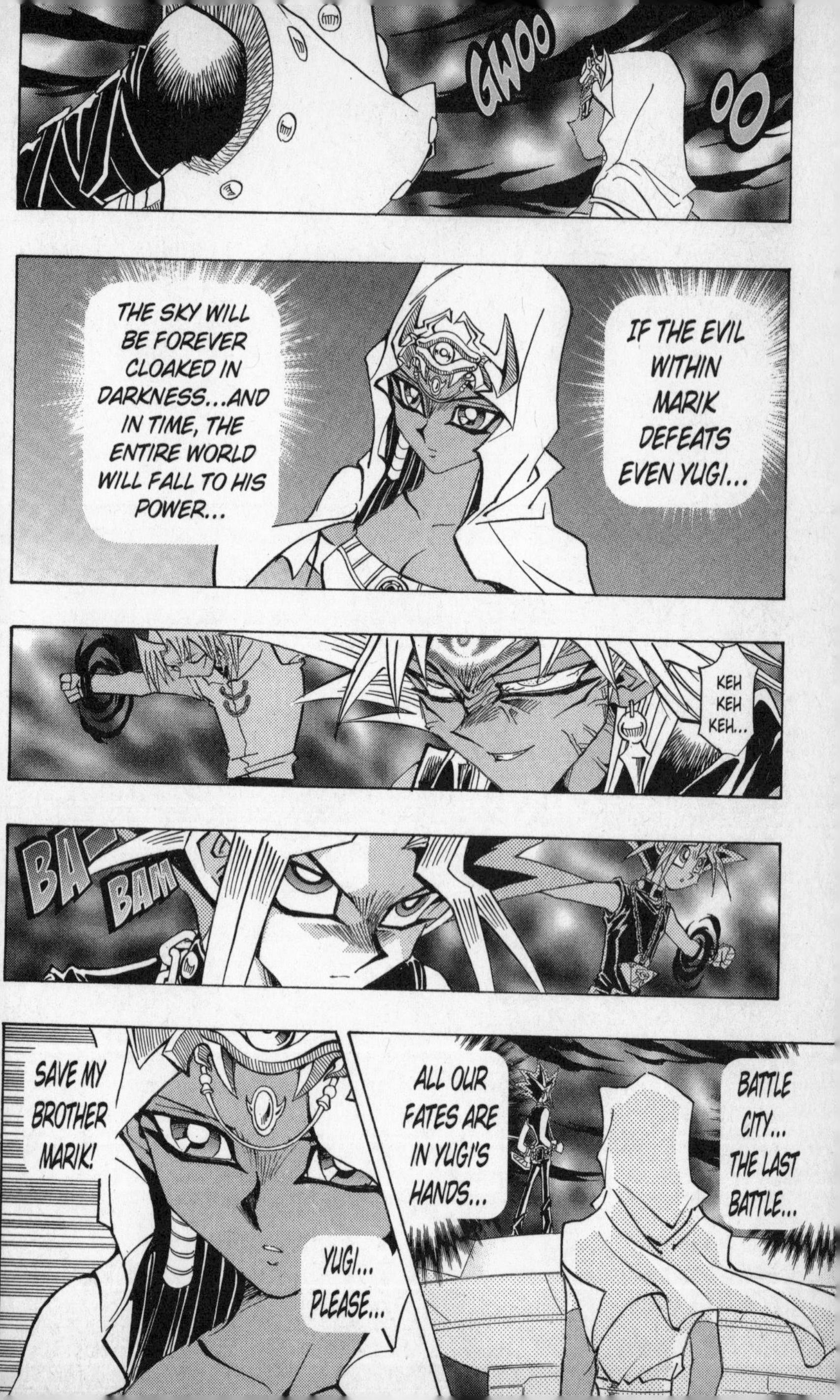
GWOO
OO
IF THE EVIL WITHIN MARIK DEFEATS EVEN YUGI...
THE SKY WILL BE FOREVER CLOAKED IN DARKNESS...AND IN TIME, THE ENTIRE WORLD WILL FALL TO HIS POWER...
KEH KEH KEH...
BA-
BAM
BATTLE CITY... THE LAST BATTLE...
ALL OUR FATES ARE IN YUGI'S HANDS...
YUGI... PLEASE...
SAVE MY BROTHER MARIK!

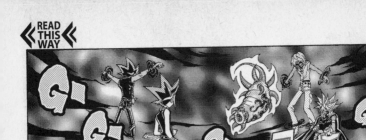

READ THIS WAY

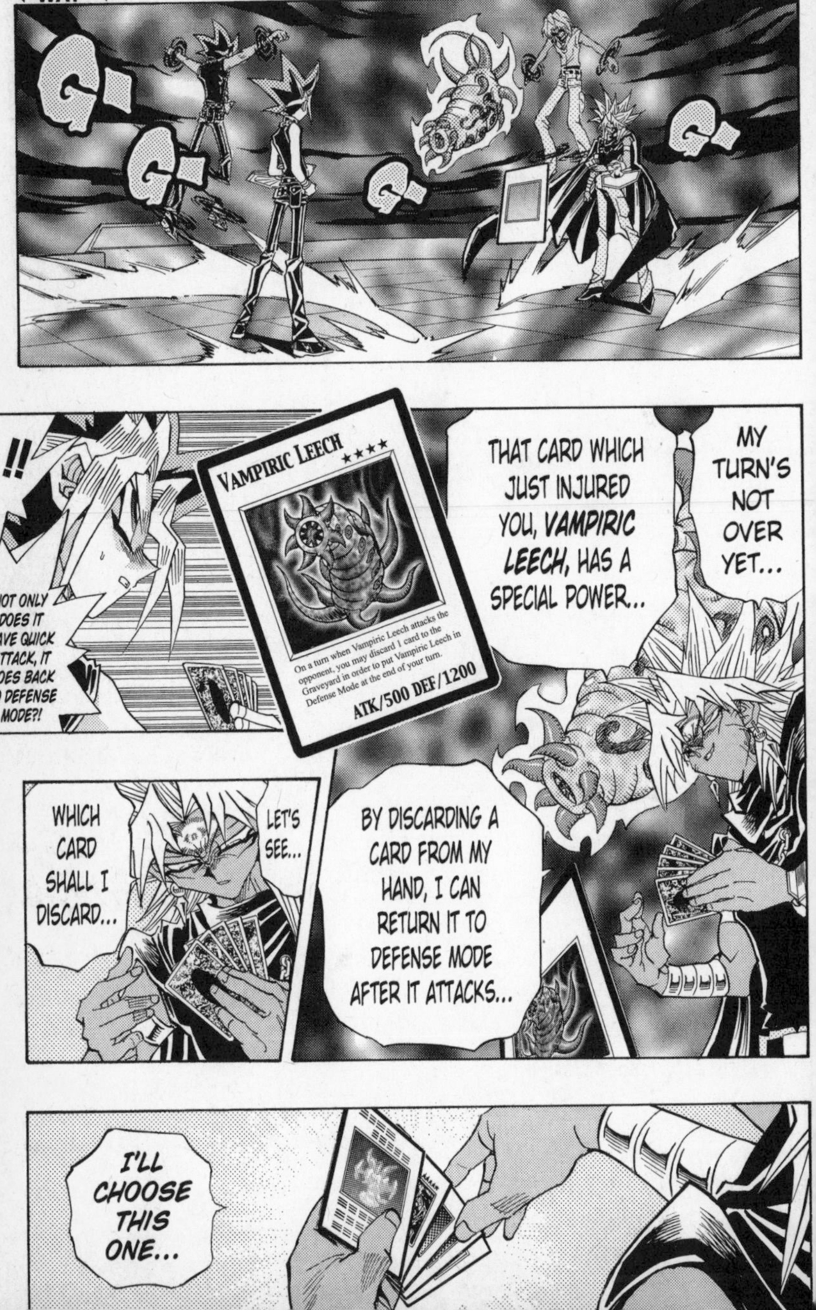

G
G
G
G
MY TURN'S NOT OVER YET...
THAT CARD WHICH JUST INJURED YOU, *VAMPIRIC LEECH*, HAS A SPECIAL POWER...
VAMPIRIC LEECH
On a turn when Vampiric Leech attacks the opponent, you may discard 1 card to the Graveyard in order to put Vampiric Leech in Defense Mode at the end of your turn.
ATK/500 DEF/1200
!!
NOT ONLY DOES IT HAVE QUICK ATTACK, IT GOES BACK TO DEFENSE MODE?!
BY DISCARDING A CARD FROM MY HAND, I CAN RETURN IT TO DEFENSE MODE AFTER IT ATTACKS...
LET'S SEE...
WHICH CARD SHALL I DISCARD...
I'LL CHOOSE THIS ONE...

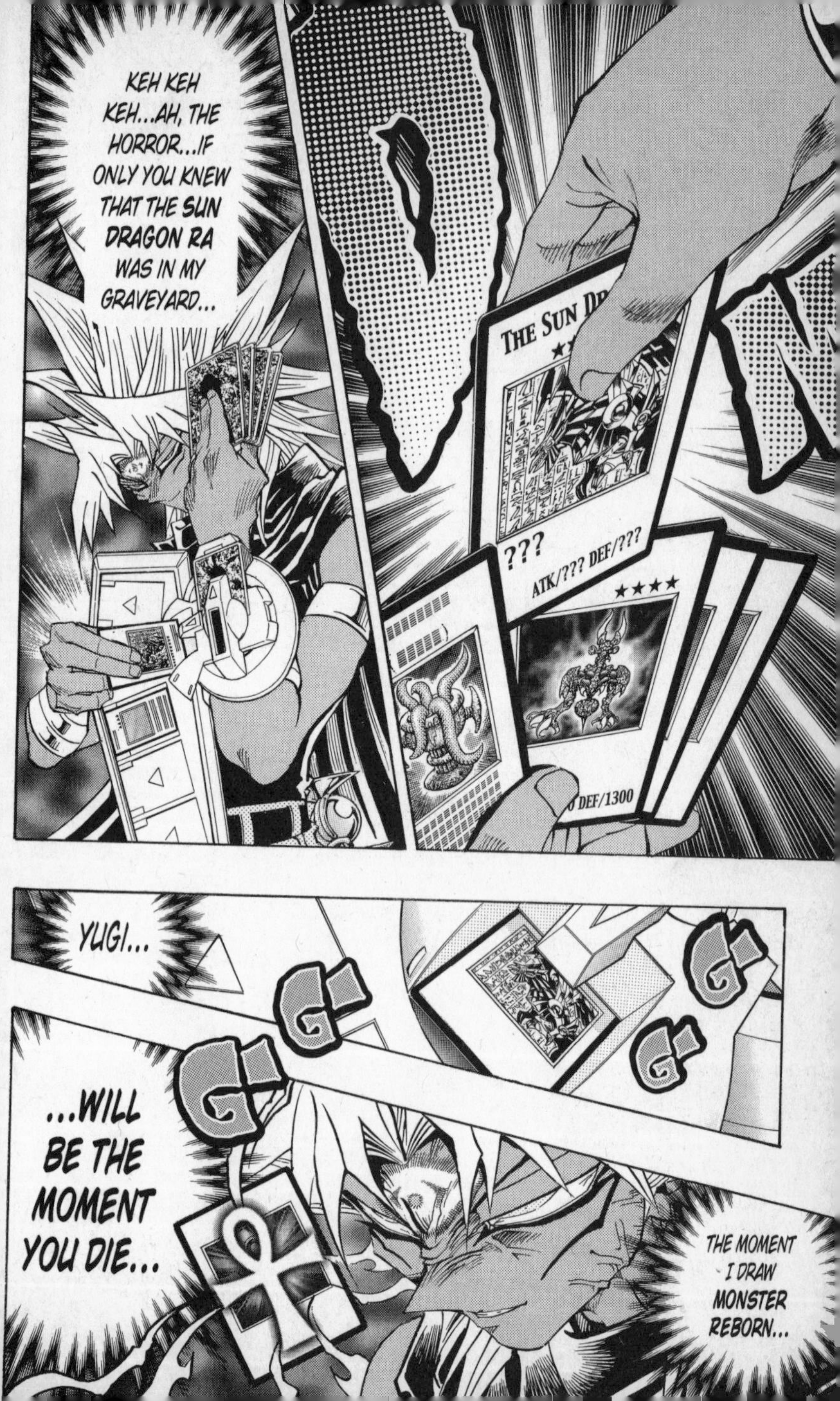
THE SUN DR
???
ATK/??? DEF/???
DEF/1300
KEH KEH KEH...AH, THE HORROR...IF ONLY YOU KNEW THAT THE SUN DRAGON RA WAS IN MY GRAVEYARD...
YUGI...
G G G G G
THE MOMENT I DRAW MONSTER REBORN...
...WILL BE THE MOMENT YOU DIE...

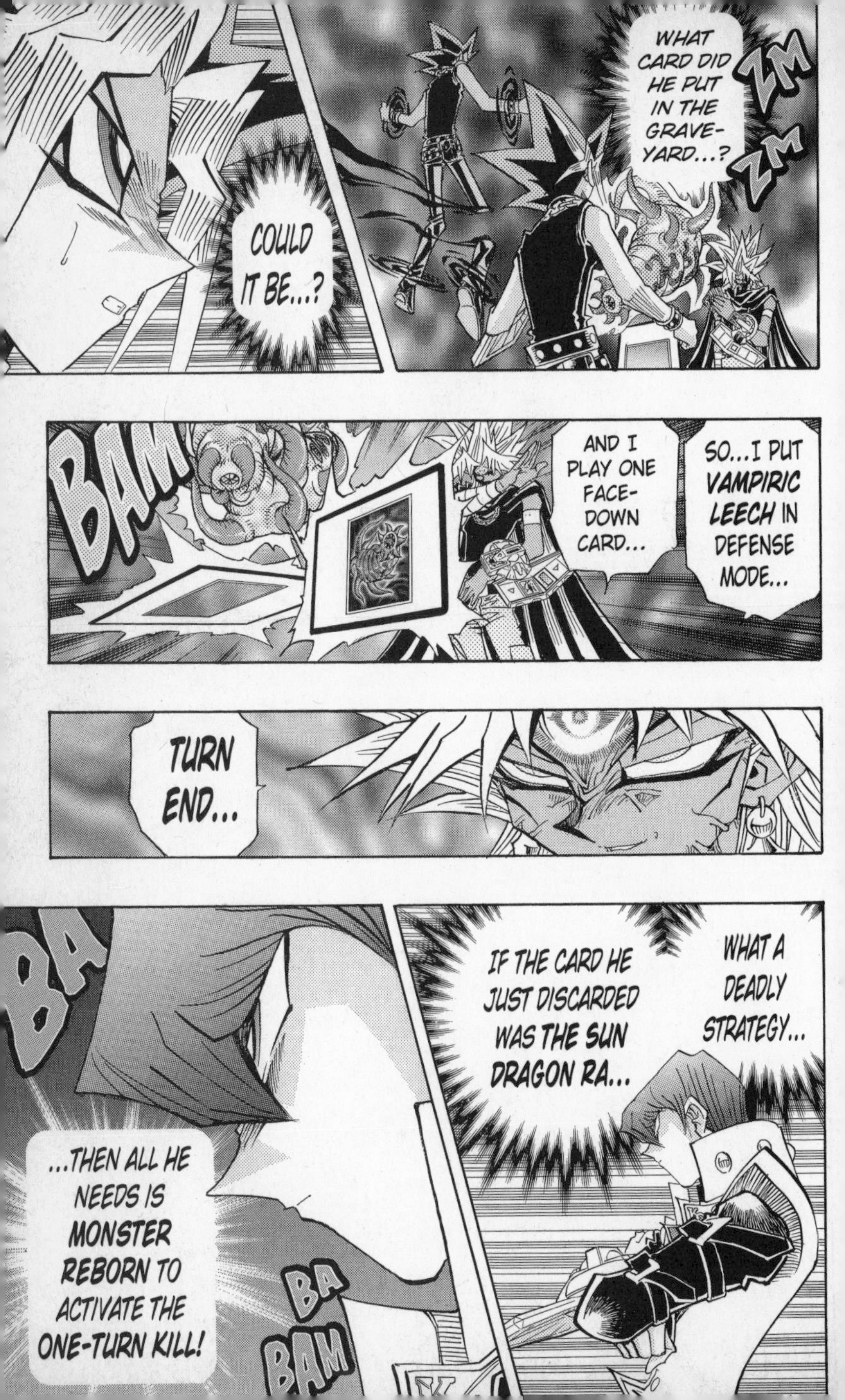
WHAT CARD DID HE PUT IN THE GRAVEYARD...?
ZM ZM
COULD IT BE...?
SO...I PUT VAMPIRIC LEECH IN DEFENSE MODE...
AND I PLAY ONE FACE-DOWN CARD...
BAM
TURN END...
WHAT A DEADLY STRATEGY...
IF THE CARD HE JUST DISCARDED WAS THE SUN DRAGON RA...
BA
...THEN ALL HE NEEDS IS MONSTER REBORN TO ACTIVATE THE ONE-TURN KILL!
BA BAM

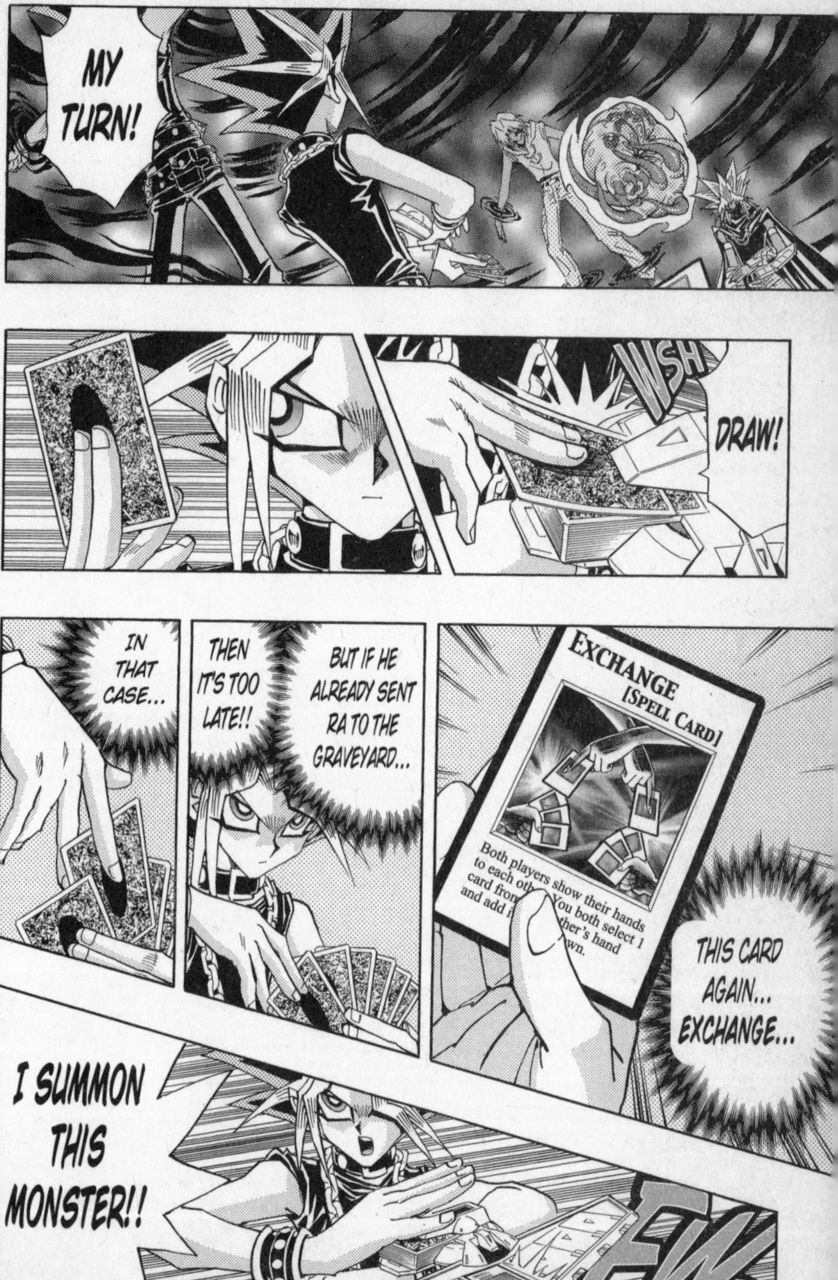
MY TURN!
WSH
DRAW!
EXCHANGE
[SPELL CARD]
Both players show their hands
THIS CARD AGAIN... EXCHANGE...
BUT IF HE ALREADY SENT RA TO THE GRAVEYARD...
THEN IT'S TOO LATE!!
IN THAT CASE...
I SUMMON THIS MONSTER!!
FWP

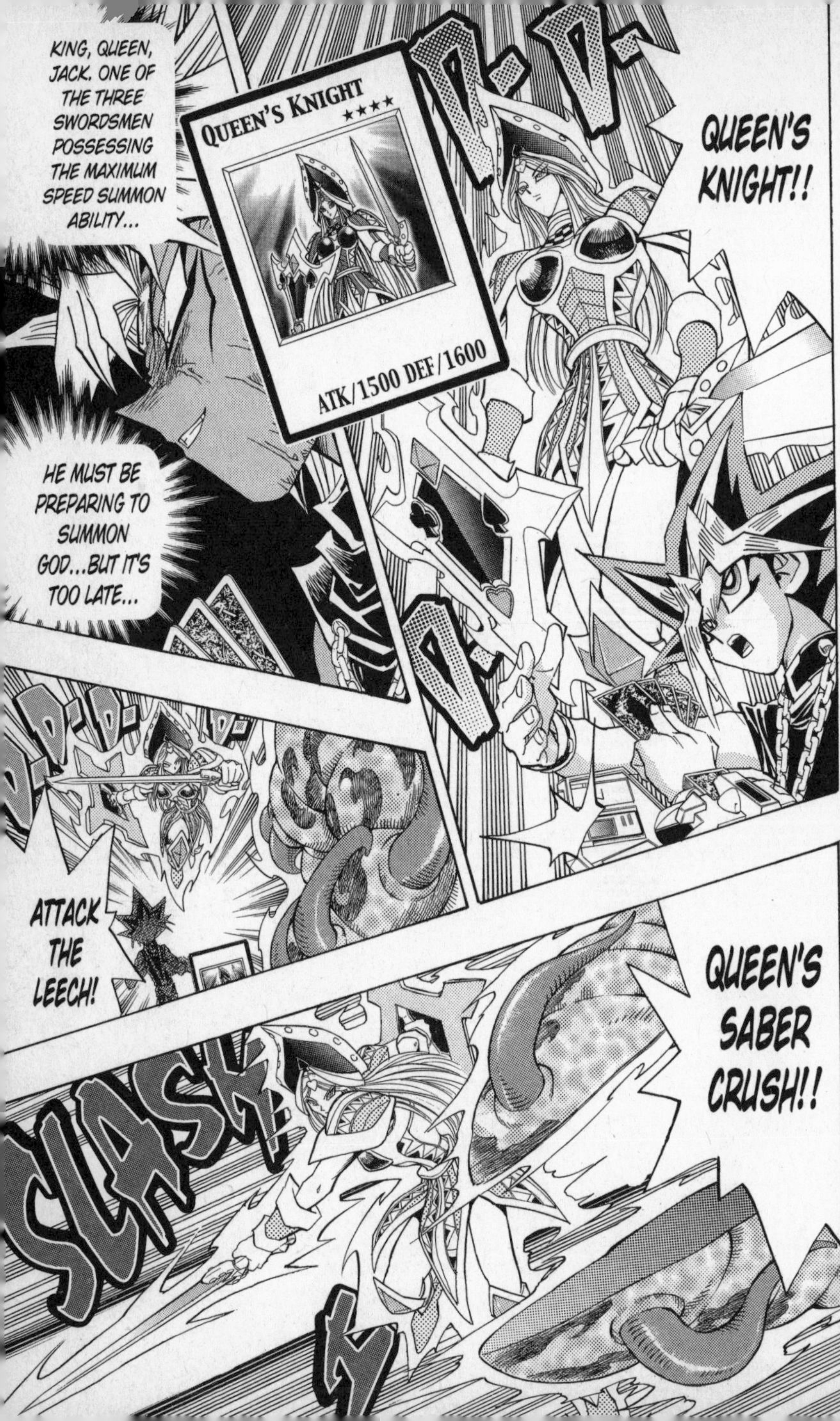
QUEEN'S KNIGHT!!
QUEEN'S KNIGHT ★★★★
ATK/1500 DEF/1600
KING, QUEEN, JACK. ONE OF THE THREE SWORDSMEN POSSESSING THE MAXIMUM SPEED SUMMON ABILITY...
HE MUST BE PREPARING TO SUMMON GOD...BUT IT'S TOO LATE...
ATTACK THE LEECH!
QUEEN'S SABER CRUSH!!
SLASH

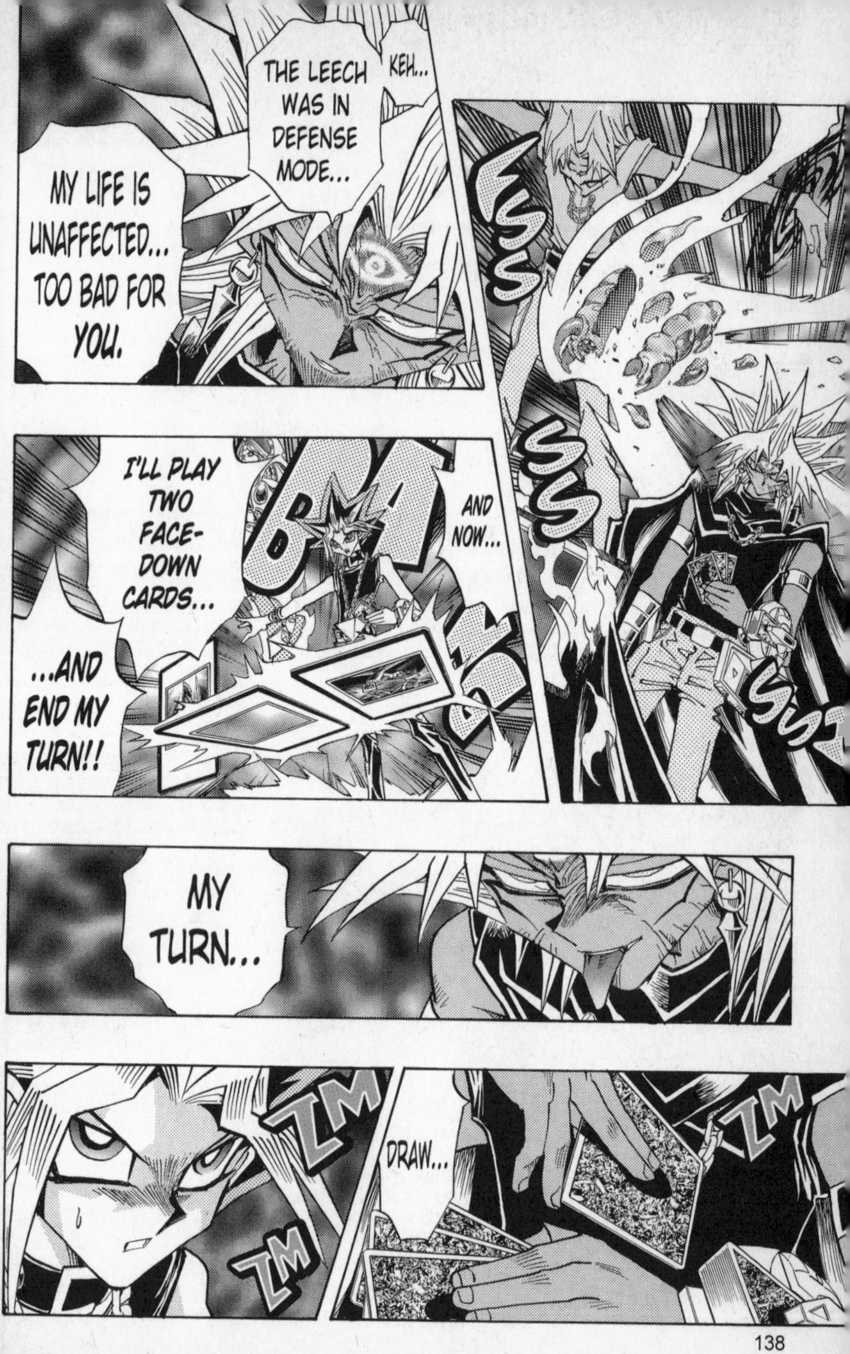
SSS
SSS
SSS
KEH...
THE LEECH WAS IN DEFENSE MODE...
MY LIFE IS UNAFFECTED... TOO BAD FOR YOU.
AND NOW...
I'LL PLAY TWO FACE-DOWN CARDS...
...AND END MY TURN!!
MY TURN...
ZM
DRAW...
ZM
ZM

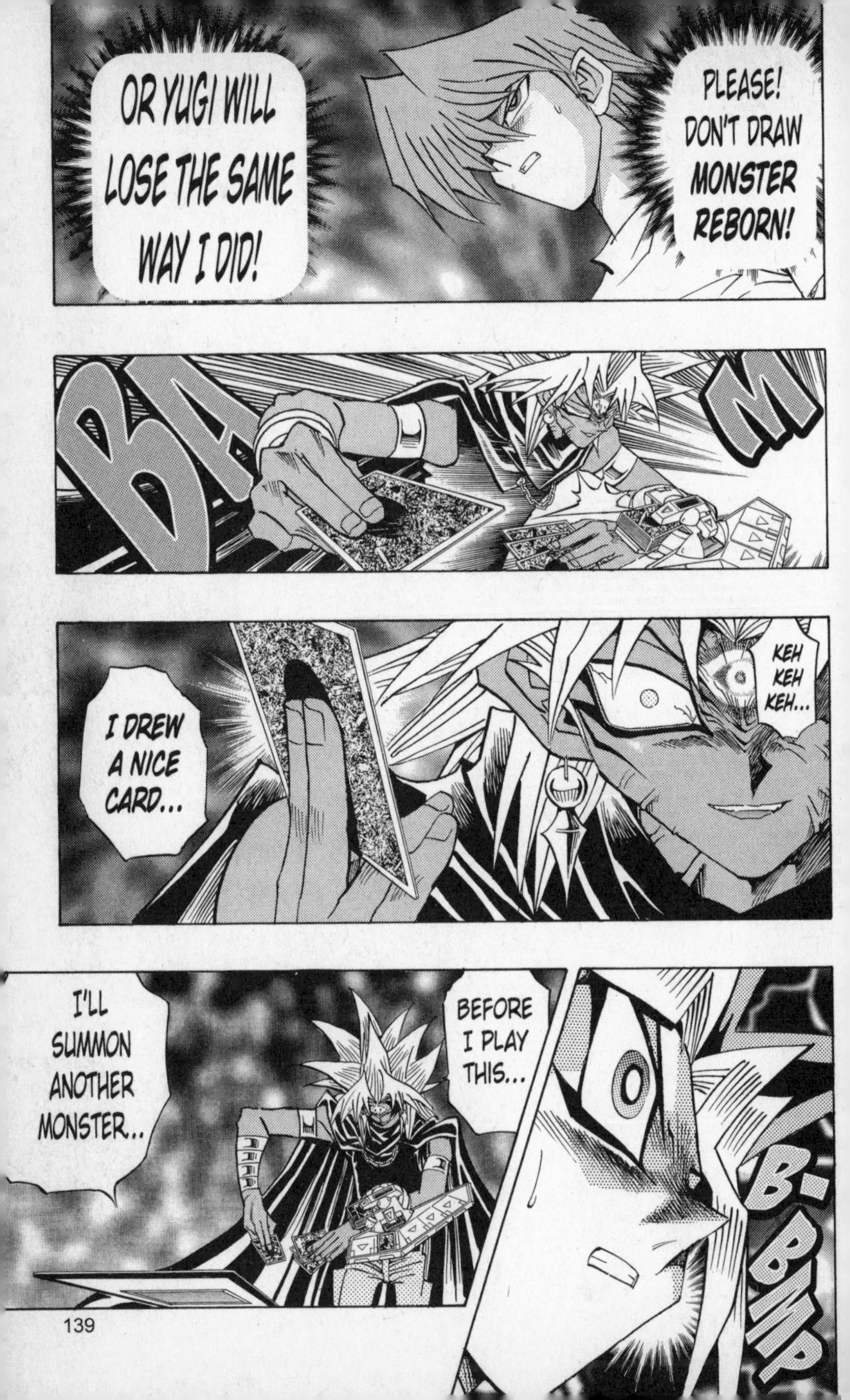
PLEASE! DON'T DRAW MONSTER REBORN!
OR YUGI WILL LOSE THE SAME WAY I DID!
BAM
KEH KEH KEH...
I DREW A NICE CARD...
B-BMP
BEFORE I PLAY THIS...
I'LL SUMMON ANOTHER MONSTER..

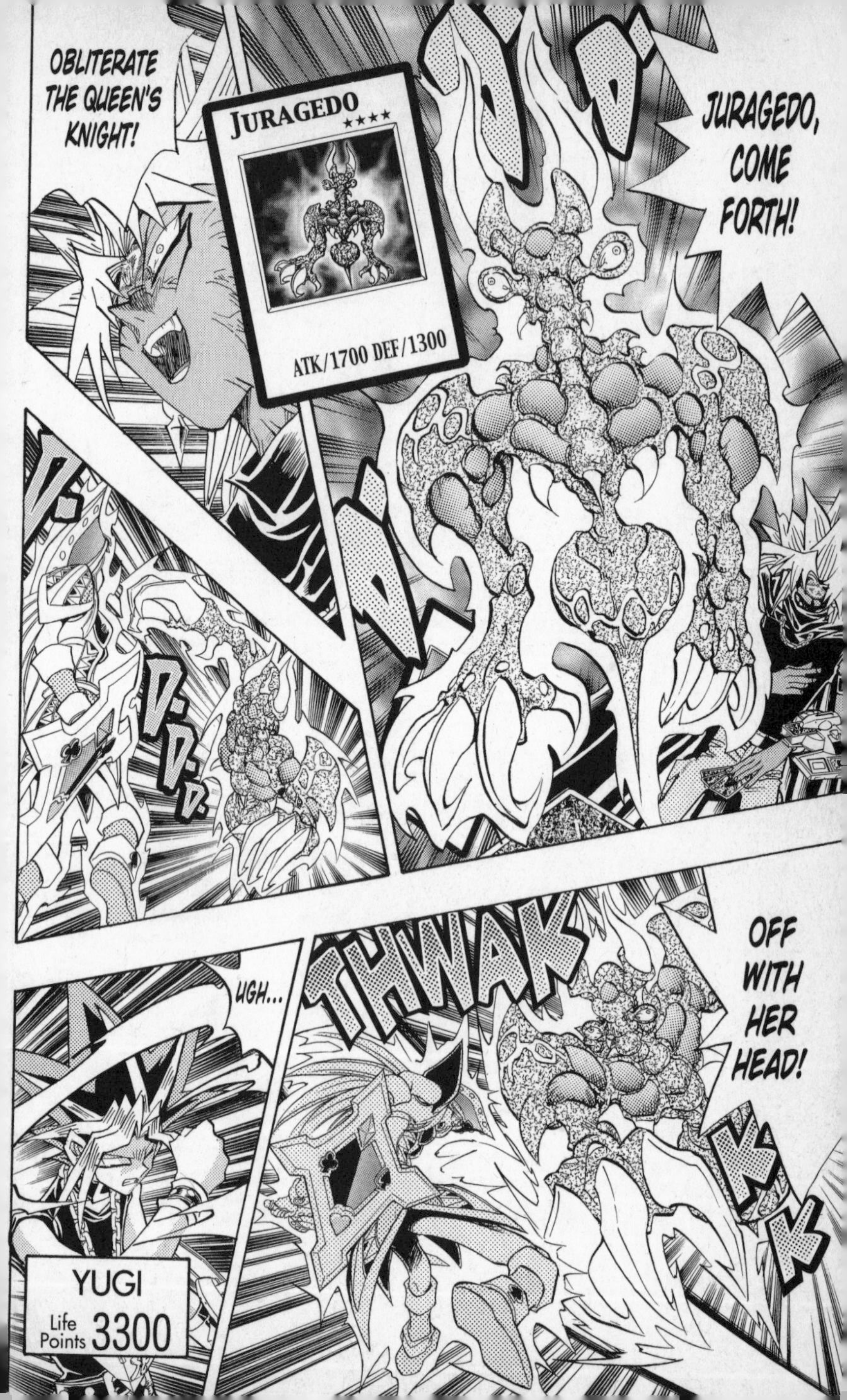
JURAGEDO, COME FORTH!
JURAGEDO
ATK/1700 DEF/1300
OBLITERATE THE QUEEN'S KNIGHT!
OFF WITH HER HEAD!
THWAK
UGH...
YUGI
Life Points 3300

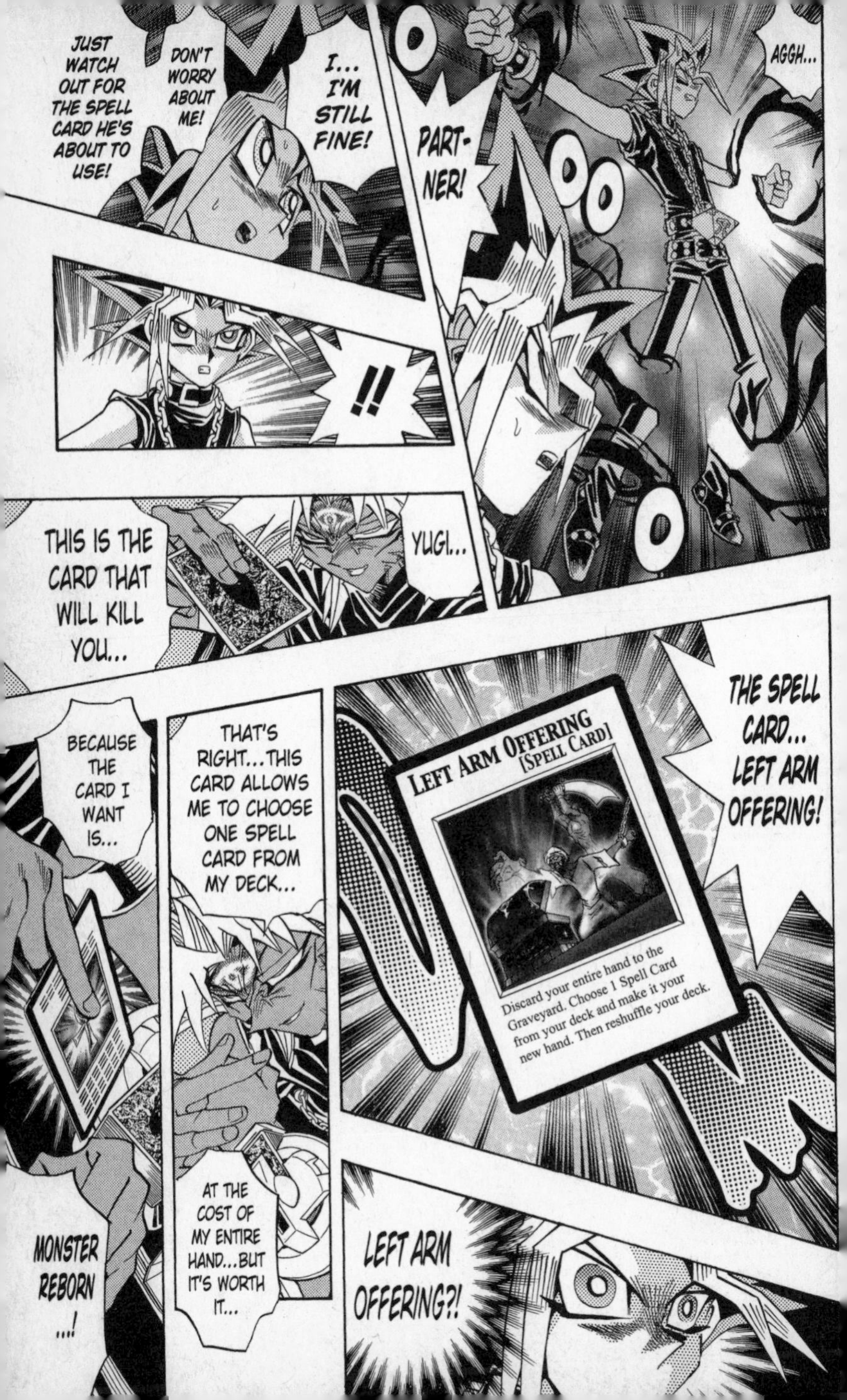
AGGH...
PART-NER!
I... I'M STILL FINE!
DON'T WORRY ABOUT ME!
JUST WATCH OUT FOR THE SPELL CARD HE'S ABOUT TO USE!
!!
YUGI...
THIS IS THE CARD THAT WILL KILL YOU...
THE SPELL CARD... LEFT ARM OFFERING!
LEFT ARM OFFERING
[SPELL CARD]
Discard your entire hand to the Graveyard. Choose 1 Spell Card from your deck and make it your new hand. Then reshuffle your deck.
LEFT ARM OFFERING?!
THAT'S RIGHT... THIS CARD ALLOWS ME TO CHOOSE ONE SPELL CARD FROM MY DECK...
AT THE COST OF MY ENTIRE HAND... BUT IT'S WORTH IT...
BECAUSE THE CARD I WANT IS...
MONSTER REBORN ...!

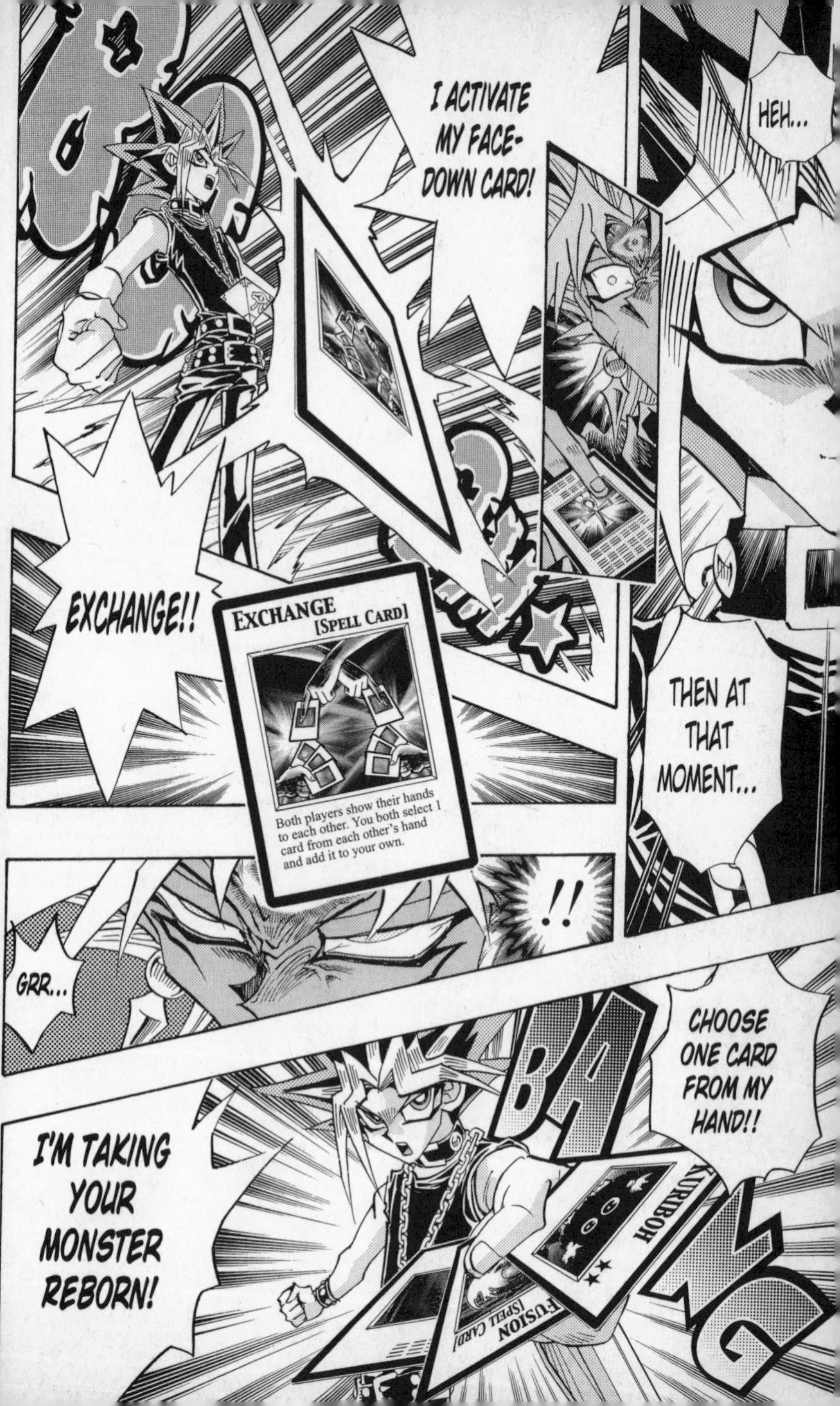
HEH...
THEN AT THAT MOMENT...
I ACTIVATE MY FACE-DOWN CARD!
EXCHANGE!!
EXCHANGE
[SPELL CARD]
Both players show their hands to each other. You both select 1 card from each other's hand and add it to your own.
!!
GRR...
CHOOSE ONE CARD FROM MY HAND!!
BA
I'M TAKING YOUR MONSTER REBORN!
KURIBOH
FUSION
[SPELL CARD]

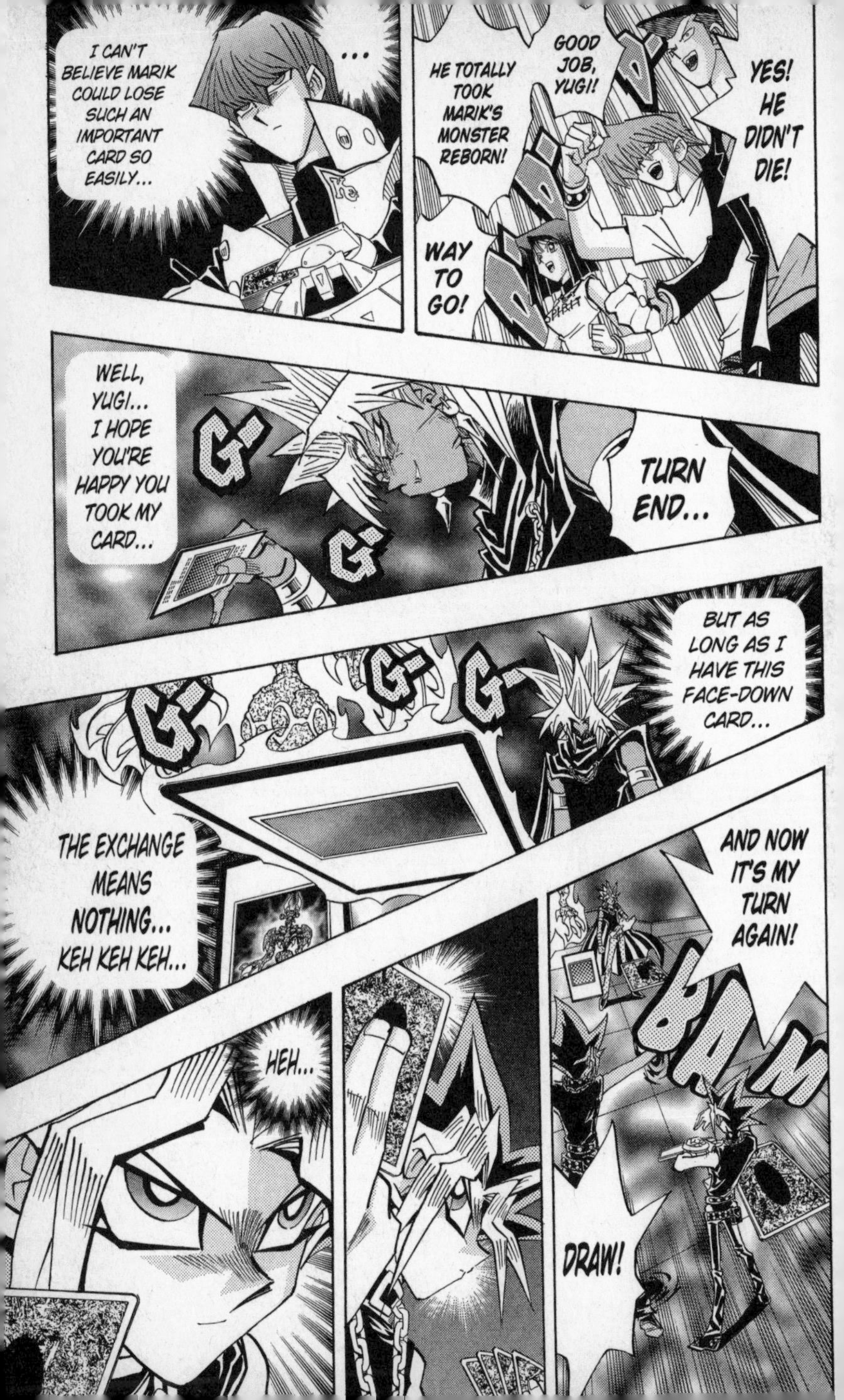
YES! HE DIDN'T DIE!
GOOD JOB, YUGI!
HE TOTALLY TOOK MARIK'S MONSTER REBORN!
WAY TO GO!
...
I CAN'T BELIEVE MARIK COULD LOSE SUCH AN IMPORTANT CARD SO EASILY...
WELL, YUGI... I HOPE YOU'RE HAPPY YOU TOOK MY CARD...
G
G
TURN END...
BUT AS LONG AS I HAVE THIS FACE-DOWN CARD...
G-
G-
G
THE EXCHANGE MEANS NOTHING... KEH KEH KEH...
AND NOW IT'S MY TURN AGAIN!
BAM
DRAW!
HEH...

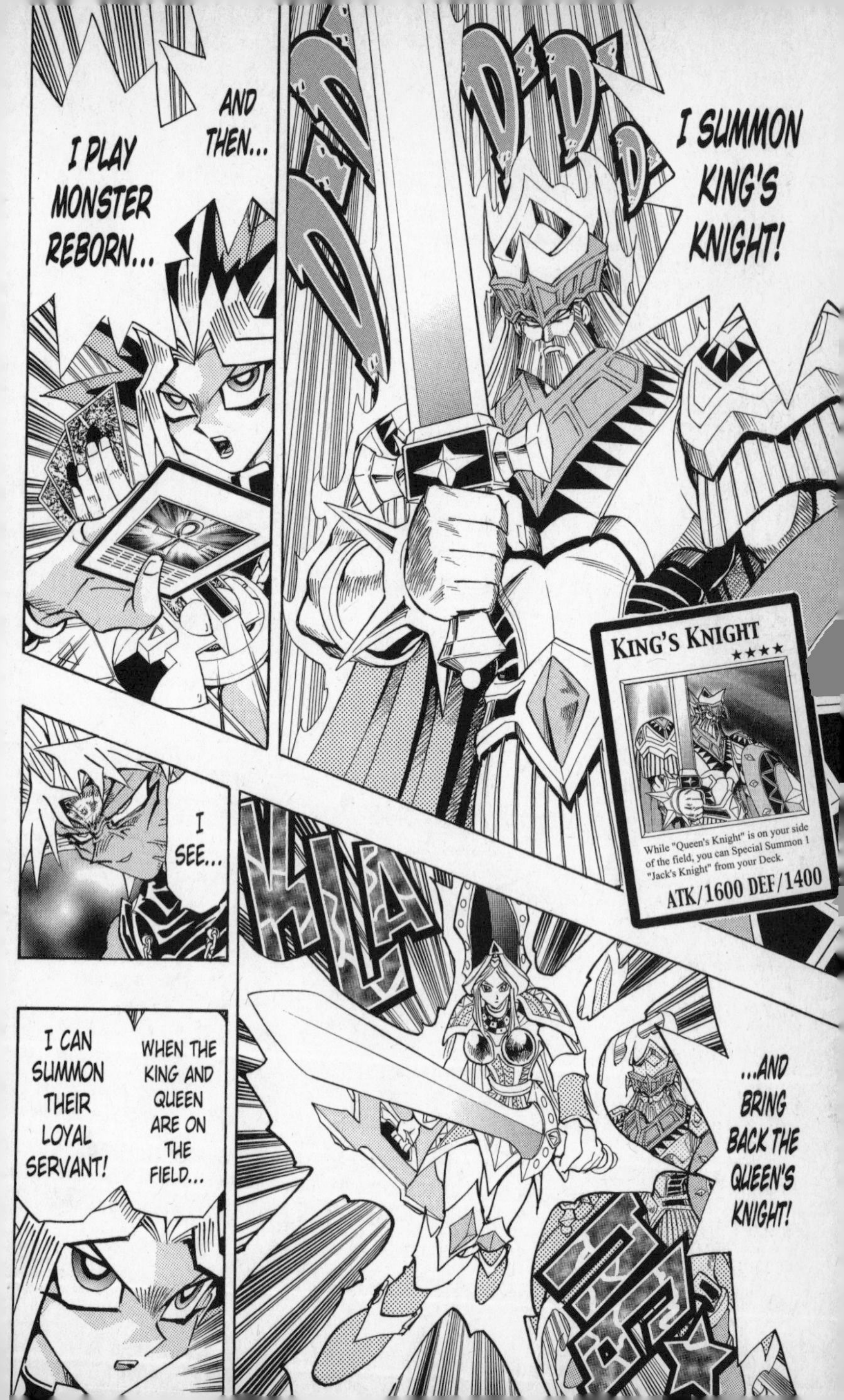
I SUMMON KING'S KNIGHT!
KING'S KNIGHT
★★★★
While "Queen's Knight" is on your side of the field, you can Special Summon 1 "Jack's Knight" from your Deck.
ATK/1600 DEF/1400
AND THEN...
I PLAY MONSTER REBORN...
WHA
I SEE...
...AND BRING BACK THE QUEEN'S KNIGHT!
WHEN THE KING AND QUEEN ARE ON THE FIELD...
I CAN SUMMON THEIR LOYAL SERVANT!

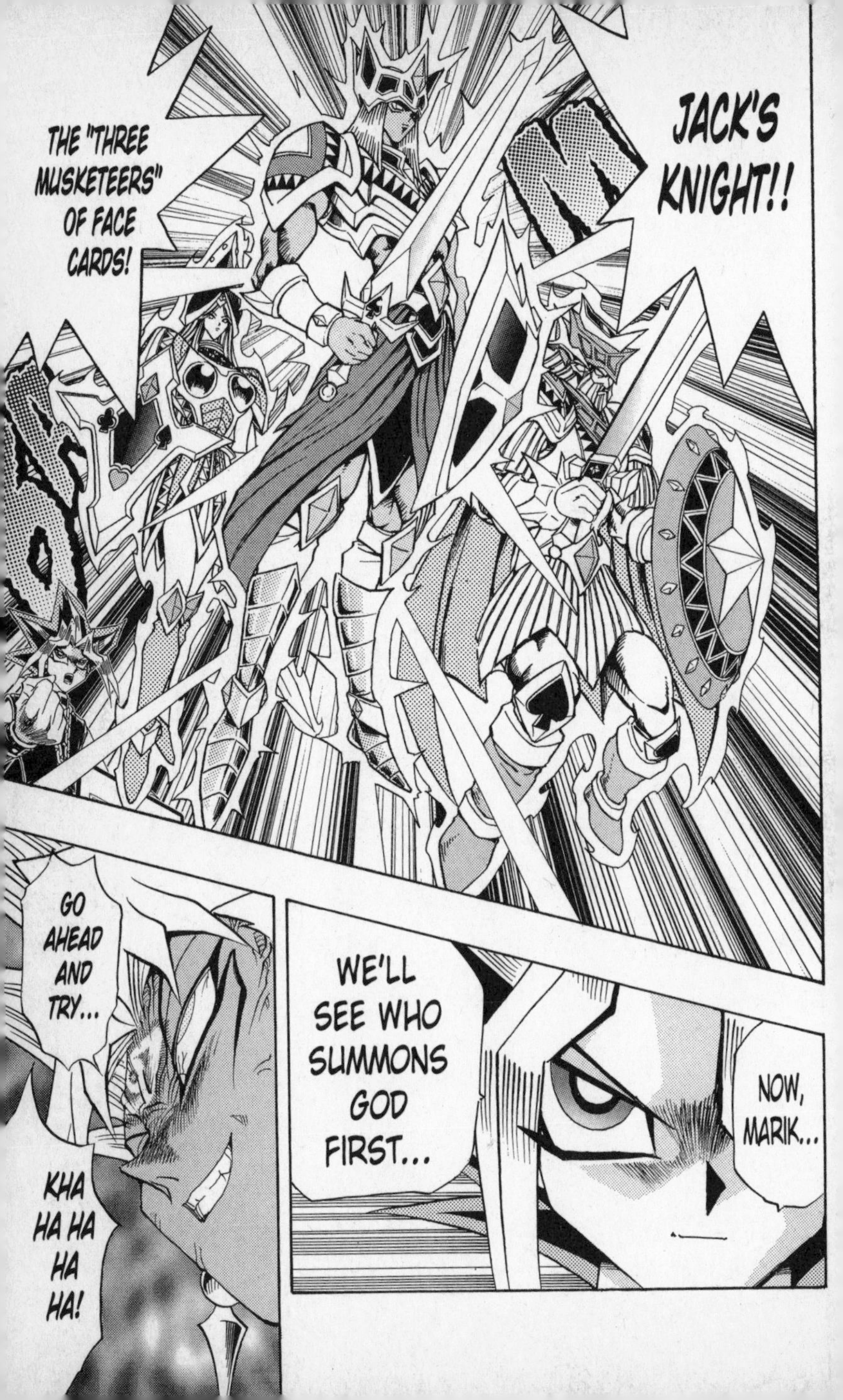
JACK'S KNIGHT!!
THE "THREE MUSKETEERS" OF FACE CARDS!
NOW, MARIK...
WE'LL SEE WHO SUMMONS GOD FIRST...
GO AHEAD AND TRY...
KHA HA HA HA HA HA!

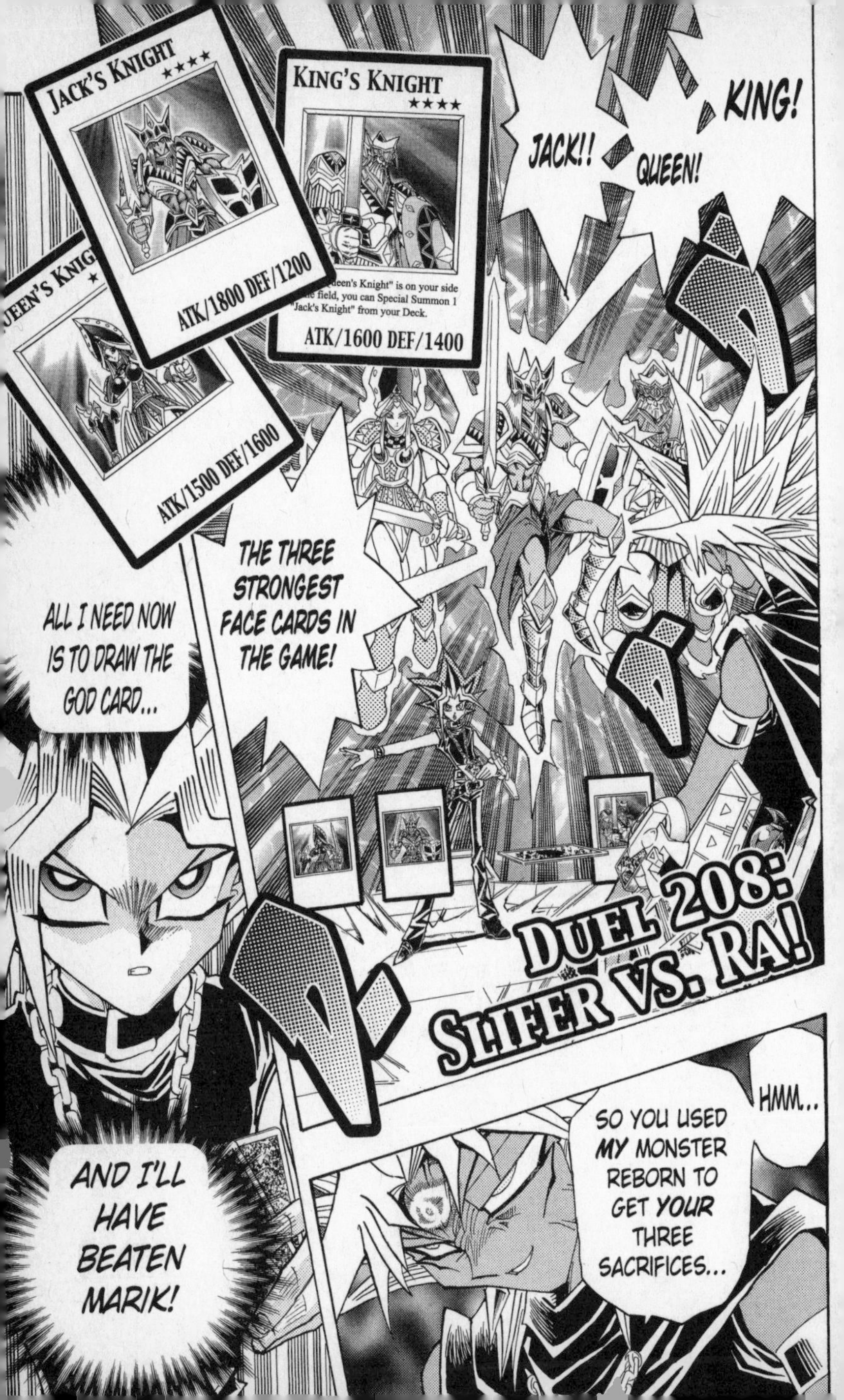
KING!
QUEEN!
JACK!!
KING'S KNIGHT
★★★★
"Queen's Knight" is on your side of the field, you can Special Summon 1 "Jack's Knight" from your Deck.
ATK/1600 DEF/1400
JACK'S KNIGHT
★★★★
ATK/1800 DEF/1200
QUEEN'S KNIGHT
★
ATK/1500 DEF/1600
THE THREE STRONGEST FACE CARDS IN THE GAME!
DUEL 208: SLIFER VS. RA!
ALL I NEED NOW IS TO DRAW THE GOD CARD...
AND I'LL HAVE BEATEN MARIK!
HMM...
SO YOU USED MY MONSTER REBORN TO GET YOUR THREE SACRIFICES...

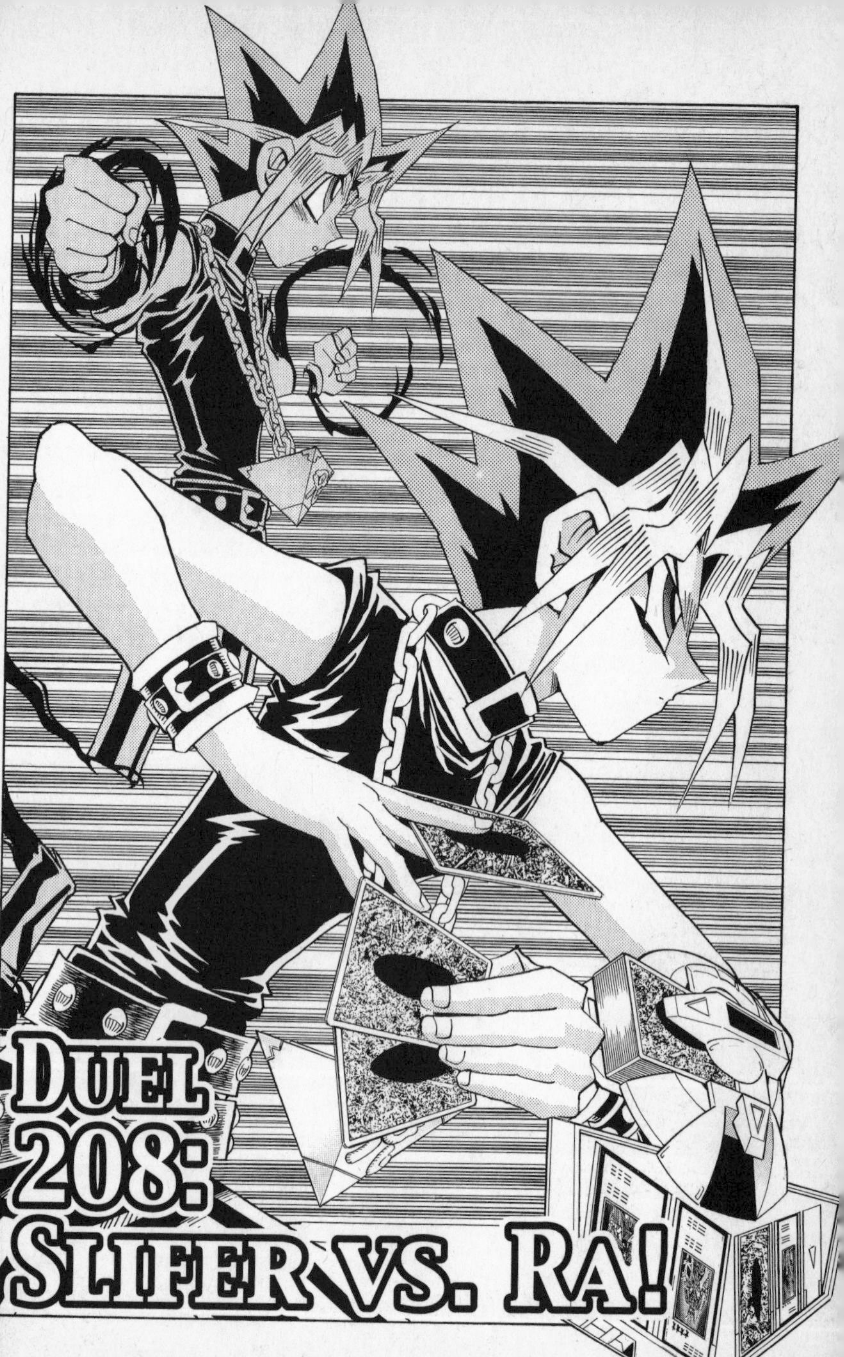
Duel 208:
Slifer vs. Ra!

READ THIS WAY

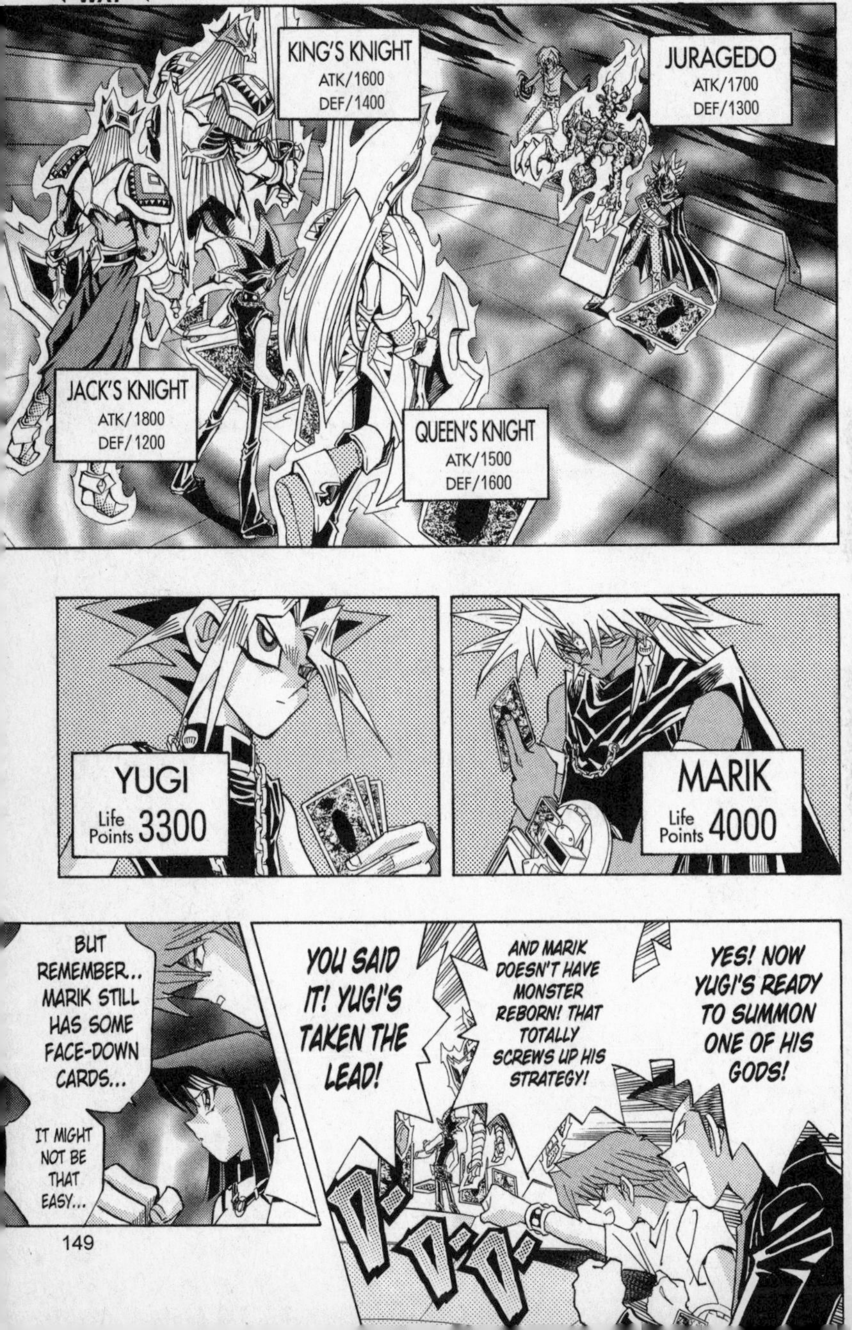

JURAGEDO
ATK/1700
DEF/1300
KING'S KNIGHT
ATK/1600
DEF/1400
QUEEN'S KNIGHT
ATK/1500
DEF/1600
JACK'S KNIGHT
ATK/1800
DEF/1200
MARIK
Life Points 4000
YUGI
Life Points 3300
YES! NOW YUGI'S READY TO SUMMON ONE OF HIS GODS!
AND MARIK DOESN'T HAVE MONSTER REBORN! THAT TOTALLY SCREWS UP HIS STRATEGY!
YOU SAID IT! YUGI'S TAKEN THE LEAD!
BUT REMEMBER... MARIK STILL HAS SOME FACE-DOWN CARDS...
IT MIGHT NOT BE THAT EASY...

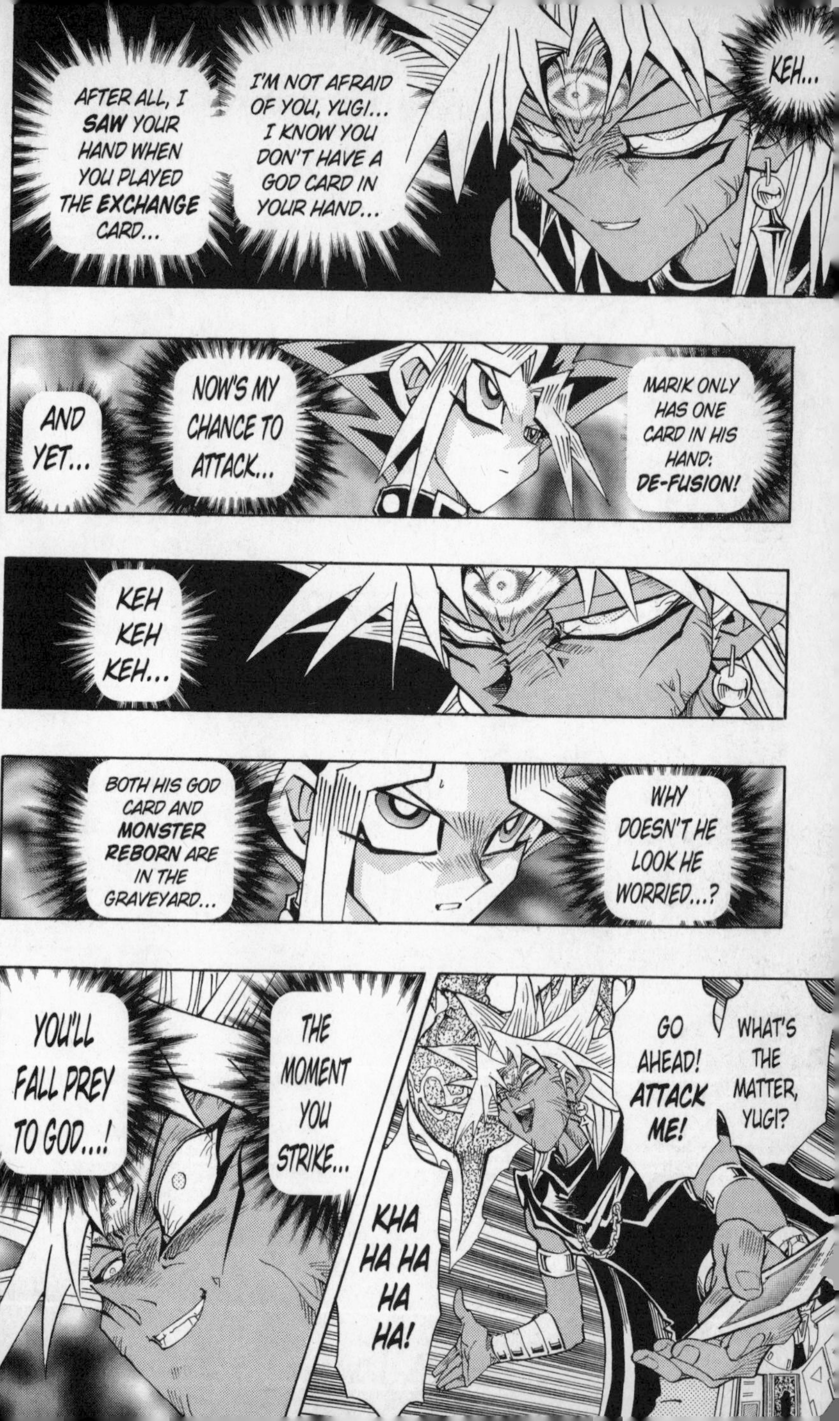
KEH...
I'M NOT AFRAID OF YOU, YUGI... I KNOW YOU DON'T HAVE A GOD CARD IN YOUR HAND...
AFTER ALL, I SAW YOUR HAND WHEN YOU PLAYED THE EXCHANGE CARD...
MARIK ONLY HAS ONE CARD IN HIS HAND: DE-FUSION!
NOW'S MY CHANCE TO ATTACK...
AND YET...
KEH KEH KEH...
WHY DOESN'T HE LOOK HE WORRIED...?
BOTH HIS GOD CARD AND MONSTER REBORN ARE IN THE GRAVEYARD...
WHAT'S THE MATTER, YUGI?
GO AHEAD! ATTACK ME!
KHA HA HA HA HA!
THE MOMENT YOU STRIKE...
YOU'LL FALL PREY TO GOD...!

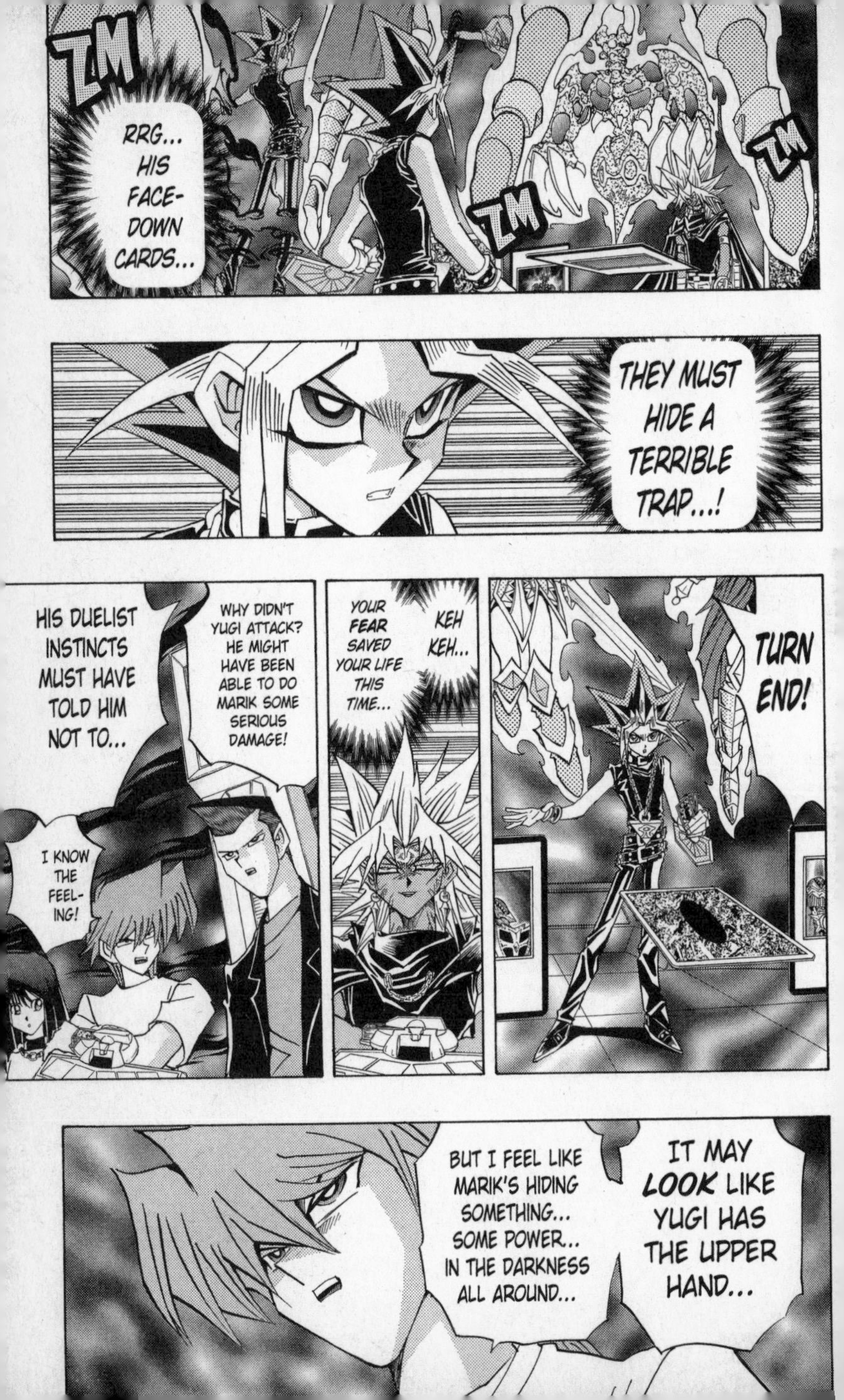
ZM
ZM
RRG... HIS FACE-DOWN CARDS...
ZM
THEY MUST HIDE A TERRIBLE TRAP...!
TURN END!
KEH KEH...
YOUR FEAR SAVED YOUR LIFE THIS TIME...
WHY DIDN'T YUGI ATTACK? HE MIGHT HAVE BEEN ABLE TO DO MARIK SOME SERIOUS DAMAGE!
HIS DUELIST INSTINCTS MUST HAVE TOLD HIM NOT TO...
I KNOW THE FEEL-ING!
IT MAY LOOK LIKE YUGI HAS THE UPPER HAND...
BUT I FEEL LIKE MARIK'S HIDING SOMETHING... SOME POWER... IN THE DARKNESS ALL AROUND...

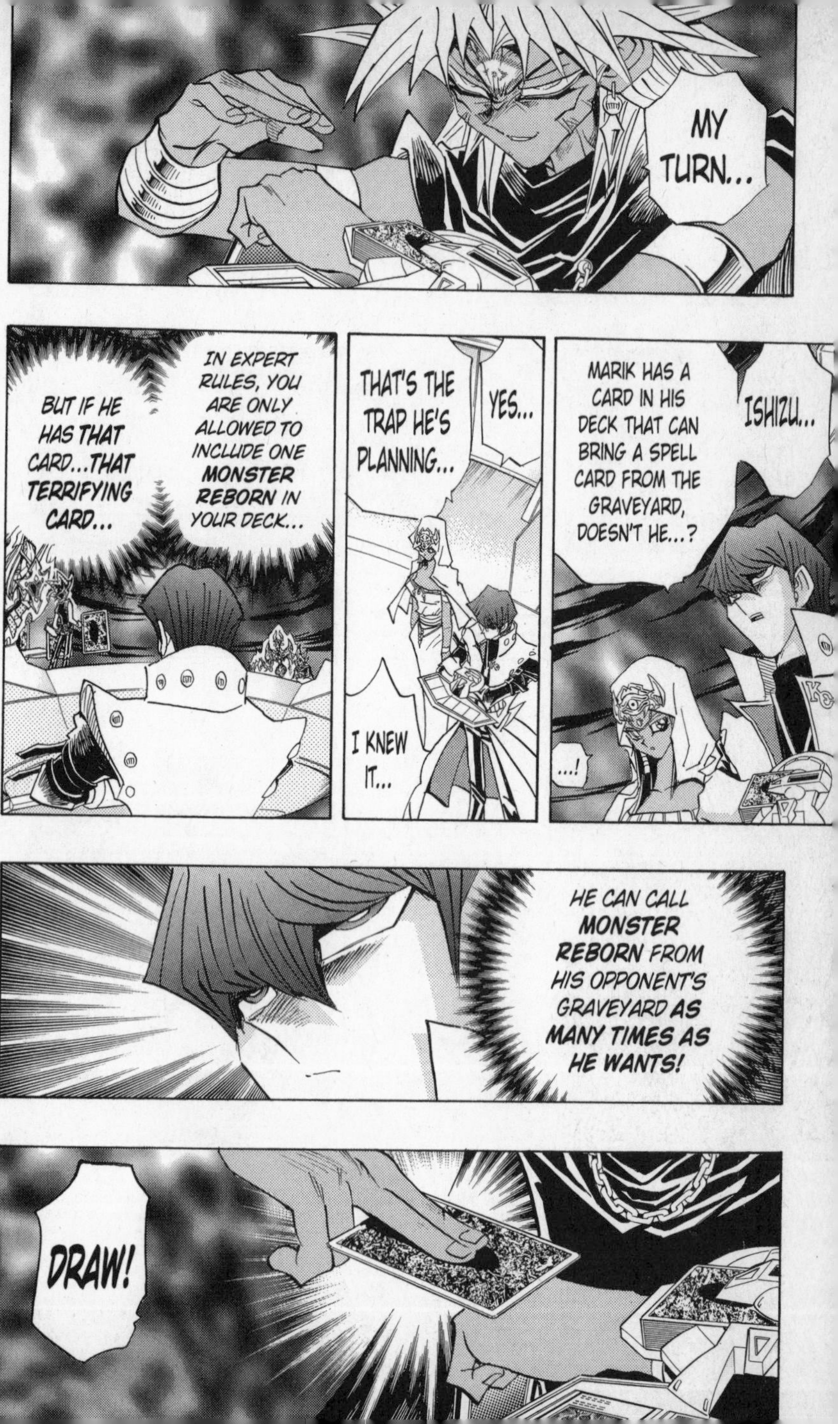
MY TURN...
ISHIZU...
MARIK HAS A CARD IN HIS DECK THAT CAN BRING A SPELL CARD FROM THE GRAVEYARD, DOESN'T HE...?
...!
YES...
THAT'S THE TRAP HE'S PLANNING...
I KNEW IT...
IN EXPERT RULES, YOU ARE ONLY ALLOWED TO INCLUDE ONE MONSTER REBORN IN YOUR DECK...
BUT IF HE HAS THAT CARD...THAT TERRIFYING CARD...
HE CAN CALL MONSTER REBORN FROM HIS OPPONENT'S GRAVEYARD AS MANY TIMES AS HE WANTS!
DRAW!

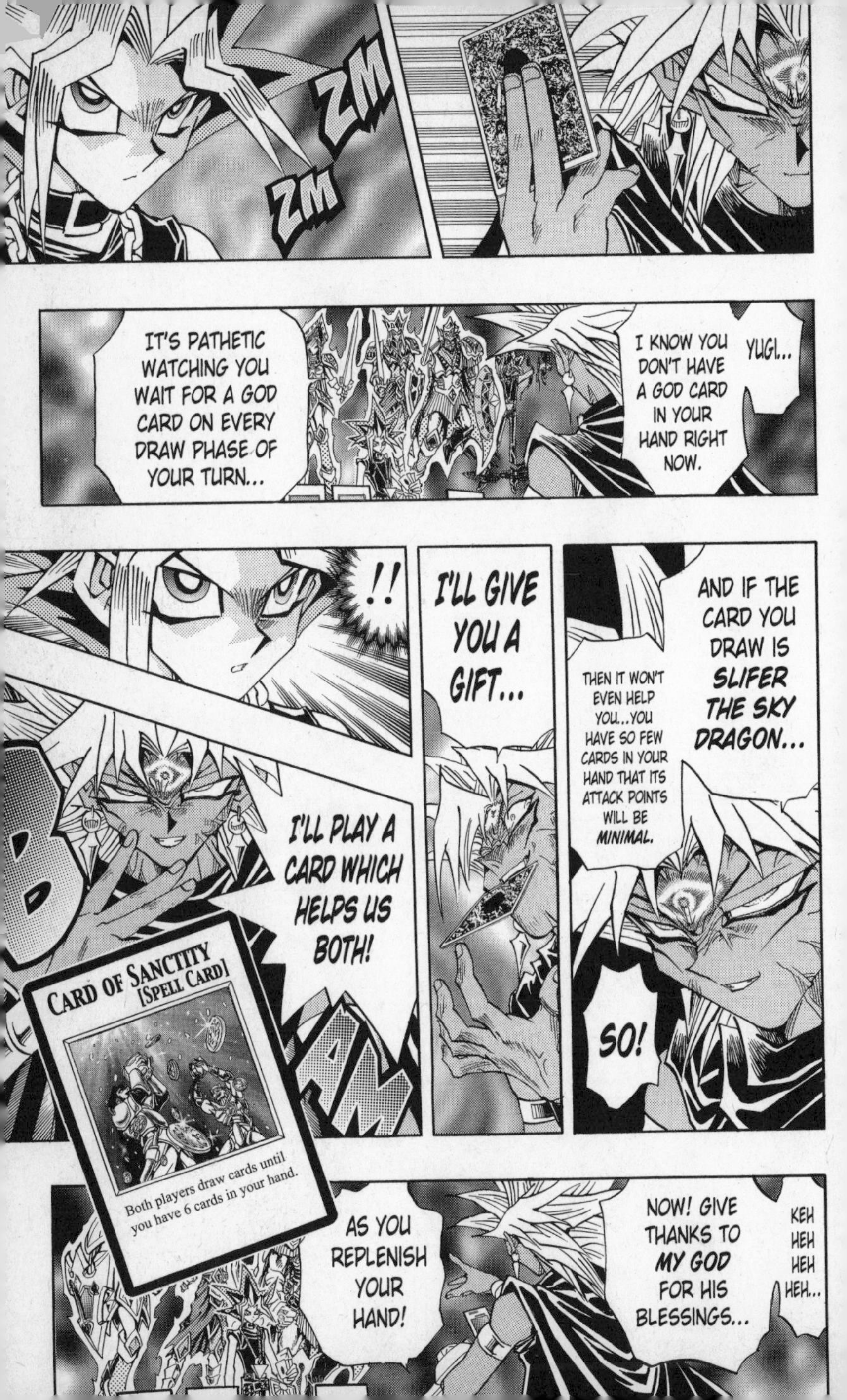
ZM
ZM
YUGI...
I KNOW YOU DON'T HAVE A GOD CARD IN YOUR HAND RIGHT NOW.
IT'S PATHETIC WATCHING YOU WAIT FOR A GOD CARD ON EVERY DRAW PHASE OF YOUR TURN...
AND IF THE CARD YOU DRAW IS SLIFER THE SKY DRAGON...
THEN IT WON'T EVEN HELP YOU...YOU HAVE SO FEW CARDS IN YOUR HAND THAT ITS ATTACK POINTS WILL BE MINIMAL.
SO!
I'LL GIVE YOU A GIFT...
!!
I'LL PLAY A CARD WHICH HELPS US BOTH!
CARD OF SANCTITY
[SPELL CARD]
Both players draw cards until you have 6 cards in your hand.
KEH HEH HEH HEH...
NOW! GIVE THANKS TO MY GOD FOR HIS BLESSINGS...
AS YOU REPLENISH YOUR HAND!

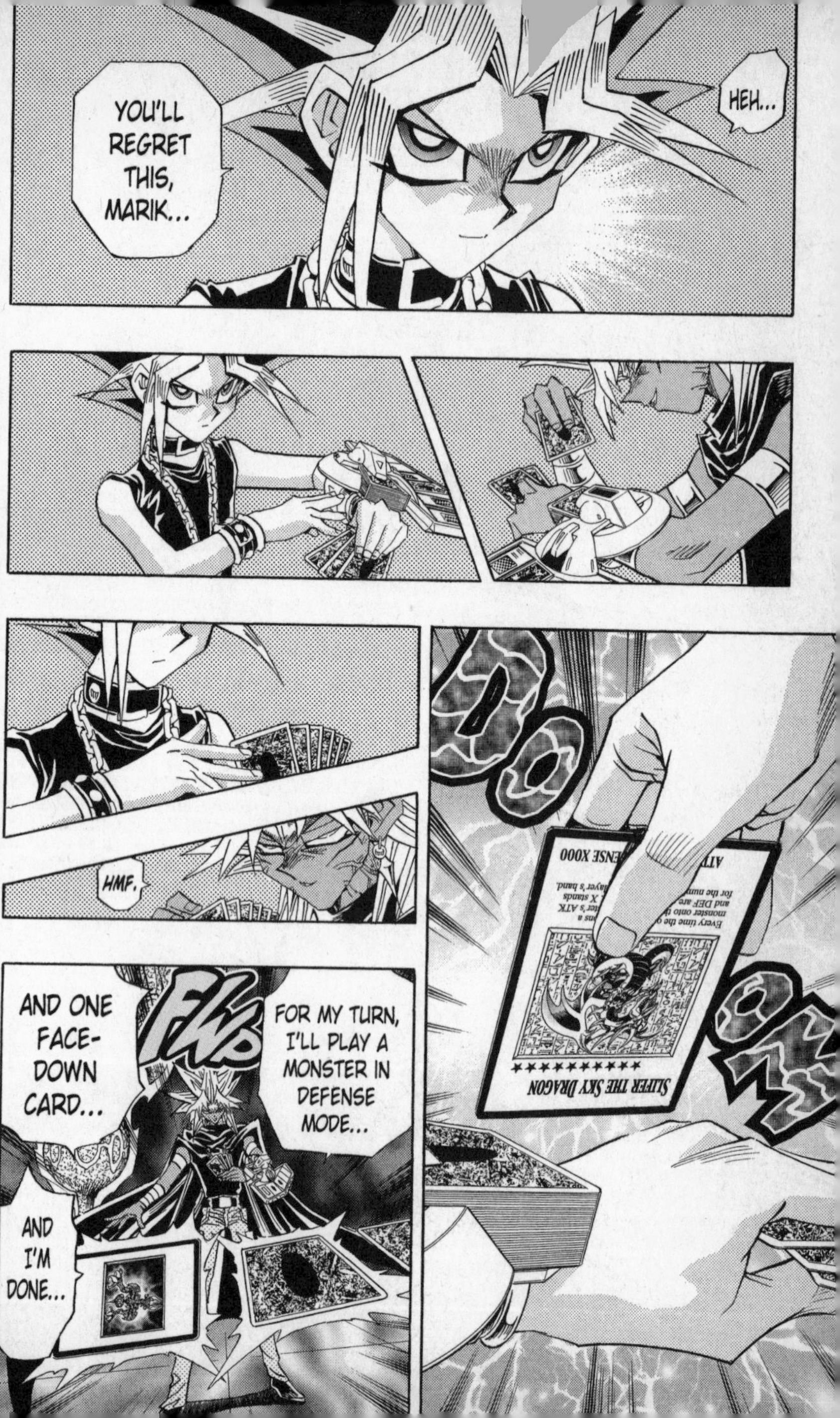
HEH...
YOU'LL REGRET THIS, MARIK...
SLIFER THE SKY DRAGON
HMF.
FWP
FOR MY TURN, I'LL PLAY A MONSTER IN DEFENSE MODE...
AND ONE FACE-DOWN CARD...
AND I'M DONE...

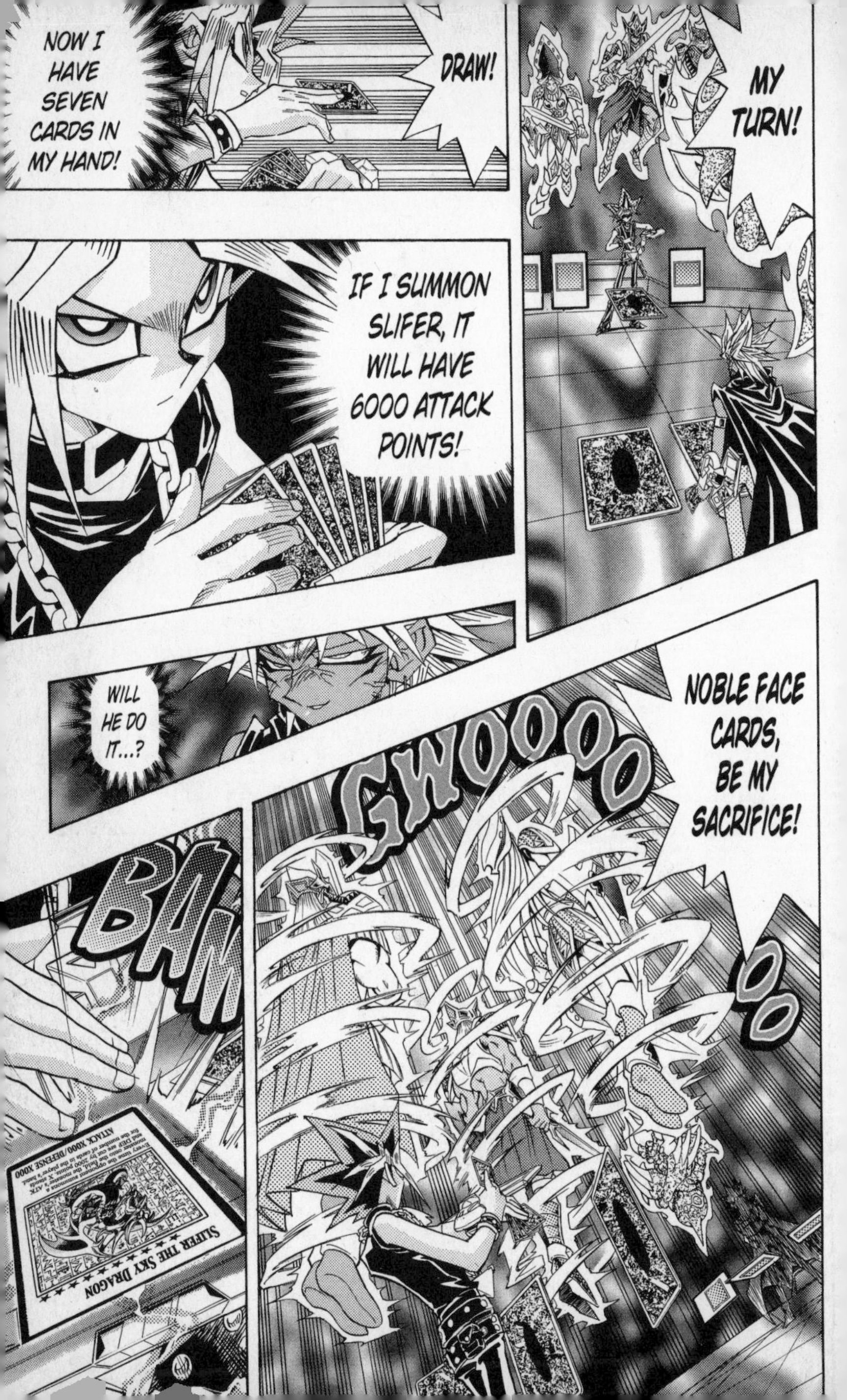
MY TURN!
DRAW!
NOW I HAVE SEVEN CARDS IN MY HAND!
IF I SUMMON SLIFER, IT WILL HAVE 6000 ATTACK POINTS!
NOBLE FACE CARDS, BE MY SACRIFICE!
GWOOOOOO
WILL HE DO IT...?
BAM
SLIFER THE SKY DRAGON
ATTACK X000/DEFENSE X000

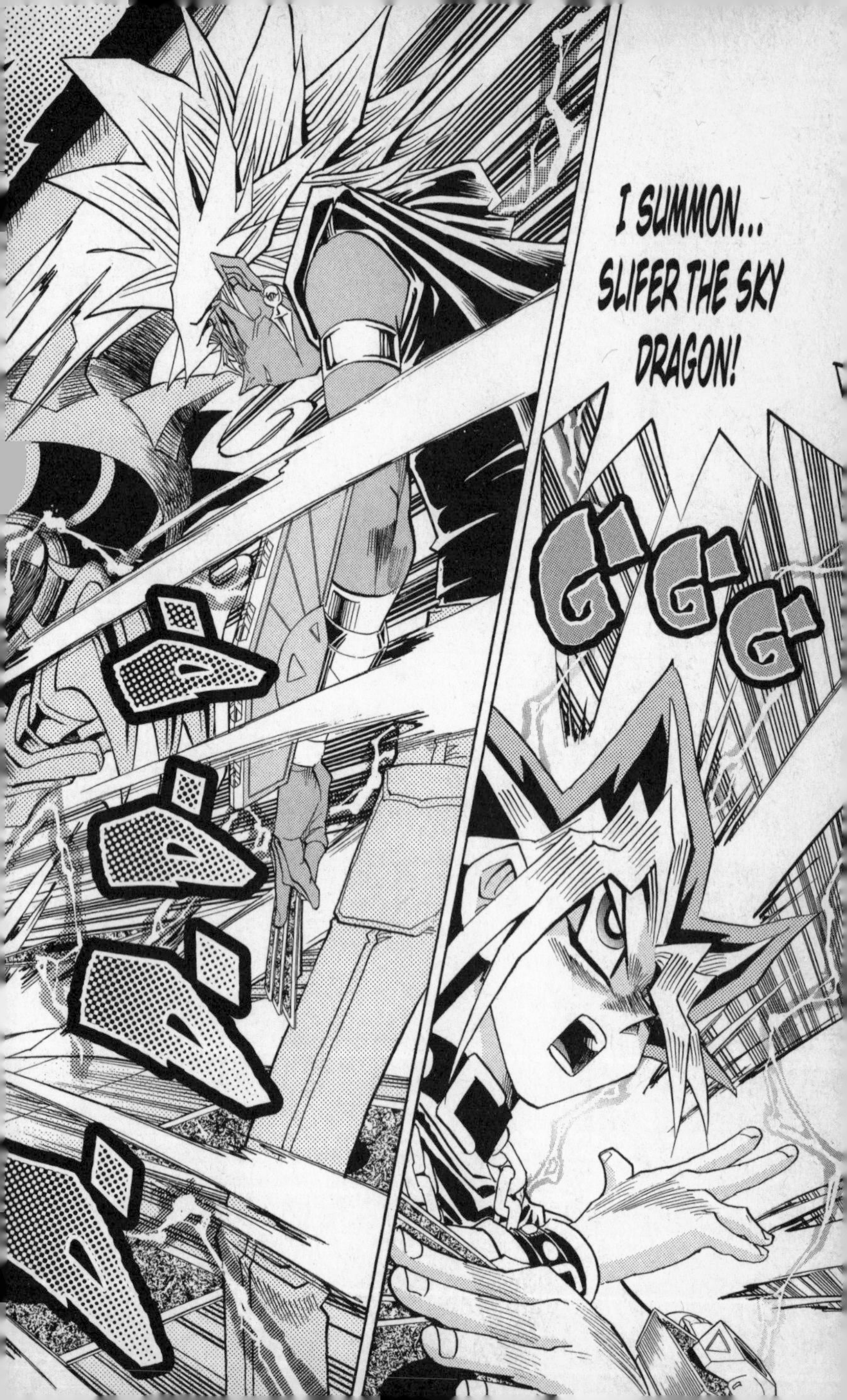
I SUMMON... SLIFER THE SKY DRAGON!
G'G'G'

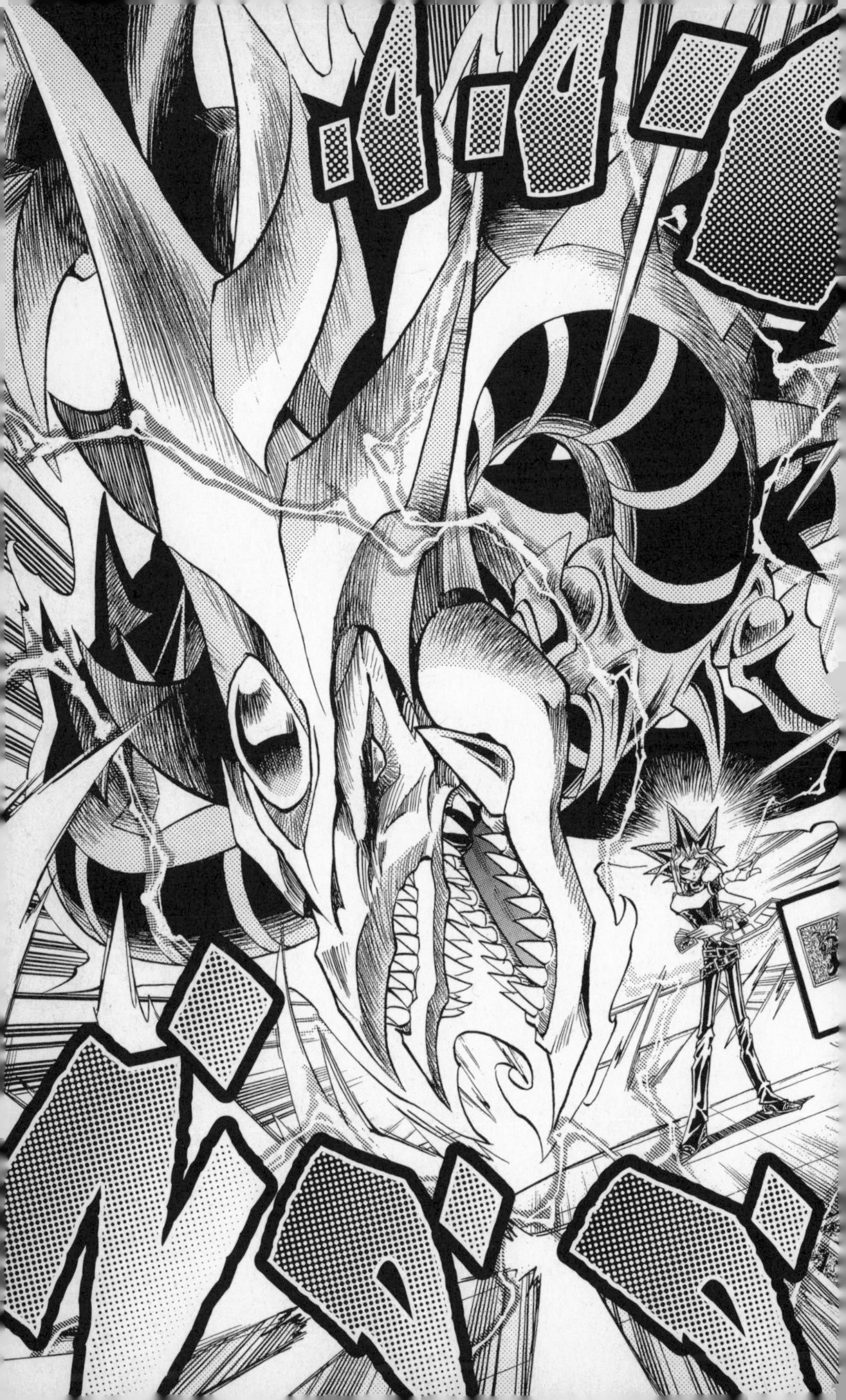

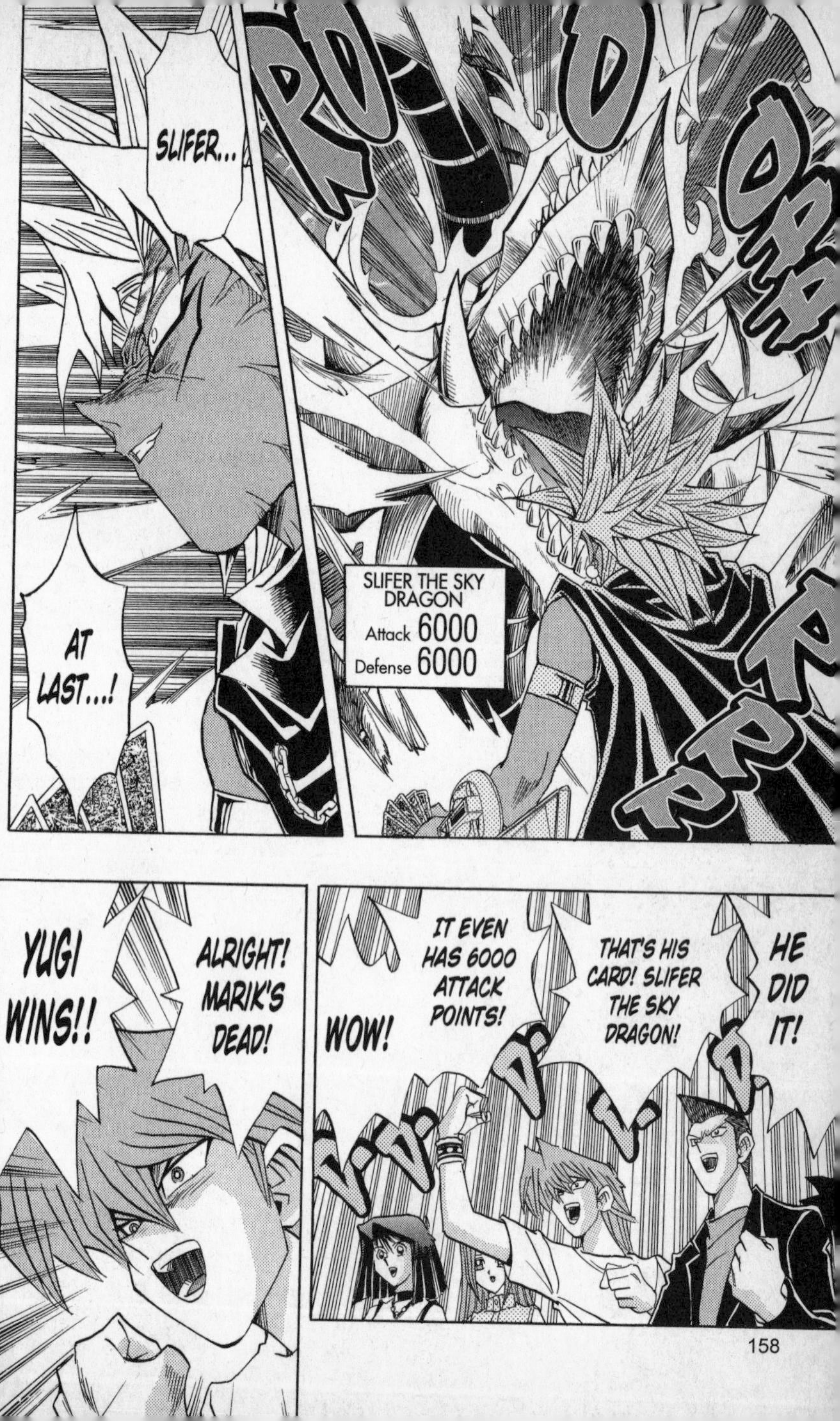
SLIFER THE SKY DRAGON
Attack 6000
Defense 6000
SLIFER...
AT LAST...!
HE DID IT!
THAT'S HIS CARD! SLIFER THE SKY DRAGON!
IT EVEN HAS 6000 ATTACK POINTS!
WOW!
ALRIGHT! MARIK'S DEAD!
YUGI WINS!!

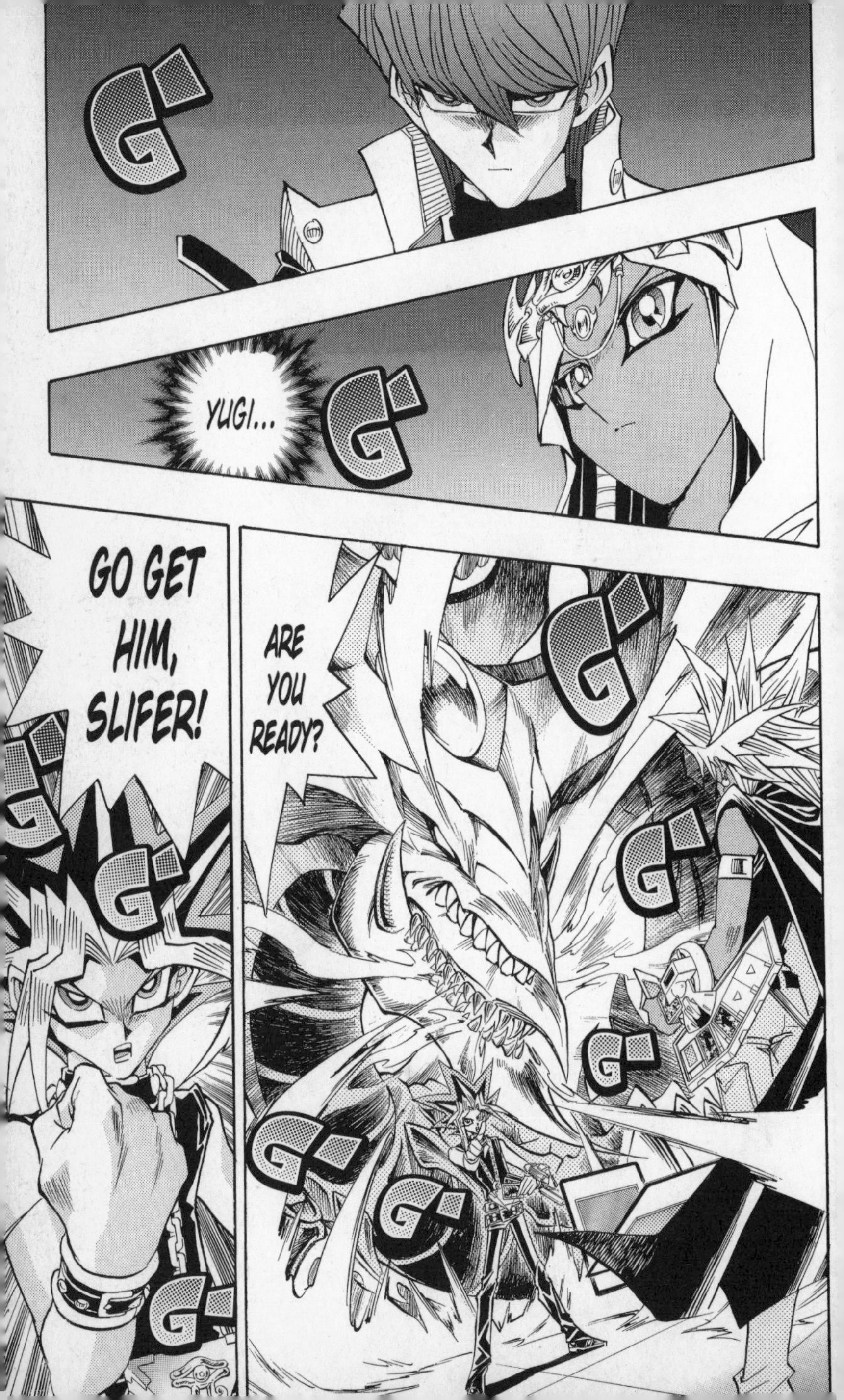
G
G
YUGI...
G
ARE YOU READY?
G
G
G
G
G
GO GET HIM, SLIFER!
G
G
G
G

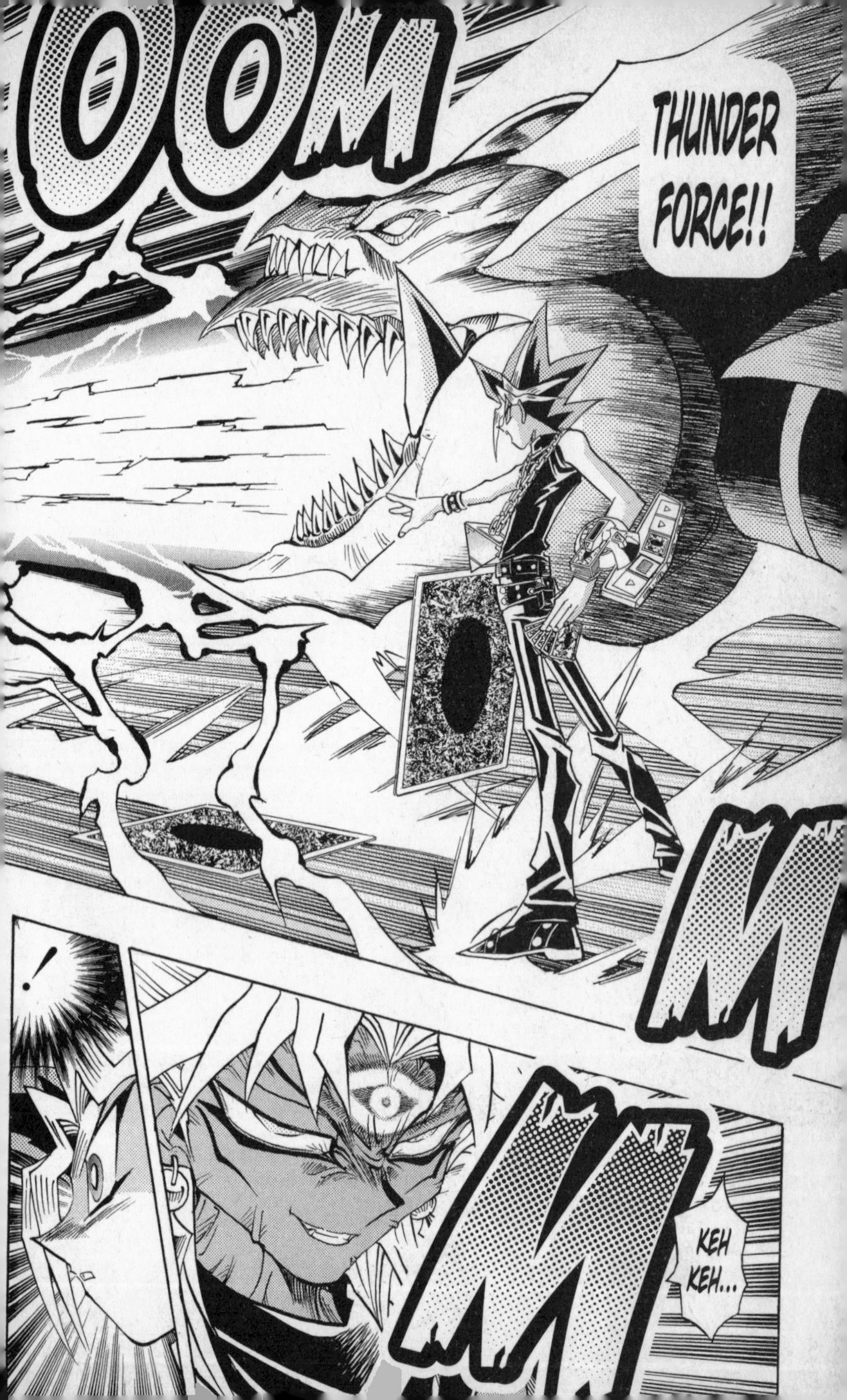
OOM
THUNDER FORCE!!
M
M
KEH KEH...
!

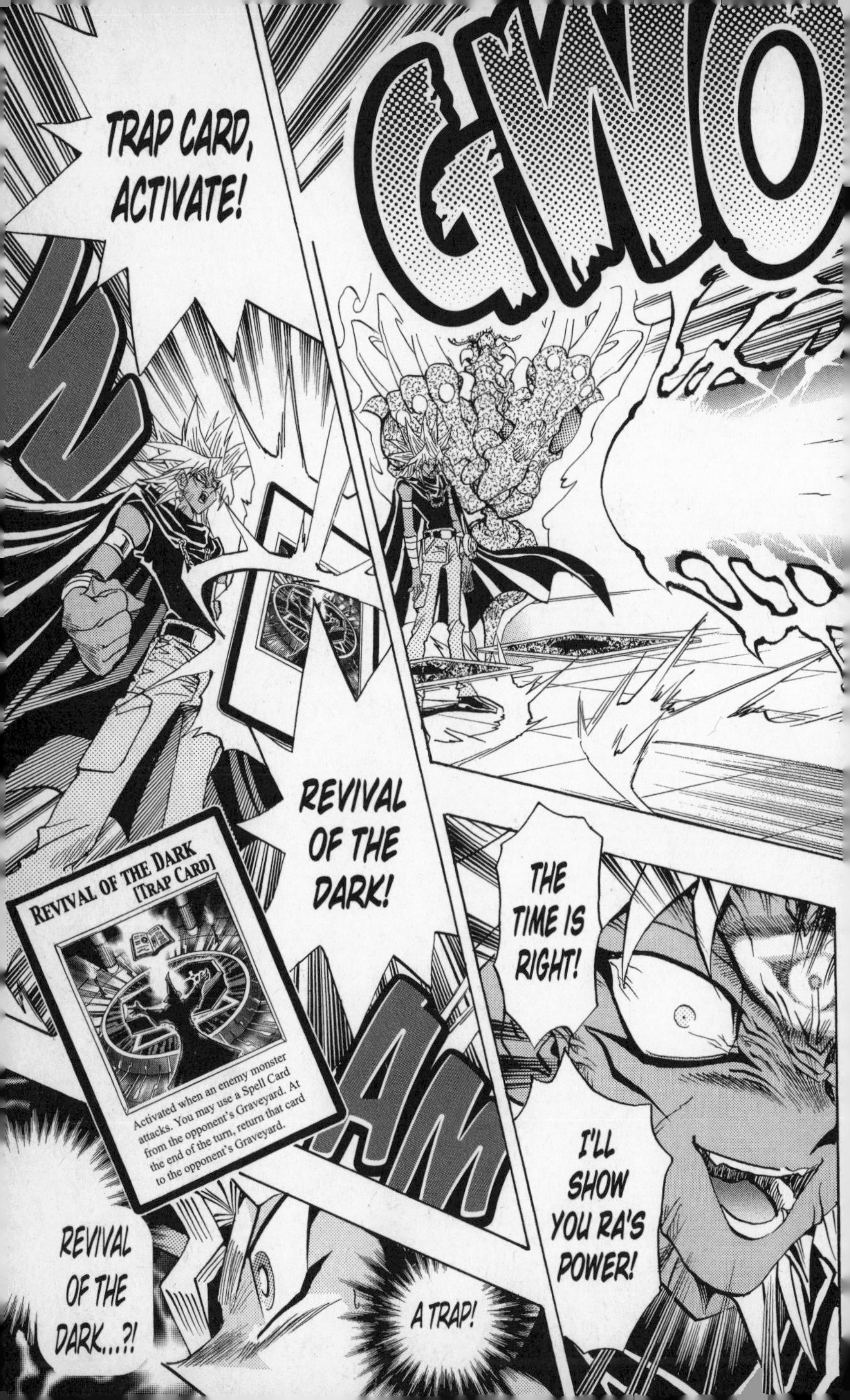
GWO
TRAP CARD, ACTIVATE!
REVIVAL OF THE DARK!
REVIVAL OF THE DARK [TRAP CARD]
Activated when an enemy monster attacks. You may use a Spell Card from the opponent's Graveyard. At the end of the turn, return that card to the opponent's Graveyard.
THE TIME IS RIGHT!
I'LL SHOW YOU RA'S POWER!
REVIVAL OF THE DARK...?!
A TRAP!

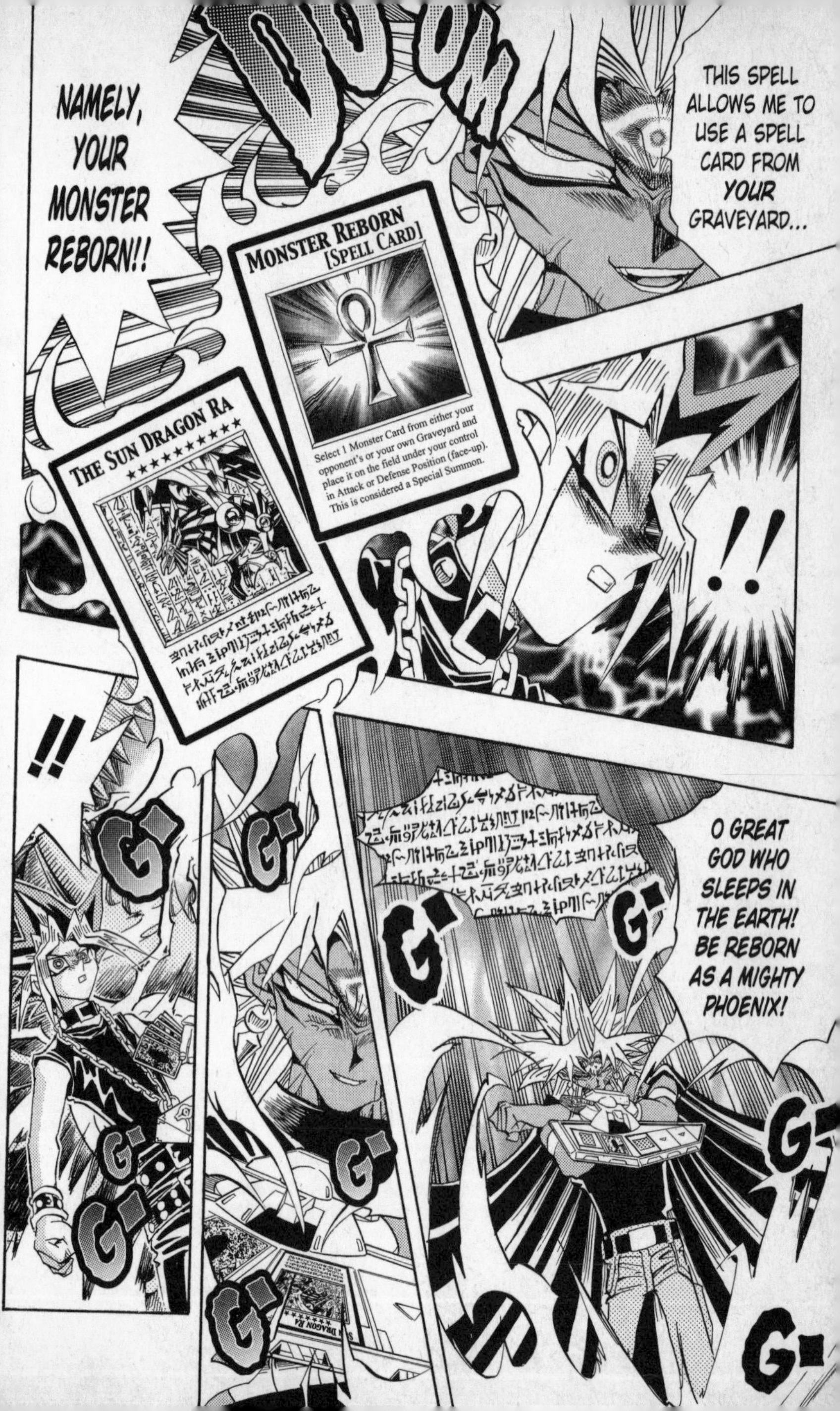
THIS SPELL ALLOWS ME TO USE A SPELL CARD FROM YOUR GRAVEYARD...
DOOM
NAMELY, YOUR MONSTER REBORN!!
MONSTER REBORN [SPELL CARD]
Select 1 Monster Card from either your opponent's or your own Graveyard and place it on the field under your control in Attack or Defense Position (face-up). This is considered a Special Summon.
THE SUN DRAGON RA
!!
O GREAT GOD WHO SLEEPS IN THE EARTH! BE REBORN AS A MIGHTY PHOENIX!
!!

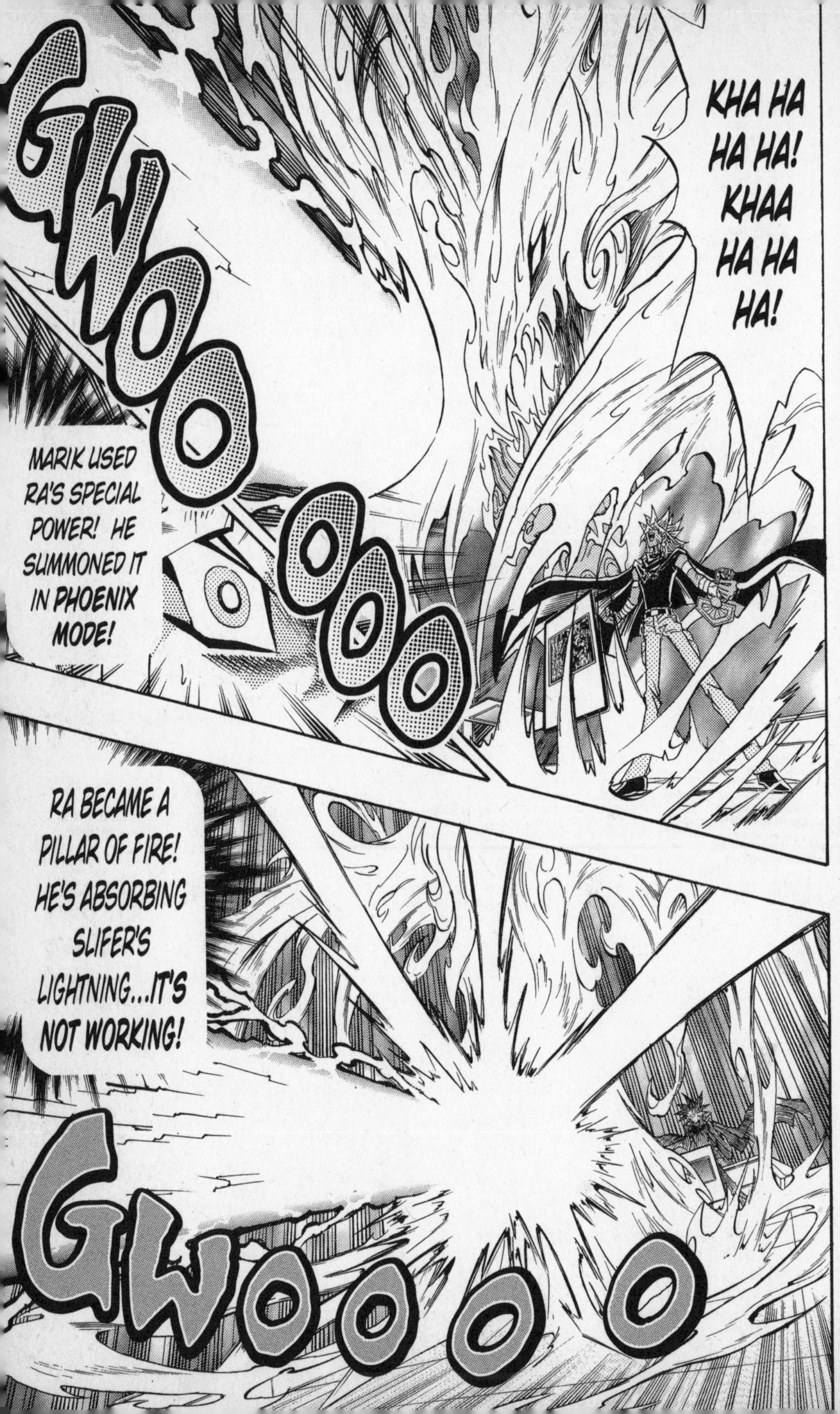
KHA HA HA HA! KHAA HA HA HA!
GWOOOOOOOO
MARIK USED RA'S SPECIAL POWER! HE SUMMONED IT IN PHOENIX MODE!
RA BECAME A PILLAR OF FIRE! HE'S ABSORBING SLIFER'S LIGHTNING...IT'S NOT WORKING!
GWOOOOO

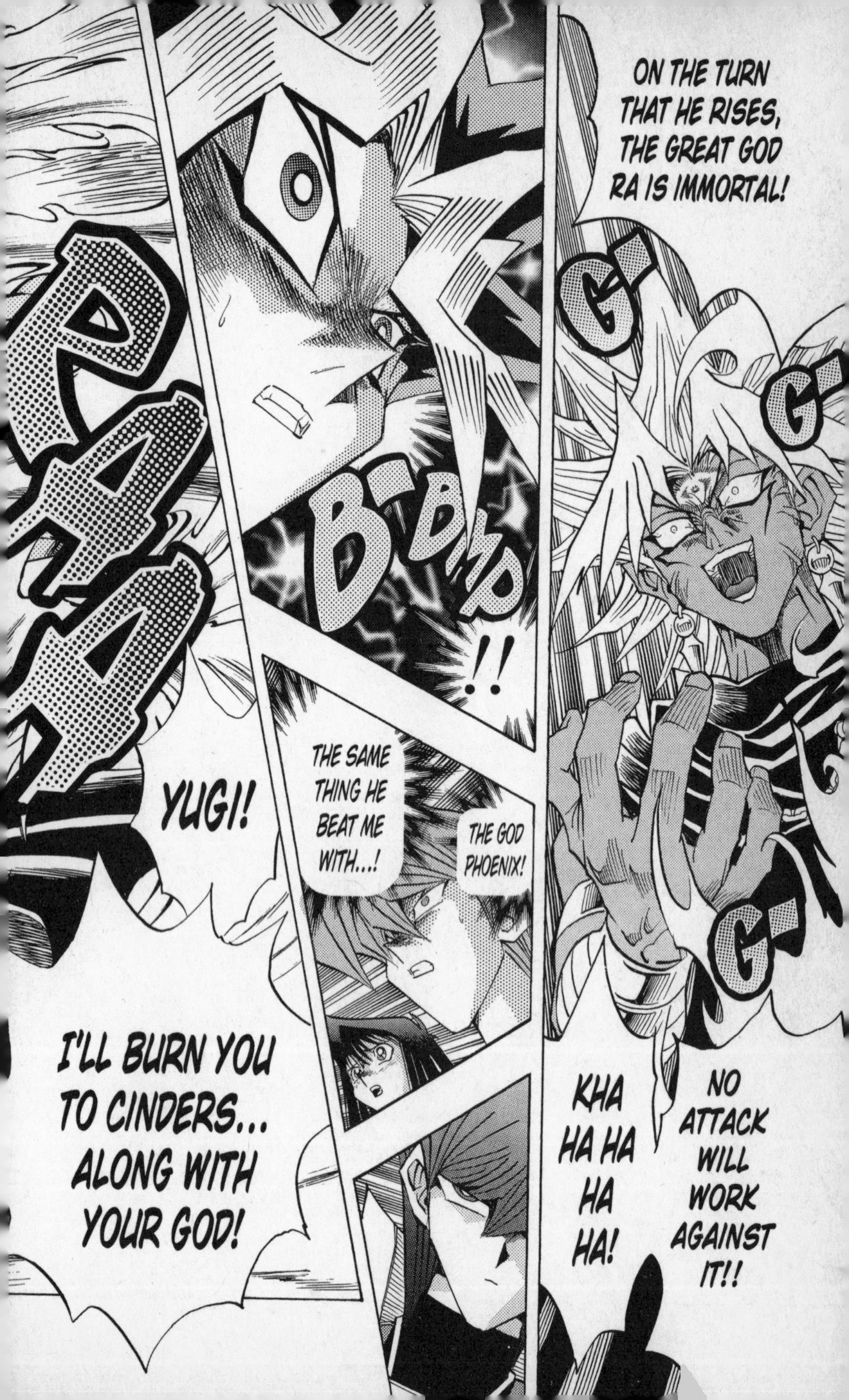
ON THE TURN THAT HE RISES, THE GREAT GOD RA IS IMMORTAL!
G
G
G
NO ATTACK WILL WORK AGAINST IT!!
KHA HA HA HA HA!
B-BMP!!
THE GOD PHOENIX!
THE SAME THING HE BEAT ME WITH...!
YUGI!
I'LL BURN YOU TO CINDERS... ALONG WITH YOUR GOD!

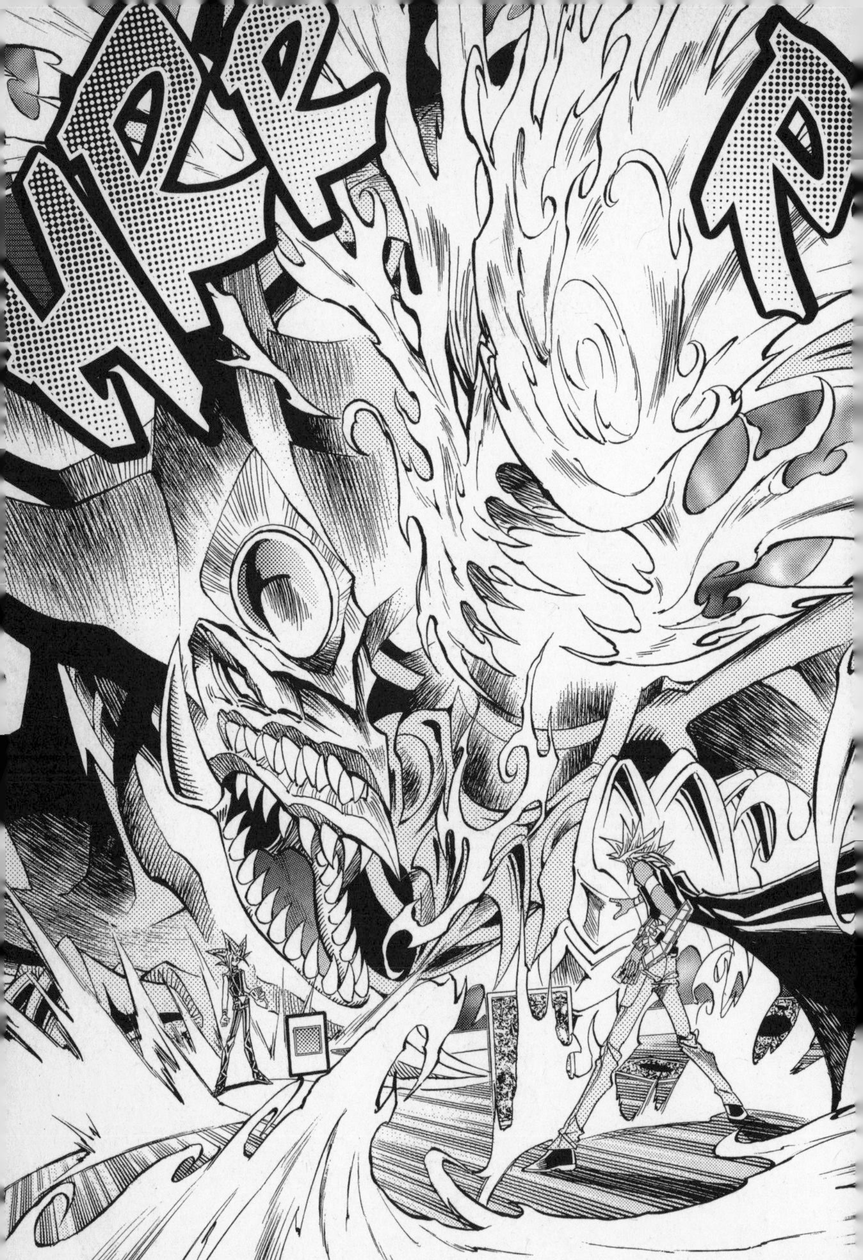

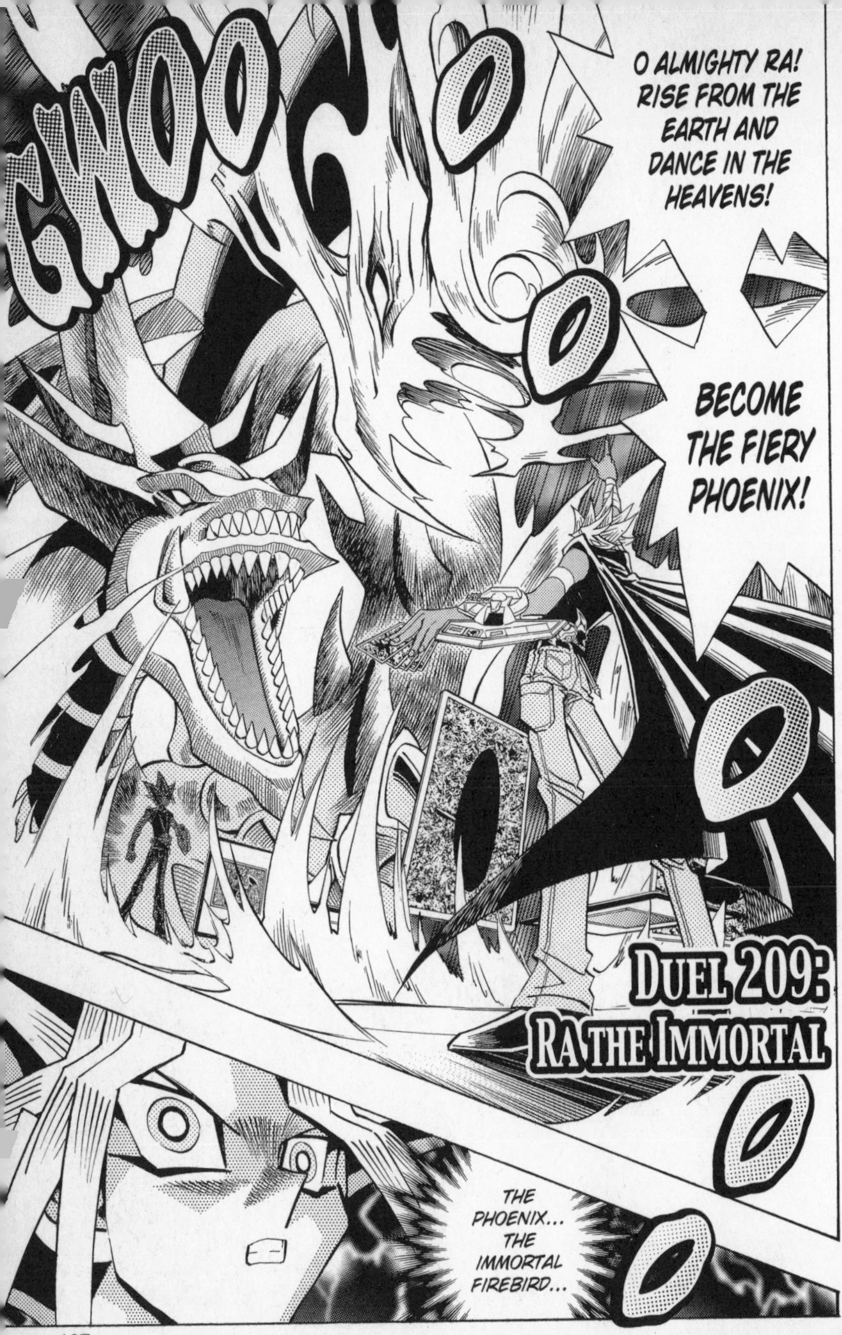
O ALMIGHTY RA! RISE FROM THE EARTH AND DANCE IN THE HEAVENS!
GWOOOOOO
BECOME THE FIERY PHOENIX!
DUEL 209: RA THE IMMORTAL
THE PHOENIX... THE IMMORTAL FIREBIRD...

Duel 209: Ra the Immortal

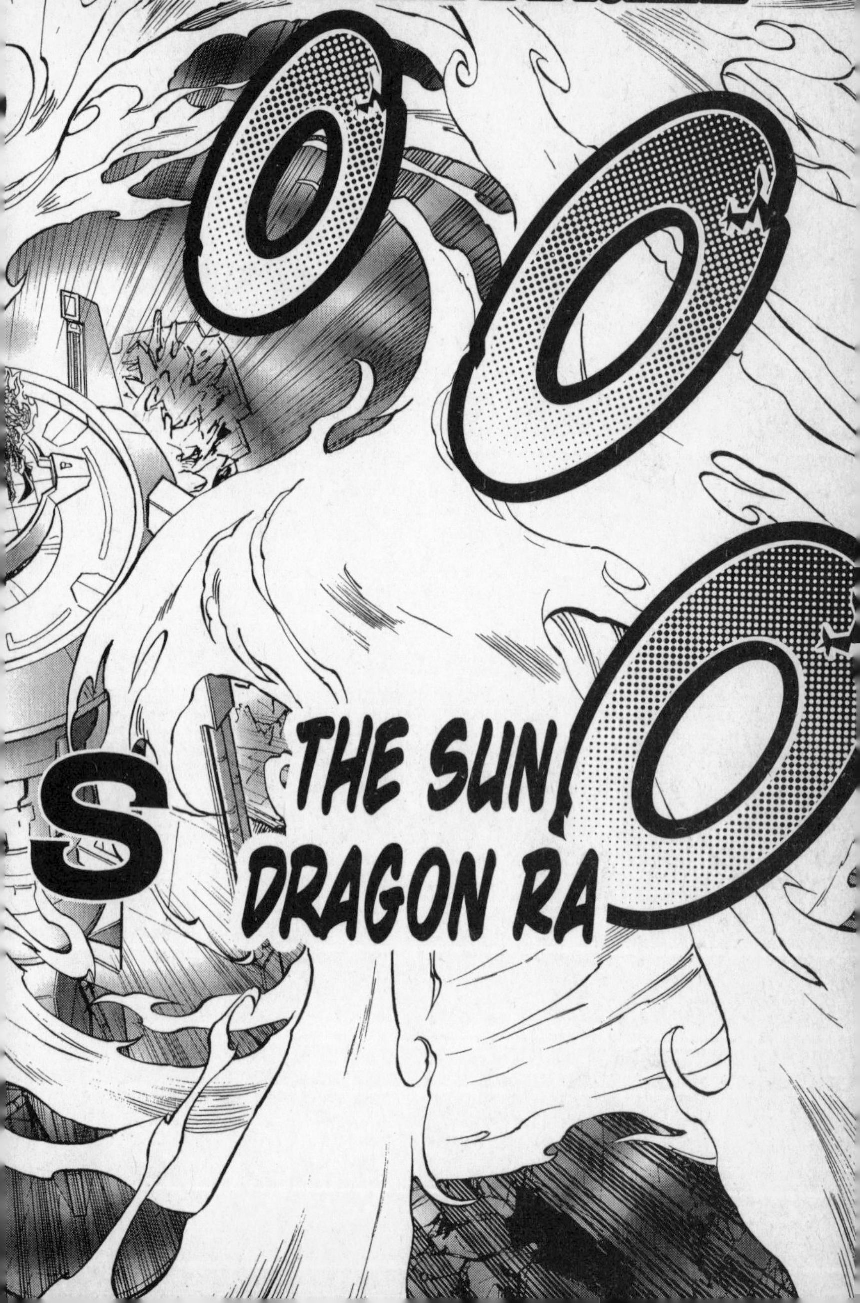
OOO
S
THE SUN DRAGON RA

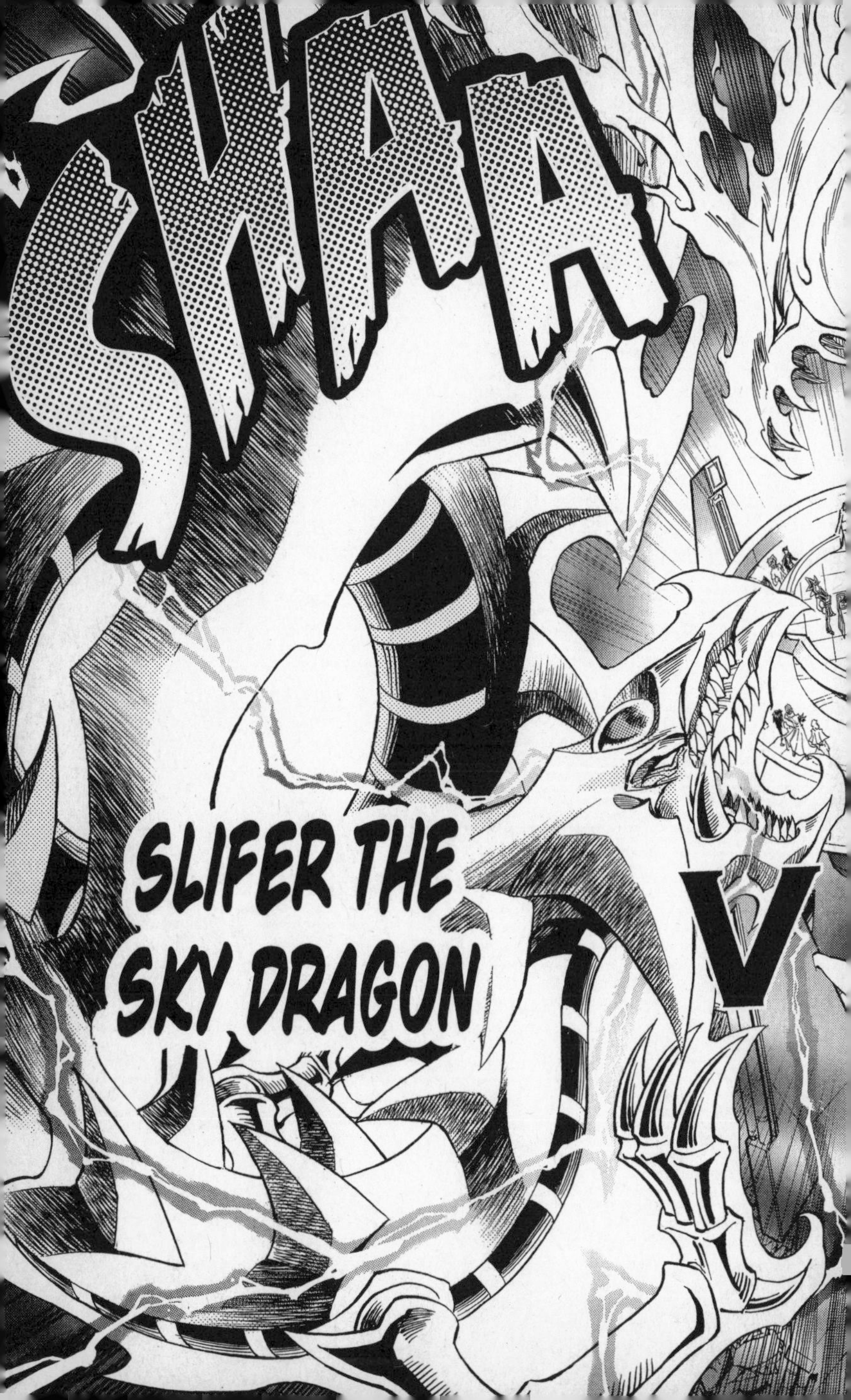

SHAA
SLIFER THE SKY DRAGON

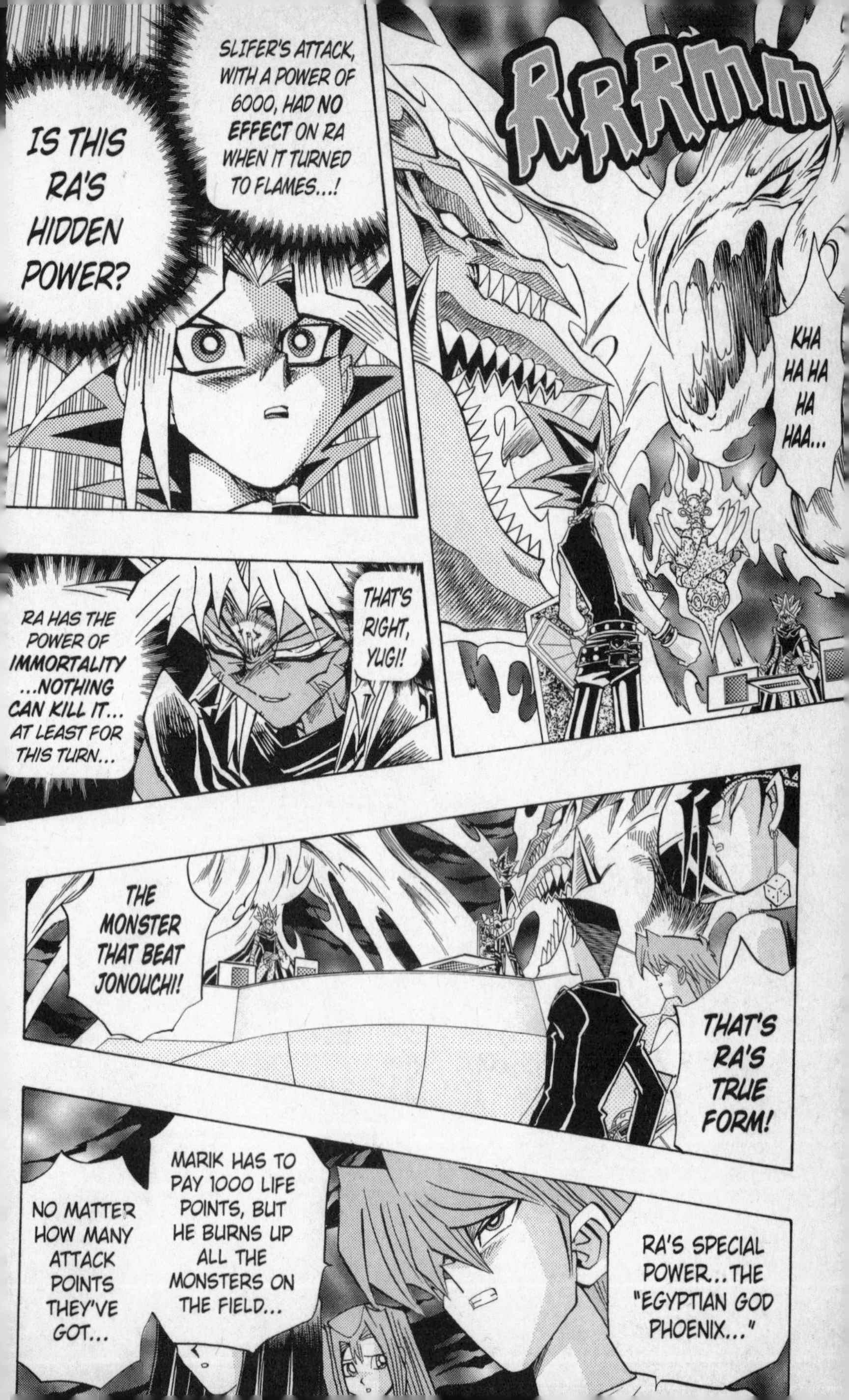
RRRMMM
KHA HA HA HA HAA...
SLIFER'S ATTACK, WITH A POWER OF 6000, HAD NO EFFECT ON RA WHEN IT TURNED TO FLAMES...!
IS THIS RA'S HIDDEN POWER?
THAT'S RIGHT, YUGI!
RA HAS THE POWER OF IMMORTALITY ...NOTHING CAN KILL IT... AT LEAST FOR THIS TURN...
THAT'S RA'S TRUE FORM!
THE MONSTER THAT BEAT JONOUCHI!
RA'S SPECIAL POWER...THE "EGYPTIAN GOD PHOENIX..."
MARIK HAS TO PAY 1000 LIFE POINTS, BUT HE BURNS UP ALL THE MONSTERS ON THE FIELD...
NO MATTER HOW MANY ATTACK POINTS THEY'VE GOT...

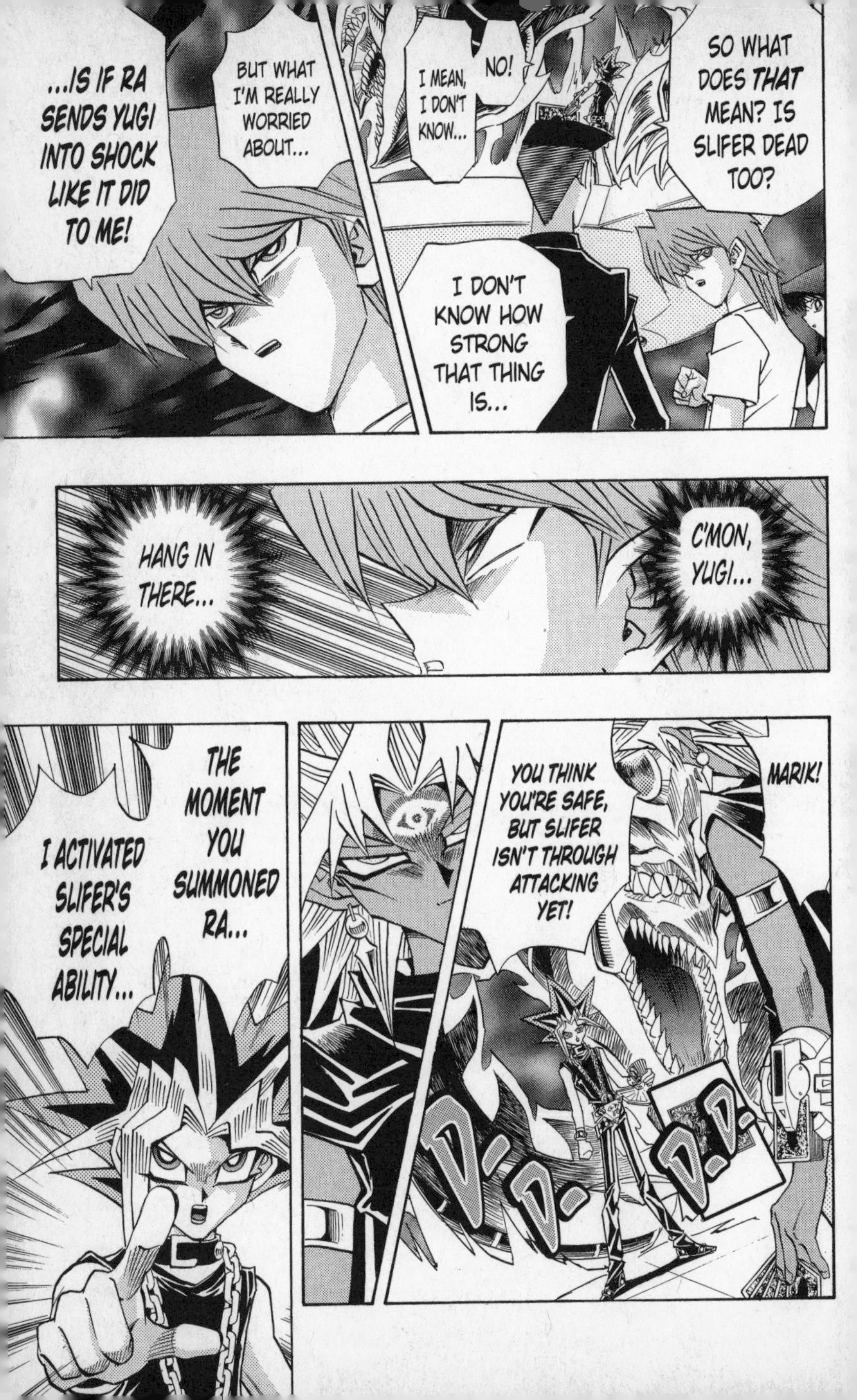
SO WHAT DOES THAT MEAN? IS SLIFER DEAD TOO?
NO!
I MEAN, I DON'T KNOW...
I DON'T KNOW HOW STRONG THAT THING IS...
BUT WHAT I'M REALLY WORRIED ABOUT...
...IS IF RA SENDS YUGI INTO SHOCK LIKE IT DID TO ME!
C'MON, YUGI...
HANG IN THERE...
MARIK!
YOU THINK YOU'RE SAFE, BUT SLIFER ISN'T THROUGH ATTACKING YET!
THE MOMENT YOU SUMMONED RA...
I ACTIVATED SLIFER'S SPECIAL ABILITY...

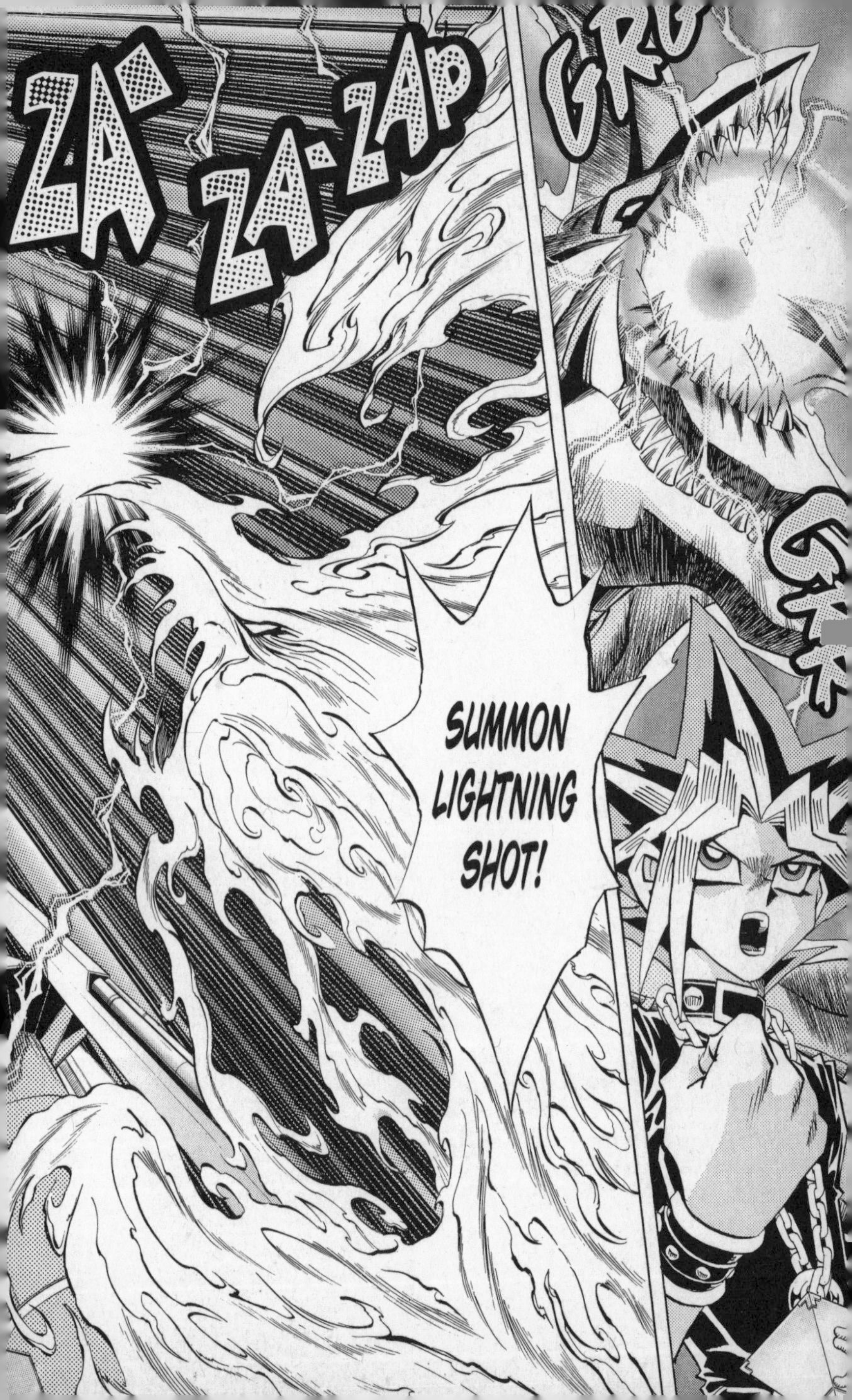
GRU
SUMMON LIGHTNING SHOT!
ZA ZA-ZAP

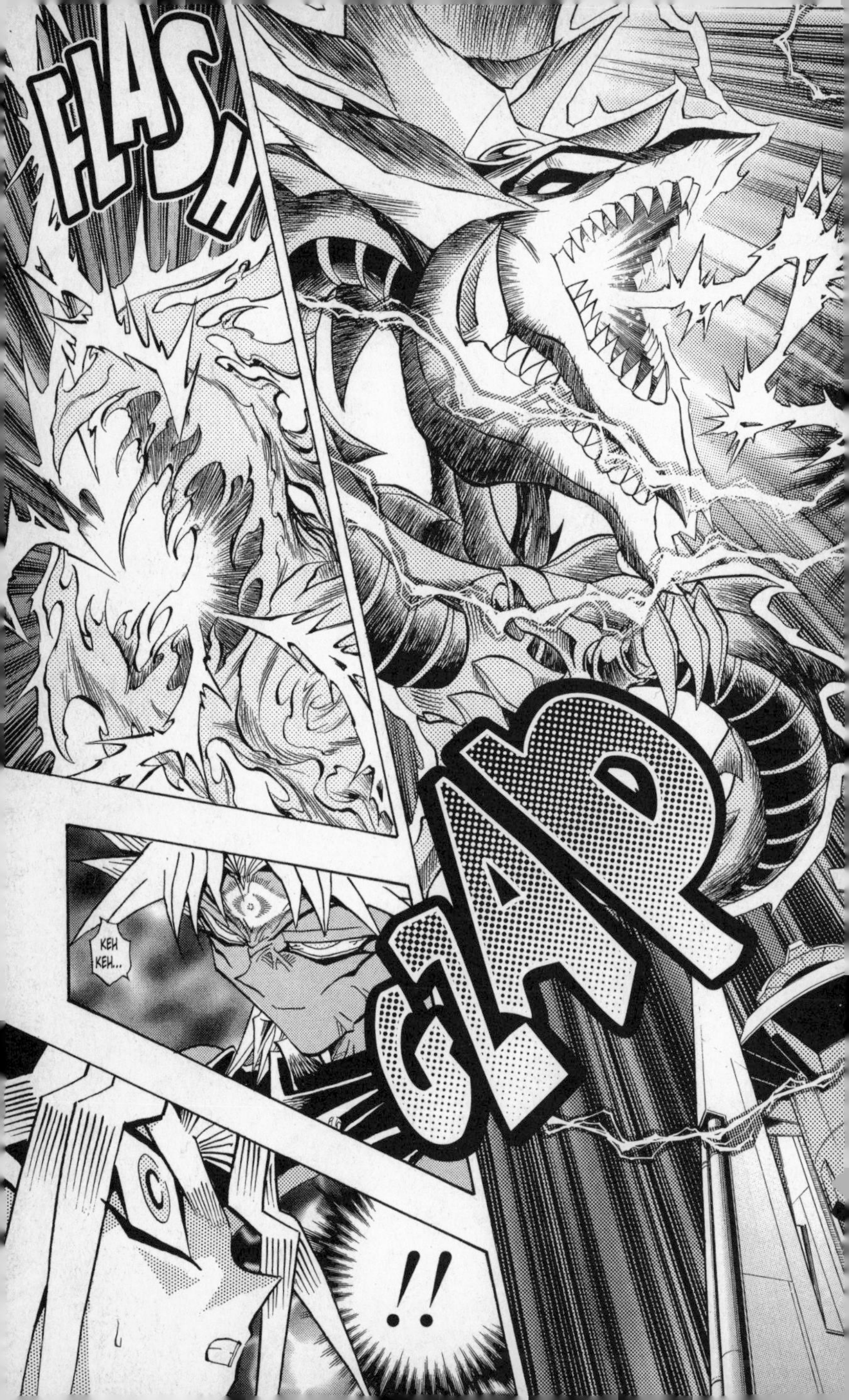
FLASH
GAP
KEH KEH...
!!

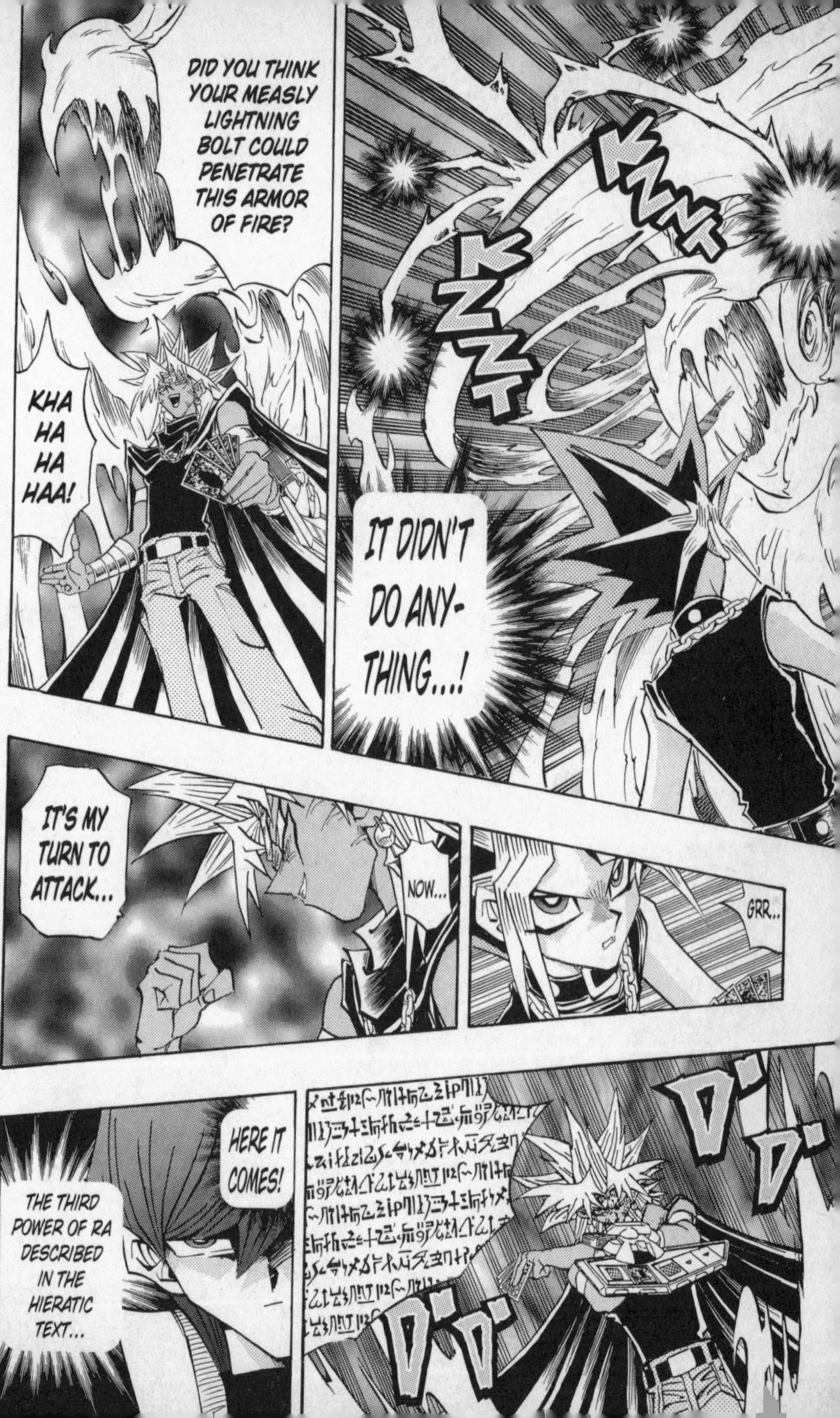
KZZT
KZZT
IT DIDN'T DO ANYTHING...!
DID YOU THINK YOUR MEASLY LIGHTNING BOLT COULD PENETRATE THIS ARMOR OF FIRE?
KHA HA HA HAA!
GRR...
NOW...
IT'S MY TURN TO ATTACK...
HERE IT COMES!
THE THIRD POWER OF RA DESCRIBED IN THE HIERATIC TEXT...

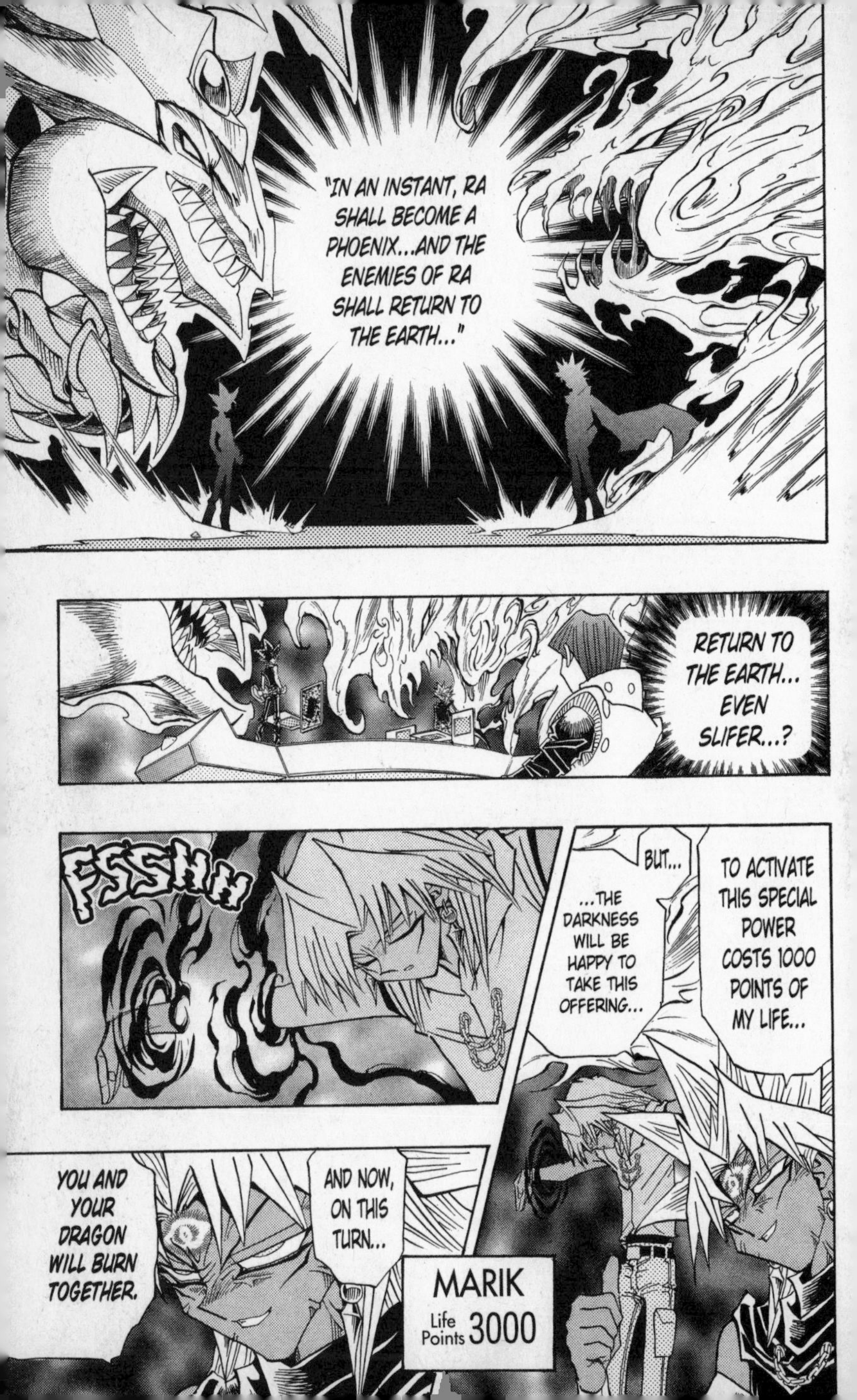
"IN AN INSTANT, RA SHALL BECOME A PHOENIX...AND THE ENEMIES OF RA SHALL RETURN TO THE EARTH..."
RETURN TO THE EARTH... EVEN SLIFER...?
TO ACTIVATE THIS SPECIAL POWER COSTS 1000 POINTS OF MY LIFE...
BUT...
...THE DARKNESS WILL BE HAPPY TO TAKE THIS OFFERING...
FSSHH
AND NOW, ON THIS TURN...
YOU AND YOUR DRAGON WILL BURN TOGETHER.
MARIK
Life Points 3000

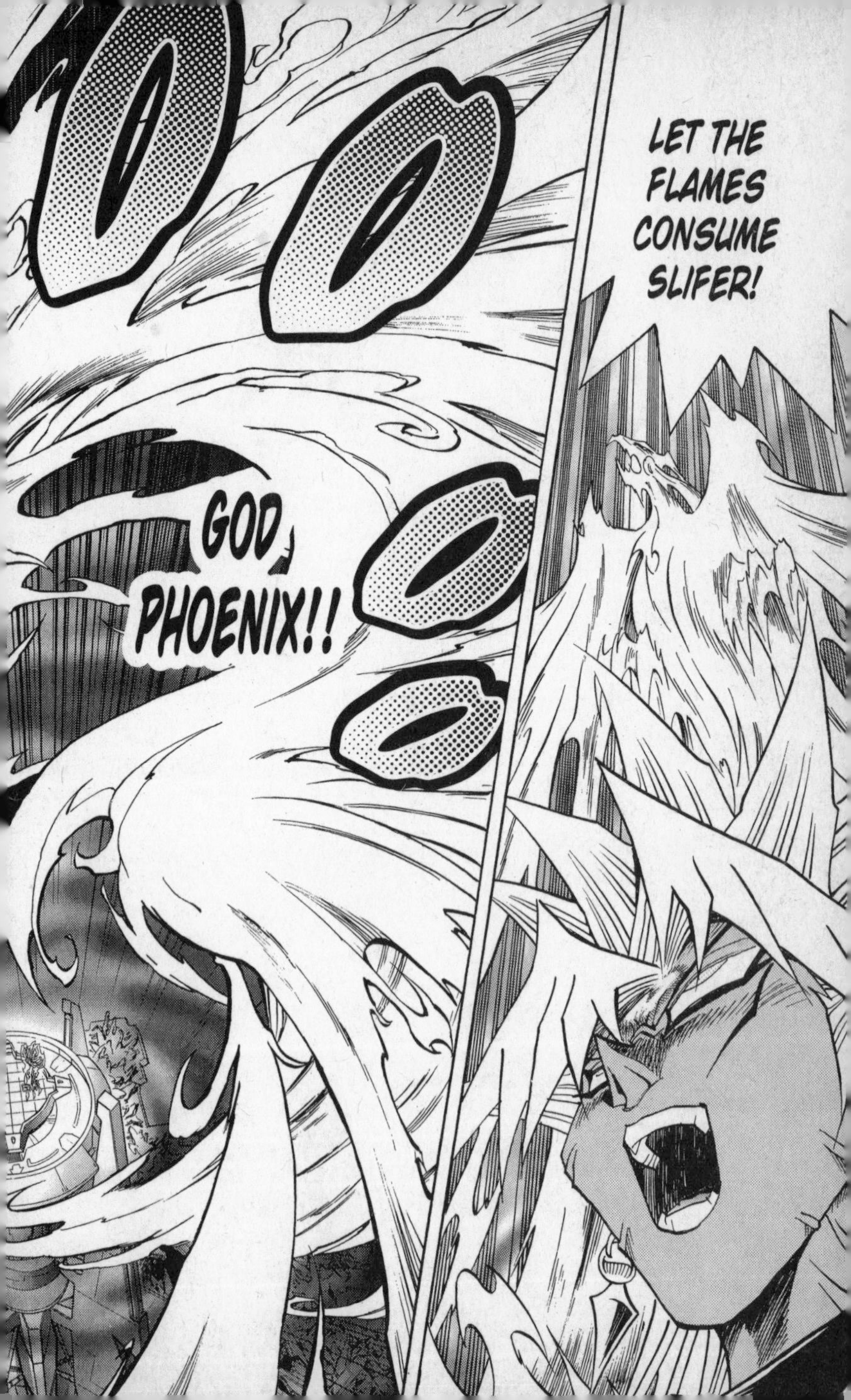
LET THE FLAMES CONSUME SLIFER!
GOD PHOENIX!!

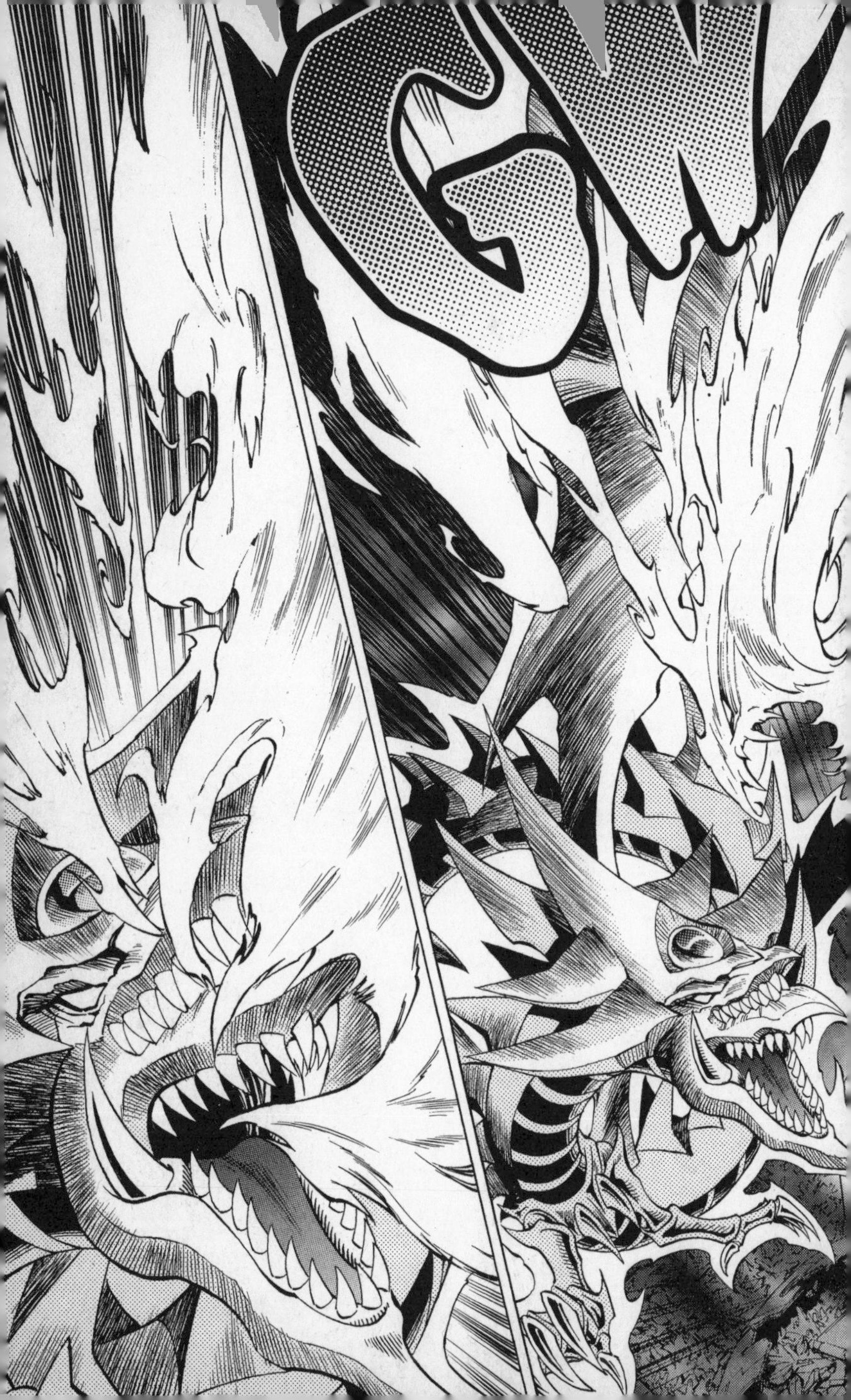

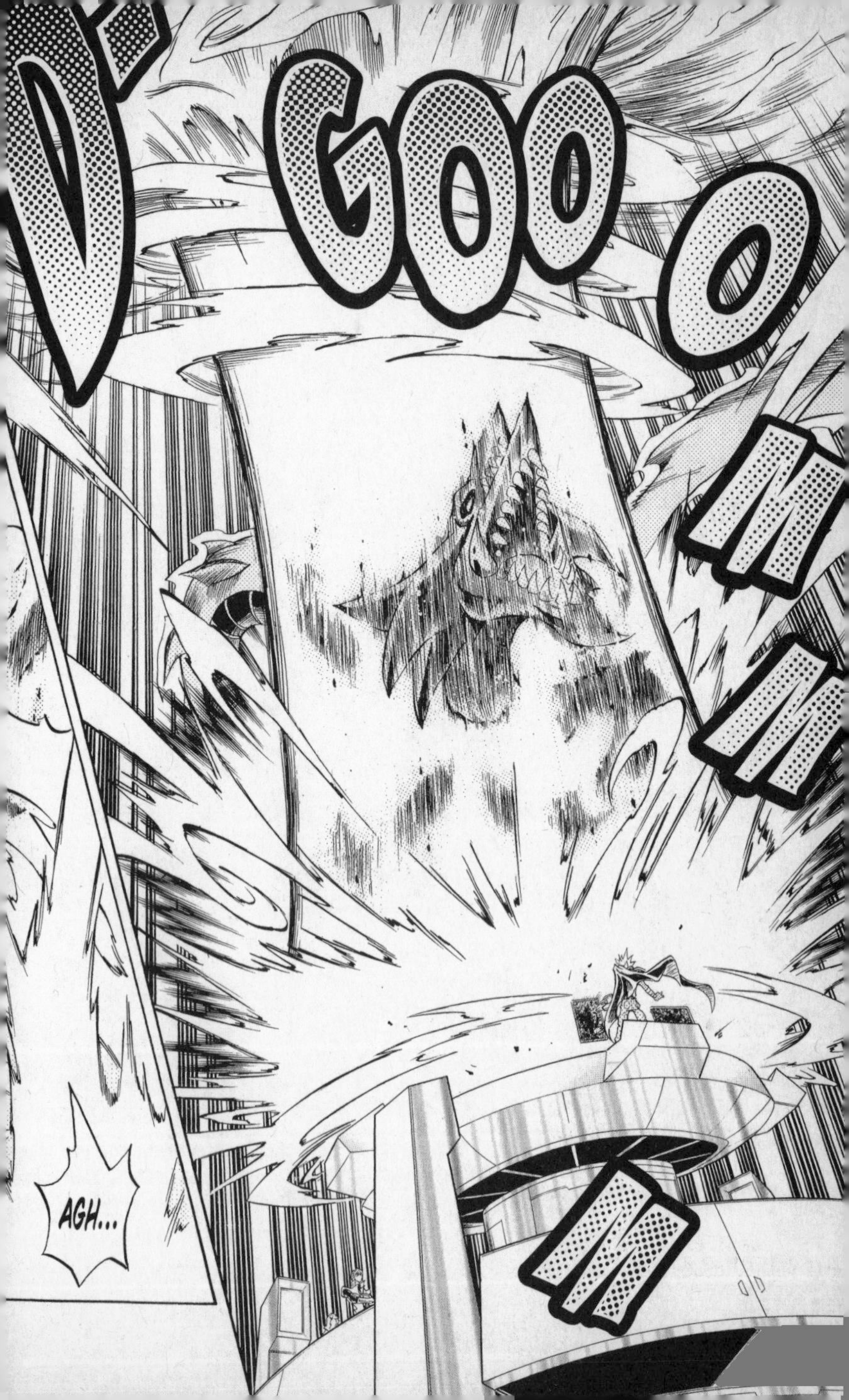
DGOOOMMM
AGH...

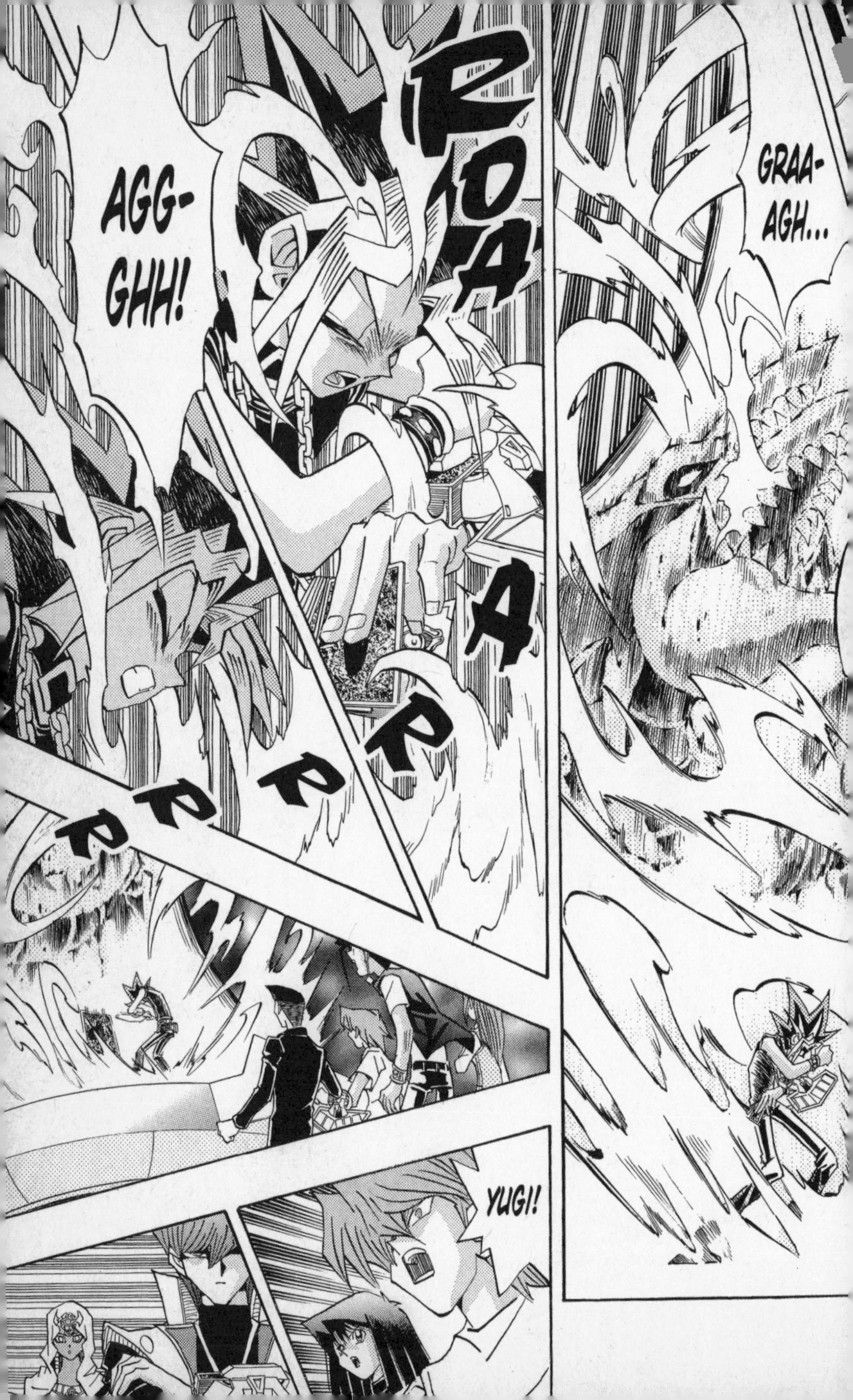
GRAA-AGH...
ROAARRRRR
AGG-GHH!
YUGI!

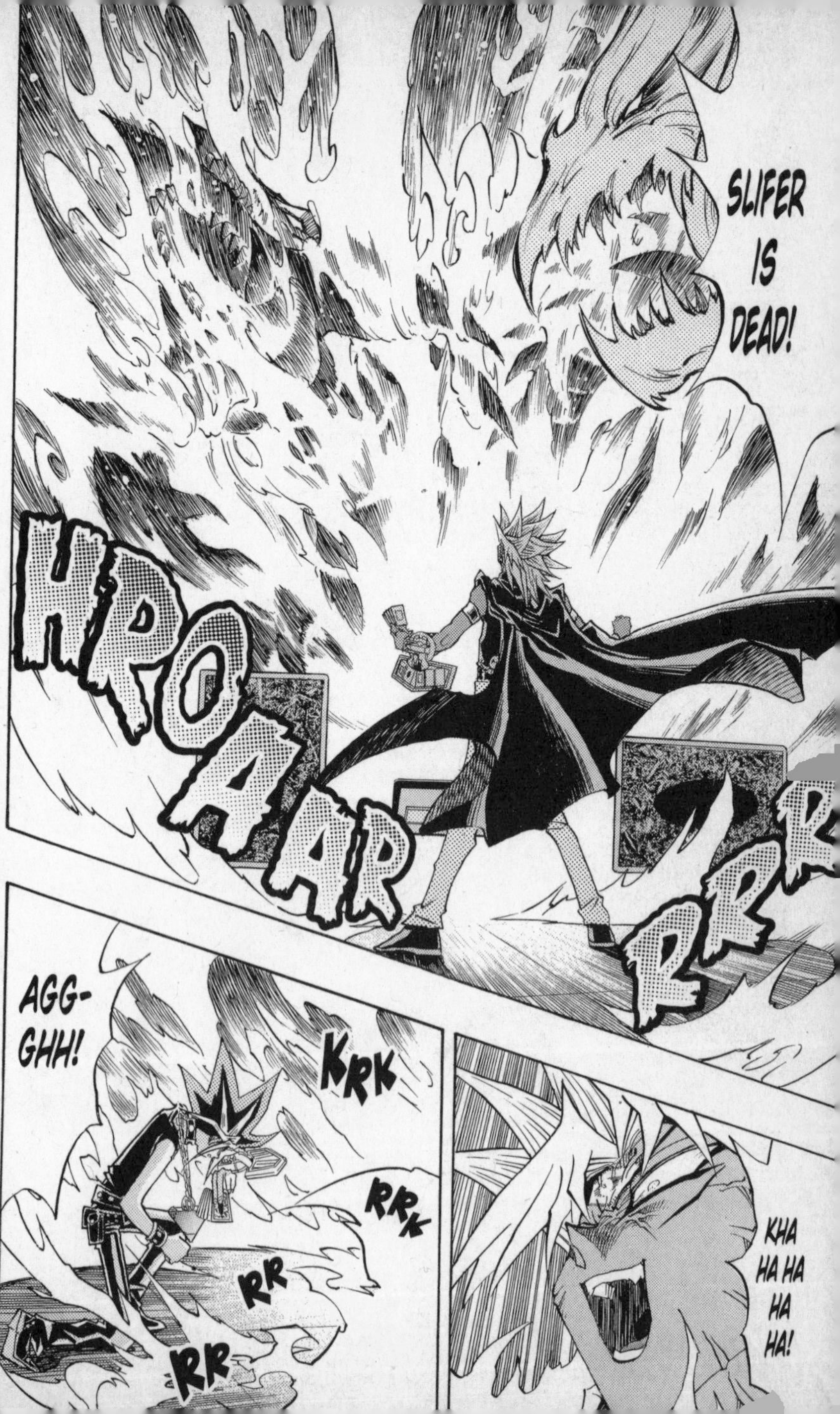
SLIFER IS DEAD!
HPOAARRRR
KHA HA HA HA HA!
AGG-GHH!
KRK
RRK
RR
RR

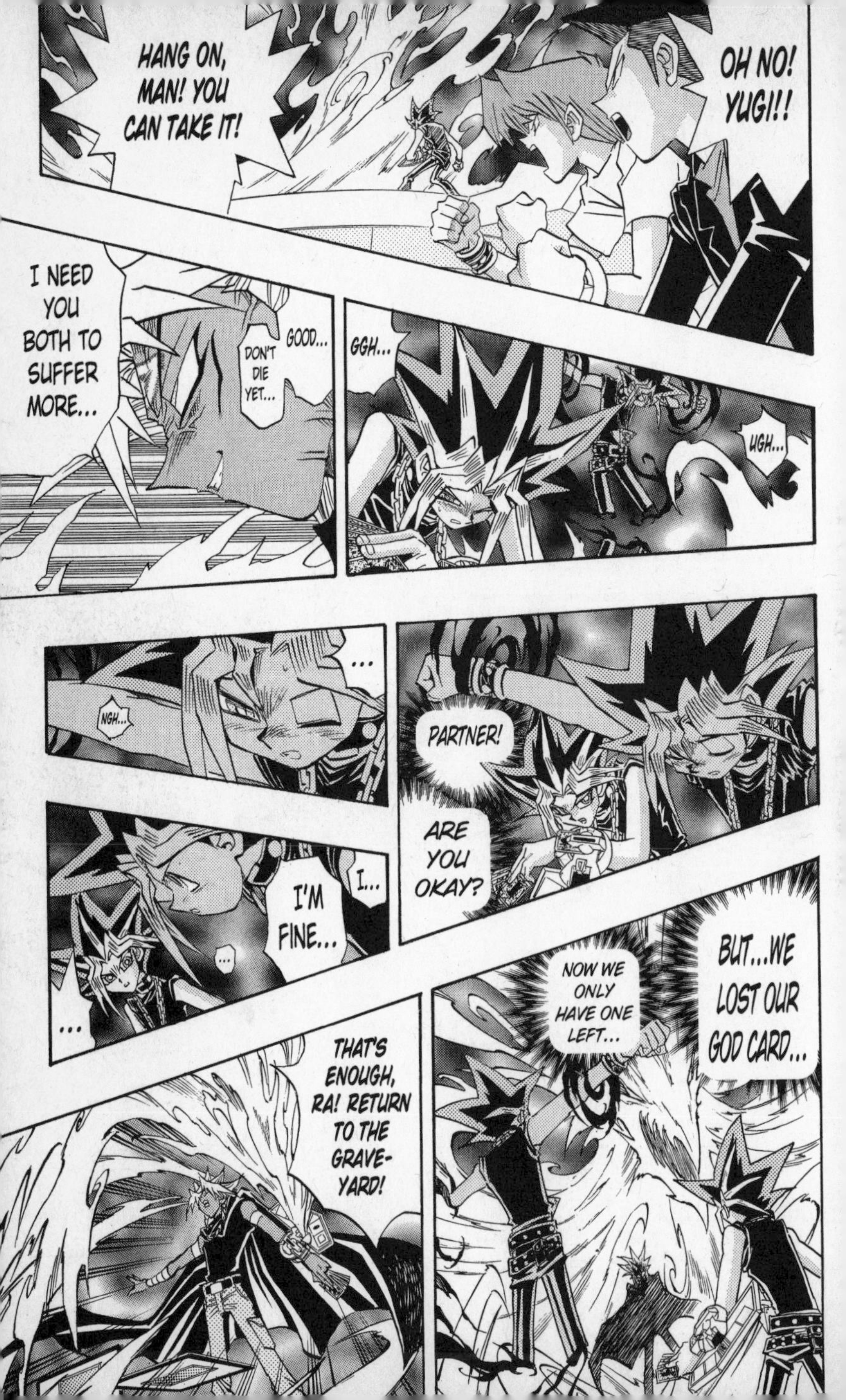
OH NO! YUGI!!
HANG ON, MAN! YOU CAN TAKE IT!
GGH...
UGH...
GOOD...
DON'T DIE YET...
I NEED YOU BOTH TO SUFFER MORE...
PARTNER!
ARE YOU OKAY?
...
NGH...
I...
I'M FINE...
...
...
BUT...WE LOST OUR GOD CARD...
NOW WE ONLY HAVE ONE LEFT...
THAT'S ENOUGH, RA! RETURN TO THE GRAVE-YARD!

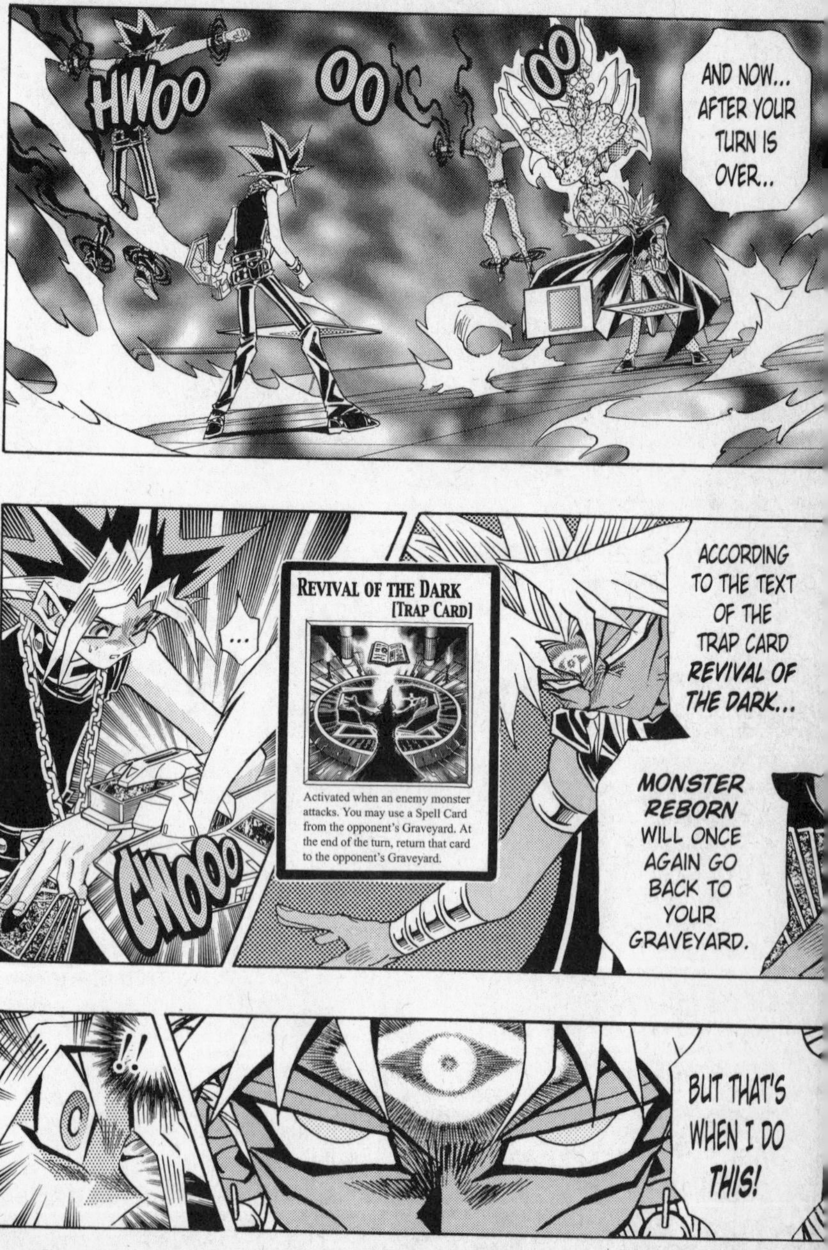
AND NOW... AFTER YOUR TURN IS OVER..
HWOO OO OO
ACCORDING TO THE TEXT OF THE TRAP CARD REVIVAL OF THE DARK...
MONSTER REBORN WILL ONCE AGAIN GO BACK TO YOUR GRAVEYARD.
REVIVAL OF THE DARK
[TRAP CARD]
Activated when an enemy monster attacks. You may use a Spell Card from the opponent's Graveyard. At the end of the turn, return that card to the opponent's Graveyard.
CHOOO
...
BUT THAT'S WHEN I DO THIS!
!!

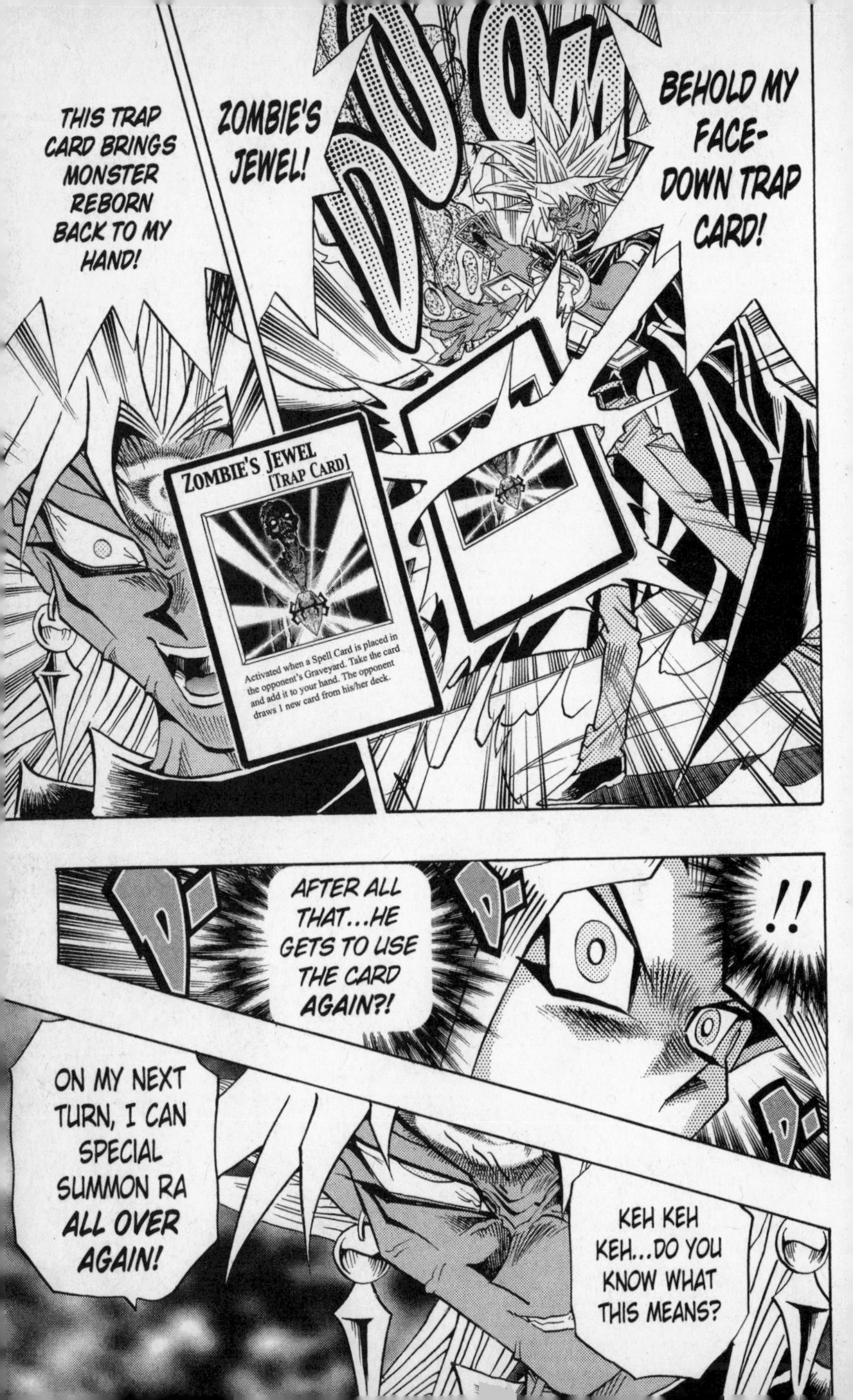
BEHOLD MY FACE-DOWN TRAP CARD!
ZOMBIE'S JEWEL!
THIS TRAP CARD BRINGS MONSTER REBORN BACK TO MY HAND!
ZOMBIE'S JEWEL [TRAP CARD]
Activated when a Spell Card is placed in the opponent's Graveyard. Take the card and add it to your hand. The opponent draws 1 new card from his/her deck.
!!
AFTER ALL THAT...HE GETS TO USE THE CARD AGAIN?!
KEH KEH KEH...DO YOU KNOW WHAT THIS MEANS?
ON MY NEXT TURN, I CAN SPECIAL SUMMON RA ALL OVER AGAIN!

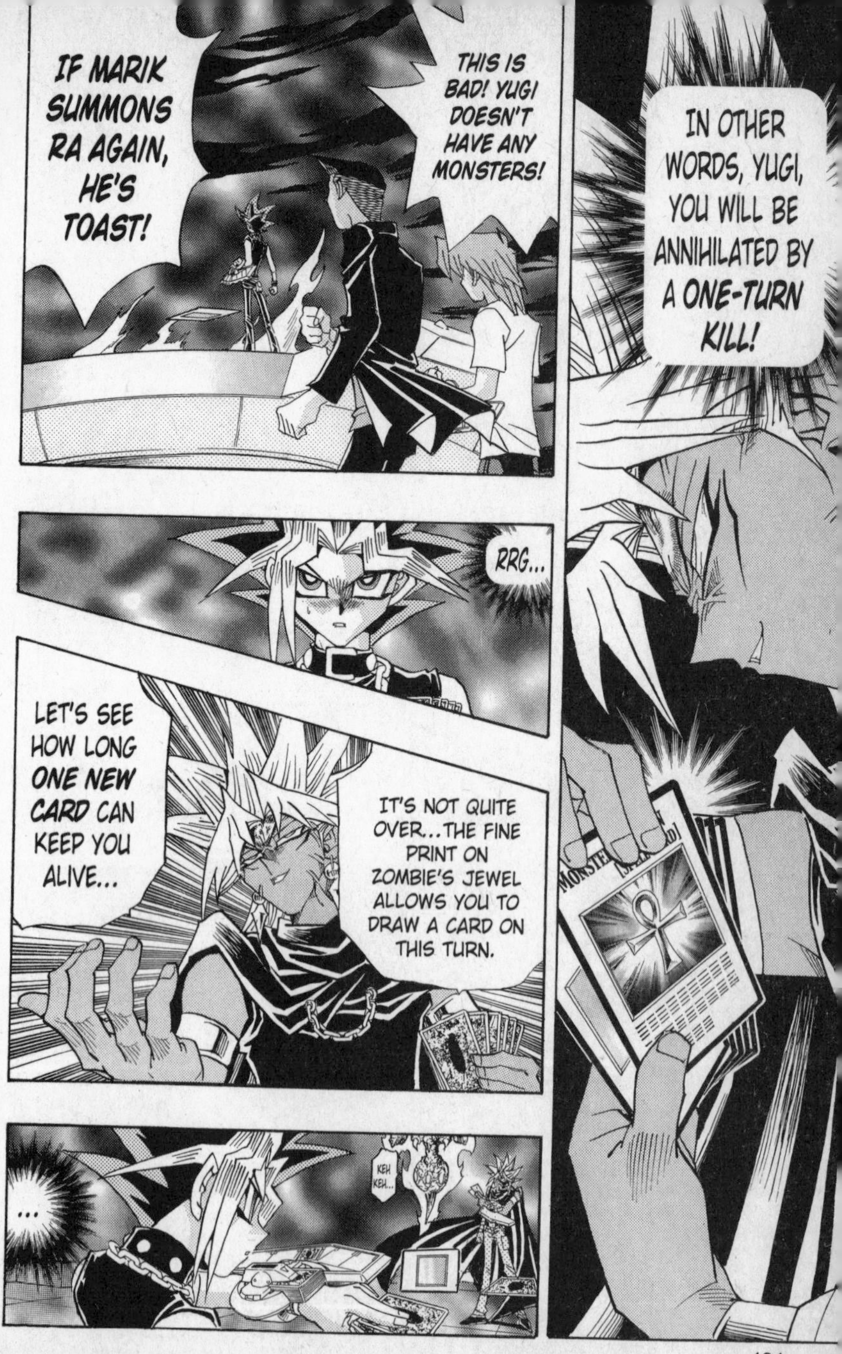
IN OTHER WORDS, YUGI, YOU WILL BE ANNIHILATED BY A ONE-TURN KILL!
THIS IS BAD! YUGI DOESN'T HAVE ANY MONSTERS!
IF MARIK SUMMONS RA AGAIN, HE'S TOAST!
RRG...
IT'S NOT QUITE OVER...THE FINE PRINT ON ZOMBIE'S JEWEL ALLOWS YOU TO DRAW A CARD ON THIS TURN.
LET'S SEE HOW LONG ONE NEW CARD CAN KEEP YOU ALIVE...
KEH KEH...
...

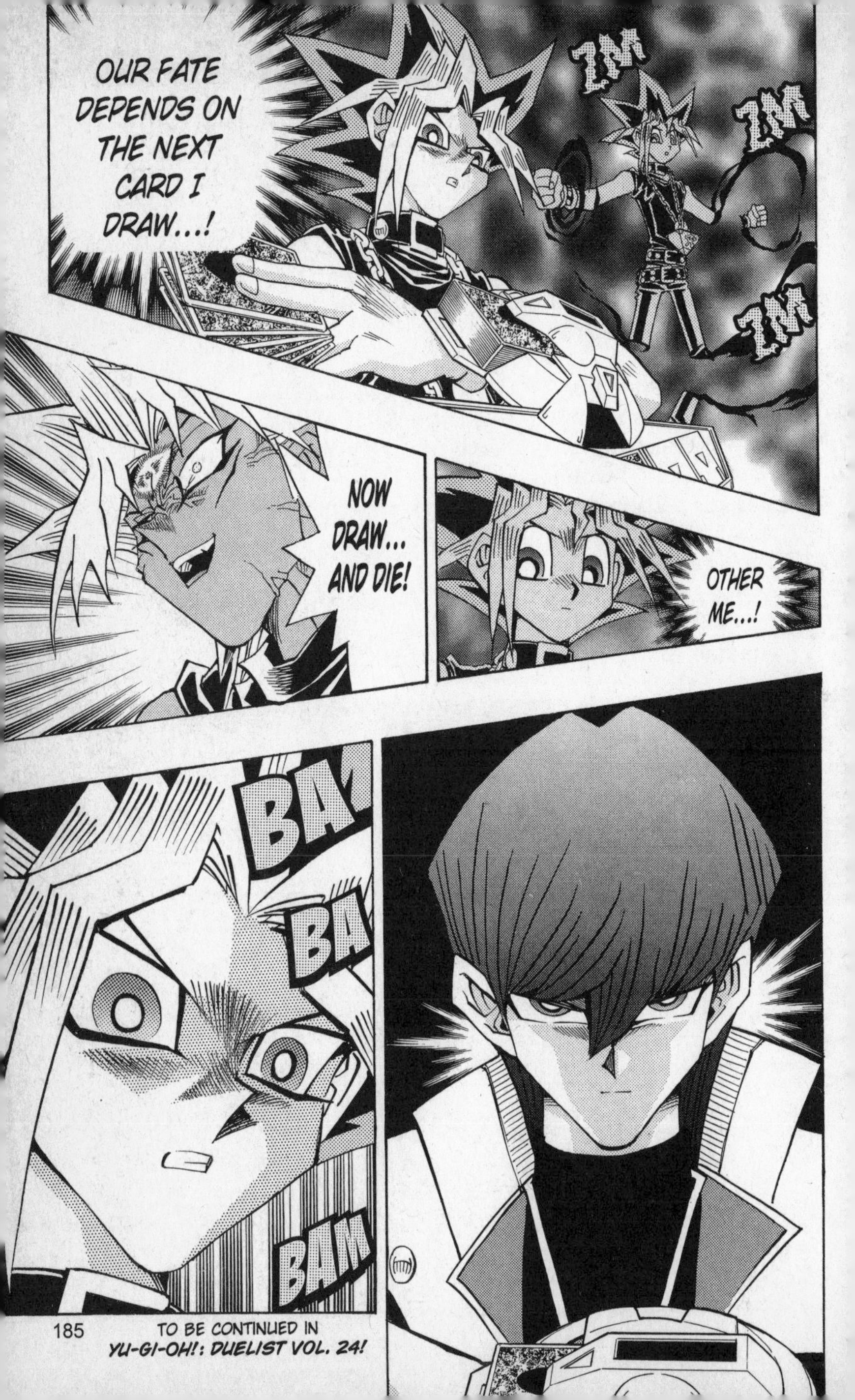
ZM
ZM
ZM
OUR FATE DEPENDS ON THE NEXT CARD I DRAW...!
OTHER ME...!
NOW DRAW... AND DIE!
BA
BA
BAM

TO BE CONTINUED IN
YU-GI-OH!: DUELIST VOL. 24!

MASTER OF THE CARDS

The "Duel Monsters" card game first appeared in volume two of the original **Yu-Gi-Oh!** graphic novel series, but it's in **Yu-Gi-Oh!: Duelist** (originally printed in Japan as volumes 8-31 of **Yu-Gi-Oh!**) that it gets really important. As many fans know, some of the card names are different between the English and Japanese versions. In case you play the game, or you're interested in playing, here's a rundown of some of the cards in this graphic novel. Some cards only appear in the **Yu-Gi-Oh!** video games, not in the actual trading card game.

FIRST APPEARANCE IN THIS VOLUME	JAPANESE CARD NAME	ENGLISH CARD NAME
p.8	*Dragon wo Yobu Fue* (Dragon-Summoning Flute)	The Flute of Summoning Dragon
p.8	*Blue Eyes White Dragon*	Blue Eyes White Dragon
p.8	*Black Magician*	Dark Magician
p.8	*Magnet Warrior Beta*	Beta the Magnet Warrior
p.8	*Lord of Dragon*	Lord of D.
p.13	*Red Eyes Black Dragon*	Red Eyes Black Dragon
p.16	*Rokubôsei no Jûbaku* (Binding Curse of the Hexagram)	Spellbinding Circle
p.16	*Majutsu no Jumonsho* (Spellbook of Sorcery)	Magic Formula

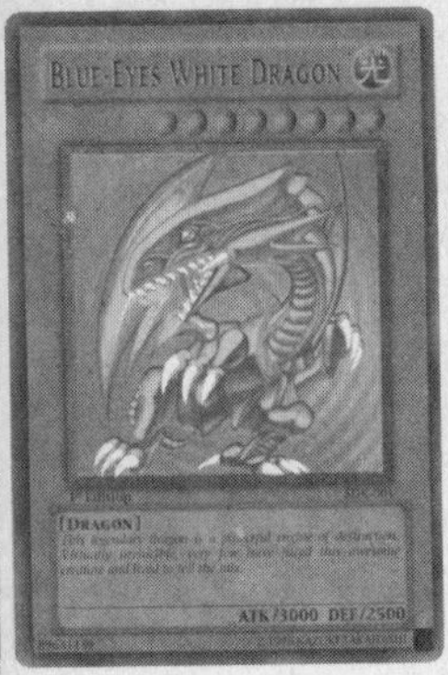
BLUE-EYES WHITE DRAGON
[DRAGON]
ATK/3000 DEF/2500
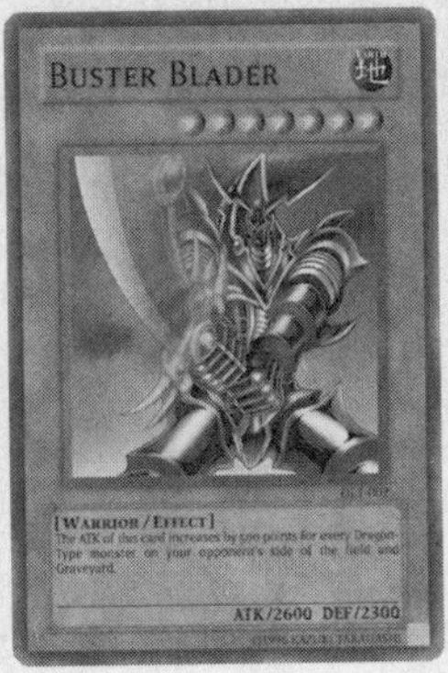
BUSTER BLADER
[WARRIOR / EFFECT]
The ATK of this card increases by 500 points for every Dragon-Type monster on your opponent's side of the field and Graveyard.
ATK/2600 DEF/2300
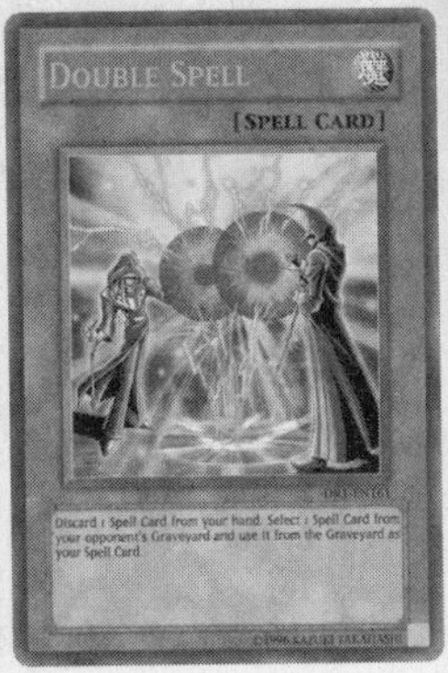
DOUBLE SPELL
[SPELL CARD]
Discard 1 Spell Card from your hand. Select 1 Spell Card from your opponent's Graveyard and use it from the Graveyard as your Spell Card.

FIRST APPEARANCE IN THIS VOLUME	JAPANESE CARD NAME	ENGLISH CARD NAME
p.17	*Magic Cylinder*	Magic Cylinder
p.29	*Double Magic*	Double Spell
p.30	*Saishû Totsugeki Meirei* (Final Attack Orders)	Final Attack Orders
p.31	*Shisha Sosei* (Resurrection of the Dead)	Monster Reborn
p.36	*Yûgô* (Fusion)	Polymerization
p.36	*Blue Eyes Ultimate Dragon*	Blue Eyes Ultimate Dragon
p.44	*Buster Blader*	Buster Blader
p.45	*Chômadô Kenshi Black Paladin* (Super Magic Swordsman Black Paladin)	Dark Paladin
p.51	*Mahô Kyûshû* (Magic Absorption)	Absorb Spell (NOTE: Not a real game card.)
p.59	*Yûgô Kaijo* (Fusion Cancellation/Removal)	De-Polymerization
p.61	*Kakusan suru Hadô* (Slicing Wave-Motion)	Diffusion Wave-Motion

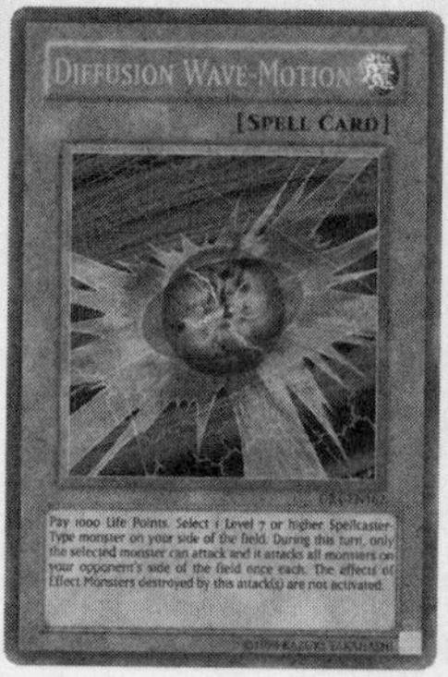
DIFFUSION WAVE-MOTION
[SPELL CARD]
Pay 1000 Life Points. Select 1 Level 7 or higher Spellcaster-Type monster on your side of the field. During this turn, only the selected monster can attack and it attacks all monsters on your opponent's side of the field once each. The effects of Effect Monsters destroyed by this attack(s) are not activated.
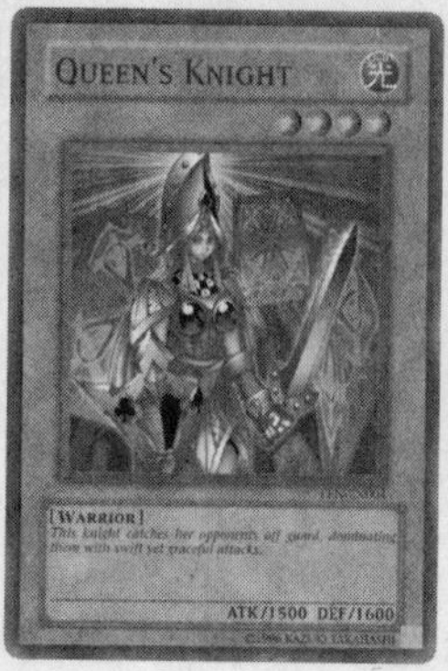
QUEEN'S KNIGHT
[WARRIOR]
This knight catches her opponents off guard, dominating them with swift yet graceful attacks.
ATK/1500 DEF/1600
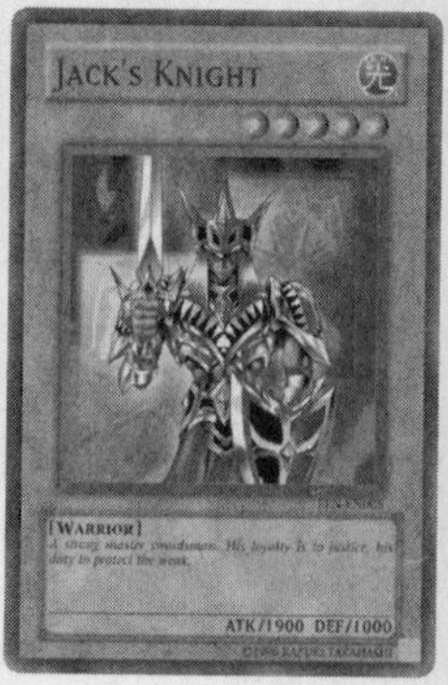
JACK'S KNIGHT
[WARRIOR]
A strong master swordsman. His loyalty is to justice, his duty to protect the weak.
ATK/1900 DEF/1000

FIRST APPEARANCE IN THIS VOLUME	JAPANESE CARD NAME	ENGLISH CARD NAME
p.75	*Obelisk no Kyoshinhei* (Obelisk the Giant God Soldier)	The God of the Obelisk (NOTE: Called "Obelisk the Tormentor" in the English anime and card game.)
p.100	*Devil's Sanctuary*	Devil's Sanctuary
p.122	*Sokkô no Kyûketsu Uji* (Quick-Attacking Blood-Drinking Worm)	Vampiric Leech (NOTE: Not a real game card.)
p.134	*Juragedo*	Juragedo (NOTE: Not a real game card.)
p.134	*Ra no Yokushinryû* (Ra the Winged God Dragon) (NOTE: The kanji for "sun god" is written beside the kanji for "Ra.")	The Sun Dragon Ra (NOTE: Called "The Winged Dragon of Ra" in the English anime and card game.)
p.136	*Exchange*	Exchange
p.137	*Queen's Knight*	Queen's Knight
p.141	*Hidariude no Daishô* (Left Arm Offering)	Left Arm Offering (NOTE: Not a real game card.)
p.144	*King's Knight*	King's Knight

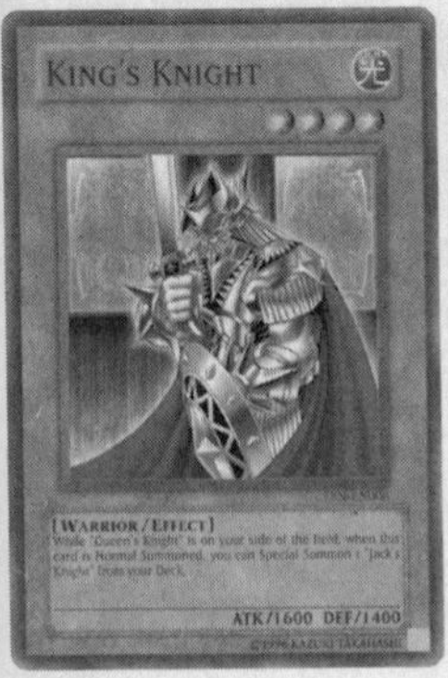
King's Knight
[Warrior/Effect]
ATK/1600 DEF/1400
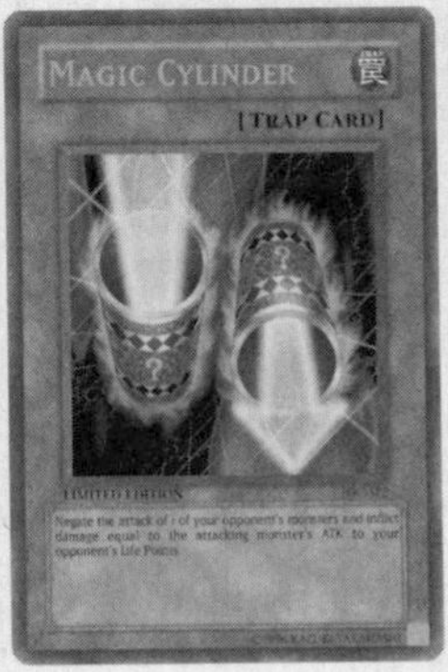
Magic Cylinder
[Trap Card]
Limited Edition
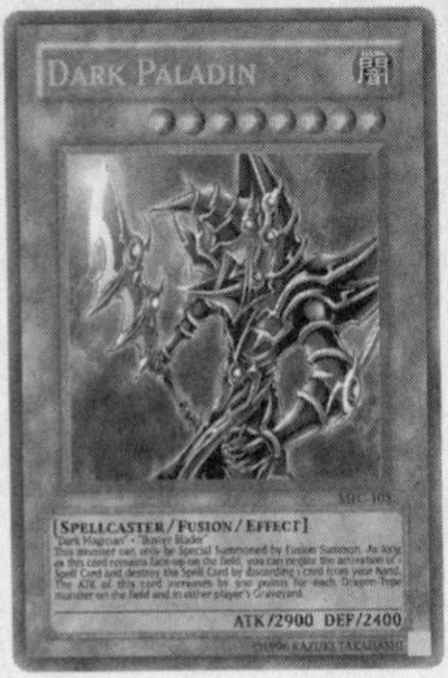
Dark Paladin
[Spellcaster/Fusion/Effect]
ATK/2900 DEF/2400

FIRST APPEARANCE IN THIS VOLUME	JAPANESE CARD NAME	ENGLISH CARD NAME
p.145	*Jack's Knight*	Jack's Knight
p.153	*Ten yori no Hôsatsu* (Treasure from Heaven)	Card of Sanctity
p.154	*Osiris no Tenkûryû* (Osiris the Heaven Dragon)	Slifer the Sky Dragon
p.161	*Ankoku no Masaisei* (Magic Revival of the Dark/Black Magic Regeneration)	Revival of the Dark (NOTE: Not a real game card)
p.183	*Zombie no Hôseki* (Zombie's Jewel)	Zombie's Jewel (NOTE: Not a real game card)

IN THE NEXT VOLUME...

Can Yugi defeat Marik's "Zombie's Jewel/Monster Reborn" combo?! Or will he fall to the terrifying fury of the Sun Dragon Ra? As the world's mightiest gamers clash, the very island may not survive the battle. The Battle City tournament ends here...but who will walk away from the ruins?

COMING DECEMBER 2007!

THE FINAL VOLUME OF BATTLE CITY!

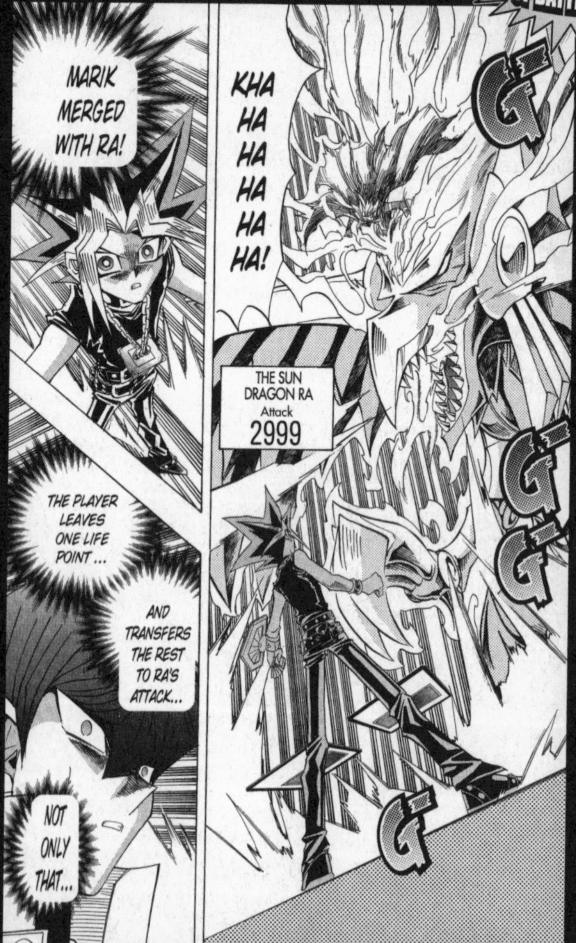
KHA HA HA HA HA HA HA!
THE SUN DRAGON RA Attack 2999
G
G
G
G
MARIK MERGED WITH RA!
THE PLAYER LEAVES ONE LIFE POINT...
AND TRANSFERS THE REST TO RA'S ATTACK...
NOT ONLY THAT...

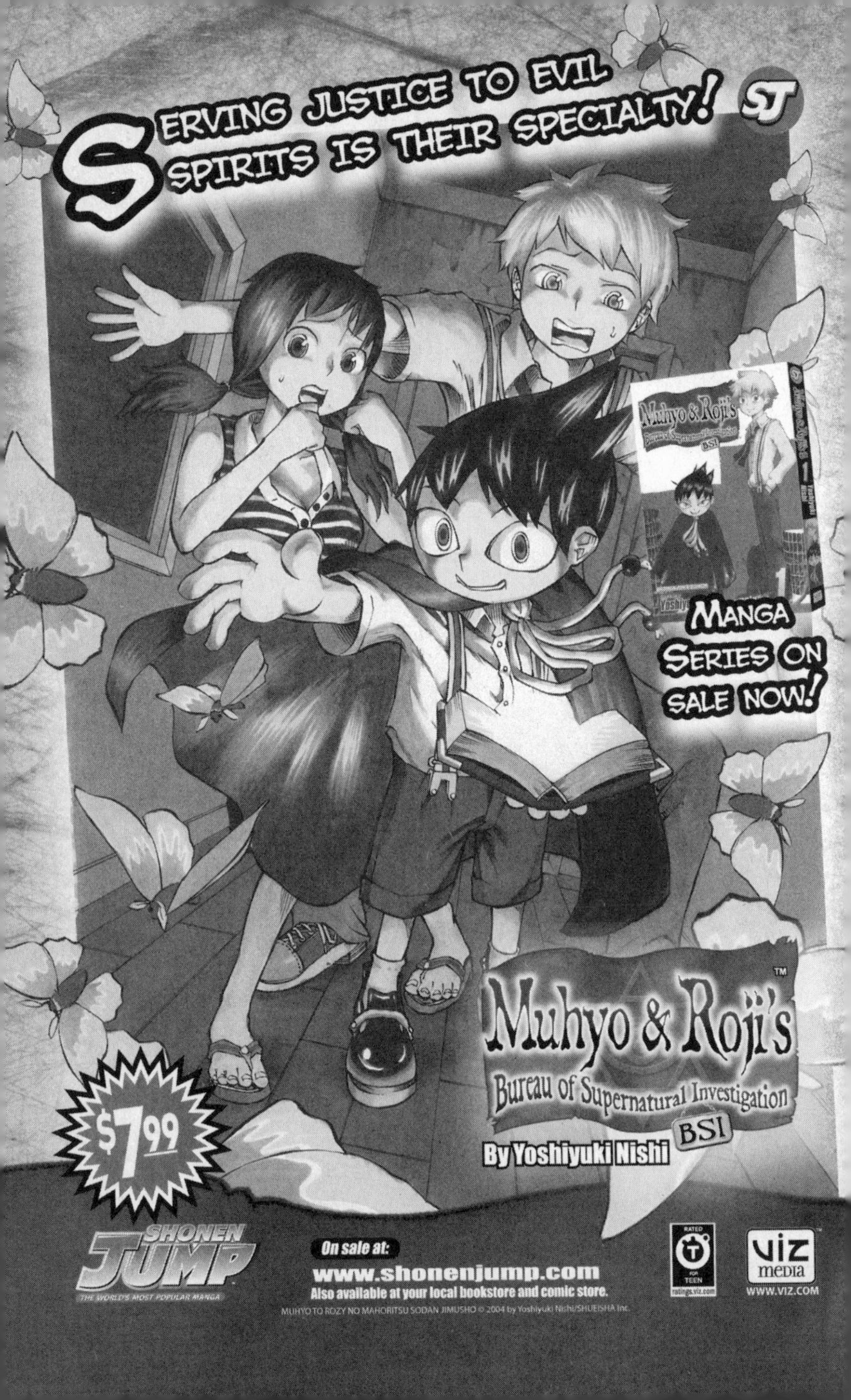
SERVING JUSTICE TO EVIL SPIRITS IS THEIR SPECIALTY!
SJ
MANGA SERIES ON SALE NOW!
Muhyo & Roji's™
Bureau of Supernatural Investigation
BSI
By Yoshiyuki Nishi
$7.99
SHONEN JUMP
THE WORLD'S MOST POPULAR MANGA
On sale at:
www.shonenjump.com
Also available at your local bookstore and comic store.
MUHYO TO ROZY NO MAHORITSU SODAN JIMUSHO © 2004 by Yoshiyuki Nishi/SHUEISHA Inc.
RATED T FOR TEEN
ratings.viz.com
VIZ media
WWW.VIZ.COM

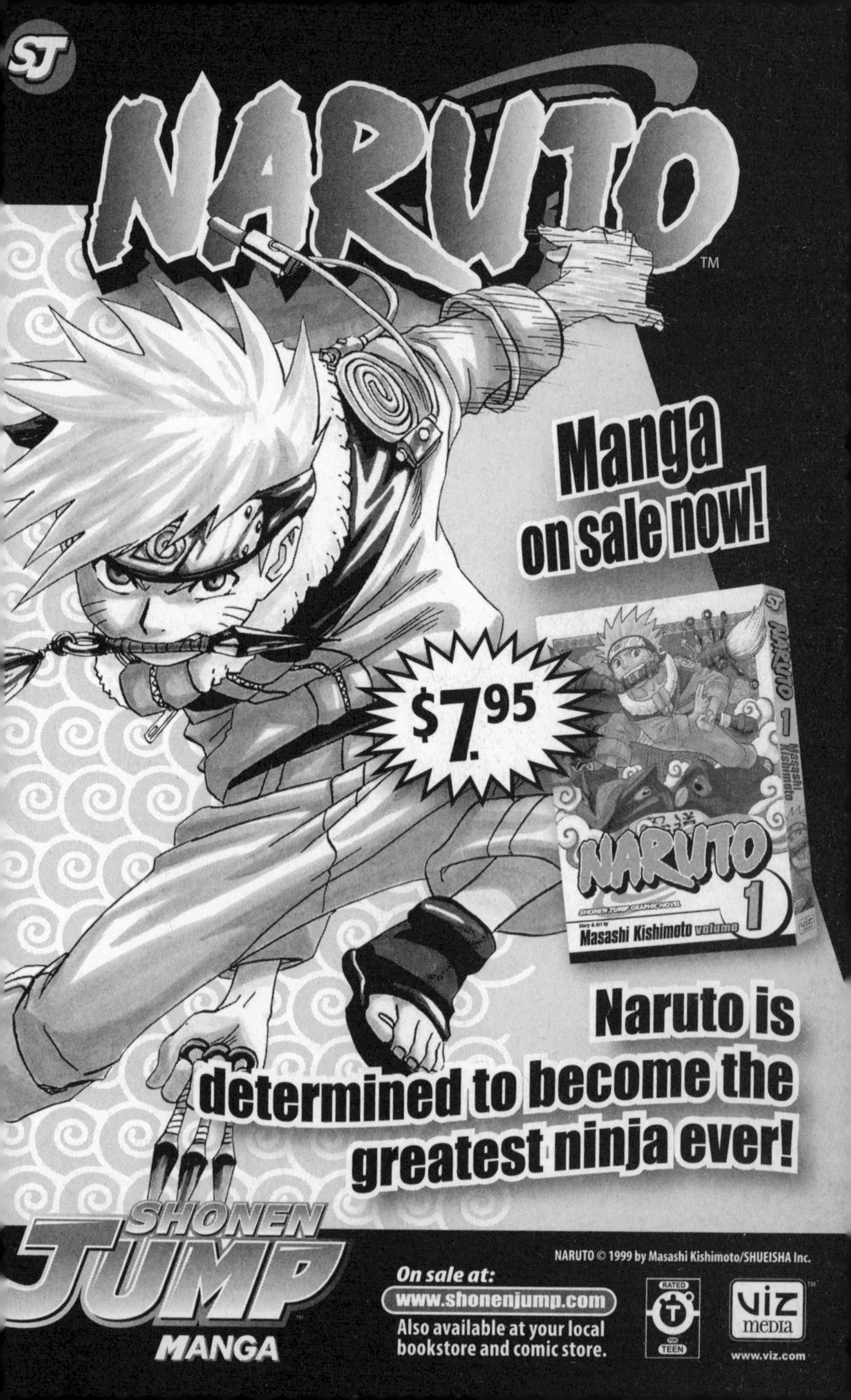
SJ
NARUTO™
Manga on sale now!
$7.95
NARUTO
1
Masashi Kishimoto volume 1
Naruto is determined to become the greatest ninja ever!
SHONEN JUMP MANGA
NARUTO © 1999 by Masashi Kishimoto/SHUEISHA Inc.
On sale at:
www.shonenjump.com
Also available at your local bookstore and comic store.
RATED T FOR TEEN
viz media
www.viz.com

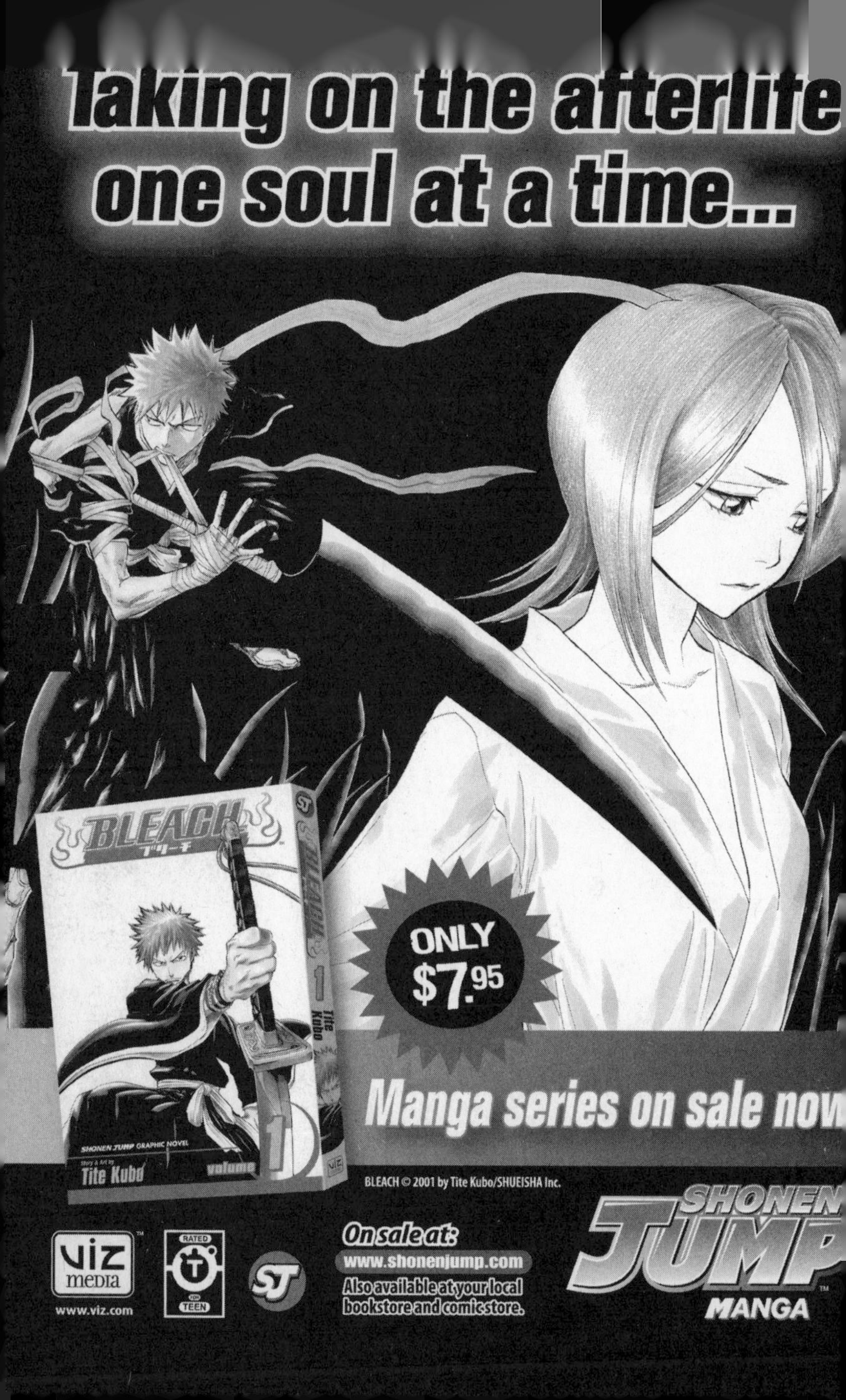
Taking on the afterlife
one soul at a time...
BLEACH
SHONEN JUMP GRAPHIC NOVEL
Story & Art by
Tite Kubo
volume 1
ONLY
$7.95
Manga series on sale now
BLEACH © 2001 by Tite Kubo/SHUEISHA Inc.
viz media
www.viz.com
RATED T TEEN
On sale at:
www.shonenjump.com
Also available at your local bookstore and comic store.
SHONEN JUMP
MANGA

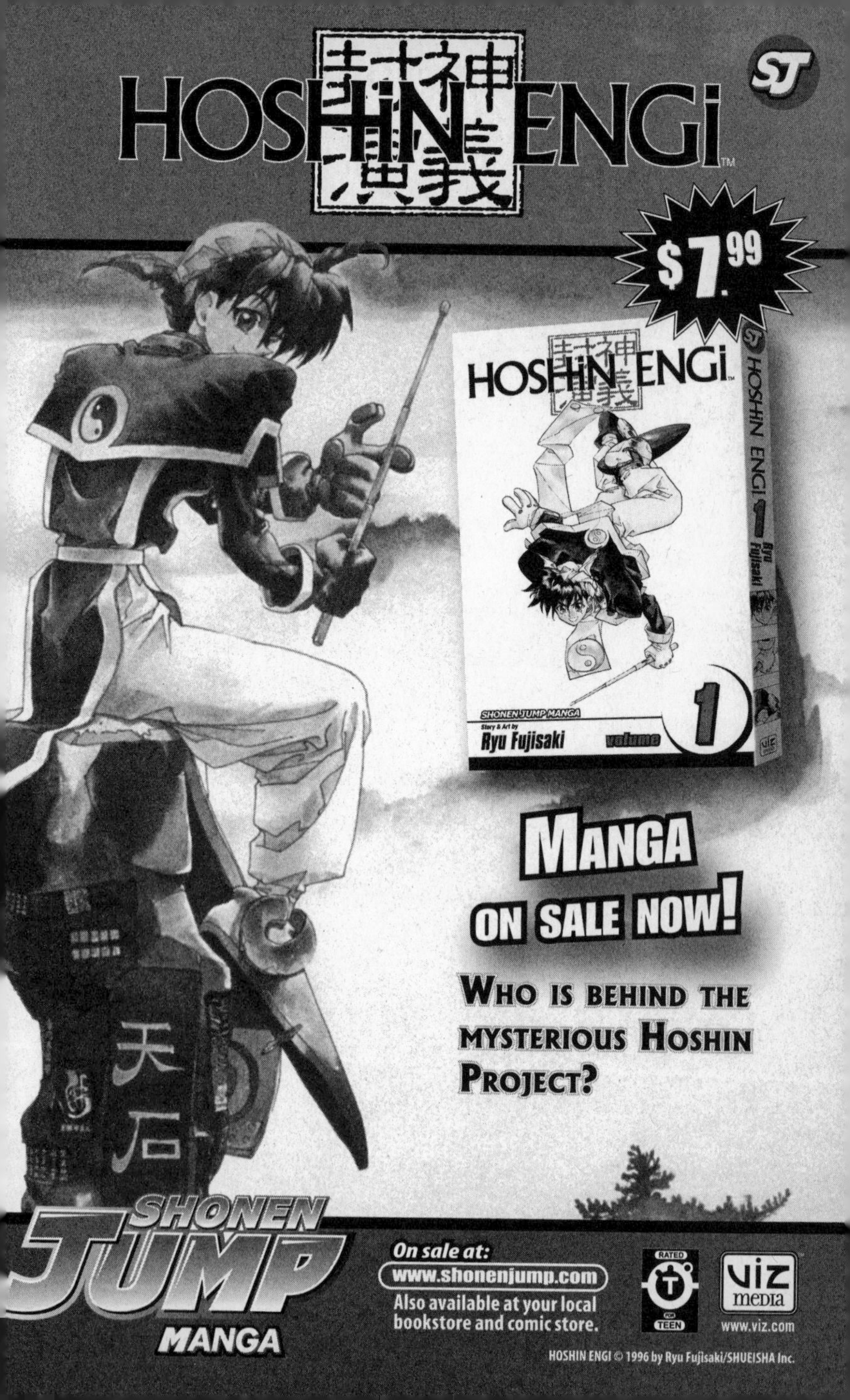

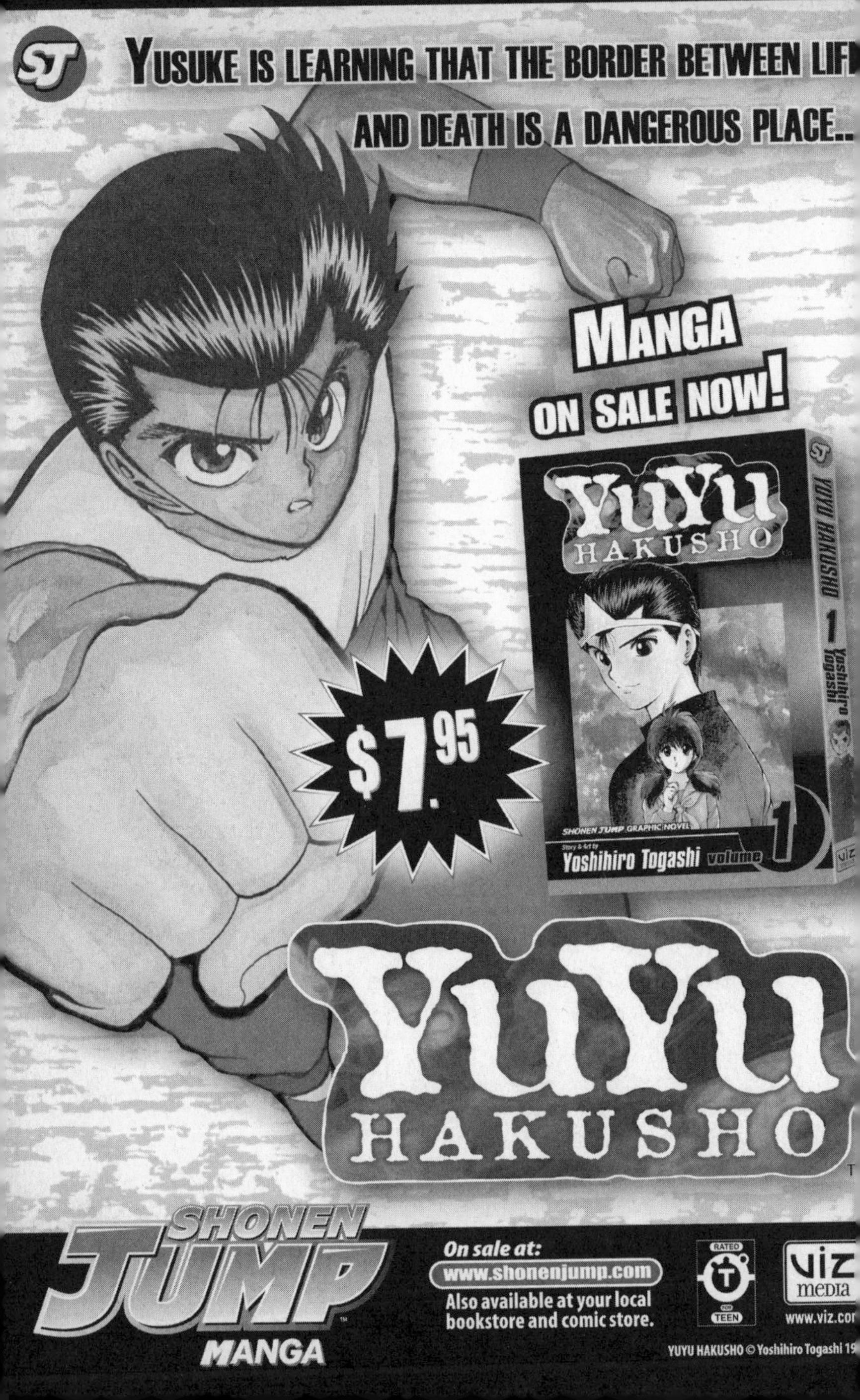
YUSUKE IS LEARNING THAT THE BORDER BETWEEN LIF
AND DEATH IS A DANGEROUS PLACE...
MANGA
ON SALE NOW!
$7.95
YUYU HAKUSHO
SHONEN JUMP GRAPHIC NOVEL
Story & Art by
Yoshihiro Togashi volume 1
YUYU HAKUSHO
SHONEN JUMP
MANGA
On sale at:
www.shonenjump.com
Also available at your local bookstore and comic store.
RATED T FOR TEEN
viz media
www.viz.cor
YUYU HAKUSHO © Yoshihiro Togashi 19

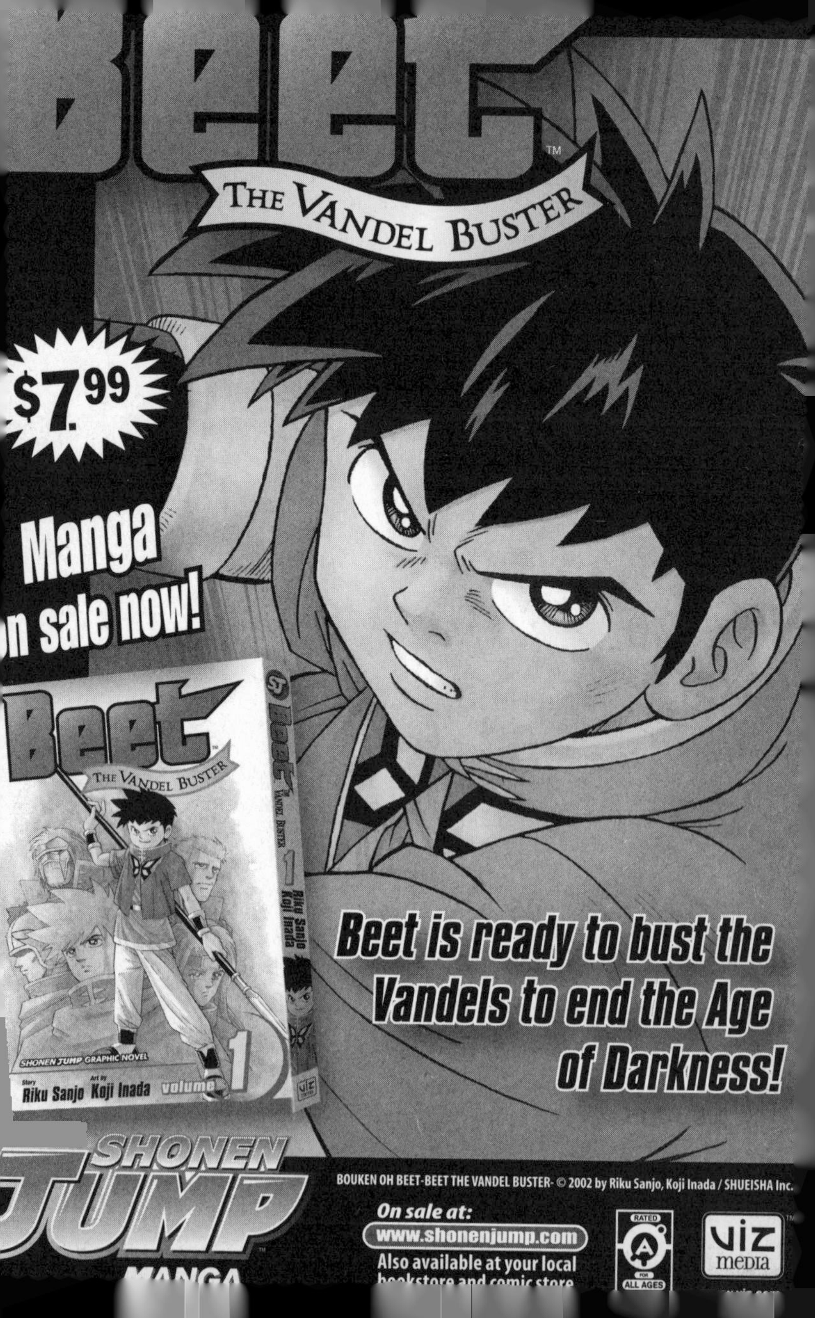

Beet™
THE VANDEL BUSTER
$7.99
Manga
n sale now!
Beet™
THE VANDEL BUSTER
SHONEN JUMP GRAPHIC NOVEL
Story Riku Sanjo Art by Koji Inada volume 1
Beet is ready to bust the Vandels to end the Age of Darkness!
SHONEN JUMP
MANGA
BOUKEN OH BEET-BEET THE VANDEL BUSTER- © 2002 by Riku Sanjo, Koji Inada / SHUEISHA Inc.
On sale at:
www.shonenjump.com
Also available at your local bookstore and comic store
RATED A FOR ALL AGES
VIZ media

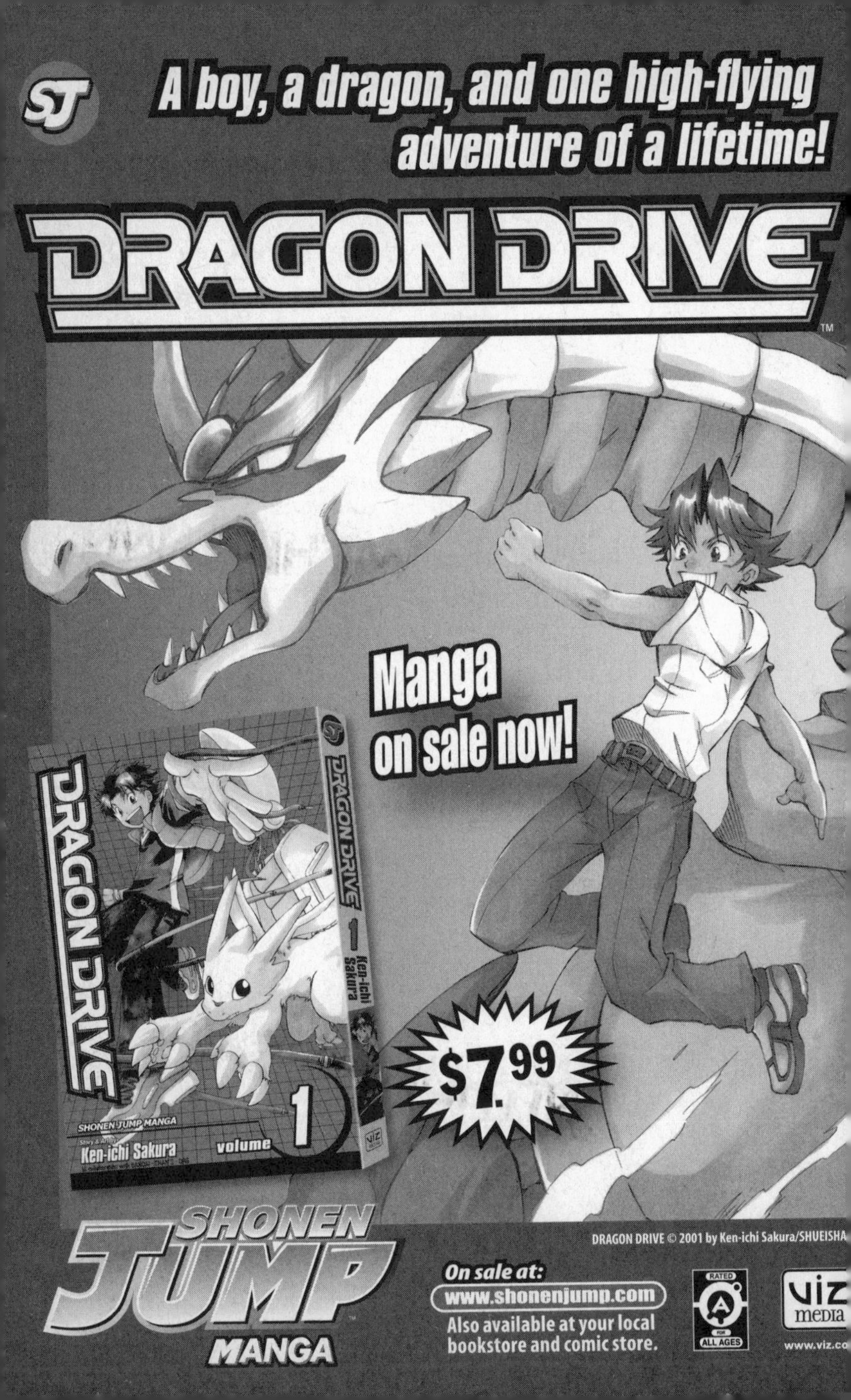

A boy, a dragon, and one high-flying adventure of a lifetime!
DRAGON DRIVE™
Manga on sale now!
DRAGON DRIVE
SHONEN JUMP MANGA
Ken-ichi Sakura
volume 1
DRAGON DRIVE 1 Ken-ichi Sakura
$7.99
DRAGON DRIVE © 2001 by Ken-ichi Sakura/SHUEISHA
SHONEN JUMP MANGA
On sale at:
www.shonenjump.com
Also available at your local bookstore and comic store.
RATED A FOR ALL AGES
VIZ media
www.viz.co

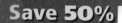

SUBSC
50% O
all the
SUBSC
conter
AVAIL

☑ YES!
(12 issue
LOW SUB
up for the

NAME

ADDRESS

CITY

E-MAIL AD

☐ MY

CREDIT

ACCOUNT

SIGNATUR

ivery.

YU-GI-OH! © 1996 by Kazuki Takahashi / SHUEISHA Inc.